RENEWALS 458-4574
DATE DUE

APR 01			
MAY 09			
GAYLORD			PRINTED IN U.S.A.

Alliterative Revivals

THE MIDDLE AGES SERIES

Ruth Mazo Karras, Series Editor
Edward Peters, Founding Editor

A complete list of books in the series
is available from the publisher.

Alliterative Revivals

Christine Chism

PENN

University of Pennsylvania Press

Philadelphia

10   9   8   7   6   5   4   3   2   1

Published by
University of Pennsylvania Press
Philadelphia, Pennsylvania 19104-4011

Library of Congress Cataloging-in-Publication Data

Chism, Christine.
    Alliterative revivals / Christine Chism.
        p. cm. — (The Middle Ages series)
    Includes bibliographical references (p.) and index.
    ISBN 0-8122-3655-6 (acid-free paper)
    1. English poetry—Middle English, 1100–1500—History and
criticism. 2. Alliteration. I. Title. II. Series

PR317.A55 C48 2002
821'.109 — dc21

                                                    2001056863

Contents

Introduction

The ghosts were not an attempt at evasion ...
Rather, the questions became more insistent,
more powerful, for being projected into the mouths
of the dead.
PAT BARKER, *The Ghost Road*

THE EPIGRAPH DESCRIBES THE ORGANIZING metaphor of this book: a drama of historical revival. It proposes that death grants ghosts an interrogative force, imbuing the impossible, unceasing communication between the dead and the living, the past and the present with fearful intimacy. For ghosts never return alone. They drag along on their mantles lost memories that compel their audiences to confront their foundational evasions, to rewrite their histories, and to renovate themselves. Ghosts trouble the strategic amnesias, substitutions, and transcendences through which history is shaped and the contours of the present are inaugurated. And the living respond, not simply because the burden of survival guilt is being tweaked, but because we construct ourselves as citizens of the present at once through our solicitation of the past and its gentle collateral forgetting. To revive the dead as the dead is to give a new shape and authority to what is lost. The revived dead distress their own erasure, goad us into self-questioning, and, like some mortifying mafia, make offers that can't be refused—this is why we summon them.

This book is about the revival of the dead and the past performed in eight Middle English alliterative poems, *St. Erkenwald*, *Sir Gawain and the Green Knight*, *The Wars of Alexander*, *The Siege of Jerusalem*, the alliterative *Morte Arthure*, *De Tribus Regibus Mortuis*, *The Awntyrs off Arthure*, and *Somer Sunday*. Five of these poems are alliterative romances; three of them, *De Tribus Regibus Mortuis*, *Awntyrs off Arthure* and *Somer Sunday* didactically meditate on alliterative romance themes and are therefore fascinating in the way they crystallize and critique the concerns of the genre. In selecting these poems I pursued a single current in the flexing, multifarious, polymorphic, widely penetrating stream that is Middle English alliterative poetry and its tributary (or cross-current), rhythmical prose.[1]

What will draw together the alliterative romances in this study is not primarily metrical, dialectical, or formal, but rather thematic: their embodied and spectacular performance of history. These alliterative romances enact an association with past traditions, histories, and languages.[2] They harness a highly sophisticated historic consciousness to a spectacular imagination. They dramatize the uses and dangers of confronting the past while remaining alert to the interests and anxieties of contemporary audiences.[3] Like their insular romance predecessors described by Rosalind Field and Susan Crane;[4] these poems (1) investigate the historical antecedents of medieval structures of authority;[5] (2) dramatize the questioning of cultural centers from outsider (or provincial) perspectives;[6] and (3) centralize the historical exigencies of a world in flux rather than aiming primarily at more transcendent concerns with the afterlife.[7] However, alliterative romances extend these themes, accentuating the mutually structuring oppositions between past and present, center and periphery, secular and religious trajectories, in order to interrogate their reciprocal debts and interdependencies. These poems animate British history by reviving past bodies—the pagan judge, the giant of St. Michael's Mount, Sir Priamus, dead fathers and mothers, and the Green Knight himself—whose potentially threatening authority must be encountered and arbitrated. Such dramatic confrontations bring into focus late fourteenth-century disjunctions between monarchy and nobility, ecclesiastic authority and lay piety, and monarchical and provincial culture.

These poems were written toward the end of a period—the medieval—that everyday parlance makes an epitome of pastness, yet which recent scholarship, mostly on Chaucer, has illuminated as a society anxiously, innovatively, and opportunistically transacting social changes, and therefore invested in recreating and forgetting its own complex histories.[8] These romances improvise a form that flaunts a traditionality in its alliteration and diction even as it innovates underhandedly in its meter.[9] They declare a genre—historical romance—preoccupied similarly both with origins and renovations. David Lawton makes a useful, if not watertight, stylistic distinction within alliterative poetry between "the plainer or 'informal' style of Langland" and his followers, and the more "ornate, 'formal' style." All of the poems that I examine are from this second group, characterized not only by its stylistic and metrical bravura but also by "extensive resources of ingenious and sometimes archaic diction."[10] Innovation meets archaism as alliterative romance performs its traditionality, coming to life in the risky transactions constituting old against new, past against present, predecessor against successor. This precarious enactment receives thematic exploration in alliterative romance's obsession with what Ralph Hanna has called "moments of historical strain . . . when political power passes."[11]

In this focus on historical strain and moments of transition alliterative romances speak to their time; they dramatize a late medieval sense of the power and danger of the past so intense that resurrecting the dead actually became a strategy for managing political transitions. A particularly freighted early fifteenth-century disinterment attests to the past's lingering political energy. Its power is not diminished by the fact that the corpse, unlike many in alliterative romance, does not actually speak after death. In December of 1413, in the first year of his reign, Henry V performed an exhumation the more eloquent for the silence of its chief exhibit:[12]

For gret loue and gedenesse, he sent to þe ffreris of Langeley, þere as his Fadir hadde do burye King Richard þe ij^{de}, and let take vp his body ayen out of the erthe, and dede bring hym to Westmynstre, yn a ryal chare couert with blak veluet, and baners of diuers armeȝ alle aboute. And al þe horsses drawyng þe chare were trappid yn black, and bete with diuers armeȝ, and mony a torch brennyng, by alle þe wey, til he come to Westmystre. And þere he lette make for hym a ryalle and a solempne terement, and buried hym be Quene Anne his wiff, as his owne desire was, on þe firther syde of Seynt Edwardeȝ schryne, yn the Abbey of Saint Petris of Westmynstre: on whose soule God haue mercy! Amen![13]

[For his great love and goodness, he [Henry V] sent to the friars of Langley, where his father had interred King Richard the II and had them take up his body again out of the earth and had him brought to Westminster, in a royal chair covered with black velvet and banners of different coats of arms all about. And all the horses drawing the chair were caparisoned in black and decorated with many coats of arms all about and many a burning torch through the whole way until he arrived at Westminster. And there he [Henry V] caused to be made for him a royal and solemn interment and buried him beside Queen Anne his wife, as he had desired, on the further side of St. Edward's shrine in the Abbey of St. Peter of Westminster; on whose soul God have mercy! Amen!]

This exhumation provoked extensive contemporary discussion. The fifteenth-century chronicler of *The Brut* makes it bespeak the "great love and goodness" of the young king. In a metrical history of Henry V, a monk of Westminster and a member of the royal household also reads it as an example of Henry V's generosity, placing it after a paean to Henry's kingly virtues and amidst a list of his benefices to Westminster Abbey. Effacing the stigma of Henry IV's usurpation, these endowments make Henry V the true heir of Richard II as they describe Henry's restoration to the abbey of a ring which King Richard had given to the shrine of St. Edward there. And in that context, the body of Richard becomes another benefice in Henry's power to rebestow as Henry removes his body from the site his father, Henry IV, had given him and restores him to the richly appointed burial site that Richard had originally commissioned for himself.[14]

These accounts show that this gesture of kingly generosity was also one of kingly authority. The fifteenth-century chronicler of *The Brut* whose account of the exhumation I have quoted stresses its political needfulness by placing it directly after the death of Henry IV and immediately before Henry V's first confrontation with the Lollard rebellion and his embarkation for France. Other, earlier chroniclers also frame it within accounts of social unrest and Lollard treason. In *The Brut* Henry V orchestrates the body's progress through London in a show of royal power carefully designed to insist upon two things: first, that this corpse was a king, and second that this king *was* a corpse. The royal chair is draped in black velvet; the heraldic banners with which the body and the horses are decorated are set off by black trappings and funeral torches. Richard II is disinterred, enthroned, and displayed to the people of London both to dramatize and to set a spectacular limit to his lingering authority.

Because linger it did—this was actually Richard's second posthumous command performance. The secrecy surrounding Richard's death had perplexed Henry IV's reign as well, sparking rebellions after his accession by subjects who would not believe Richard was dead or who would not accept his successor. In 1402 Henry IV hanged a group of friars for spreading rumors about Richard's continued survival; the following year, large numbers of Richard's personally favored Cheshiremen flocked to Shrewsbury to die in Henry Percy's rebellion. John Froissart describes Henry IV's futile efforts to nip in the bud rumors of a kingly revenant. Henry IV also displayed Richard's body for the Londoners, laying him in a black-draped chair and proceeding from the Tower of London to Cheapside where the chair rested for two hours and enormous crowds came to see him: "Thyder came in and out mo than xx. M. persons, men and women, to se hym where as he laye, his hedde on a blacke quisshen and his visage open." [Thither came in and out more than 20,000 people, men and women to see him as he lay, his head on a black cushion and his visage open.] [15] After that, the body was taken from London in haste and buried at Langley.[16]

But more than a decade later, the specter of Richard was still haunting the realm. The chroniclers note the currency (and sometimes the ridiculousness) of these rumors. Thomas Elmham and Walsingham both depict the accused Lollard rebel, John Oldcastle, as justifying his rebellion by claiming that Richard was still alive nearly twenty years after his reputed death in prison.[17] Paul Strohm compellingly describes the realm's inability to absorb the king's death and its astonishing need to believe in his phantasm.[18] In contemporary accounts, Richard's continuing influence becomes a danger to Henry's authority, grist for the mills of malcontents. It was crucial for Henry V to differentiate himself from his father (reputedly Richard's murderer and usurper), efface this troubled paternity, and seek further into the past for a more immaculate political predecessor. Henry V cannily followed his father's funeral with the reburial of Richard II because he needed not only to demonstrate Richard II's death but also to appropriate Richard as a father. Walsingham suggests this when he describes Henry's conviction that he owed as much veneration to Richard as he did to his own father, Henry IV.[19] Another detail makes this fatherly substitution even more overt. Margaret Wade Labarge cites the Issues of the Exchequer for Henry's reign to show that "the banners to be placed on the hearse carrying Richard were hurriedly borrowed from Henry IV's tomb at Canterbury."[20]

Henry V thus raises the body of a past authority in order to dramatize a claim to its power before laying it decisively to rest under his own re-invigorated authority. The spectacle is passional, expressing his veneration to his old patron, his uneasiness with the shadow of his own father's usurpation, and his anxiety about the atmosphere of rebellion and distrust. By exhuming and displaying the body of Richard's royal authority, Henry deliberately invokes both past and contemporary challenges to his own kingship in order to re-dress them (literally, in his father's trappings) and affectively defuse them.[21]

And the Lancastrians are not the only late medieval kings led by uneasy ghosts to mine the ideological power of their predecessors. The uses of the dead emerge provocatively in the war of precedents waged between Richard II and the Lords Appellant. Richard II was fascinated by the legal controversies of Edward II's monarchy and admired Edward II's model of kingship; throughout his reign he attempted to resurrect the image of the deposed and discredited king and have him canonized.[22] His enemies, the Lords Appellant, responded in kind, reeling Richard in before the Merciless Parliament by reminding him of Edward's deposition and, not very subtly, intimating its repetition if the magnates' counsel was not respected.[23] Potentially this process could be repeated ad infinitum. In October of 1397, after Richard had executed Arundel on the same spot where in 1388 Arundel had executed Richard's former tutor Simon Burley, Richard foiled what looks like a resurrection attempt on Arundel's behalf.[24] According to Walsingham, Richard was haunted by uneasiness over Arundel's lingering specter. Rumors of sainthood were circulating, including assertions that the beheaded earl's head had been miraculously reattached to his body. In the middle of the night, Richard was driven to commission an exhumation of the body, sending four dukes and an earl to inspect the corpse. At the Augustinian convent church on Bread Street where it was buried, they woke the friars, opened the grave, and found that the head and body of the corpse had been sewn together.[25] Richard exiled six of the Augustinian friars and ordered the grave paved over.[26]

Such political resurrections are powerful not just because they effectively rewrite history but because they rewrite it while concretizing, confirming, ritualizing, and extending its cultural power. Genealogies can be inflected and symbolically revised as each ruler suppresses the legacy of an immediate but intractable predecessor in order to affirm the power of a more distant, manipulable, and legitimate one. The very reverence and traditionality of the funerary ritual or the canonization process can become vehicles for political challenge and transformation.

Alliterative romance dramatizes similar revivals but can give its embodied pasts a much more disquieting scope. They allow the specters of past authorities to descend from the processional chair and roam at large in the world to challenge all comers. However, unlike the corpse of Richard—resurrected to finalize the symbolic transfer of power that would complete his death and lay him to rest once and for all—the revived bodies in these poems often resist symbolic reinscription and work to confound the transfers of power that will render them inert. They enact mortal dramas, corporealizing resistance in the impossible materiality of their own riven but animate bodies. They refuse to surrender and stay dead, and thereby gain a terrifying power over their killers and successors. The Green Knight treats decapitation as a passing inconvenience, the pagan judge in *St. Erkenwald* enjoys a posthumous conversation and baptism, Anectanabus in *The Wars of Alexander* prophesies after his death to delimit his murderer's power, the Jewish people in *The Siege of Jerusalem* intimate the brutality of their Christian besiegers in the protracted liquidation of their flesh and their city, while in *De Tribus Regibus Mortuis* and *The Awntyrs off Arthure,* the walking, disintegrating, and blazing dead implicate their children in cautionary exchanges.

These poems are simultaneously curious about the past as other, delighted by the particularities of historic re-creation, and anxious to assimilate or overwrite the unfamiliar, to make the past theirs. The ideological rewards are great when the past yields to such assimilation: connection, continuity, lineage, the uninterrupted translation of power and authority, and consolation from the disjunctions of history. But the narratives become even more fascinating where the past is intractable. It can entrap its interlocutors in the face of their own mortality, miring them in clinging impotence or flinging them onto a gerbil wheel of frantic, futile evasion. The narrative suspension between historic connection and catastrophic rupture allows these poems to soft-shoe the line between nostalgia and iconoclasm. To characters such as St. Erkenwald, controlled connections to an assimilable pre-Christian past become a source of hope and renewed authority, while to insurgent characters such as Alexander or Titus and Vespasian from *The Siege of Jerusalem* such connections must be violently exorcized. If late medieval literature often expresses a persistent sense of indebtedness to and inadequacy before more illustrious pasts, these romances show that the counterpoint of that indebtedness could be insecurity, anxiety, and a need for re-tribution (in both its etymological senses: gift-return and vengeance), by matching ancestral achievements or, more darkly, obliterating the debt with the lender.

As they transact these temporal exchanges, these alliterative romances realize the past both as other and as familiar. Monika Otter asserts the mutual interdependence of these historical conceptualizations: "A narrative asserting historical continuity would not be needed unless other cultural and psychological factors suggested the opposite; conversely, a narrative about disruption and historical loss presupposes a desire for continuity."[27] Alliterative romances enjoy a similar historiographic ambidexterity. On the one hand, these romances mobilize the continuities between past and present. They suggest the contemporaneity of the past, tracing what Augustine suggestively calls "the present of past things."[28] To write the past is always to address the past's uses for the present, to animate the writer's own desires and fears concerning the past.[29] The past, whether it is shaped into memory or history, is continually reinvented for present consumption. These poems treat the past as prologue rather than difference when they create protagonists who implicate late medieval identities, anxieties, and ideals—Erkenwald, Gawain, Titus and Vespasian, Alexander, and Arthur—imagining, through these characters, relationships between past and present that are identificatory, lineal, exemplarizing, flexible, and productive.[30]

On the other hand, however, the central conflicts of these poems are energized by a sense of the past as radical difference, against which these contemporaneous figures must struggle to define themselves and with which they must come to terms.[31] These temporal conflicts vary in character from poem to poem. *St. Erkenwald* sets a pagan predecessor/bishop against a Christian successor—with the church's institutional role in mediating salvation hanging on the outcome. *Sir Gawain* sets a veteran knight against an ingénue court—with definitions of chivalry as "safe" game or life-or-death venture at issue. *The Wars of Alexander* sets a threatening Eastern father against a rebellious, iconoclastic, and conflicted son—with escape from patriarchal containment, a limiting cycle of generational rise and fall, and, finally, mortality itself at issue. *The Siege of Jerusalem* sets Jewish and Roman forefathers against Christian claimants—with control over both religious and imperial heritages at issue. The alliterative *Morte Arthure* sets Arthur against a range of the historical and genealogical predecessors of his empire, in order to test the limits of chivalric imperial self-fashioning. Both *De Tribus* and *Awntyrs* set dead parents against their children to provoke social and moral reform. In each of these permutations, different contemporary problems are approached but the conflict is basically a drama between a different or threatening past—embodied as predecessor, as veteran, as ancestor, as parent—and the present. It is here that the past appears most dangerous, foreign, conflicted, and mysterious—where these poems dwell on the powerful alterities of the pagan judge, the Green Knight, the Jews, Anectanabus, and the dead fathers and mothers.

And yet the poems do not wholly alienate these "past" figures—that would make them too easy to dispatch. These romances embody the dialectical interdependencies of concepts of history as continuity and history as rupture when they make their revenants disquietingly or aggressively contemporaneous. That doesn't lessen their challenge; it intensifies their uncanny power—makes them intimate provocateurs on the border where *heimlich* and *unheimlich* shade into each other.[32] When the Green Knight erupts into Arthur's Christmas feast, he looks like a vegetation god cross-fertilized by a primeval British giant, yet he is also an exquisitely coiffed and costumed contemporary nobleman. In *The Siege of Jerusalem* the Jews are at once powerful predecessors to the Christians and their contemporary rivals for empire, as are *The Wars of Alexander's* Anectanabus, Darius and Porrus to Alexander, and virtually every enemy Arthur fights in the alliterative *Morte Arthure*. Both *Gawain* and *Wars of Alexander* further literalize this thrusting together of past and present by giving their revenants double lives. Each revenant speaks familiarly in contemporary language and with a finely tuned and manipulative insight into how to make his audience jump. These temporal conjunctions are deliberately flagrant, theatrical, and bizarre; they slip the challenge of the past into the skin of the present. By playing history as continuity and history as gap insistently against each other, these alliterative romances make the past culturally resonant, questionable, and compelling to their audiences—and they energize contemporary issues by projecting them into such distant, vast, and spectacular historical theaters.

Thus as these poems work their strange spectacles, they summon fourteenth-century modes of identity and authority to judgment. Ralph Hanna brilliantly describes how alliterative poetry's incessant exploration of the historic tyranny of rule implicates late medieval constructions of lordship.[33] And such critiques resound farther because the very range and acuity of these poems' historic consciousness stake a claim to authoritative reassessment. Patrick Geary has shown how to talk about the past is to claim a particular kind of social power—to perform a depth of experience, learning, or memory which commands respect, if not obedience.[34] In alliterative romance, this power can be mobilized to validate and reify particular social identities, but it can also work against dominant social grains to provoke startling interrogations.

In these poems, therefore, as the past is negotiated, it also becomes a means of renegotiating the world.[35] Like Will, the seeker of Langland's alliterative allegory, *Piers Plowman*, the alliterative romances imaginatively claim dual citizenship of "London and opelond bothe" (C, V, 44) and with a similar category-perplexing energy.[36] Not confining themselves to a single locus of challenge, such as that between the monarchy and the barony (*pace* J. R. Hulbert),[37] the poems define and strategically manipulate relationships between city, province, nation, and world.[38] They explore a matrix of interests both local and national, both historic and contemporary, both political and transcendental, both conservative and innovative. They raise questions that make visible not just the social work done by these powerful binaries but the dialectical transactions that continually reconstitute their poles. Pursuing these questions allows the poems to explore more deeply, precisely, intensely, and self-consciously not only the lingering power of the past, but also the contemporary desires, insecurities, curiosities, and self-questionings which it enkindles. Thus, by invoking the past to reinforce or challenge contemporary ideologies, these poems make history an intensely political and socially interrogative force.

Methodologies

This book's title, *Alliterative Revivals*, puns both on these interests in reviving the past and on the enigma of the alliterative revival, literary history's much-questioned attempt to explain the apparent suddenness of alliterative poetry's appearance on the English literary scene in the latter half of the fourteenth century. This poetry has been a crux of medieval scholarship; the debates about the continuity of an oral or lost alliterative tradition combined with the problems of wresting provenances from unique, late, and dialectically transmigrated manuscripts have atomized attempts to read alliterative poems together—the very existence and nature of an alliterative revival is still hotly debated.[39] The pluralizing of the book's title, therefore, urges a critical shift. Rather than trying once again to solve the enigma by proposing an explanatory theory, this book works to redirect the treatment of fourteenth-century alliterative romance from explanation—whether, why, and where does it occur?—to interpretive exploration, and from a concentration on meter, dialect, and provenance to one on shared themes, poetic voice, and audience address. It works to discover the interests these poems share and the social work they do.[40]

Methodologically this book pursues a dual trajectory. The first trajectory is an "inward" close reading of textual passages to illuminate the particular confrontations between past and present that I argue are crucial to a poem. The second trajectory is a "lateral" exploration of the late medieval social developments that, in my view, inform, parallel, and are reimagined by means of these temporal confrontations. Reacting against the nationalist impulses of older historicists of alliterative traditions, Elizabeth Salter has urged alertness to alliterative poetry's "wide range of particular, and probably differing, literary and social backgrounds," their variety of cultural address.[41] Therefore this book does not interpret these poems solely in reference to emerging nationalisms or events at the royal court or to any single nexus of social tensions—between lay and clerical cultures, Latinity and vernacularity, king and aristocracy—however encompassing its social and political effects. Rather it seeks to illuminate the complexity of the richly textured and interlayered localities—cathedral and city, court and province, priory and pagandom, east and west—that these poems so intricately traverse.

To do this, the book pays attention to the poems' stated settings which are, for medieval romances, unusually explicit and geographically specific. I was interested in the ground they cover and, even more crucially, the boundaries they erect and shatter.[42] This range of settings structures the book. Broadly speaking, the chapters move from more localized to less: from *St. Erkenwald*, which sets all of London surging toward the churchyard of St. Paul's Cathedral, to the international blitzkrieg of the *Morte Arthure*. The settings also gave me the cues I followed in selecting areas of late medieval culture to place in dialogue with the poems. *St. Erkenwald* stages its churchyard drama before an unruly London mob; its chapter accordingly investigates late fourteenth-century relationships between cathedral and city (rather than, for instance, wide-ranging contemporary debates about the salvation of pagans or the relationships between the king and the city of London). *Sir Gawain* moves its hero from Arthur's court to the remote provinces of Lancashire and Cheshire in a topographically explicit journey; its chapter therefore considers the interactions between royal court and provincial gentry central to the poem. *The Siege of Jerusalem* moves "internationally" between Jerusalem, Marseilles, and Rome — exoticizing Judaism and demonizing pagan Rome as it does so — therefore, I examined it in the larger contexts of Jewish/Christian and East/West relationships. The same is even more true of *The Wars of Alexander* and the alliterative *Morte Arthure* which launch international conquests and examine the violent foundations of world empires. The only poems in which a figurative rather than a physical setting became more crucial to my argument were *De Tribus Regibus Mortuis* and the *Awntyrs off Arthure* where the most critical boundaries are between life and death, which acquire their own eerie landscapes.

Alliterative poetry both invites and resists this kind of historicization. The rich contemporary resonances and geographical specificities provoke inquiry about specific dates and provenances; the poems' invocations of fictional audiences and narrators make identification of historical ones almost impossible except in the broadest strokes. Broad strokes and larger developments — spanning twenty-year periods or longer — are therefore what I have attempted to descry in their movements. This actually made for more interesting history; the typical historicist snap-shot is not even a possibility, and thinking in terms of decades forces the realization of how continuously changeable were the social, political, and religious landscapes of this time. I tried to resist as much as possible fixing the poems to particular dates by pointing out correspondences that are too exact, or flattening them into political allegories referencing specific events, mostly because I was concerned to pursue a sense of these poems' depth, breadth, and multiplicity of engagements. Many of these poems were probably written and revised over years in any case, just as *Piers Plowman* was. For tentative dates and provenances, I have relied upon the speculations (often divergent) of editors and textual scholars; they are summarized in footnotes towards the beginning of each chapter.

Chapter 1, "Alliterative Romance: Improvising Tradition," treats the critical history of the so-called alliterative revival, arguing that it is useful to consider alliterative romance as a genre invested in testing the present by reinventing the past, formally, metrically, thematically, and performatively. Chapter 2, "The Body in Question," examines the way *St. Erkenwald* invokes a revenant from the pagan past in order to consolidate the civic authority of the fourteenth-century Cathedral of St. Paul. In Chapter 3, "Heady Diversions," the focus shifts to the late fourteenth-century tensions between the British monarchy and the provinces in *Sir Gawain and the Green Knight*. Here, the Knight and the other provincial characters represent an older, more experienced but internally riven and perplexed form of chivalry with legendary overtones, with which Gawain, and by extension, the youthful Arthurian court, are asked to come to terms. In Chapter 4, "Geography and Genealogy in *The Wars of Alexander*," the eponymous hero/patricide attempts to erase and subjugate both his eastern progenitor and all the oriental kingdoms whose exotic paternities complicate Alexander's own chivalric authority. In Chapter 5, "Profiting from Precursors in *The Siege of Jerusalem*," the provincial Christian Romans face and obliterate two different forefathers and rivals for power, the Jews and the pagan Roman emperors. Chapter 6, "King Takes Knight: Signifying War in the Alliterative *Morte Arthure*," considers Arthur himself as a critical revival of Edward III, and examines Arthur's confrontations with a whole series of historic figures that challenge Britain's status and draw it into international conflict—from the giant of St. Michael's Mount, to the Greek knight, Priamus, to the emperor of Rome himself. In the course of these ancestral confrontations the poem criticizes the way the king channels the lives and energies of his dearest knights into his own programs of national war. Finally Chapter 7, "Grave Misgivings," examines the ways *De Tribus Regibus Mortuis*, *The Awntyrs off Arthure*, and *Somer Sunday* confront powerful kings and queens with the moldering corpses of their royal fathers and mothers, bringing intimations of mortality to monarchies. The dead attempt to draw the living into mutually profitable exchanges to provoke social reform. They target monarchs, enticing them to reconnect themselves to the social body by acts of redress both to those to whom they owe their fortune and those they govern, the dead and the poor.

Throughout its length, the book weaves other alliterative poems—*The Parliament of Three Ages*, *Winner and Wastoure*, *Richard the Redeless*, *Gologras and Gawain*—episodically into chapters to illuminate particular points and to underscore the ways that these poems play well together. Even as they range over the fascinatingly variegated landscapes of late medieval society, they work through abiding preoccupations—history, spectacle, genealogy, sovereignty, honor, and challenge—whose collective force deserves consideration. As it searches these late medieval terrains, this book seeks to illuminate what links these romances to the concerns of other socially invested late fourteenth-century works and also what sets them apart—the spectacular intensity with which they riddle the late medieval present by projecting their questions into the mouths of the dead.

I

Alliterative Romance: Improvising Tradition

AT THE BEGINNING OF *St. Erkenwald* an Anglo-Saxon construction crew digging the foundations of a new Christian cathedral unearths an ancient tomb graven with mysterious writing.

> Hit was a throgh of thykke ston thryuandly hewen
> With gargeles garnysht aboute alle of gray marbre.
> The sperl of þe spelunke that spradde hit olofte
> Was metely made of þe marbre and menskefully planed
> And þe bordure enbelicit with bryȝt golde lettres;
> Bot roynyshe were þe resones þat þere on row stoden.
> Full verray were þe vigures þere auisyd hom many
> Bot all muset hit to mouth and quat hit mene shuld,
> Mony clerke in þat close with crownes ful brode
> Þere besiet hom aboute noȝt to bryng hom in wordes. (Erkenwald, 47–56)

[It was entirely made of thick stone gracefully hewn, garnished about with gargoyles all of grey marble. The fastening of the tomb that sealed it on top was fittingly made of marble and becomingly smoothed, and the border embellished with bright gold letters. But mysterious/runic were the words that stood there in a row. Full clear were the letters where many studied them there but all wondered aloud what it meant. Many a wide-tonsured clerk in that close busied himself to no avail to make words out of them.][1]

This passage shows the fascination of ancient inscription especially when it can no longer be read. The excellence, smoothness, and exquisite artifice of the tomb are brilliantly apparent, but their import is lost with the writing that adorns but cannot elucidate them—some antique worthiness has been ritually cherished but whose and why?

The paradox of familiar letters but mysterious words might well describe a fourteenth-century clerk's attempt to read the ancient writing of Britain and the dialects of Anglo-Saxon, probably indecipherable to fourteenth-century readers.[2] However, this passage suggests that ignorance of an ancient writing does not beget indifference. In *St. Erkenwald* the compulsion exerted by the tomb reflects its prior and consummate artistry in a land barely converted to the new work of Christianity. Viewed across the break between a forgotten past and a barely incipient present, both the break and the incipience intensify the need to know. Two lines later all of London converges on the tomb in an inquisitive wave of global proportions: "Þer comen þider of all kynnes so kenely mony / Þat as all þe worlde were þider walon within a hondequile" (64–65) [There came there eagerly so many people of all stations / that it was as if all the world had swarmed there in an instant]. There follows the energetic but futile attempt of the "broad crowned" Latinate clerks to parse that past writing, to "brynge hom in wordes." That they cannot do so perhaps hints that a more vernacular reader is needed. Their interpretive failure leads to their penetration of the wonderful tomb and its eventual transformation into what the poem demands it should become, a ruin holding only dust and fittingly replaced by the cathedral foundations.

As D. Vance Smith has pointed out, the inscription never is interpreted—it is pried off and discarded in the opening of the tomb and effectively replaced by the drama of the speaking corpse.[3] The inscription's glossy and unglossable wholeness at its first moment of unearthing gives way to the gaping tomb from which an ancient corpse will dramatically speak. This loss that becomes a conduit—the disappearance of the beautiful inscription—the opening of the mouth of the dead—performs the mystery of the alliterative romances' formal relationships with their own poetic predecessors. These relationships confound traceable genealogy but nonetheless bear identifying traits—alliteration, a tendency to four (and sometimes five) stress meter—that have, siren-like, cried their heredity to the puzzled ears of medieval scholars for a century. In this chapter I will argue that the alliterative poets, unlike the clerks in the passage, knew their insular vernacular traditions sufficiently to read the letters and also to mimic the lineaments, the "verray vigures" [true figures/letters] whose shapes can be discerned and admired despite their mysterious import. That is, while the alliterative poets may not have understood (or wanted to emulate) Anglo-Saxon or its long line—the beautiful inscription remains lost—alliteration itself becomes a marker of antiquity.[4] They were canny and curious enough about the deep-structures of ongoing vernacular alliterative traditions in England to be able to put together an alliterative long line that looked convincingly archaic, traditional, and glamorously illustrious when they wished to do so—and inventive enough to experiment continually with its inflections. This flexibility of aim is expressed in the metrical variability across poems and genres. *The Destruction of Troy* poet holds with brisk monotony to the narrow beam of an atypically unvarying meter. The Gawain-poet gives himself a felicitously experimental license. The *Joseph of*

Arimathie poet pushes license to the verge of metrical chaos or works out a different theory of meter entirely.[5] Other alliterative poems experiment with stanzas, intricate rhyme schemes, and with the freer metrical structures of the ongoing popular traditions of alliterative rhythmical prose. I will argue that the fourteenth-century formality of these romances is a deliberate archaism, the invention of a tradition convincing enough in its features that it would seem to bridge the gaps between past and present, and mimic the intonations of the dead—but the voice, the metrical structure, the reworking of genre are innovative and contemporary. These poems stage a drama of revival, creatively, strategically, and spectacularly improvising insular traditions rather than faithfully reconstituting them.

The Alliterative Revival: Questions and Theories

The following list comprises the most salient features upon which theories about the alliterative revival rest:

1. The fourteenth-century alliterative long line has rhythmical affinities with the early Middle English long line and with vernacular rhythmical prose traditions but does not develop in any traceable way from the Anglo-Saxon long line. However, it does show correspondences with some of its elements despite the changes attendant on the transformation of English from a more synthetic to a more analytic language. While working out distinctive and elaborate rules for metrical patterns (combinations of strong dips—several consecutive unstressed syllables—and stresses) that differ between half-lines, it retains the dominant Anglo-Saxon alliterative patterns of aa/ax and ax/ax, even as it enriches its alliteration by extending half-lines and indulging in ornamental alliteration on unstressed syllables.[6]

2. Much alliterative poetry exists only in single and/or fragmentary manuscripts with the exceptions of *Piers Plowman* (about fifty manuscripts) and *The Siege of Jerusalem* (nine). Manuscript survival for this poetry was clearly sporadic, if not extraordinary, and we are therefore missing a great deal and should be wary of judging too much from the few manuscripts that we have. The whole apparent fourteenth-century "revival" may be a fluke of the record.

3. Loose alliterative poetry (rhymed and unrhymed) and its analogues in rhythmical prose (homiletic and otherwise) are ubiquitous and exuberantly variable in prose, homily, and drama throughout the whole period.

4. There are elaborate alliterative verse forms in the contemporary vernaculars of Irish and Welsh that might have served as analogues. In
Anglo-Norman, the *laisse* offers an interesting metrical parallel, a classical epic ten- or twelve-syllable long line gathered into irregular *laisses*.[7]

5. There is no surviving external evidence for or against a continuous
structured oral alliterative tradition that served as an inspiration for or
was transformed into the written alliterative long line.

6. If one exemplary artist (a Chaucer of alliteration) inspired a fourteenth-
century outbreak he has utterly vanished; if there were a series of evo-
lutionary steps for the development for the fourteenth century long
line, they have virtually no trace in the surviving manuscript record
(though scholars such as Derek Pearsall have sought with arguable
success quotes and cross-references proving they did exist).

7. Alliterative poetry abounds with neologisms, *hapax legomena*, and
archaisms found nowhere else in Middle English but existing in
Anglo-Saxon. If Anglo-Saxon is unavailable, where do the poets get
this vocabulary? From local oral retention? From regional dialects?
From the importations of venturesome translator-wordsmiths? From
the more elusive Old Norse loan-words surviving (or remembered)
within ancient Danish settlement areas? Or from a sustained and energetic lexical conscription using any or all of the above in order to
expand and vary alliterative possibilities for every letter?

8. The alliterative lexicon is also very up-to-date, drawing vocabulary from
the rich efflorescence of late fourteenth-century vernacular writing: Lollard treatises, chivalric manuals, technical and occupational vocabularies
(armor-making, siege-warfare, and hunting, for example)—a professional contemporaneity analogous to that of Chaucer's *General Prologue*.

Four important theories negotiate these facts and absences. The eldest
was proposed by R. W. Chambers, who believed that the fourteenth-century
alliterative revival was the sudden and only partially surviving reemergence
into writing of a three-century-long continuum of strictly structured, oral,
alliterative verse—a living native poetic tradition invisible to manuscript
culture.[8] This is a lovely hypothesis and a crux of questions about the relationship between orality and literacy, but it is inherently unprovable. Furthermore, if Chambers is right (and if the flowering of alliterative poetry
in the fourteenth century is not merely produced by the vagaries of manuscript survival), the question remains: why should poets have decided to
commit this living oral tradition to written form? Is there a different kind
of cultural authority and permanence associated with manuscript culture

which they wanted to graft onto oral literary practice—the ancient (and possibly threadbare) *scop* clasping hands with the learned clerk?

More recently, Derek Pearsall suggests that a continuous written tradition of alliterative poetry was, in fact, preserved in monastic libraries of the southwest Midlands through the late twelfth, thirteenth, and early fourteenth centuries but that it has not left any surviving manuscripts. In support, he points to the number of unique manuscripts that define the later tradition (non-survival of previous manuscripts would therefore not be surprising) and to evidence of alliterative borrowing within the thirteenth-century chronicle attributed to Robert of Gloucester. Arguing for the role of monasteries as source collections for alliterative poetry, he outlines the close ties between monastic and aristocratic culture.[9] Pearsall's argument for monastic involvement is persuasive; in fact, Ralph Hanna and David Lawton have managed to trace a manuscript of *The Siege of Jerusalem* to Bolton Priory in Yorkshire.[10] Pearsall's more general idea of a non-surviving written alliterative tradition is also persuasive, and more recent scholarship has pursued the continuities between alliterative poetry and more widely spread alliterative styles as they appear in prose sermons, proverbs, and chronicles.[11]

Thorlac Turville-Petre proposes a different, less continuous model: that alliterative poetry of the fourteenth century self-consciously recreated a recognizably "classical" form of poetry associated specifically with English poetic history, drawing on contemporary oral and written rhythmic prose, alliterative rhymed verse, and logically devised metrical practices that distinguished it from its predecessors and adapted it more fittingly to the state of late Middle English.[12] Turville-Petre supports his theory of the fourteenth-century development of alliterative technique by identifying (somewhat tentatively) earlier alliterative works like *Joseph of Arimathie*, *Alexander and Dindimus*, and *Alisaunder of Macedoine* with sporadic use of strict alliterative form and relatively limited vocabulary and contrasting them with more metrically consistent and lexically ingenious, possibly later, works.[13] Turville-Petre's discussions of how fourteenth-century poets might have recreated self-authorizing precedents parallels and informs my own argument, but his larger generalizations about a revival have not sparked unanimous approval. While acknowledging his book's importance, Derek Pearsall dryly points out in his 1982 essay that several of Turville-Petre's reviewers doubted whether it could or should have been written.[14]

This is because belief in the existence and critical usefulness of an alliterative revival has gone out of style. This final theory arguably exerts the most current power; it has certainly discouraged attempts to treat alliterative poems as distinctive groups. It claims that there is no alliterative revival to explain; the medievalists of the first part of this century, W. P. Ker, R. W. Chambers, and J. R. Hulbert created a needless mystery when they assumed the revival's existence as a fourteenth-century movement, whether nativist, baronial, or vigorously, if vestigially, Anglo-Saxon. Elizabeth Salter moved increasingly towards this view and became its first influential proponent. In 1978 her deliberately pluralized essay, "Alliterative Modes and Affiliations," argued strongly that rather than treating these poems as a coherent school or a self-conscious revival, we should attend to alliterative poetry's diversity and openness, "the easy commerce it traditionally maintained . . . with other forms of composition" (171). She cautions against the "scholarly patriotism" that would mold these poems into indomitable nativist lineages and urges attention instead to "features of extreme detail in the literary landscape" (170). In her analysis, the formal alliterative long line is only one manifestation of a rich and multiform alliterative culture encompassing both rhythmic prose and verse, "norm and high art" (171). It should be most profitably viewed in those diverse local contexts rather than artificially isolated as a separate literary tradition.[15] Ralph Hanna's assessment of alliterative poetry in the *New Cambridge History of Medieval English Literature* strongly reprises and adds to these objections; the preeminence of its inclusion in that admirable and energetic volume attests to this theory's currency.[16]

It will be clear from this summary that all of these theories, unsurprisingly, communicate as much about the altering imperatives of twentieth-century medieval studies as they do about fourteenth-century alliterative verse. And without further evidence—a fuller manuscript record, the discovery of a shadowy league of fourteenth-century Anglo-Saxon antiquarians, the surfacing of a lost methodological treatise on alliterative meter—no theory is sufficient to the evidential gaps. Each theory is powerful and promising not because it solves the mystery but because it enables profitable textual and historical interpretation. Given that depressing—or exciting—presumption, I would like to urge a critical change in direction; to beg temporarily the etiological questions traditionally asked of fourteenth-century alliterative poetry as a group: "how did it come about? who wrote it? where and in what dialect?" and move to more blatantly interpretive questions. Do these poems share common interests? Do the worlds they create resonate with each other? Can we balance fidelity to their "features of extreme detail" with an observance of their larger generic affiliations?

What can these tell us about the interests of the writers and the cultural work of the writing? How do the narrators of these poems assess their own labors, capacities, and obligations as literary and social *makers*? How do these poems constitute, entice, and work their internal and external audiences? The next sections outline the features I believe these poems share, working them to enable what I will argue is their larger generic enterprise: to constitute and perform the past as an arena both of spectacular worth and restless questioning for the present.

Shared Themes: Dramatized Temporality

If, as the *Gawain*-poet famously declares, "A ȝere ȝernes ful ȝerne, and ȝeldez neuer lyke, / Þe forme to þe fynisment foldez ful selde" (498–99) [A year passes apace, and proves ever new: / First things and final conform but seldom], these alliterative romances are determined to call attention to that fact, obsessively folding "forme" to "fynisment" as spectacularly as possible.[17] One of the most dramatic aspects of these poems' historic imaginary is its use of mortal bodies as registers of change, a strategy that makes temporal disjunction intimate. In these poems the elusive, constitutive, absent presence of history is given a local habitation and a name in the uncanny bodies that communicate its disjunctive force. Readers encounter fey bodies, garrulous corpses, headless bodies lifting their heads by the hair to let them speak more projectively, horses frantically galloping while tripping on their own intestines, corpses that are both piteously ephemeral and appallingly vigorous. Their combination of liveliness and mortal scarring differentiates them from the bodies that serve so compellingly in recent criticism as inscriptional or vulnerable sites for social power plays— even for medieval romance these bodies are unusually bizarre and miraculous.[18] They differ also from those powerful symbolic bodies that serve as collective metaphors for political, social, or religious institutions, working to integrate the interdependencies and hierarchies of their fractious (and sometimes violently dissident) parts.[19] They cannot signify wholeness because they are not whole, they cannot focus dissident particularities into powerful unities because they are not singular. These bodies are not synchronic and structural, but radically diachronic and historical. They cannot exist but, in their appalling palpability, they are not virtual or phantasmatic either. They incarnate mutability, but they differ from the fecund and regenerative carnivalesque bodies of Bakhtinian analysis that bring renewal out of death. Alliterative bodies adumbrate fatality as easily as festivity;

they reek of mortality. They are body as rupture and their effect is to communicate with maximum impact the inevitability of temporal disruption, at once provoking and troubling the impossible continuities generated to surmount it.

These bodies become uncanny by forcing into simultaneity states that we are accustomed to separating: life and death; youth, prime, and age; power and powerlessness; past, present and future. They both invoke and confound temporal aspects of narrative, synchronizing historic change. They erase the narrative transitions and structural emplotments that organize temporal moments and that trope historic narratives as tragedy or comedy, romance or irony.[20] In these bodies, the little disruptions and alterations of time which work their metamorphoses more profoundly because of their imperceptibility erupt into brutal visibility. They highlight the otherness of the past and the future to the present. And they communicate this inevitability of change with the unanswerable authority of the Green Knight's severed head lifting its eyelids and opening its mouth across the gulf of death to summon Gawain to a fatal rendezvous.

But such disrupted bodies are only the most dramatic aspect of a more general obsession with temporality in these poems. In addition to embodying temporal disruptions, these poems continually narrate them. They employ retrospective frames, nostalgically revisit their own origins, punctuate the poems' present with historic flashbacks and with cautionary forebodings. They weave narrative tapestries of memory, history, and prophecy. These temporal narrations also correct for the elusiveness of historic change, alerting readers to the inescapable mutability of lived experience, and they do so not simply to issue Augustinian injunctions to journey through history with the wary itinerancy of a pilgrim, nor to urge us to cherish the moment, nor even to respect the past, but more profoundly to teach the otherness of the past in a way that summons us to account for our own use of time and passage through history. This emerges with particular intensity in *Sir Gawain and the Green Knight*'s famous description of the passing of a single year which intercedes between the beginning of the Green Knight's beheading game and its end. Here the year itself assumes the turbulent shape of British history, becoming an competitive struggle between interlocked and opposing forces, a round robin of two-party combats.

> Forþi þis 3ol ouer3ede, and þe 3ere after,
> And vche sesoun serlepes sued after oþer:
> After Crystenmasse com þe crabbed lentoun,
> Þat fraystez flesch wyth þe fysche and fode more symple;

But þenne þe weder of þe worlde wyth wynter hit þrepez,
Colde clenges adoun, cloudez vplyften,
Schyre schedes þe rayn in schowrez ful warme . . .
After þe sesoun of somer wyth þe soft wyndez
Quen Zeferus syflez hymself on sedez and erbez,
Wela wynne is þe wort þat waxes þeroute,
When þe donkande dew dropez of þe leuez,
To bide a blysful blusch of þe bry3t sunne.
Bot þen hy3es heruest, and hardenes hym sone,
Warnez hym for þe wynter to wax ful rype;
He dryues wyth dro3t þe dust for to ryse,
Fro þe face of þe folde to fly3e ful hy3e;
Wroþe wynde of þe welkyn wrastelez with þe sunne,
Þe leuez lancen fro þe lynde and ly3ten on þe grounde,
And al grayes þe gres þat grene watz ere;
Þenne al rypez and rotez þat ros vpon fyrst,
And þus 3irnez þe 3ere in 3isterdaye mony,
And wynter wyndez a3ayn, as þe worlde askez,
        no fage. (498–506, 516–31)

[And so this Yule to the young year yielded place, / And each season ensued at its set time; / After Christmas there came the cold cheer of Lent, / When with fish and plainer fare our flesh we reprove; / But then the world's weather with winter contends: / The keen cold lessens, the low clouds lift; / Fresh falls the rain in fostering showers . . . / And then the season of summer with the soft winds, / When Zephyr sighs low over seeds and shoots; / Glad is the green plant growing abroad, / When the dew at dawn drops from the leaves, / To get a gracious glance from the golden sun. / But harvest with harsher winds follows hard after, / Warns him to ripen well ere winter comes; / Drives forth the dust in the droughty season, / From the face of the fields to fly high in air. / Wroth winds in the welkin wrestle with the sun, / The leaves launch from the linden and light on the ground, / And the grass turns to gray, that once grew green. / Then all ripens and rots that rose up at first, / And so the year moves on in yesterdays many, / And winter once more, by the world's law, draws nigh.][21]

This passage makes the passage of time a series of battles between embodied seasons, each displacing its predecessor only to be ousted in its turn—a genealogy of conquest recalling that with which the poem opens. Its last grim chord is sobering within the narrative as Gawain's fateful rendezvous draws near, but powerful as a knell in its implications for the overall trajectory of British history. Winter both encloses and governs the passage of the seasons, casting a cold shadow on the year. As "wynter wyndez again," the poet's pun on "wynde" equates the process of the turning of the year with the "wroþe wynde of þe welkyn" that wrestles the sun into submission. Time becomes a fundamental winter; the poet describes a cyclical but declining temporality, diverging from the axis of

winter in frantic, lovely sorties that become the more precious for their
bleakly-framed brevity. Gawain's oblivious lethargy as he plays this year
away at court emerges in stark contrast and becomes terrible. With everything "ȝirning" [slipping/yearning] so violently, gorgeously, and inexorably away, what does he think he is doing?

Such dramatic narratives of temporal disjunction implicate the present
reader not just when they remember the inevitability of mortality but when
they shimmer forth a vision of its impossible opposite. At the climax of
Alexander's campaigns, *The Wars of Alexander* takes its hero out of historic
time into a high plateau governed by a lord who blends the vigor of youth
with the white-haired wisdom of age. There Alexander is led into a time-
transcending garden which contains the prophetic trees of the sun and
moon and other trees so enormous and beautiful that they seem set up
by the hands of angels. Blending mourning and reparation like the flowers
that grow on the grave of the lost child in *Pearl*, these trees shed tears
whose ravishing smells promise health and pleasure (5101–4). In the midst
of this garden, Alexander finds an image of what he longs for, an identity
that is self-generating and everlasting. As they walk through the copiously
weeping trees, they find an oddity, a single barren one. It is 150 feet tall,
leafless, barkless, and rindless, but lovely in its bones, and it bears a marvelous bird:

> of a port of a paa with sike a proude crest,
> With bathe þe chekis and þe chauyls as a chykin brid,
> And all gilden was hire gorge with golden fethirs.
> All hire hames behind was hewid as a purpure,
> And all þe body and þe brest and on þe bely vndire
> Was finely florischt and fair with frekild pennys,
> Of gold graynes and of goules, full of gray mascles. (5110–16)

[with the figure of a peacock with just such a proud crest, and both the cheeks
and the jowls resembled those of a chicken. All gilded was her throat with golden
feathers, and all her plumage behind was colored purple. All the body, the breast,
and the underbelly were finely adorned and lovely with freckled feathers with gold
kernels and red, full of grey speckles.]

This bird is a creature of opposites, peacock and chicken, imperial gold/
purple and stern grey. As she lightens her barren tree with the effulgence
of her plumage, Alexander is completely fascinated by her: "Þan waitis
on hire þe wale kyng and wondire him thinke, / Was in þe figure of hire
fourme noȝt ferlid a littil" (5117–18) [Then the proud king pauses before
her and thinks it a wonder; he marveled not a little at the shape of her
figure]. The lord is impatient at Alexander's wonder:

"Quat loke ȝe?" quod the ladisman, "do lendis on forthire;
ȝone is a fereles foule a Fenix we call." (5119–20)

["What are you looking at?" asked the guide, "come along further. That is a peer-
less bird we call a phoenix."]

Alexander is hustled firmly away from the phoenix, which in medieval bes-
tiaries symbolizes eternal life, immolating herself each hundred years to
rise reborn from the ashes of her funeral pyre. Like the lord, she combines
life and death, youth and age, red-gold and grey, a body instinct at once
with mortality and its transcendence. Although she is denied to Alexander,
his own flaming arc of meteoric rise and sudden tragic fall both recalls
and becomes brighter next to her placid, glittering continuance. And her
fleeting appearance shows forth his most ardent desire: the tantalizing
possibility of continuity through time, which is the obverse of the poem's
obsession with mortality.

This spectral promise impels these romances' performances as they
extend their own questions across time. Why else make their historic representations so alluringly figurative, so outrageously spectacular—and so
challengingly enigmatic? Here the poem animates Alexander's aversion
from his inevitable mortality with a performative flair that is both analyt-
ically restrained (since we are denied complex interior exploration) and
figurally prodigious (why is the tree barren? why does a phoenix have
cheeks like a chicken? why is it both gold and mottled grey?). We are
placed in Alexander's position to wonder after answers we must create
ourselves. These romances abound with such spectacular and enigmatic
figures, with provocative displays, with the bodily extremities of combat
and death. This theatricality binds them to the honor culture which is
the assumed (though not always actual) milieu for the genre of romance,
with all of its emphasis on spectacle, conspicuous consumption, the theaters of love, tourney, and war, and the externalized identities of insignia
and device. Yet even as the alliterative romances indulge in flagrant theatricality, they often tease at the mechanics of such theater by their sheer figurative and bodily excess. They perform both the power and the failure of
signs, their arresting illegibility, the ways they can exceed a single interpretation or, in Alexander's case as he gazes longingly at the phoenix, a
reader's ownership. They externalize and figuralize identity in order to
whittle away its moorings—as in *Gawain* with the mutually complicating
signs of pentangle and the girdle, or the *Morte Arthure* with its unassign-
able insignia. And this figural complexity has a counterpart in the difficult, gorgeous, abstruse meter and diction that become hallmarks of these

romances.[22] Both stylistically and figurally the alliterative romances invite readers to pause in wonder, grapple with, and reanimate through their own reading the quandaries of old and new that the poems present.

Other Coherences: Meter, Genre, Voice, Audience

1. Meter

There is no consensus about methodologies for analyzing alliterative meter let alone any agreement on conclusions to be drawn from it. Just how little we know has been trenchantly assessed by Stephen A. Barney, who argues that the whole century of scholarship on alliterative meter has been both unsystematic and disastrously cagey about revealing its operant assumptions about methodology and data.[23] Scholars have not even agreed on what should be included in the corpus of Middle English alliterative poetry. They have worked at cross-purposes inventing their own metrical systems, notations, and terminologies (often not defined). They have concocted individual databases with different assumptions for inclusion, analysis, and projected rationale (How should the data be used? As a way to systematize editorial emendations? As a heuristic for linguistic problem-solving? As a method of metrical analysis?). Barney outlines over fifty multifaceted questions in five different areas of investigation that have remained unsystematically treated and thus largely unanswered. He ends with a call for methodological consensus and full disclosure of both data and the governing assumptions for its analysis that would allow the replication of results by other scholars. He hopes that the data-crunching force of computer-driven statistical analysis will shed some light on the viability of the fascinating hypotheses that have recently been proposed and open up new possibilities of analysis.

This is because hypotheses by Hoyt Duggan and Thomas Cable have recently galvanized the field of alliterative metrical studies that had been previously shaped by the magisterial metrical genealogy of J. P. Oakden.[24] Oakden sought and found considerable continuity between Old English and late Middle English in both rhythmical and alliterative patterns, with the most likeness between early and late Middle English.[25] According to Oakden, the most significant break in the alliterative tradition comes between late Old English and early Middle English as widespread vernacular traditions of rhythmic prose exert a pull on the alliterative poetry. Late Middle English alliteration as a whole continues early Middle English patterns, including its experimentation with other stanzaic, rhyming, and rhythmic traditions. However, late Middle English *formal* alliterative styles discard the vestiges of the popular rhythmical form, unstructured rhyming couplets, and rhyme words linking half-lines. As a result, the fourteenth-century formal alliterative long line at first looks more like a return to classical Anglo-Saxon than some of its rhythmically influenced predecessors, but Oakden's survey concludes that it actually extends early Middle English alliterative patterns.[26] He bases his rhythmical analysis on Eduard Sievers's breakdown of Old English poetry into five types of rising, falling, rising-falling, and clashing lines which he believes becomes increasingly flexible over time. Oakden's sense of poetic continuity may have been accentuated because he privileged alliteration in the interweaving of metrical, morphological, rhythmical, formulaic, and syntactic features that have emerged as cruxes of metrical definition. Alliterative patterns show the least change over time, and the "classical" Old English patterns aa/ax and ax/ax still dominate in fourteenth-century formal alliterative poetry.[27] Oakden has come under heavy fire in the last decade. Cable criticizes Oakden for privileging alliteration as a marker of stress and challenges his thesis of continuity. Barney castigates Oakden for failure to define his corpus, methodology, terminology, arguments, and assumptions, and above all for refusing to disclose the evidence on which he based his conclusions so that other scholars could examine it, winding up the devastation with "it is clearly wrong, but even if it were right it is unusable."[28]

In a series of articles written from the mid-1980s to early 1990s, Hoyt Duggan usefully moved the emphasis to rhythm and syntax as "at least equally fundamental to the line, perhaps in some way 'deeper' in the structure of the line itself than the alliteration."[29] Positing a caesura between half-lines and different rhythmical expectations for the metrical patterns of the a-line (first half-line) and the b-line (second half-line), Duggan discerned a more rigid patterning in the b-line. His anatomy of the b-line comprises two stresses (of which the first must and the second may alliterate) and between one and three dips (unstressed syllables) of which one (and only one) of the first two must be strong (with several consecutive unstressed syllables), and of which the last must be null or weak (with only one unstressed syllable).[30] His articles express a regularizing impulse that dictates the coincidence of alliteration and stress, finds an unvarying aa/ax alliterative pattern (he excludes *Piers Plowman* from his corpus here), and finds generally two stresses in each half line, with particular patterns of dips distinguishing a- and b-lines.[31] He attributes variations from these patterns to scribal error, and wishes to mobilize his metrical system for the editorial emendation of manuscripts back to "original" metrical norms.[32]

Thomas Cable independently came to some of the same conclusions about alliterative metrical structure at roughly the same time. Like Duggan, he decentralizes alliteration and foregrounds rhythmical pattern, describing a system that rhythmically differentiates a-lines and b-lines according to mutually exclusive patterns of stresses and strong dips. In his system, the a-line can be either normal (with two metrical stresses and two strong dips) or extended (with three stresses and any pattern of dips). His b-line rules resemble Duggan's, with two metrical stresses of which one and only one can be prefaced by a strong dip. Unlike Duggan, Cable also finds that the b-line must end with a single unstressed syllable.[33] Cable disputes Duggan's linkage of metrical analysis to editorial emendation and his soliciting of scribal error to explain irregularities. Cable wishes to grant the alliterative poets more metrical license even as he attributes to alliterative poets the evolution both of careful metrical rules and a high level of linguistic consciousness of the historical morphologies and derivations of words.

Cable's description of alliterative metrical development from Old English to Middle English, meets neither Duggan's nor Barney's criteria for argumentative rigor.[34] However, it usefully counters Oakden's emphasis on continuity and accords with my argument that the fourteenth-century alliterative poets were improvising a lost tradition rather than actually following one. In brief, Cable's snapshot history of alliterative meter finds that Old English poetry is fundamentally syllabic, compounded of four positions (of which the first or second allow minor syllabic expansion) and nine to ten syllables or their resolved equivalents. This view counters prevailing descriptions of Old English poetry as stress-based. In Cable's view, stress becomes fundamental to alliterative meter only in early Middle English, when (as Oakden also noted) a strongly stressed rhythmical prose tradition exerts its influence upon alliterative poetry. Between Old and Middle English, alliterative verse moves from a fairly simple, structured syllabic system to a very flexible line patterned by strong stresses, two to each half-line and varying numbers of unstressed syllables between. A rhythmical preference develops to alternate metrically stressed syllables with varying numbers of unstressed syllables, thus eliminating Old English "clashes" of consecutive metrically stressed syllables. In early Middle English alliterative poetry, syllable count only matters in establishing a minimum half-line length of at least five syllables. In this move from a syllable-counting meter to a stress meter alternating strong stresses with strong dips (several consecutive unstressed syllables),[35] Cable sees not only a decided break with Old English poetic methodologies but also possibly a self-conscious one. For instance, patterns of simple four-syllable verses are avoided in

Middle English alliterative verse for "the reason . . . that they are too close to the patterns of other meters (both Old English and iambic pentameter), and the Middle English poets were concerned to forge their own unambiguous meter."[36]

This self-conscious break with other poetic forms hallmarks Cable's description of fourteenth-century alliterative verse as well. In his view, the fourteenth-century alliterative long line is unprecedented in its formality and metrical challenge:

Middle English alliterative meter is even more highly controlled than the Chaucerian meter. Certain patterns of stressed and unstressed syllables turn out to be appropriate only for the first half-line and other patterns only for the second half-line. This distribution is the main evidence for a new paradigm of Middle English alliterative meter. (4)

Amidst this invention of a challenging new poetic form, however, Cable sees a backward-looking impulse. Cable discerns in fourteenth- and early fifteenth-century alliterative poetry a careful cultivation of past and passing morphologies. In evolving rules for the mutually exclusive subsets of metrical patterns allowable in a- and b-lines, Cable finds "a correlation between the number of unstressed syllables that occurred in a word *historically* and the placing of that word in the long line" (emphasis added; 68). Retention of voiced final -*e*, the last residue of lost grammatical case endings in many word classes, becomes crucial to Cable's argument, even though most linguistic histories posit that final -*e* gradually became unvoiced in the fourteenth century. Cable thus connects his arguments that "(1) the phonology of the West Midlands alliterative poetry is more conservative than the standard grammars indicate and (2) the fourteenth-century alliterative line is more highly regulated in its patterns of unstressed syllables than prosodists of the modern period have understood" (76). One hypothesis relies upon the other; voicing final -*e* in designated classes of words regularizes the metrical patterns of the fourteenth-century long line.

Cable further argues that this conserving of past morphological forms was a deliberate, and not always entirely successful, reconstruction of previous linguistic usage. He notes that the *Wars*-poet cultivates a historical final -*e* consistently in weak and plural forms of monosyllabic adjectives, but neglects to use it for the suffix -*full*, in contrast to the usage of alliterative poets writing a generation earlier (notably the *Alexander A*-poet). He concludes that this shows an error in the *Wars*-poet's learning of an earlier form of language:

The poet who wrote *The Wars of Alexander* had to learn a language during a period of extraordinary changes. Final *-e* was disappearing, but final *-e* did not disappear the way the members of an endangered species do, any one of which is alive or dead. It disappeared in changing configurations of grammatical categories from speaker to speaker. The evidence suggests that the poet's grammar retained *-e* on the present and past participles and on words with *-lich*, but there is no positive evidence . . . that he retained *-e* in *-fulle*. The lack of positive evidence is evidence itself, though inferential, because positive evidence occurs in other poems. A plausible explanation, then, for what Peirce calls "strange facts" is that the poet of *The Wars of Alexander* constructed a grammar which in most of its details replicated the grammars of the earlier generation. On at least one small point, however, the poet as language-learner missed a category that retained final *-e*. (109–10)

This suggestive picture of conservative reconstruction during a time of linguistic change remains at the level of hypothesis but it suggestively links to other "backward-looking" features of formal alliterative poetry noted by scholars: diction, formulaic phraseology, and subject-matter, and also suggests an ongoing improvisation of the past.[37] Cable disavows Duggan's need to regularize, allowing for an Eliot-like poetic license and flexibility of metrical usage, even amidst his description of rules.[38] The picture that emerges from Cable's discussion thus allows for a range of linguistic sensitivity, reconstructional expertise, and performative license on the part of alliterative poets. This admission of license prevents Cable's hypotheses from gelling into implacable rules (and promises to complicate the statistical analysis for which Barney calls). At the same time it brings Cable's pattern-discerning hypothesis more into line with many scholars' impressionistic sense of alliterative poetry's capacity for formal flexibility and experimentation.

I find Cable's thesis suggestive because it describes a group of poets interested in reconstructing past forms even as they are elaborating a meter different from both early Middle English and Old English alliterative meters. It yields a view of an alliterative poetry both challengingly structured (laying down expectations for different sets of metrical patterns admissible within each half-line) and flexible (allowing hundreds of different combinations of a-line and b-line patterns, and thus a very wide range of line forms). It can be both innovative (departing rhythmically from both Old English and early Middle English alliterative poetry) and backward-looking (linking its half-lines with archaic-seeming alliterating letter patterns as well as reconstructing past morphologies). It can toe a purist long line but it can also take poetic license to adopt the freer manners of alliterative rhythmic prose common in homiletic and devotional writing (in

Richard Rolle, for example, who actually adapts Latin to English alliterative meter).[39] If it performs a tradition it also claims the improvisational mastery to adapt, embroider, and depart from it.

2. *Genre*

Just as fourteenth-century meter looks backward to perform insular alliterative traditionality even in the midst of rigorous innovation, alliterative romance as a genre both reprises and revises insular romance traditions as it continues to test the exigencies of chivalric, religious, historical, and artistic authority in a constantly changing world.[40] The first often noted feature shared by these poems is their concern with history, a generic axis which I treat as distinctively dramatic, spectacular, embodied, and interrogative. Rosalind Field notes how the alliterative romance obsessions with historical and legendary matters do not fit comfortably within descriptions of romance deriving from continental traditions of *fine amor*—although individual poems, particularly *Sir Gawain and the Green Knight,* knowingly solicit and critique those traditions.[41] Their large-scaled historical concerns also disarticulate alliterative romance from insular Anglo-Norman and Middle English ancestral romances dramatizing the antecedents of particular illustrious and usually baronial families, usually fabricated from convention or drawn from local legend (57). By contrast, the alliterative romance poets flaunt their learned and often Latinate bookishness and thereby express a notable sense of the worthiness of their literary enterprise: "the list of subjects of alliterative romance reads like a programmatic elaboration of the theme of the Nine Worthies, drawing on the biblical, classical and Arthurian material that made up 'the common inheritance of fourteenth-century Englishmen.'"[42]

Yet alliterative romances also express affinities with insular Anglo-Norman and Middle English romance's sense of heroic provinciality. These emerge in their sharp awareness of the sometimes conflicting interests dividing monarch from aristocracy and their often critical treatment of Arthur (68); especially if he does not recognize the vast extent to which his power requires the support, strength, and separate authority of his barons and provincial knights. Susan Crane agrees with Field's basic conclusions about insular romance but elaborates them further. She accentuates the social work of insular romance as she works out the relations of Anglo-Norman and Middle English romances in her 1986 *Insular Romance.* In it she describes an English romance tradition constelling four concerns (1) history as a guarantor of lineal authority and legitimacy; (2) a provinciality interested in the prerogatives of baronial culture and critical of the royal court's self-universalizing politics and poetics; (3) religiosity but in a mode that ultimately harnesses the earth-transcending work of faith to worldly (and specifically baronial) purposes; and (4) the historically altering needs of a particular baronial audiences and their class-conscious but also individualizing opportunisms.

I will argue that alliterative romance as a genre mobilizes essentially these same four concerns, but that it also complicates and interrogates them until they become less generic descriptors than generic dramas of questioning. First, alliterative romances are as obsessed with history as their insular predecessors but as Field shows, they solicit histories that are vaster, more worthily learned, more portentous. In addition, I will argue, their attitudes toward history are more complex: the past is no longer unambiguously illustrious, safely dead, and easily solicited. Instead we find a fractured series of unquiet pasts—pagan, primeval, Jewish, non-chivalric, admirable, alien, pathetic, and threatening. Thus, the alliterative romances are often as interested in revising their lineages as in soliciting them.

Second, they still, by and large, place themselves outside an increasingly questionable royal court, but their reading of continental Arthuriana has given them a Matter of Britain more appropriable to monarchical critique than before and they seize it with gusto. The four most substantial romances in this book, *Sir Gawain and the Green Knight*, *The Wars of Alexander*, *The Siege of Jerusalem*, and the alliterative *Morte Arthure*, expand provincialism into a trope one might (mischievously) call "caveat imperator," dramatizing how great things may come from apparently insignificant outlying regions to topple empires. *Sir Gawain* and *Morte Arthur* delight in scenes that disturb the royal court-centered universe by receiving royal emissaries with a provincial "sparcity" whose spectacular extravagance daunts and beggars their monarchical or imperial guests. *The Wars of Alexander* and *The Siege of Jerusalem* use less gentle means to show how provincial upstarts are forces to be reckoned with. And the monarchy is not the only altering site of authority that attracts these romances' attention—the city of London and its rowdy citizenry threaten the bishop's civic authority in *St. Erkenwald*.

At the same time, these poems put pressure upon simple divisions between center and province. The provincial gentry is internally riven by royalist affiliations in the Cheshire and Lancashire of *Sir Gawain and the Green Knight*; the poem explores a strikingly self-conflicted late medieval chivalric consciousness. And the alliterative *Morte Arthure* brings those concerns to the heart of the monarchy itself, even as it reflects its insular roots by showing a king so heavily dependent on the chivalry of his baronial comrades that without them he declines to the impotence of a grieving widow. Meanwhile, *The Siege of Jerusalem* and *The Wars of Alexander* gesture critically at the international scope of late medieval monarchical ambition, while *De Tribus Regibus Mortuis* and *The Awntyrs off Arthure* somberly acknowledge the limited lordship of all kings and adjure their leaders to recognize the charity they owe their social inferiors.

Third, as for their religious trajectories, religious values are still subjected to worldly ends but no longer as easily. Rifts open continually to show troubling disparities between historically transcendent signs, identities, soteriological concerns, and chivalric ambitions, and the worldly governance they are invoked to ratify. This is most noticeable in *Sir Gawain and the Green Knight*, which weaves religious ritual into noble household life with almost terrifying ease, and in the alliterative *Morte Arthure,* which uses the language of sacrament to trouble and intensify its military drama.[43]

Fourth, in all this, alliterative romances reflect and reimagine a social world anxious and alight with change: tug-of-wars between monarchy and magnates, unprecedented social mobilities (both vertical [social climbing, clinging, and falling] and horizontal [laborers and artisans roaming town and country for better wages despite statutory legislation to control their movements]), mercantile opportunisms, contractual chivalries, newly authorized vernaculars, spreading literacy, and claims to religious agency by the laity.

The opening of these generic markers as questions alters and extends the way that alliterative romances can pitch their distinctive narrative voices to assert cultural authority and appeal to and work on targeted audiences. A drama foregrounding the authority of provincial outsiders, for example, can work in unprecedented ways to encompass religious outsiders or romance others. The traditional romance preoccupation with unknown knights and non-chivalric (or non-Christian) sources of authority can be pursued even farther and to far more culturally adventurous (or discomfiting) extremes. In this vein, Stephen Shepherd interestingly suggests the possible interchanges between the romance fascination with alterity and *Piers Plowman*'s adventurous address to pagan salvation, dramatized in *St. Erkenwald* as well.[44] When alliterative romances imaginatively invest themselves in the outsider challenges that enliven their historical confrontations, a field of fascinating risk and speculation opens out, which can be traversed both to encompass outsiders within newly invigorated hegemonies or to reject them and in the process show forth the functional cracks, gaps, and sutures that riddle dominant ideologies (or historical narratives) when they make themselves explicit to do social work.[45] By centralizing outsider challenges, these poems thus can work to both conservative and socially interrogatory ends—sometimes simultaneously—often laying bare, in Michel de Certeau's phrase, "the ingenious ways in which the weak make use of the strong."[46]

3. Poetic Voice: Antiquity, Authority, and Craft

These alliterative romances differ from earlier Middle English romances in their poetic and lexical virtuosity, their sheer verbal spectacle. They show an unprecedented belief in the self-evident value, interest, and allure of their craft. Turville-Petre comments on the unusual sense of solemnity claimed by the alliterative poets for their works: "The poems share . . . a sense of their own value that is far from universal in fourteenth-century poetry, a conviction sometimes openly expressed by the poet that what he communicates is important and is being treated with dignity and seriousness."[47] In later alliterative poetry one finds very few of the disclaimers so typical of Chaucer and his followers, for whom professions of modesty, innocence, lack of skill, or feeble imitation of older, better masters become identifying *topoi*. Where Chaucer in particular registers problems of poetic authority (which can of course be exploited for a multitude of underhandedly self-promoting ends) by offering himself as a dreamer, a reporter of others' words, or an appellant to multiple (and surprising) gods, goddesses, furies, and muses, the alliterative poets show no hesitation in grandly invoking the greatest foundational moments in European history. By writing in such meter on such illustrious topics, they are claiming a recognizable cultural authority whose antiquity becomes ground enough for its own dramatic reenactment.

This claim rings most clearly in their swaggering opening gestures, whether they sweep the listener directly onto the burning battlefields of Troy or take a more leisurely route, preambling about the pleasures and profits of storytelling in fine company. Implicit in these introductory lines is an act of conjuration; the poets fabricate personae for both themselves and their audiences and construct a relationship between them that is both lulling in its familiarity and flexible in its effects: the professional poet addressing the demanding, discerning, postprandial, aristocratic audience:

> When folk ere festid and fed, fayn wald þai here
> Sum farand þinge eftir fode to fayn[en] þare hertis
> Or þai ware fourmed on fold or þaire fadirs oþir.
> Sum is leue to lythe þe lesing of sayntis
> Þat lete þaire lifis be lorne for oure lord sake.
> And sum has langinge of lufe lay[e]s to herken,

> How ledis for þaire lemmans has langor endured.
> Sum couettis and has comforth to carpe and to lestyn
> Of curtaissy, of knyȝthode, of craftis of armys,
> Of kyngis at has conquirid and and ouircomyn landis;
> Sum of wirschip, iwis, slike as þam wyse lattis,
> And sum of wanton werkis, þa þat ere wild-hedid;
> Bot if þai wald on many wyse, a wondire ware it els,
> For as þaire wittis ere within, so þaire will folowis. (*Wars of Alexander*, 1–14)

[When folks are feasted and fed, they are eager to hear of some pleasurable matter to gladden their hearts after food, something that happened before they walked the earth or their fathers either. Some like to listen to the redemption of saints who gave up their lives for the sake of our lord. And some long to listen to lays of love, how men for their lovers have endured hardships. Some desire and enjoy discussing and hearing matters of courtesy, knighthood, and weapon-craft, of kings that have conquered and overcome lands. Some prefer worshipful things, certainly those who consider themselves wise, and others prefer wanton deeds, those that are wild-headed (frivolous). It would be a wonder if they did not like many different things; for as their wits are within, so their will follows.]

In this opening passage from *The Wars of Alexander*, the feast becomes the operant trope as the poet sketches the various trajectories of aristocratic desire at the moment of their transformation from gustatory to literary. Audience and story interpenetrate as the poet channels subjectivities and sensibilities into a rich cornucopia of literary possibilities all of which serve the appetites of aristocratic literary culture. The narrator emerges as a distinct voice, observant, detached, a little ironic, alert to the vagrant diversities of both audience and narrative. The passage ends with a theatrical moment of choice. Amidst all these possible generic delicacies, which will he select?

> And I forwith ȝow all ettillis to schewe
> Of ane emperoure þe aȝefullest þat euir armys hauntid;
> Þat was þe athill Alexsandire, as þe buke tellis,
> Þat aȝte euyn as his awyn all þe werd ouire;
> For he recouerd quills he regnyd þe regions all clene,
> And all rialme and þe riches into þe rede est.
> I sall rehers, and ye will, renkis, rekyn ȝour tongis
> A remnant of his rialte and rist quen vs likis. (15–22)

[And here before you, I intend to tell of the fiercest emperor that ever pursued arms. That was the noble Alexander, as the book tells, that claimed as his own all the world over, for while he reigned he wholly gained possession of all regions and all realms and their wealth unto the red east. I shall recite a small part of his royalty and you, people, pay heed to your tongues, and we will rest when it pleases us.]

The bravura of this moment of choice is calculated, even stagey; for a moment the narrator is the carnival barker adjuring silence, and soft-selling his product, which in the spirit of the most dextrous salesmanship gradually transforms into a pleasantly communal enterprise. The poet lays down the rules but solicits compliance not because of his own stature but because his matter is both monumental and richly, wonderfully extravagant.

Yet that monumentality is itself a production; the poet is constituting not only his narrator and his audience but, retrospectively, the very literary traditions which he invokes and from which he draws his authority—in this case the Matter of Alexander. Pierre Bourdieu describes a similar process of boot-strap self-legitimation as doubly representational, performing an "alchemy of *representation* (in the different senses of the term) through which the representative creates the group which creates him: the spokesperson endowed with the full power to speak and act on behalf of the group . . . is the substitute for the group, which exists solely through this *procuration*."[48]

If the Alexander-poet's world-creating strategy mobilizes an analogous kind of representational authority, the fictional "group" that the Alexander-poet at once represents and constitutes becomes the elusive and semi-mythical tradition of the professionally recognized and recompensed poet as guardian and transmitter of history and cultural identity—an authoritative stance. That this is a fictional group at this time in England, there is very little doubt; evidence for widespread patronage of poets (as opposed to musical minstrels) in the late fourteenth century at any level of society—royal court, baronial household, or manor—is tenuous at best. Nonetheless, it is an identifiable tradition and one whose very literary fossilization paradoxically guarantees its recognition as a convention and grants it at least the temporary hearing that it requests.

And to the constitution of such a tradition, the choice of formal alliterative meter is key. With its performance of antiquity and the unusual breadth of vocabulary, artistry, and onomatopoesis, formal alliterative meter exercises a visible and verbal expertise that attains in several poems to coloratura performance. This meter wears its artistry on its courtly and elaborate sleeve—a visual poetic authority that poets would not find in such a showy form in the French-derived syllabic end-rhymed meter that had been catching on in London writing workshops and the southeast as an acceptable vehicle for romance.[49] When poets performed an ancient insular metrical form, they took the dignity of the *scop* as an indigenous cultural historian and wed it to the stability and clerical prestige of writing, altering the form to do this. In support, Oakden suggests that the unusual

preference of fourteenth-century alliterative poetry to alliterate predominantly identical vowels (as opposed to earlier forms that allowed any vowel
to alliterate with any other) reflected a desire to present alliteration for
delectation of the reading eye as well as for the listening ear—exhibiting
additional skill in the process.[50] And the sometimes extraordinary artistry
of formal alliterative performance vindicates this attempt—poetic skill
becoming its own authorization in the spectacular hybridization of oral
and written traditions.[51] The opening of the most beautiful and intricate of
the poems, *Sir Gawain and the Green Knight* makes this explicit. After its
grandiose invocation of the history of British settlement the poet addresses
his fictional audience:

> If ȝe wyl lysten þis laye bot on littel quile,
> I schal telle hit as-tit, as I in toun herde,
>   with tonge,
>   As hit is stad and stoken
>   In stori stif and stronge,
>   With lel letteres loken,
>   In londe so hatz ben longe. (30–36)

[If you will listen to this lay but a little while, I shall tell it at once, just as I heard
it told in town aloud, as it is set down and fixed in story brave and strong, fastened
with true letters, in this land from time immemorial. (translation mine)]

This description claims both an oral and a written source for the poem.
Where the meter lilts in the unrhymed long line, the story is oral and
almost accidental; the poet heard it "in toun," possibly as a new story
circulating in London. However in the rhymed and alliterated wheel
where the meter is battened down into iambic steps, the poem is doubly
inscribed and fastened, "stad and stoken." The story itself becomes more
substantial. "Stif and strong" are fighting words; the story has suffered and
endured the buffets of time. The last couplet completes the anchoring
process by suggesting the antiquity of the meter as a native tradition. The
poem wants it both ways, claims both types of poetic legitimacy: speaking
tongue and written letter, comparative metrical flexibility and rigidity,
"toun" and "londe," eye and ear, innovation and tradition.[52]

And this dual character intensifies self-consciousness about the poem's
relationship to precedent and tradition. As transmitter of an oral narrative circulating like gossip, each teller is free to embroider, to thicken with
other sources, to edit and curtail without fear of compromising the traditionality and antiquity of the story itself. Its historicity can be asserted,
even as it is changed. The poems thus resist the rigidity of their inscription. Their performance of orality helps to broaden their imaginative

license, allowing them to relax their clerical moorings and evade the anxiety of literary genealogy and precedent that so besets other contemporary writers. We see another author vividly choosing the same strategy in Chaucer's *House of Fame* where the narrator "Jeffrey" similarly abandons the rigid pillars and unstable favors of the House of written Fame and leaps eagerly and "alderfastest" into the circulating clamor of Rumor's tatty labyrinth, inaugurating a new, ventriloquent, and resilient poetic voice, thriving on indeterminacy.

4. Implied and Probable Audiences

To be both oral and written also gives alliterative writing a kind of hyperpoetic status; many of the poems begin by entreating their noble audience to listen while simultaneously flaunting their literary and clerical dexterity, referring to (or simply using) sources (often in Latin and French) which have often been translated or elaborately collated.[53] They address simultaneously an audience of listeners and readers. Thus this insistence on the flagrant fictionality of the poetic performance bleeds into this hybridized and virtual audience. Most evidence indicates that alliterative poets were not professional minstrels or court poets (who were having their own occupational difficulties with an endemic absence of patronage systems), but rather clerics or functionaries associated with the households of provincial knights, gentry, or monastic establishments.[54] Moreover, the actual audiences/readers of these poems were most probably not the greater nobility whose halls the poems invoke as their milieu, but rather well-off landowners, clerics, and country gentlemen—the traditional barony, gentry, and clergy who were also addressed, according to Susan Crane, by the insular romances. These figures resemble, as Turville-Petre notes, Chaucer's banquet-giving Franklin more than Arthur's noble "douth" on the dais.[55] If franklins, lesser knights, or household clerks are the poem's most likely audience—which is still an open question—another question still remains: why do alliterative poets create implied audiences of aristocratic listeners?[56] Why an invitation to play these particular roles? Are the poets simply offering the private pleasure of imaginatively ascending the social ladder for an evening?

I think that is only part of the answer. The fictional narrator plays the professional poet that the writer is not, a contradiction that places him in the peculiar position of someone who claims to represent a tradition but is perceptibly outside it—both authority and interloper. Bourdieu points out that the effectiveness of the performative utterance depends on an a priori recognition of the social authority of the speaker—his institutional investiture. Lacking such socially apparent investiture, the alliterative writer must not only create himself, a desirous audience, and the tradition he represents, but also make that creation alluring to as many different kinds of audience engagement as he can. Artistry, illustrious subjects, claims to the authority of older indigenous literary traditions, and displays of clerical skill all play their part in this. But appealing to an audience of prosperous country gentlemen and educated clergy in positions of local authority need not mean simply pandering to their social ambitions. The poet can draw them in even more compellingly by encompassing the wide-ranging and peculiar tensions and oppositional desires that perplex their particular social experience.

And there is a fair amount of evidence for the conflicted experience of this nebulous class.[57] In a discussion of the social agency of Chaucer's Franklin, Susan Crane analyzes the effects of the Franklin's liminal status vis-à-vis the aristocracy and the aristocratic literary genre of romance. In her argument, this liminality gives the Franklin a marginal perspective which allows him to register both collusion with the aristocracy and resistance to them. He both profits from and is uncomfortably subordinated by the dominant aristocratic hierarchies that he cannot easily penetrate, but to which he must retain a relationship. The Franklin does this through two strategies. The first strategy is performative: daily feasts—which attain meteorological proportions—to demonstrate his liberality. The Franklin dramatizes a wealth and prestige which does not rest on the aristocratic foundations of land and lineage. The Franklin's second strategy is literary: his selection of a romance as his tale for the pilgrimage. Yet the romance he tells and the way he shapes it allow him to make visible not only the virtues of aristocratic hierarchies but the crippling constraints with which they can rack the social ladder, delimiting the agencies of women, squires, and clerks, not to mention the Franklin himself.[58] Crane's point can be extended to suggest that alliterative poetry, directed to an audience most likely of the Franklin's social level, performs a similar self-inclusion within late medieval aristocratic culture, yet like the Franklin's tale it can also register detachment from, criticism of, and resistance to that culture. And this would perhaps explain the curiously contradictory strategies with which many alliterative poems open and which seem to highlight the flexibility and imaginative agency of the poets—their capacity both to capitalize upon and interrogate the traditions and social structures they invoke, highlighting both their strengths and their limitations as they are brought face to face with their own authoritative predecessors.

Summation

Given the gap-ridden, theory-riddled critical history of alliterative romance, I return to the hypothesis of performed archaism with a certain wariness— a curiosity about its many and varied uses, an unwillingness to assimilate these poems solely to nativist or nationalizing traditions, an alertness to Salter's call for attention to each poem's local detail, and a sense of the rightness of Turville-Petre's arguments for informed re-creation. Even Salter concedes—with an understandable weariness born of the drum-beating on archaism by "scholarly patriots"—that "there may be departments of alliterative verse-writing which lay some genuine claim to self-conscious literary 'antiquarianism,' or to other forms of self-conscious literary refinement upon older patterns newly rediscovered" (171). Now that such scholarly patriots have been rendered a little less shrill by becoming analytical objects in the recently burgeoning study of medievalisms, we can return to such an antiquarian and aesthetically refined "department" within alliterative verse-writing and trouble the parameters of its implied self-enclosure. Here, Salter opposes the formal and archaic alliterative romances to "others whose part in a 'revival' is less well-defined, and whose affiliations . . . speak rather of transformatory processes" (171), but earlier, she usefully suggested their inescapable contemporaneity: "Though it has a ground base of metre with a long and redoubtable ancestry, the distinction of this Middle English verse is its power to invest an old measure with contemporary splendour and relevance. Like the art of the illuminated psalters commissioned by the baronial families, the English poetry written either in or near to their castles has links with the past—but more decisively caters to the tastes of the present."[59] Even the most formal and antiquarian poems retain an urgent presentist commerce.

I think that these alliterative romances make antiquarian retrospection a means of contemporary social preoccupation and thereby share in the interests of other socially invested fourteenth-century texts. Yet they also distinguish themselves from other fourteenth-century poetic traditions in the provocative spectacularity of their historic consciousness, their reinvention of insular metrical and romance traditions, and the ways they perform and constitute poetic voice and audience. Their spectacularity distinguishes the alliterative romances not only from the poetry of Gower and Chaucer but also from the plainer styled and more dialectically driven alliterative, allegorical dream-visions of *Pier's Plowman* and its imitators, and the equally elaborate but more didactic *Pearl, Patience,* and *Cleanness.*

Their historical and provincial concerns link them to insular romance, but insular romance does not stage temporal disruption with such dramatic and formally ornate persistence. In bringing together these two concerns—spectacle and history—alliterative romance establishes a peculiarly vivid and difficult arena for interrogating a late medieval society heavily invested in the cultural power exerted by both.

St. Erkenwald
and the Body in Question

A ROMANCE OF BRITISH CHRISTIAN foundation, *St. Erkenwald* is startlingly willing to capitalize on that foundation's belatedness, its innovative
status as "New Werke" (38) in a land far older than itself.[1] And that "werke"
is energized by its specific location: St. Paul's Cathedral in London. The
poem tells the story of the original construction of the cathedral that will
become not only a conduit of salvation but also a strong center of urban
authority for the city of London.[2] It tests the foundations of episcopal control of the city in the person of Erkenwald, a bishop and saint whose shrine
in St. Paul's drew pilgrims and revenue for the cathedral in the fourteenth
and fifteenth centuries. However, in the poem the bishop's authority is
not preordained but emerges through a chancy dialogue with a dead man
discovered in the cathedral's foundations. This corpse in its lovely and loving entombment at first bespeaks a forgotten past of wondrous alterity but
grows increasingly and disquietingly familiar in the course of the conversation, eventually adumbrating to the bishop his own posthumous career
as foundational relic. The poem underscores the interrogatory force of
this strange disinterment. Monika Otter vividly describes the "tremendous
nervous energy . . . a general mood of wonder and questioning" that the
poem radiates.[3] Ruth Nissé highlights its overwhelming anxiety.[4] Before
the venerable mirror of that reverently invested, pagan body, the bishop's
own institutional vulnerabilities emerge sharply; his questions delve at the
foundations of fourteenth-century ecclesiastical prerogatives to shepherd
the city and solely mediate its salvation. Yet even as all of his questions
are answered their intensity lingers; the poem spotlights the tremendous
desire and fear directed toward this revenant from the pagan past and the
historical risk that any genuinely new work must transact.[5]

The poem begins in Anglo-Saxon London with the first construction
of St. Paul's Cathedral upon the site of an ancient heathen temple. The
workmen are digging new foundations when they unearth a gorgeous and
mysterious tomb in the churchyard. This discovery incites a riot of curious
London folk. So tumultuous is their influx that the Bishop of St. Paul's,

Erkenwald, is recalled from a progress through the provinces and hurries back to London to quell the disturbance. The rest of the poem recounts the long conversation between the corpse and the bishop. The corpse reveals himself to be an ancient pagan judge whose concern for righteousness was so profound and socially productive that after he died the people of his London buried him as a king. His body, miraculously uncorrupted after centuries, gives a divine stamp of approval to his very real social accomplishments. The bishop questions the corpse more narrowly: does this mean that the pagan judge has achieved salvation by his own virtue? It turns out not; the blissfully uncorrupted body traps a tormented soul that will never achieve Heaven because the judge lived without knowing Christian grace. The tension and pathos of this conversation finally move the bishop to tears of pity which fall upon the corpse to enact a posthumous baptism. The pagan's body crumbles to dust and his soul flies up to God. The bishop leads the citizens of London out of the churchyard, and the bells of St. Paul's ring over all of London.

Why should the civic and secular authority of the church emerge so visibly in a poem that seems so self-evidently a tale of divine mercy?[6] I argue that the poem works to quell assertions of civic and religious agency from London laity. These assertions troubled the administration of St. Paul's in London throughout the late fourteenth century when Lollards had friends in high places, nailed their Conclusions to the cathedral door, and circulated their pamphlets. The poem also responds to the late century social mobilities—physical, occupational, and class-jumping—that were recreating the London civic landscape. The 1380s were a time of unusual tension between both civic and ecclesiastical authorities and an unusually restless London commons. If the poem was written around 1386, it was composed only five years after the Rising of 1381, when the rural rebels drove through London and other cities in England, targeting ecclesiastical dignitaries for their special outrage, killing Archbishop Sudbury in London, and pillaging the rich monastic estates in Canterbury, St. Albans, and Bury St. Edmunds.[7] When the insurgents stormed through the gates of London, they were welcomed by their city cousins, urban artisans, and itinerants disaffected both with the multiple ecclesiastical and parish controls and with the hierarchical and exclusive structures of their own gild and city governments.[8] *St. Erkenwald* distantly echoes the memory of such civic disorder when it depicts the city-wide insurgency of frantic movement towards the discovered tomb. The memory of this riot and the terror it inspired had a lasting influence on the policies of both sacred and secular authorities, leading not only to stern reprisals against the ringleaders of the rebellion but also to a long-lasting return to conservative city government policies.[9]

Yet the Rising of 1381 was only an extreme manifestation of far more widespread social unrest in the late fourteenth century and fifteenth century. And London was a particularly fraught nexus of social confrontation, proximal to the royal government at Westminster, protective of its own hierarchies of civil administration with their peculiar liberties, and porous to the different artisans, laborers, merchants, and landed gentry who sought advancement within its walls. The 1370s had been distressed both by poor harvests and recurrences of the plague that are believed to have destroyed between thirty and fifty percent of the indigenous populations. Although barriers between town and country were already flexible, these circumstances intensified migration to the cities as immigrants responded to rumors of unprecedented access to citizenry and urban advancement.[10] This exceptional social mobility incited widespread attempts at control. When laborers and artisans attempted to control their own economic circumstances by refusing to work for wages legislatively frozen at pre-plague levels and by traveling to find better terms, they were characterized as malicious and socially subversive. The 1352 Statute of Laborers and subsequent legislation—especially the ambitious and ideologically explicit Statute of 1388—transformed the laborers' social initiative into particularized and personal sins of fraudulence, sloth, and ingratitude.[11] As the turn of the century neared, poverty became associated with Lollardy, which many members of church and seigneurial government were increasingly labeling as a perverted and seditious doctrine, transforming it from a reformatory movement operating within ecclesiastical, scholastic, and governmental structures to a socially destructive religious and political heresy.[12]

Many urban establishments linked poverty with moral turpitude in order to extend and justify their control. In the city of London, within the urban craft gilds after the Rising, dissension over wages between the gild heads and the lowlier members intensified to the point that craft masters were unable to contain the arguments over wages and had to call for civic and national legislation to back them up. This legislation bristles with moral indignation, accusing the miscreants of "behaving ill," plotting "to the damage of the commonalty and the prejudice of the trade," and plotting together "under false color of sanctity," a reference to illegal attempts to organize as religious fraternities.[13] These movements within the cities simultaneously widened the gaps between classes and intensified social mobility. At a time when itinerants and traveling craftsmen were seeking the city in increasing numbers only to be turned away or funneled

into lengthy and low-paying apprenticeships, moderately wealthy taxpay-
ers sought more powerful positions in city and ecclesiastical government.
They were then faced with the problem of maintaining their new status,
forced to draw and redraw the shifting boundaries they themselves had
trespassed and promote the kinds of social legislation that had previously
excluded them. This fed an atmosphere of fierce conservatism that further
alienated the disenfranchised, solidified the social hierarchies, and yet at
the same time, made the recent newcomers' positions more precarious.[14]

The insecurity of this new conservatism surfaces in the overtly ideological focus of writing associated with it. In such writing, social dilemmas
are translated into moral and religious condemnations. This emerges
vividly in contemporary accounts of the Rising of 1381 written by clerics
associated with such centers of ecclesiastical control as St. Albans and
Westminster. They fabricate the rebels at best as sinners against a natural
order and at worst as ravenous beasts. In these writings the rebels' class-
specific, historically motivated, and justifiable reasons for social revolution
are carefully transmogrified into a historically undetermined, inexplicable
and irrational will to disorder which disrupts tradition and legal precedent
and attempts to rewrite history, thereby justifying its own violent suppression and witnessing to the need for even more rigorous social control.[15] A
similar translation of social tension into moral imperative is at the heart of
St. Erkenwald's construction of the ecclesiastical authority of St. Paul's.

Battling for the Saint

Like London itself, St. Paul's Cathedral was a porous network of competing administrations, with its own governmental affiliations, and many
smaller parish churches whose sponsors were often the local parish gilds.
In the late fourteenth and fifteenth centuries the gilds began exercising an
unprecedented authority over parish priests, controlling their salaries and
tenures. Caroline Barron discusses this as part of an increasing eagerness
for lay participation in parish affairs, and speculates that the prospect of
such control may have been a strong inducement to join parish fraternities.
For a parish fraternity, having one's own priest signaled both authoritative religiosity and social status; prosperous gilds such as the gild of the
Virgin at St. Dunstan in the East strove to keep them and modest ones
such as the gild of St. Austin hoped to afford them.[16] The ability to provide a living for a parish priest had an additional charm—the power to
select or dismiss him. Barron argues that "more than most of the clergy

within the late medieval church, [the parish clergies'] livelihood depended upon the whim of lay people. If the brotherhood failed to hold together, or if its members disliked their chaplain, then his salary might not be forth-coming."[17] Barron describes increasing opportunities for friction between London parishioners and the cathedral bureaucracy by the late fourteenth century. And this was a battle where the cathedrals lost more and more ground. During the fifteenth century, the parish fraternities became in-creasingly active in parish life, establishing lectureships and preachers at various London churches, including St. Paul's Cross.[18]

In *St. Erkenwald*, the poet works to reverse this tendency. Through-out his poem he underscores the London laity's lack of qualifications for religious leadership by painting them as an unruly mob, easily awed by the tomb-wonder, yet without the power or the ability to comprehend it. By making a bishop the hero of the poem, he defends the rights of the cathedral, designing his poem to invoke piety and respect for the London episcopal administration. And he selects St. Erkenwald to be that bishop very cannily. St. Erkenwald was strongly identified with the civic pride of London itself; he was known as the "light of London." The twelfth-century *Vita Sancti Erkenwaldi* devotes much of its narrative to an extended fight over the corpse of the bishop-saint.[19] At first the battle is limited to differ-ent interests within the church as two monasteries endowed by Bishop Erkenwald endowed argue about which has the better right to his relics. The author of the *Vita* accentuates the bitterness of their rivalry and the extent to which it divides the church that the saint had spent his life con-solidating through his pastoral care. Soon, however, the monastic struggle widens to encompass the citizenry of London who become impatient with the quarreling monasteries and claim the saint for the city "where he was ordained prelate and appointed to that office by Rome."[20] The strife becomes sharpest when a more specific segment of the London citizenry takes action—the lay people.

While this was going on, the lay folk of London ran forward eagerly and, with divine consent, carried off with them the body of their bishop. And the monks and nuns, grieving that the dead man's corpse had been taken from them, followed after, weeping and wailing for the body of the blessed man. Just as they were leav-ing the convent there arose a great storm of wind and rain, as if to manifest the man's worth; and it was so violent that people could scarcely stand upright.[21]

The *Vita* shows that when clergy and lay citizenry come to odds over the saint their struggle assumes the dimensions of a natural catastrophe; a fierce wind blows out all the candles on the saint's bier, dramatizing how completely the saint's peaceful influence has been destroyed by the contention over his body. The storm is so violent that no one can cross the river Hile. The non-urban monastic folk read this storm as an expression of divine disfavor. They jeer at the Londoners on the brink of the river, comparing their behavior to the way "famished wolves burst in upon the fold of a flock of sheep, pursuing, seizing, and mangling whatever sheep they can find, and then devouring and consuming them: even so, raging and full of threats, you rushed in among us, and then you robbed our church of this good and great man."[22] Such indignation would not have been out of place in *St. Erkenwald* where the London mob rages into the churchyard with such force that the sexton is forced to close the sanctuary. Yet the author of the *Vita* carefully vindicates his Londoners by allowing them to speak for themselves with chivalric eloquence, grace, and a justified civic pride:

"We would have you know that we are not like wolves but rather we are like strong and vigourous men who will burst at full tilt through the midst of battle-lines of warriors, and even batter, undermine and overturn cities heavily fortified with men and weapons before we will give up the servant of God, our protector. For truly we, and all the people of London and of the province, and especially the church metropolitan which he governed with justice and holiness for a long time, we all strongly believe and trust that through him, with God's mercy and his protection, we will be rescued and delivered from the snares of our enemies now and in the future. Therefore, we ourselves intend that such a glorious city and congregation should be strengthened and honored by such a patron."[23]

This speech not only rebukes the mocking of the monastery folk, but also presents the Londoners as a folk to be reckoned with, both militarily and spiritually. Only after this speech does the struggle die down, as a London cleric reminds all the contenders that the question can only be settled if they remember the purpose of the saint's life—love. They join together in a prayer for divine intervention; the clergy intone the service and the people prostrate themselves upon the ground and "with groans and tears beseeched God's mercy, that he might put an end to this great strife and upheaval."[24] God parts the waters of the river in a second Red Sea crossing, the candles around the bier miraculously light again and the body goes from the quarreling monks to the Londoners.

In the *Vita*, there is little division between the London lay folk and the London clergy; their interests in the saint coincide. The saintly relics are accorded to both the London lay people and the metropolitan church. However, it is the lay folk who get the most narrative space with their dignified arguments and fervent prayers. They are the ones whose tears actuate a miracle. They affirm London's pride, and welcome the saint into the city, "singing hymns and canticles, jubilant that their own city should have been honored with the burial rites of the shepherd who was so much revered."[25] The author of the *Vita* makes the lay folk a powerful and positive force in the final allocation of the saint's body and in turn St. Erkenwald becomes an asset to strengthen the pride and status of the city of London as a newly consolidated body of devotion.

However, by the late fourteenth century the interests of church and laity were aggressively at odds in the city of London; all the parties were maneuvering to gain access to the cultural power of religious symbols. The poet of *St. Erkenwald* is alert to these contemporary tensions as he rewrites the *Vita*'s ending and reappropriates the saint firmly for the cathedral against the city lay folk. In his poem it is the bishop who becomes a soldier for the church; his tears, not theirs, enact miracles. And a crucial transfer of self-determination takes place. The bishop-saint becomes a living leader rather than an inert (if powerful) relic; at the same time the Londoners lose their powers of speech and argument, dwindling from articulate unity to an avid mob desperately in need of governance. The *Erkenwald*-poet alters the saint's past hagiography in order to initiate a "new werke" of his own. In the 1380s the metropolitan church was trying to stage a comeback for the famous London saint. His shrine at St. Paul's had been rebuilt elaborately in the early fourteenth century and was already a prosperous center of pilgrimage, but in 1386, Robert Braybroke, Bishop of London, began a campaign to promote the observation of St. Erkenwald's feasts and those of St. Paul simultaneously.[26] Both Bishop Braybroke and the poet link the saint and the bishop famed for conversion to shore up the foundations of the cathedral and to model a new and passional conversion of the laity of London—from the wild inquisition of the mob to the fervent piety of the congregation.

Old Foundation/Newe Werke

In its selection of a historical setting, the poem engineers an interesting mirroring effect. It dramatizes the discovery of a strange and distant past by figures from a more familiar past which in turn becomes a legitimizing model for the poem's contemporary readers. The poem, therefore, both distances and fascinatingly refracts the immediacy of contemporary tensions over city and cathedral governance by invoking an analogous past transfer of power—the planting of the church in pagan British soil. To do this the poem draws upon ecclesiastical histories of early Britain that describe a city of London where the urban commons had not yet become a strong political force. The church provided an irresistible locus of authority for the city, and within the church, authority was vested overwhelmingly in the person of the bishop.[27] However, while the poem alienates itself from fourteenth-century civic tensions, it does not ignore them. Only by restaging these conflicts can the foundations of an enduring Christian establishment be laid, an urban church that works not only as a savior of souls but as a center of civic government.

Moreover, as it investigates the foundations of St. Paul's, the poem dramatizes its own fascination with and wariness of British history. The poem seeks after pure foundations, seeking to remake history in a way that strengthens rather than threatens the ecclesiastical hegemony of St. Paul's. Ruth Nissé shows how the poem critiques medieval historiography with its exclusive focus on monarchy and genealogy, and quests for more inviolate origins.[28] In her view the poem reshapes British history when it constructs the character of the virtuous pagan. It replaces the conquerors of monarchical genealogy with an idealized cultural figure who can function as a worthy predecessor to the new Christian community, an "Old Law" to the "New Law" of the Christian saint.[29] This rewritten genealogy reveals a perception of not only the uses of secular history but also its possible dangers.[30] I would press this point a little further and argue that as the poem reworks British history it is intensely aware that even a purified origin can be threatening. The transition of power from Old Law to the New Law is fraught with anxiety. The poem dramatizes the confrontation between the present and the past to underscore a threat to the civic hegemony of the bishop that actually increases with the pagan's spotless virtue.

The poem begins with a series of interested temporal transpositions. It takes the erection of the Newe Werke of St. Paul's Cathedral (which was a project begun in the thirteenth century) and displaces it six hundred years in the past, describing its construction on the site of a seventh-century pagan temple. This anachronism has been read predominantly as a universalizing gesture, an example of how the miraculous processes of divine grace transcend time.[31] Yet I would like to examine more closely the way the poem depends upon historical difference. It draws attention to both the incongruities and uncanny resonances between different histories as it layers together the past and present: an ancient pagan cheek by jowl with an Anglo-Saxon saint and an incipient fourteenth-century cathedral. We have no source that credits Bishop Erkenwald with the original building of St. Paul's; he was primarily associated with the conversion of pagans and the endowment of monasteries. By linking the bishop with the cathedral, the poem shows how episcopal and ecclesiastical foundations reinforce each other: the institutional edifice foregrounds the authority of the bishop and the demonstrable holiness of the bishop validates the elaborate and expensive construction of the cathedral.[32] The poem, in fact, rewrites history to reflect the fourteenth-century architectural and spatial centrality of the shrine within the cathedral, its imposing position behind the high altar. There, the shrine of St. Erkenwald loomed with an impressive monumentality that drew pilgrims from all over Europe. William Dugdale's description gives weight to the material and economic organization supporting

This glorious Shrine . . . [and] the Iron Grate which inclosed it, extending to 5 feet, 10 inches in height, having Locks, Keys, Closures, and Openings, and was also tinned over . . . which Grate weighing 3438 pounds at the rate of 4 d. a Pound, amounted to 64 l. 2 s.; and that it might be kept in this beautiful Condition, Thomas de Evere, Dean of this Cathedral, in anno. 1407, by his Testament bequeathed 100 l. for the Building of Houses in Knightrider St. to the end that the Revenue of them should be employed upon the Reparation thereof, and the Maintenance of Lights burning about it, on the two feast days of St. Erkenwald, as also for the Support of a Chaplain celebrating for the fraternity of that blessed Confessor.[33]

At his death, Bishop Braybroke was entombed at the entrance to the Lady Chapel, not ten yards from and directly opposite to the shrine of his saint, forming a triumvirate of high altar, Anglo-Saxon saint, and fourteenth-century bishop. Thus, in the late fourteenth and fifteenth century, cathedral, saint, and bishop were associated not only in their status and authority but even in their physical proximity.

In constructing origins for this association, the poem locates it at a historical crux—an unstable moment between regimes when power transfers are possible. Such cruxes abound in earlier chronicle histories and persist in subsequent poetic histories from Laȝamon's *Brut* to Lydgate's *Troy Book*. Geoffrey of Monmouth explores a striking instance in the image of Vortigern's falling fortress, a frustrated foundation that crystallizes the futility of Vortigern's efforts to establish a kingdom founded solely upon his usurping ambition. *St. Erkenwald,* like many other fourteenth-century alliterative romances, follows Geoffrey in depicting early British history as a restless succession of foundations and refoundations by rulers who cannot make their regimes last; like Vortigern's fortress they only stand the length of a ruler's day. And the poem actually intensifies the sense of historical insecurity by describing a series of whirling changes that actually accelerate with the coming of Christianity.[34]

For [the temple] hethen had bene in Hengyst dawes
Þat þe Saxones vnsaȝt haden sende hyder.
Þai bete oute þe Bretons and broȝt hom into Wales
And *peruerted* all þe pepul þat in þat place dwellid;
Þen wos this reame renaide mony ronke ȝeres,
Til Saynt Austyn into Sandewich was send fro þe pope.
Þen prechyd he here þe pure faythe and plantyd þe trouthe,
And *conuertyd* all þe communnates to Cristendame newe,
He *turnyd* temples þat tyme þat temyd to þe deuell,
And clansyd hom in Cristes nome, and kyrkes hom callid.
He *hurlyd* owt hor ydols and hade hym in sayntes. (7–17)

[(emphases added) For the temple had been a heathen one in the days of Hengist whom the unappeased Saxons had sent hither. They beat out the Britons and drove them into Wales, and perverted all the people that dwelt in that place. The realm was apostate for many rebellious years until Saint Augustine was sent into Sandwich by the pope; then he preached here the pure faith and planted the truth and converted all the communities anew to Christianity. He turned temples around that for a time had been loyal to the devil, and cleansed them in Christ's name and renamed them churches; he hurled out their idols and had saints brought in.]

At first glance, this stanza appears to tell the story of an effective conversion. The original Britons, perverted to heathendom after the Saxon invasions, are converted back to Christianity by St. Augustine, who "plants" the truth of Christianity in a stable and lasting way. But the passage puts up considerable lexical resistence to this planting in the ensuing vocabulary of turning, whirling and hurling. The idols fly out; how long will the saints cling on against the centrifugal forces of historic change? And as the communities spin like tops between the Saxon perversion and Augustinian conversion, the past is transformed by a cosmetic reversal more gestural and linguistic than essential; the temples are "turned" but not fundamentally altered, "clansyd" but not reconstructed. Despite the violence of the gestures, there is little sense of a fundamental alteration in religious practices. Can saints simply *replace* idols? Isn't that exactly what the late century Lollards were accusing? The conversion accomplished by St. Augustine leads to a Christianity that rests easily in Britain without changing the shape of pagan worship. The poet barely touches on it long enough to establish it as a lasting social force.

This insecurity infects the nominal transformations of the next lines as St. Augustine establishes the new regime by weirdly rechristening heathen idols and churches:

He hurlyd owt hor ydols and hade hym in sayntes,
And chaungit cheuely hor nomes and chargit hom better;

Þat ere was of Appolyn is now of Saynt Petre,
Mahoun to Saynt Margrete oþir to Maudelayne,
The Synagoge of the Sonne was sett to oure Lady,
Jubiter and Jono to Jesu oþir to James. (17–22)

[He hurled out their idols and had saints brought in, chiefly changing their names and refurnishing them better. The one that used to honor Apollyon is now for St. Peter, Mohammed was changed St. Margaret or to Mary Magdalene. The Synagogue of the Sun was dedicated to our Lady, Jupiter and Juno changed to Jesus or James.]

Here conversion is signaled by a baptism of the mere letter and some improved furnishings. Apollyon slips easily into St. Peter; the other heathen idols become the most sacred Christian saints with unnerving facility, the transfer governed by the arbitrary associations of alliteration. It doesn't even matter if it's James or Jesus; both saints and idols seem interchangeable. But if the poet was punning when he gave our Lady the synagogue of the "Sonne," the conversion becomes even more destabilizing, the pagan and the Christian deities indistinguishable even by sound. And Augustine's Adam-like renaming of the churches lacks Adam's authority because the churches, unlike the animals, have previous names which infiltrate their new christenings through those shared initials. All these underhanded likenesses undercut the "planting of Christian truth" as a distinctive entity, a genuinely "newe work."

As this initial conversion expands to include the town, the disturbing resonances deepen. The reader expects some apotheosis to culminate the conversion, fulfilling it and stabilizing its movement. Instead, the wheel appears to turn backward:

Now þat London is neuenyd hatte þe New Troie,
Þe metropol and þe mayster-toun hit euermore has bene;
Þe mecul mynster þerinne a maghty deuel aght,
And þe title of þe temple bitan was his name,
For he was dryghtyn derrest of ydols praysid,
And þe solempnest of his sacrifices in Saxon londes.
Þe thrid temple hit wos tolde of Triapolitanes:
By alle Bretaynes bonkes were bot othire twayne. (25–32)

[Now London is named, called the New Troy, and since that time has been the chief city and capital. The great minster of the city was owned by a mighty devil and his name was given to the temple itself. For he was a great lord, the most noble of idols worshiped, and the most solemn and holy of his sacrifices in all the Saxon lands. It was counted the third temple of the Three great cities; on the shores of Britain there only two others.]

The last two lines have caused considerable interpretive speculation among the poem's editors. Ruth Morse offers the most intriguing reading. By mentioning three great pagan centers, the poet is "again making the past like the present. London, York, and Canterbury were the three most important ecclesiastical centers in the England of his day."[35] In this reading, pagan and fourteenth-century ecclesiastical structure approach and merge, each with a tripartite (not to say Trinitarian) structure. Yet the poet's placement of a pagan structure at the culmination of a Christian conversion deflects the trajectory of that conversion at its climax. Most crucially, who is the "maghty devel" who gives the temple its name? Why does the poet throw the absence of that name into such high relief by claiming that the temple was named after it and then refusing to give it? And if the poet is layering his present with Britain's pagan past, what fourteenth-century equivalent could there be to this "dryghtyn derrest of ydols praysid?"

An interesting answer surfaces in the lexicon the poet deploys. It mimics the rhetoric of the Lollards who continually infuriated Bishop Braybroke by affixing anti-clerical manifestos on the doors of St. Paul's Cathedral throughout his tenure.[36] Idolatry was precisely the charge they leveled at the late fourteenth-century church, both in explicitly Lollard writings and in other anticlerical treatises. The church was accused of taking signs for essences and of promulgating the worship of images which it used magically and idolatrously to maintain a monopoly of piety. And in Lollard writings this distrust of images fastened upon reverence toward saints:

But þus don false men þat lyuen now in þer lustis to color wiþ þer owne cursid lif by þis false peyntyngis; and herfore þei lyen on seyntis, *turnyng þer lif to þe contrarie* to counfort men in worldly pride and vanyte and lykyng of her wombe and eȝen and other lustus.[37]

[But thus do false men that live now for their own pleasures—they make their own cursed lives appear better by these false paintings, and therefore they misrepresent saints, turning their lives to the contrary to comfort men in their worldly pride and vanity and delights of the belly and eyes and other pleasures.]

The same gestures of turning, perversion and idolatry haunt Lollard characterizations of ecclesiastical practices. In a treatise against miracle plays from the same manuscript, the writer inveighs against priests playing in interludes, using a language of perversion and conversion that strikingly recalls *Erkenwald*'s prologue:

The same wise myraclis pleyinge, al be it þat it be synne, is oþere while occasion of *conuertyng* of men, but, as it is synne, it is fer more occasion of *peruertyng* of men, not only of oon synguler persone, but of al an hool *comynte*.[38]

[(emphases added) The same (the capacity of ill deeds to bring forth good and vice versa) is true of miracle plays; even if it is sinful, it could sometimes be the occasion of the converting of men, but since it is sin, it is far more often the occasion of men's perversion, and not only the perversion of a single person but of a whole community.]

"Converting," "perverting," "commynte" ("communnates" in *St. Erkenwald*): this treatise levels at the contemporary church the same accusations that the poet attributes to the heathen Saxon leader. The use of the word "perversion" is highly significant. According to the *Middle English Dictionary*, the word "perversion" was first introduced into English only in 1381 in the Wycliffite Bible. By using it in this context, the poet deliberately echoes a Lollard complaint against the church. And the administration of St. Paul's Cathedral was much concerned with the threat of Lollardy. Bishop Braybroke spoke out fiercely against them. One tower in the cathedral was adapted for their examination and imprisonment. In his sixteenth-century chronicle, Stow describes the "Lollard tower," supposedly located at the west end of the church, conveniently next to the bishop's palace: "At either corner of this West end is . . . a strong tower of stone, made for bell towers; the one . . . toward the south is called the Lowlarde's Tower, and hath been used as the Bishop's Prison, for such as were detected for opinions in religion contrary to the faith of the Church."[39]

Familiar with fourteenth-century St. Paul's, the *Erkenwald*-poet knowingly uses Lollard rhetoric in his description of England's initial conversion to put contemporary insecurities about ecclesiastical authority on the line. If the initial conversion to Christianity of England is merely cosmetic, if the idolatrous practices of the past are allowed to infiltrate the shape of Christian practice, then the Lollards' complaints gain a stinging accuracy. They strike true when they nail their accusations to the cathedral of the saint most dramatically associated with a profound and permanent conversion from persecutor to apostle. In their view a cathedral historically infected with idolatry is egregiously perverting Paul's authority back from apostle to persecutor again. The mighty devil who gives the temple its name remains significantly nameless because that indeterminacy heightens the risk, allows the present to bleed backwards into the past, and even entices anticlerical supposition by hinting at a pagan adumbration of St. Paul or St. Erkenwald himself.

Having deliberately upped its ante, then, the poem launches a new scheme, a destruction down to the foundations and a reconstruction from that "fundement on fyrst" (42). It engages in a stage-managed confrontation with a more graspable history, a dialogue with a past that will enable rather than subvert contemporary ecclesiastical control. This confrontation is played out before the eager eyes of the entire community of Londoners, the crucial audience whose conversion to faith and obedience to the church is most at stake.

Cathedral and Shrine

St. Paul's Cathedral is a fine choice for this dramatic confrontation. In the late fourteenth century, St. Paul's was not merely a sanctuary but also a forum for religious dispute and even political violence; in the late fourteenth century bishops were fighting to preserve the privilege of the church as sacred ground.[40] And St. Paul's had a particularly vivid history of contention. In its precincts, bishop and chapter, cleric and lay, gild-controlled parish church and cathedral staff, gild master and urban disenfranchised, all met and negotiated. The cathedral administration had very close ties to the government at Westminster and many of its canons sought government employ. St. Paul's also belonged to the merchant class and the commons of London who gathered in its churchyard to fight out their factional rivalries, particularly in the 1380s and '90s.

This social openness could be damaging even to the cathedral's structure. Sir William Dugdale, in his eighteenth-century history of the cathedral, describes the efforts of Robert Braybroke, appointed Bishop of London after the Rising, to control the behavior of the people within the cathedral. Bishop Braybroke mandated "that no Person whatsoever should defile it, or the Church-Yard, with Piss or other Excrement; nor presume to shoot Arrows, or throw Stones at Crows, or any Birds making Nests thereabouts."[41] This popular iconoclasm hurts the windows and images of the cathedral; the birds are shot, arousing an administrative indignation whose force is explained when we discover that during the celebration of Pentecost at St. Paul's an actual pigeon was released inside the cathedral to signify the holy spirit.[42] Braybroke was not the only cathedral administrator who attempted to control such irreverence; later, the walls of Old St. Paul's itself were graven with the warning: "Hic locus sacer est; hic nulli mingere fas est," courteously translated beneath as "This house is holy; here unlawful 'tis / For anyone here on her walls to piss."[43]

St. Paul's Churchyard also became a battle site for opposing civic factions. Ruth Bird mentions numerous instances when churchyard disputes led to larger battles between craft gilds controlled by Northampton, who wanted to break down the monopoly of the merchant oligarchy, and by

Nicholas Brembre, who supported it.[44] Often these battles amounted to riots.[45] When Brembre was elected mayor, Northampton "began conspiracies and confederacies in St. Paul's Churchyard and St. Michael Quern, in order to get another election."[46] And when later, Northampton summoned a meeting of 500 gildsmen and led them through London, it was at St. Paul's Churchyard that Brembre's servants found them.[47] St. Paul's Churchyard was associated with conflict between not only craft gilds, but also London citizenry. Historically the citizens of London had "of Ancient time held a certain court there, called the folkemot," and bells were rung to summon meetings there.[48] The open air pulpit of St. Paul's cross functioned as an exhortatory channel between cathedral and London citizenry—and both sides seized it. When Robert Braybroke was trying to raise money for the repair of that weather-beaten monument, he describes it as "the high cross . . . where the word of God was wont to be preached to the people."[49] But it was there that Richard fitzRalph delivered anti-fraternal sermons in 1356 and 1357.[50] On at least three occasions mobs gathered and fights broke out, involving not only the London commons but the ecclesiastical administration itself. In 1377, John Wyclif himself was brought to trial at the cathedral in an encounter that pitted his patron, John of Gaunt, Duke of Lancaster against the aristocratic London bishop, William Courtney and a crowd of Londoners. C. L. Brooke describes the proceedings:

John of Gaunt . . . insisted on accompanying Wyclif when he appeared before his judges in the Lady Chapel in St. Paul's on 19 February 1377. The duke had to make his way through a hostile crowd to get to the Lady Chapel, and his temper was badly frayed before ever he arrived . . . In the end he fought his way out of the cathedral and the court adjourned with nothing accomplished.[51]

These accounts underscore how violently fraught and socially open was this cathedral close. If the poet wrote the poem at the end of the fourteenth century, he might have witnessed this confrontation, and with his intimate knowledge of London and the cathedral, would certainly have heard about it.

And the reputation of St. Paul's as a site of urban chaos rather than a sanctified space only intensified as time went on, defying both the Reformation, and the destruction and rebuilding of the cathedral itself. In 1692, Bishop Earle published his "Microcosmography," which made the central nave of the cathedral a microcosm of all that was chaotic and illicit in London society:

It is a heap of stones and men, with a vast confusion of languages, and were the steeple not sanctified, nothing liker Babel. The Noise in it is like that of bees, a strange humming or buzz mixed, of walking, tongues, and feet; it is a kind of still roar or loud whisper. It is the great exchange of all discourse, and no business whatsoever but is here stirring and afoot . . . It is the general mint of all famous lies . . . All inventions are emptied here, and not a few pockets. The best sign of a temple in it is, that it is the thieves' sanctuary, which rob more safely in the crowd than in the wilderness, whilst every searcher is a bush to hide them. [52]

The *Erkenwald*-poet deliberately invokes a similarly extreme contemporaneous sense of urban chaos when he describes the discovery of the miraculous tomb. Its excavation sparks off a city-wide disturbance amounting to riot as all leave their work and come racing to gape at the marvel:

> Quen tithynges token to þe toun of þe toumbe-wonder
> Mony hundrid hende men highid þider sone;
> Burgeys boghit þerto, bedels and othire,
> And mony a mestersmon of maners dyverse;
> Laddes laften hor werke and lepen þiderwardes,
> Ronnen radly in route with ryngande noyce;
> Þer comen þider of all kynnes so kenely mony
> Þat as all þe worlde were þider walon within a hondequile. (57–64)

[When tidings came to the town about the wonderful tomb many hundred gentlemen rushed there immediately, burgesses followed thereto, with beadles and others, and many man indentured to craft gilds of all diverse kinds. Lads left their work and lept thither, running quickly in a mob with ringing noise. So many people of all kinds came there so quickly that it was as though everyone in the whole world converged there in an instant.]

The poet underscores the violent jubilee of this motion which brings together different ranks and classes in one tremendous gathering. High-ranking men, the prosperous city merchants, heralds, craftsmen of all different kinds, their lads and apprentices—all join the mob that presses toward the tomb. So violent in its curiosity is the gathering that the sexton closes the sanctuary to the public.[53] The sheer noise, mass, and exuberance of this rout recall the social melees that are apt to erupt without warning in *Piers Plowmen* or the wild chase of the fox in *The Nun's Priest's Tale* that evokes the 1381 Rising itself. The "ryngande noyce" of the people in the churchyard becomes more threatening if we remember that in the time of Simon Montfort, the bells of St. Paul's were rung to summon citizens of London to the churchyard to revolt against King Henry III.[54]

The poem further highlights the potential for civil disruption in the lines dealing with the "laddes," the apprentices who are indentured to the craft gilds and perhaps still belong to the class of London foreigns, those who are disenfranchised or have not yet received citizenship. These lowly creatures leave their work and "leap" noisily into the fray with a

precipitous energy that defies the straining hierarchies of their gild organization. At this time the urban disenfranchised were causing disturbances
not only within the city but within their own gilds, separating off into
mini-brotherhoods and electing their own leaders. The more prosperous
artificers were lobbying increasingly for city-wide and even monarchical
legislation to help keep them in check. R. A. Leeson recounts several cases
where the less prosperous gildsmen gather in force to levy wage changes.
In 1415, a particularly violent dispute broke out in the gild of tailors when
a number of yeomen broke away from the jurisdiction of their masters
and set up for themselves near St. James's Church. According to Leeson
"they lived like fighting cocks, beating any unfortunate master who dared
reprove them, assaulting Sheriffs' men who arrested them, and rescuing
prisoners. The tailors told the Mayor they simply wished to continue the
customs of their fraternity and the Mayor after lecturing them on being
'youthful and unstable' told them to be under the 'governance and rule' of
their master."[55] In the poem, when the boys flock towards the churchyard,
they similarly leap away from such "governance and rule" and join the rest
of London in irresistible civic chaos.

Moreover, this scene of exuberant convergence on the "tombe wonder" becomes an antitype of pilgrimage, attesting to the anxieties that popular pilgrimage aroused, even in the Church that encouraged it.[56] It
invokes contemporary critiques of pilgrimage—that it takes people away
from their rightful work to far places where they fall into sin, that it
foments idolatry and that "summe men don it of her owne grett will rather
to se faire cuntreys þan for ony swete deuociouns in her soule to God or
to þe seynt þat þei seken."[57] [Some men do it because of their own great
desire to see fair countries than for any sweet devotions in their soul to
God or to the saint that they seek.] To critics of the ecclesiastical institutions, any pilgrimage sparked by curiosity rather than devotion leads to
both economic and spiritual dissolution. Thus, even as the poem promotes
a saint lavishly enshrined at St. Paul's whose cult there was second only
to that of St. Paul himself, it defamiliarizes the mechanics of pilgrimage
by making a dead pagan the object of the citizens' curiosity rather than a
Christian saint.[58] In effect, the poem repeats the same destabilizing strategy that undercut its description of the initial establishment of Christianity in Britain; it explores the more subversive social valences of pilgrimage
before going on to refigure them in ecclesiastically validating ways.

To establish St. Erkenwald's effectiveness as a saving mediator, the
poem does not recount the miracles at his shrine as does the twelfth-
century *Vita*; instead it innovatively shows him performing miracles at the

anti-shrine of the pagan tomb.[59] The pagan corpse rises to an uncanny life, urged to speak "with a drery dreme" (191) [with a mournful voice], not only by the bishop's sanctity but by the fierce intensity of his interrogatory need. And this eerie exchange shadows the recuperative congress between present and past, living and dead that a saint's shrine offers, where the living come to prove the miraculous power of the saint's fragmented body to heal the disruptions of death, illness, and sin. The staging in St. Paul's excavated churchyard reminds the reader that the Cathedral opens crucial transactions not only between the restless living but with the unseen dead. Even amidst the social bustle, disputing, sermonizing, ball playing, and bird shooting, the Cross was erected there in order to "put good People, passing through such Cemeteries, in mind to pray for the Souls of those, whose Bodies lay there interred."[60]

The wonderful tomb of the pagan also holds up a weird mirror to the fourteenth-century shrine of St. Erkenwald itself. Its beautiful surfaces, glowing figures, and occult inscriptions recall Lollard accusations that shrines promoted sorcerous idolatries; its runic letters incite a frenzy of futile research. Virtually every critic comments on its unfathomability and notes that only the bishop through the grace of God possesses the power to go beyond the magical runes and speak to the body within. Yet if the tomb is meant to recall a saint's shrine then the association is not unidirectional. The fourteenth-century shrine of St. Erkenwald with its impassible grate and long inscriptions might just as well echo the inscribed tomb's invocation of a remote and alien divinity. Indeed, because its inscriptions were in Latin, they would have been as unfathomable to most lay viewers as the "roynyshe resones" on the mysterious tomb. Within the poem the clerks and canons of the cathedral, armed with their command of Latin and their knowledge of British history are forced to view the tomb of the pagan as a fourteenth-century lay person who did not know Latin would view a shrine. The reader, as well, is situated by the poem just as the fourteenth-century administration of St. Paul's wished to position the lay people of London, maneuvering them into dependency on the bishop's interpretive power.

Yet the universal curiosity, the clamorous questioning, and stunned wonder this tomb excites are excessive enough to raise doubts about even Bishop Erkenwald's capacities for interpretive containment. With the clerics at an interpretive loss and great "troubull in þe pepul / And suche a cry aboute a cors crakit euermore" (109–10) [great trouble among the people and such an outcry about the corpse battering incessantly], the bishop is sent for immediately to quell the disturbance. In the ensuing confrontation this strange predecessor, illustrious in its accomplishments, violent in its allure, is subjected to the bishop's interrogation and made to speak itself with such mortal drama that it risks overshadowing the poem's more ideological urgencies.

A Question of Sanctity

The poet first underscores the fact that the corpse (unlike the bishop) is unknown both to ecclesiastical histories of institutional expansion and to secular histories of dynastic governance. His kingly clothes only highlight his absence from monarchical history, "bot one cronicle of þis kyng con we never fynde" (156) [but any chronicle describing this king we could not discover]. Instead, the poet invokes an unknown origin, London's pre-Christian civic past. The poem's theologically inclined readers contrast the poem's conservative treatment of the question of pagan salvation with the more radical valances of versions of the Trajan story in Dante and Langland.[61] But Frank Grady persuasively suggests that both *Piers Plowman* and *St. Erkenwald* make their virtuous pagans speak most trenchantly not as theological models but historical ones, serving as connecting fulcra between pagan past and Christian present through their power as illustrious secular ethical exempla.[62] The poem makes this corpse just such a historical crux, but, I would argue, in an anxious and discontinuous way. The poem's vision of past civic governance is pagan but unitary—a secular city where perfect justice is not only achievable but also lustrously and enviously apparent. The poem's present, on the other hand, is Christian but civically turbulent. This difference invades the means by which each civic leader signifies himself. The bishop, whom we see exhorting his clerics, adjuring the pagan corpse, spectacularizing his authority, and stage-managing the people, seems less like the "Light of London" than a troubled administrator. The pagan, by contrast, is a just governor who apparently does not have to construct his authority; the ancient Londoners' act of posthumous coronation sealed a virtue that spoke itself to his people with the unmediated intensity of a beam of light. The poem demonstrates the salvific impotence of this ancient virtuous governor before an audience of contemporary Londoners in order to induce a transfer of that lost civic unity. It seeks to subsume the Londoners' initiative at once to the bishop's salvific charity and civic governance. And that civic agency of the people of London to chose and coronate their just governor is what the poem at once craves, appropriates, and works to deny.

The implicit threat posed by this pagan authority emerges only gradually in the course of Bishop Erkenwald's interrogation of the corpse. The
confrontation is a carefully engineered dramatic spectacle. If the bishop can
demonstrate the celebrated pagan's need for the church's ministrations,
then the watching mob of London folk who are not such paragons will
accept their own dependence on the church. The poet takes care to establish the bishop's credentials not only as a worthy episcopal ruler but a
genuinely involved and holy man whose feelings are caught up in his
office. Before the confrontation begins, we see the bishop weeping and
praying all night, begging God for enlightenment. Once the narrator has
established the genuine faith that affectively grounds the bishop's authority, he dramatizes that authority, extending it visually and materially over
the unruly Londoners. The bishop times the confrontation very carefully,
going out to the churchyard at dawn, after an elaborate mass dramatizing
his Christly lieutenancy.[63] The bishop must not be out-dressed by the marvelous gold-clad body within the tomb so the poem invests him with pon-
tifical splendor and gives him an audience of "mony a gay grete lorde . . .
the rekenest of the reame" (134–35) [many a gay great lord . . . the noblest
of the realm]. As he emerges from the mass "þer plied to hym lordes, /As
riche revestid as he was" (138–39) [Lords bowed to him there who were
as richly appareled as he was]. But the real target of this display of spectacular nobility emerges when he has the churchyard unlocked: "pyne wos
with þe grete prece þat passyd him after" (141) [There was trouble/ferment
with the great crowd that came after him].

During the confrontation, the poet deliberately heightens the similarities between the bishop-saint richly arrayed before the tomb and the
richly arrayed pagan speaking within. The description of the pagan's body
reaches beyond splendor to sanctity:

> a blisfull body . . .
> Araide on a riche wise in riall wedes;
> Al with glisnande golde his gowne wos hemmyd,
> With mony a precious perle picchit þeron,
> And a gurdill of golde bigripid his mydell;
> A meche mantel on lofte with menyuer furrit,
> Þe clothe of camelyn ful clene with cumly bordures,
> And on his coyfe wos kest a coron ful riche
> And a semely septure sett in his honde.
> Als wemles were his wedes withouten any tecche
> Oþir of moulyng oþir of motes oþir moght-freten,
> And als bryȝt of hor blee in blysnande hewes
> As þai hade ȝepely in þat ȝorde bene ȝisturday shapen;

And als freshe hym þe face and the flesh nakyd
Bi his eres and bi his hondes þat openly shewid
With ronke rode as þe rose and two rede lippes,
As he in sounde sodanly were slippide opon slepe.
Þer was spedeles space to spyr vschon oþir
Quat body hit myȝt be þat buried wos ther. (76–95)

[A blissful/blessed body, arrayed in a rich manner in royal garments: all with glistening gold his gown was hemmed, with many a precious pearl placed thereon, and a girdle of gold begripped his waist; a great mantle was over that, furred with miniver, the cloth of pure camel hair with comely borders; and on his coif was set a very rich crown, and a seemly scepter was set in his hand. All spotless were his clothes without any blotch, either of mildew or of blemish, nor was it moth-eaten. And his body was bright of complexion with as much glowing color as if he had quickly in that church-yard been laid only yesterday. And all fresh was his face and the bare flesh near his ears and his hands that was clearly visible was fresh with the copious red of a rose, and the two red lips also, just as if he had suddenly slipped into a sleep only then. There was much ineffectual wrangling as each person asked the other what body it might be that lay buried there.]

Resting in an elaborately inscribed shrine amidst the odor of sanctity, this corpse not only wields the kingly authority of crown and scepter but is an unauthorized copy of St. Erkenwald himself. And this saintliness only intensifies as the body opens its eyes in answer to the bishop's prayer and answers the bishop's questions by describing a virtuous life as stainless as the pagan's clothes—and without benefit of clergy. His answers to the bishop's questions slowly construct him as a figure who incarnates a socially palpable virtue to a city (familiarly) riven by disorder and brutality. The tension increases. His answers afflict the bishop with an ambiguous torment—does he feel pity or pain as he interrogates the corpse "with bale at his hert" (257)?

After asking about his identity and his kingly regalia and receiving provocative explanations of unswerving governance during times of ancient trouble, for which he was honored after his death by the people's unanimous coronation, the bishop comes to the crux of the matter: the pagan's body. How does it come to be preserved? Is the pagan embalmed so that his miraculous freedom from corruption comes about "by monnes lore" (264)? "No," answers the corpse, drawing out the moment, "if renkes for riȝt þus me arayed has, / He has lant me to last þat loues riȝt best" (271–72) [if men had arrayed me thus (reverently) for justice, / He who loves justice best of all has granted it me to last]. The bishop doesn't dwell on the answer, refusing the obvious conclusion (and its reference to his own future sainthood and enshrinement in St. Paul's).[64] He presses further:

"bot sayes þou of þi saule" (273) [but tell now of your soul]. And at this
question the corpse's authority suddenly disintegrates: "Þen hummyd he
þat þer lay and his hedde waggyd, / And gefe a gronyng ful grete" (281)
[Then he who lay there muttered and his head shook and he gave a very
great groan]. This sudden pang deepens into a chilling picture of his
sojourn in hell which above all is a place of hunger.

> "Quat wan we with oure wele-dede þat wroughtyn ay riȝt,
> Quen we are damnyd dulfully into þe depe lake,
> And exilid fro þat soper so, þat solempne fest,
> Þer richely hit arne refetyd þat after right hungride?
> My soule may sitte þer in sorow and sike ful colde,
> Dymly in þat derke dethe þer dawes neuer morowen,
> Hungrie inwith helle-hole, and herken after meeles
> Long er ho þat soper se oþer segge hyr to lathe." (301–8)

["What did we win with our good deeds, we who worked justice always, when we
are damned dolefully into the deep lake and exiled thus from that supper, that
solemn feast, where those who hungered greatly after justice are richly refreshed
with food. My soul may sit there in sorrow and sigh full cold, dimly in that dark
death where day never dawns, hungry within hell-hole and harken after meals, long
before she may see that supper, or any man to invite her."]

In this passage, the bishop's misgivings about the necessity of his office are
gratifyingly dispersed. The corpse abruptly diminishes from the bishop's
unauthorized double to Dives begging in hell; this leaves an authoritative vacuum into which the bishop can step. The corpse's hell-hunger connects him instead with the unsuspectingly spiritually famished London
citizens whose fierce curiosity made the tomb-wonder dangerous in the
first place. The poem tightens the sympathy between the corpse hunger-
ing in hell and the onlooking Londoners by extending his despair and
hunger over the watching crowd; they begin to weep as they listen, and the
bishop himself, here a man of the people, is shaken with sobs and ready to
baptize the corpse on the spot. But God forestalls him; when the bishop's
pitying tears fall on the corpse, the suffering soul is ravished into the heavenly feast, praising God and thanking the bishop profusely, and the body
falls instantly into dust, a physical dissolution that culminates the poem's
subversion of his ecclesiastically unsanctioned authority. It is a graphic,
carefully detailed putrefaction:

> Bot sodenly his swete chere swyndid and faylid
> And all the blee of his body wos blakke as þe moldes,
> As roten as þe rottok þat rises in powdere.
> For as sone as þe soule was sesyd in blisse,

Corrupt was þat oþir crafte þat covert þe bones,
For þe ay-lastande life, þat lethe shalle neuer
Devoydes vche a vaynglorie, that vayles so litelle. (342–48)

[Suddenly his fresh visage vanished and faded, and all the complexion of his body turned black as the mold, as rotten as a decayed thing that rises in powder. For as soon as the soul was taken into bliss, corrupt was that other element that covered the bones; for the everlasting life that shall never cease makes void all such vainglory that avails so little.]

This is the moral that many of the poem's critics take out of the poem—earthly vainglory must fade in contrast to the everlasting life beyond history and society. Yet this pious interpolation is a moment of striking textual instability; it contradicts the poem's focus on the power of precisely those earthly vainglories to communicate reverence—and not just for the corpse. Just as the blissful soul leaves the corrupt body, essence flees away from sign in a way that invalidates it, leaves it empty and disintegrating. This sudden reversal moves a step toward the Lollard suspicion of spectacle as magical sign, the anticlerical critiques that distrust priest and bishop in their regalia and regard them as corrupt actors in a deceptive play. And, significantly, the poem ignores its own moral, both before and after the corpse's dissolution, immediately reconfirming the continuity between inner holiness and the visible signs of wealth and status. Far from disdaining the corporeal, it enlists its figurally unifying power as it incorporates a new body to replace that corrupt "other craft" of the pagan's corpse. As the pagan body dissolves, the civic body is dramatically reconstituted with the bishop at its head. He replaces the pagan king of civic justice with his own image as the Christian king of civic mercy, a necessary mercy that his contemporaries hunger for and need, even if—*especially* if—like the pagan judge in life, they see themselves as working to institute social justice in troubled times. The drama played out between the pagan and the bishop melts into the drama played out between the bishop and the citizens of London as the bishop leads them in a procession that makes visible a newfound civic unity and a return to due process. The structured procession away from the emptied tomb counters and redeems the wild influx of the curious world toward it. Under the bishop's benign jurisdiction:

Þay passyd forthe in procession and alle þe pepulle folowed,
And alle þe belles in þe burgh beryd at ones. (351–52)

[They passed forth in procession and all the people followed and all the bells in the city rang in unison.]

The poem ends with a procession like the Corpus Christi processions that both celebrated the feast of Christ's body and dramatized the unity of the civic body. The threatening "ryngande noyse" of the rout toward the churchyard is harmonized into the ringing unity of the church. Bishop Erkenwald has accomplished the true conversion that Augustine did not; he has reconstructed the Christian church by truly confronting the authority of its pagan predecessor. And this conversion is not a mere name change (the pagan remains startlingly nameless) but rather a transformation, literally, at the bone. By doing this the bishop legitimates his own position, and that of the bishopric of St. Paul's, as head of the civic body he has reconstructed.

In this ending the poet works to elicit responses that are at once deeply felt and culturally scripted, strengthening and channeling a civic-minded piety by openly dramatizing its sometimes difficult vindication. Its tale of fleeting mortality and divine love becomes more powerful through the adduction of contemporary religious and civic conflicts, the dramatic tensions between the bishop, the corpse and the restless London spectators that put the bishop's authority on a trial with contemporary resonances. The poem enacts the chivalric presumption that fortune favors the brave and, with deliberate brinkmanship, pushes its test of the bishop's ecclesiastical authority to the balance of a hair. Had the pagan proved as "blissful" as he looked, it would have justified the fourteenth-century anticlerical writers who maintained that there was no need for the elaborate sacramental edifice of the church as a conveyor of salvation. But by testing the church so severely, the poet makes its victory that much the stronger. The poem recreates the sacrament of baptism not as an empty form or even as a magical ritual, but as a true crux where the divine and human interpenetrate. Human pity catalyzes the poem's miracle; by divine intervention the bishop's tear becomes the baptismal font. This commingling of bodily and sacred water bespeaks not only the divine mercy of salvation but also the bishop's affective part in mediating it. And in validating the bishop's sacramental authority, the poem foregrounds his civic authority, his natural place at the head of the procession of devoutly improved London citizens.

And yet we never learn who the pagan judge was; his name remains unspoken, his inscription laid aside and unread. The bishop's interrogation reveals more about the bishop than it does about the corpse. The bishop conjures the corpse to answer the questions troubling his own heart, and touchingly, obediently, the corpse finally gives the answer the bishop most desires to hear. Yet the mysteries this ancient pagan represents, as Monika Otter attests, overreach the poem's ending "as if a big question mark hangs over the entire poem."[65] The speaking "spelunke" (49, 217) [tomb] still echoes with the profound hunger so dramatically witnessed by the body before its fleeing soul ascended to God's plenitude. Was that bodily hollowness entirely sealed and filled by the bishop's healing tears and the soul's feast? Or was it horrifically fulfilled in that sudden dissolution? Should we mourn the lost civic community to which the corpse witnesses, where the people lovingly ratify leaders who lead the people with an impartial justice perfect and palpable in its self-deprecation—where there is no need for ideological self-justification, no need for manipulative spectacle? The living body of the civic procession leads us from the gaping fissure of a still not quite known past holding its terrible, sign-dissolving putrefaction, and we are uncertain.

3

Heady Diversions: Court and Province in
Sir Gawain and the Green Knight

THE PAST WE ENCOUNTER IN *St. Erkenwald* is, however inconclusively, already colonized. The ancient foundations have been breached, the pagan temples converted, and the old gods thrown out.[1] But what would happen if it were one of these gods that the bishop unearthed in St. Paul's churchyard? Imagine a British aborigine, divorced from the classical traditions of secular justice that sanitize *Erkenwald*'s virtuous pagan, a figure both native and uncanny, "an alvysh man" [an elvish man] perhaps, or "half etayne in erde, I trow" [Half a giant on earth I hold him to be].[2] This, of course, is the Green Knight from another poem of the late fourteenth century also written in the dialect of the North West Midlands and bound in the same manuscript as *St. Erkenwald*. In this chapter, I argue that, like *St. Erkenwald*, *Sir Gawain and the Green Knight* solicits the British past to challenge and prove contemporary ideologies. Like the Erkenwald-poet, the Gawain-poet carefully locates his poem at a historical moment that resonates with contemporary tensions. Here the conflict is played out between a royal court becoming increasingly alienated from traditional seigneurial modes of chivalry and a conservative and insecure provincial gentry, whose status, livelihoods, and careers were increasingly coming to depend on careers at the royal court. The testing of Arthurian chivalry is catalyzed by a revenant from the past but one who also has a life in the present as a provincial outsider to Arthur's court. The Green Knight's double life links the strengths and powers of Britain's legendary history to those of its remote provinces. And unlike *St. Erkenwald*'s pagan judge, the Green Knight never fully yields himself up for questioning. The plot in which he embroils Sir Gawain shifts deceptively and masks its own cruxes, the reciprocity his games promise is an illusion, and his very identity as an incarnation of mythical authority is the result of a trick. As the poem spins out its gorgeous web of indirection, it explores the tensions between past and present, innovation and tradition, and royal court and provincial gentry, in a quest to define and socially locate true chivalry—and tests the claims of the royal court to embody it.[3]

The poem's characterizations of both royal and provincial courts undergo constant revision as the poem proceeds. For this reason, definition is strikingly difficult. The provincial characters in particular, the Knight/ Bertilak and the Lady/Morgan, are revealed to be doubles that perplex attributes of past and present, youth and age. The provincial landscape itself is riven with temporal disjunctions, fashionably modern courts twinned with ancient gaping barrows, forests of tangled oaks with beautifully tended hunting parks. To increase the confusion, the poem negotiates the relationships between these disparate temporal sites in incommensurate ways within the two embedded plot-lines of the poem. In the "outer" plot of the beheading game, the Green Knight gains the dramatic authority to test Arthur's court by assuming the patina of an wild and self-regenerating natural/chivalric sovereignty. But the poem reveals that he is just a contemporary nobleman in an ancient magical costume. In the "inner" plot of the winnings-exchange, the beguiling Lady depends on her youthfulness and knowledge of the language of aristocratic fashion to entice Gawain to a self-knowledge that he both samples and resists. But by the poem's end her sexual/textual magic yields to the less attractive machinations of Morgan le Fay, revealed not simply as Gawain's aunt and Arthur's half-sister, but towering abruptly over the narrative as "Morgan the Goddess." An unsightly old lady becomes an ancient deity, a suitable consort to the inimitable Green Knight in his first incarnation, even as she subsumes him (and everyone) beneath an absolutism all the more threatening for its intimacy to Arthur's court.

Because of this chiasmic movement it is difficult to argue that the provinces can represent in any unconflicted way an older traditional chivalric authority that has the right to administer knightly accolades to anyone, let alone the reputed pinnacle of chivalry, Sir Gawain. This chapter argues instead that the poem makes the provinces a place where the past is at issue, always powerful, always dangerous, always immanent, highlighting the vivid inevitabilities of change, consequence, and death, and, fascinatingly, teaching delight in their uncertainties. This is opposed to the royal court which seems to connect itself to nothing—genealogically or geographically—beyond its own self-enclosed and prescripted games, skipping from festival to festival in blissful ignorance both of its violent origins and its impending end. By ending on this palpable gap, the poem adumbrates the intensification of late fourteenth-century tensions between the provincial gentry and the royal court, their long-term impact, and their ultimate costs.

King Arthur and Richard II: The Young and the Restless

Sir Gawain and the Green Knight is intensely, if obliquely, implicated in the mindsets and anxieties of its late fourteenth-century provincial milieu.[4] The poem constructs its central characters to invoke and amplify contemporary tensions between the royal court and the provinces of the North West Midlands. Its picture of Arthur in particular resonates with the self-presentations and cultural perceptions of Richard II, opening at the same time to a range of late medieval anxieties concerning monarchical self-definition.[5] Clearly apprehending Richard's self-promoting strategies, the poem pursues their contradictory effects upon the provinces of Cheshire and Lancashire—provinces which were intimately tied to the King and his family (Richard was the Earl of Chester and John of Gaunt the Duke of Lancaster) and yet also remote from the ideology of royal self-sufficiency Richard was promoting.

The poem stresses Arthur's youth and inexperience, his ignorance both of the farther reaches of his realm and of his own historic predecessors. The poem begins with a retrospective summary of the foundation of Britain, from its roots in the ashes of Troy to the branching line of belligerent kings that culminate in Arthur. From the very beginning, this history proceeds by repeated cataclysms; its first verb—"watz sesed"—gives the impression, as Ian Bishop puts it, of "the slamming shut of a volume of history."[6] This halting march of violence, treachery, and ancient glory sketches out a history when heroes pushed westward, establishing kingdoms as they went and breeding both great warriors and cruel violence: "Bolde bredden þerinne, baret þat lofden / In mony turned tyme tene þat wroȝhten" (21–22) [Bold boys bred there, in broils delighting, / that did in their day many a deed most dire].

Arthur is to crest this unruly wave of ancient British warrior-kings. The poet promises a tale of "Arthurez wonderez," fostering expectations of a typical conquest poem that features brave warriors, violent combat, and valor in battle—in other words a poem that would continue the epic tradition of foundation with which it opens, similar to that of Laȝamon's *Brut* perhaps. But as the focus sharpens on Arthur's court, we find a very different, much more continental romance atmosphere: feasting, gaming, lovely ladies, elaborate ornaments, and a king renowned not for his strength at arms or fortitude under adversity, but because he is "þe comelokest kyng þat þe court haldes" (53) [The comeliest king that holds court]. Additionally, Arthur is not where we expect him to be, enthroned on the dais beside Gwenore (i.e., Gwenever). Instead he is hovering hyperkinetically over the feasting knights of his court, displaced from his ancestral position of heroic authority and control.[7] We are forced to approach him by leaving the dais and moving in among the celebrating gentlefolk. As we sidestep the court games of knights and ladies and bow briefly in the queen's direction, we find another surprising detail—Arthur's restless youthfulness, "so joly of his joyfness, and sumquat childgered" (86) [So light was his lordly heart, and a little boyish]. By the time we reach this passage, we have moved from the militaristic imperatives of the foundational epic into the newer, more verbal imperatives of the court-centered romance—from battle to debate—and from insular romance (which avoided Arthur) to continental romance (which reveled in, obsessed over, and frequently pinioned him).[8] This self-conscious generic shift highlights the incongruity of a young, untried, and over-eager king endowed with authority over an ancient, riven, bloodstained land—a king at once innocent and alienated.

To my knowledge, this picture of Arthur has few literary analogues. He differs from the older, inert, stolid king of the continental romances who provided a foil to his risk-taking and thus more chivalrically interesting knights. He diverges from British chronicle traditions which followed Geoffrey of Monmouth in depicting a militarily experienced conqueror in the prime of life. But a historical prototype suggests itself: Richard II as several of the chronicles present him in the early 1380s, when the English government had just emerged from the jurisdiction of the continual council and before the hostilities between the king and his greater magnates that culminated in the Merciless Parliament had become sharply defined.[9] When the poet imbues Arthur with Ricardian characteristics, he animates the poem with questions that perplex the relations of king and nobility throughout the 1380s and '90s—anxieties about the definition of nobility and of the nobility's role in government. The poet was clearly implicated in seigneurial interests and perspectives; he is thought to have been attached to a provincial household in Cheshire or South Lancashire, and the poem targets a chivalrically knowledgeable audience.[10] When the poem interrogates the royal court's reputation as the nonpareil of chivalry, it invites attention from the nobility, the commons, and especially the provincial gentry of the North West Midlands, who were subject to a uniquely conflicting set of pressures with regard to the royal court.[11]

Throughout the first part of the 1380s, Richard II's ambition was to establish the royal household as an autonomous power in its own right, as free as possible from control or reliance upon those established nobles and magnates who had previously exercised such dominance over his own sovereignty. The disorganization of the governing council during his minority helps explain his later avoidance of magnatial dependence.[12] After the council was dissolved, Richard gradually opened the government to a new combination of competing interests from the king's informal counselors. The king's chamber knights gradually acquired positions and influence throughout the early years of the 1380s due partly to a lack of both ministerial and magnatial leadership—and partly to the new opportunities for political leadership that opened up after the Rising of 1381. In 1380–81 a number of important ministers of state resigned and their positions were filled by relatively inexperienced replacements. As for the magnates who had dominated politics throughout the previous decade—Gaunt, Buckingham, and the Earl of March—all had planned expeditions which were to keep them abroad at least until the following year. The events of the Rising and its aftermath reestablished the king's household as a locus of authority in the land. When he faced the peasants at Smithfield and directed their dispersal and the round-up of their ringleaders, Richard himself became more conscious of his status as king and of the personal loyalty he could command. In the years that followed the Rising, he began to assert himself actively, attempting to expand the royal household and increase its financial independence from the Commons-dominated Exchequer. He took the initiative in endowing his chamber knights with favors, lands, and offices, in what amounted to a deliberate campaign to divorce the throne from dependence on anyone but his own young protégés.[13]

There are interesting parallels between the Richard who emerges from the works of chroniclers such as Walsingham, the Monk of Westminster, and the author of the *Vita Ricardi Secondi*, and the characterization of Arthur and his court at the beginning of the poem. Most suggestive is the general youth of Arthur's court. The Green Knight laughingly dismisses Arthur's challenge to battle because "Hit arn aboute on þis bench bot berdlez chylder" (280) [There are about on these benches but beardless children]. Correspondingly, Richard's household court in the early 1380s was composed of relatively young and unestablished chamber knights—a fact that gravely troubled both the Commons and the nobility, and was a point of continuing dispute. Walsingham famously echoes the Green Knight's dismal opinion of the court's capacity for mature deeds of arms by dismissing them as knights of the bedchamber rather than the battlefield.[14] But while such military snobbery shows the extent to which Walsingham was aligning himself with a conservative noble perspective, others were also voicing similar sentiments. The Commons, chiefly distressed about household expenditure, attacked Richard's extravagant patronage of young and relatively inexperienced courtly careerists, periodically accusing him of overindulging weak or evil counselors who were leading the kingdom to ruin. The anonymous poet of *Richard the Redeless* bemoans Richard's youthful appointments.

The cheuyteyns cheef þat ye chesse euere,
Weren all to yonge of yeris to yeme swyche a rewme. (175–76)

[The greater lords that you always appointed were all too young in years to rule such a realm].

This indictment recalls the monarchical alienation with which *Sir Gawain and the Green Knight* begins—the immature king and his coterie of young chamber knights reinventing government in a kingdom whose governing traditions intricately negotiate the power balances between an unusually organized monarchy and fiercely defended regional baronial control of land ownership and law enforcement.

In addition to youth, the Gawain-poet gives his Arthur other Ricardian touches. The Arthur of the poem is courageous, quick-tempered, and hasty. He blushes furiously under the Green Knight's mockery: "þe blod schot for scham into his schyre face / and lere; / He wex as wroth as wynde" (317–19) [The blood for sheer shame shot to his face, and pride. With rage his face flushed red], just before snatching the ax from the Green Knight's hand and brandishing it wildly about. Arthur's violent responses would awaken familiar associations in contemporary observers of Richard II. The Westminster chronicler relates an incident of 1384 in which during a council session, Arundel, the Archbishop of Canterbury, castigated Richard for relying too much on his informal household counselors. Stung by this imputation of royal weakness, Richard lept up and attacked him with personal threats. Later in the day, while taking an after-dinner boat-ride on the Thames, Richard and his party encountered the archbishop on his own barge. When Arundel repeated the charges, Richard lost his temper completely, drew his sword, and tried to run the Archbishop through. When his companions, Sir John Devereux and Sir Thomas Trivet, attempted to restrain him, he turned his anger on them to such effect that they lept from Richard's boat to the archbishop's.[15] Although this incident is the most dramatic, similar exhibitions enliven the chronicle accounts of Richard's reign, even those composed before his deposition in 1399.[16]

In the poem, however, the most suggestive parallel between Arthur and Richard emerges not in a speech from Arthur but one from Sir Gawain. It is the first time Gawain speaks, and in this speech he makes the king the single source and center of his seigneurial identity.

"I am þe wakkest, I wot, and of wyt feblest,
And lest lur of my lyf, quo laytes þe soþe—
Bot for as much as 3e ar myn em I am only to prayse,
No bounté bot your blod I in my bodé knowe;
And syþen þis note is so nys þat no3t hit yow falles,
And I haue frayned hit at yow fyrst, foldez hit to me;
And if I carp not comlyly, let alle þis cort rych
      bout blame." (354–61)

["I am the weakest, well I know, and of wit feeblest; / And the loss of my life would
be least of any; / That I have you for uncle is my only praise; / My body, but for
your blood, is barren of worth; / And for that this folly befits not a king, / And 'tis
I that have asked it, it ought to be mine, / And if my claim be not comely let all
this court judge, in sight."]

This speech has been treated either as a conventionally chivalric profession
of humility or as a sidelight on Gawain's personal courtesy and self-control
in contrast to Arthur's hot-headedness. However, it also establishes a more
broadly applicable model for relations between king and noble subject.
From the very beginning, Gawain draws attention to his own humble
dependence on his uncle's word, favor, and blood: "Bot for as much as 3e
ar myn em I am only to prayse, / No bonté bot your blod I in my bodé
knowe." In this speech Gawain departs significantly from conservative definitions of aristocratic identity. We can come to a fuller understanding of this
departure if we contrast it to a similar but quite differently accented performance, the dedication to Richard II with which the Earl of Gloucester—
later to become a notable thorn in Richard's side—opened his *Ordenaunce
and Fourme of Fightyng within Listes*. Pursuing his duties as constable of
England he wrote a treatise for the Court of Chivalry on the protocols
governing trial by combat, and offered it for the king's authorization.[17]

I, the seid humble liege and youre conestable, offre unto your seide roial maieste
this litill booke of ordenaunce and maner of fightyng armed within listes before
you, not for that it is so wisely nor of so goode avisement ne discrecion made, but
that it may bee lightly amendyd, in requiryng your noblesse as humbly as I may or
can, that it please your benigne grace for to ovirsee, corect, and amende the seide
booke, and to put or to make lesse as it shall seeme you gode with gode maner
deliberacion, and avisement of the moost wise, valiantes, and sufficiant lordis and
knyghtes of your reame, which of dedes of armes have the most knowlege. But hou
sumevir I have begune this dede, I have not taken upon me such witte nor such
worthynesse that I am woorthy such thynges to undirtake, but for asmuche as it
longith to my seide office.[18]

In this dedication, Gloucester interweaves humility with a certain stubbornness about who is most qualified to judge modes of chivalry—and it

is not simply the king. At once conscious of the dignity of his position, like Gawain he performs humility: he made the treatise "aftir the litill power and witte that I have hadd."[19] However, even as he offers the treatise to the editorial authority of the king, he urges the king to seek advice from a more valuable source of chivalric authority: the "moost wise, valiantes, and sufficiant lordis and knyghtes of your reame, which of dedes of armes have the most knowlege."

Gawain's speech, on the contrary, makes the king the chief broker of chivalric authority. While Gloucester maintains the nobility of his own enterprise, Gawain regards his undertaking as a foolish ("nys") game which the king should not sully his hands with, let alone be so desirous ("talenttyf") of undertaking. And although he does proffer his speech itself to the aesthetic and social judgment of the listening courtiers whose war-strength he flatters, he does not constitute them as a communal audience of nobles whose expertise the king should solicit. The speech marks Gawain as one of the new court-centered nobility—a courtier who draws his power directly and solely from the king's generosity.

It was this kind of courtier that Richard II was actively seeking to create throughout the 1380s. His distrust of the traditional nobility prompted him to expand the royal household, doubling the number of chamber knights who looked to him for grants and offices. By installing these men in positions of authority throughout the land, he could bypass the jurisdictions of the greater nobility and command a base of support that was independent of their control. Later in his reign, he sought to establish military independence as well when he made Cheshire a recruiting ground for troops that were uniquely tied to the throne. Such attempts to alienate the throne from reliance on the existing nobility dismayed magnates such as Gloucester and Arundel. They felt that by creating direct affinities and dependencies among his subjects, the king was threatening their own networks of patronage and obligation and indulging in a dangerous absolutism.[20]

Their response is understandable. Richard was eroding two crucial links in the conservative ideology of feudal relations—that the king should cultivate his nobility for council and military support (as Edward III had done in his prime) and that the nobility had a natural right to participate in the government. Richard was quite explicit about his rejection of this ideology. In the 1385 patent that made Michael de la Pole the Earl of Suffolk, he envisions a nobility entirely dependent on the king: "We believe the more we bestow honors on wise and honorable men, the more our crown is adorned with gems and precious stones." [21] In this scenario, the king grants the favors to wise and honorable (not necessarily noble) men; they become inert ornaments for the crown and exist to glorify it. Royal favor becomes the chief route to advancement.[22]

However, even as Gawain reduces himself to an unworthy monarchical appendage, his royal blood in itself would mark him to a fourteenth-century audience as one of the great hereditary magnates, commanding the respect of even conservatively minded fourteenth-century nobility. In Edward III's reign all the dukedoms except that of Henry of Grosmont were firmly in the hands of members of the royal family, and the nobility bitterly resented what they considered to be Richard II's reckless and outlandish ennoblements of figures without royal blood.[23] Gawain's relationship to the royal family prevents him from sinking to the level of court flunkey. His status makes him recuperable from an aristocratic perspective. If he can be brought to see that true nobility is not given or granted but won, and won not from the king at the royal court but in the more dangerous lands outside its enclosure, then perhaps he, and by extension, Arthur's court can be brought out of their ignorant alienation and into consonance with the land and history they are reputed to crown.

The Provinces: Rifts in the Landscape

Even as it frames a provincial test of the royal court, *Sir Gawain and the Green Knight* simultaneously dramatizes contemporary problems of provincial identity and self-determination.[24] It vividly depicts Cheshire and south Lancashire—the setting of its central episodes—as landscapes of contradiction, and their rulers as duplicitous shapeshifters, strategists, and magicians. The provincial terrain Gawain traverses is uncultivated, ancient, and formidable. Yet in the middle of that grim wilderness he miraculously finds a castle that exhibits the newest in castle technology with all the modern conveniences where he is welcomed with a flawless courtesy. In the course of the poem, the poet repeatedly highlights this double face of the province, the disjunctions between bleak and ancient wilderness and up-to-the-minute courtly cultivation. This section focuses upon the divided character of provincial identity, arguing that it expresses and explores a historical disjunction in provincial culture at the time of the poem's composition—the dilemma created for the local gentry by Richard II's attempts to strengthen his ties to the North West Midlands in a campaign of patronage that induced the provincial gentry increasingly to depend on royal support for their careerism.

One of the most memorable and least discussed passages of the poem describes Gawain's solitary journey from the royal court through North Wales into the wilderness of the Wirral in Cheshire. The poem stresses at the outset the sheer remoteness and isolation of the provincial locale from the royal court. As Gawain journeys outward, the poet follows his itinerary carefully through North Wales, past the "iles of Angelsey," over the ford at "Holy Hede" and into the wilderness of the Wirral.[25] At that point Gawain falls off the map and into a landscape untouched by human nomenclature or history. Only nature has left its traces there.

> Mony klyf he ouerclambe in contrayez straunge,
> Fer floten fro his frendez fremedly he rydez . . .
> Bi a mounte on þe morne meryly he rydes
> Into a forest ful dep, þat ferly watz wylde,
> Hiȝe hillez on vche a halue, and holtwodez vnder
> Of hore okez ful hoge a hundreth togeder;
> Þe hasel and þe haȝþorne were harled al samen,
> With roȝe raged mosse rayled aywhere,
> With mony bryddez vnblyþe vpon bare twyges,
> Þat pitosly þer piped for pyne of þe colde. (713–14, 740–48)

[Many a cliff must he climb in country wild; / Far off from all his friends, forlorn must he ride . . . By a mountain next morning he makes his way / into a forest fastness, fearsome and wild; / High hills on either hand, with hoar woods below, / Oaks old and huge by the hundred together. / The hazel and the hawthorn were all intertwined / With rough raveled moss, that raggedly hung, / With many birds unblithe upon bare twigs / That peeped most piteously for pain of the cold.]

In this passage the poet portrays the desolation of the uncleared oak forests of the North West Midlands, virtually untouched even by the late fourteenth century. The passage shadows this tangled fecundity with overpowering bleakness. This English winter landscape in Gawain's eyes becomes a foreign land ("contrayez straunge") in which Gawain wanders ("floten") far away from his friends. As the passage progresses, the poet intensifies the sense of Gawain's separation by leaving behind even the enemies, woodwos, dragons, giants, and wolves that enlivened the earlier part of his journey. All contact, civilization—even time itself—are lost in a disorder of ancient trees which even the natural inhabitants, the birds, find bleak and cruel.

Yet it is in this desolate landscape that Gawain comes upon Bertilak's castle, floating delicately above the trees like a cut paper model. The poet stresses the castle's mirage-like apparition: "hit schemered and schon þurȝ þe schyre okez" (773) [it shimmered and shone amid shining leaves], a miraculous answer to Gawain's prayer. This castle is as modern, hospitable, and carefully crafted as the forest is ancient and wild. It features fashion-able architectural innovations like the chimneys, private chambers, and machicolations that were becoming widespread in England only in the latter half of the fourteenth century.[26] Gawain's reception there mingles smooth pageantry with warm hospitality, as he is welcomed in, relieved of his travel-stained garments, and personally conducted to his room by his solicitous host—a rapid reinsertion into human society and history.

In the poem, similar divisions characterize the provincial society of the West Midlands and constitute its presiding spirit, the Green Knight/Bertilak.[27] There are many indications that the Green Knight/Bertilak can be read as a member of the provincial gentry. Foremost is the placement of Bertilak's castle somewhere in the North West Midlands, in the fourteenth century a sparsely settled region partitioned out and governed mainly by numerous gentlefolk rather than great local magnates with extensive estates. The poem also teases at Hautdesert's courtly provincialism when it describes Gawain's reception at Hautdesert. In public, the castlefolk are exaggeratedly wide-eyed and respectful of this royal visitation, kneeling on the cold earth to welcome him. Privately, they are rubber-necking and whispering in corners, anticipating with relish a royal exhibition of chival-ric love speech.

Like the provincial landscape he rules, the Green Knight is an amal-gam of nature and culture, both ancient and contemporary. His two courts both reflect and relate these divisions. Their names adumbrate each other: the green-lawned estate of Hautdesert with its superb modern hall and chapel, and the "high wasteland" of the ruinous Green Chapel. As an elvish giant and barrow haunter who wields the magic of the "Goddess" Morgan le Fay, the Knight radiates aboriginal enchantment. Yet he is also a paragon of modern fashion, clad in silk and gilt, his long green hair beautifully coiffured; and in his Bertilak persona he perfectly exemplifies the tradi-tional life of the gentry, hearing mass, exercising the intricate protocols of venery, and celebrating Christmas with appropriate Christian revelry. His initial description vividly and hypnotically communicates these divisions. Every change of light and shift of tassel is recounted with a cinemato-graphic specificity that makes the image both dramatically gripping and epistemologically ungraspable—an inundation of conflicting detail that confounds synthesis.[28] And as the poem proceeds, these temporal disjunc-tions are widened and literalized by the actual splitting of the provincial characters into paired opposites: Bertilak/Green Knight, and the Lady and Morgan le Fay who enter the text hand in hand as linked extremes of beguiling youth and ancient beguilement.

This consciousness of historic perplexity resonates with the experience of the fourteenth-century provincial gentry of Cheshire and Lancashire, who were continually balancing on the tremulous fault-line between tradition and innovation. Their success was based equally upon the authority of ancient seigneurial precedent and upon the need to work ceaselessly at creating new sources of revenue and patronage. They carefully preserved their links to a kind of mythologized traditional feudalism at the same time as they seized upon the capitalistic "bastardizations" that continually complicated feudalism throughout its practice. Michael J. Bennett shows that in the provinces of Cheshire and Lancashire the opportunities of a money economy existed concurrently with the most exemplary of feudal practices; and the gentry sought revenue and influence not only by the conventional customs of seeking service in other households and contracting advantageous marriages but also by venturing into trade.[29] Bertilak indulges in time-honored seigneurial flourishes—sealing his bargains with drink, pursuing the art of venery, and offering Gawain a princely hospitality. At the same time, he introduces Gawain to a world where relationships must be renegotiated at every turn and contracts have to be constantly redrawn and re-rehearsed according to changing circumstances. He seems to distrust any binding system to keep his compacts firm in the minds of the royal courtly participants even overnight.[30]

Why does the Green Knight show such eagerness to set up such detailed and superintended contracts with Arthur's court? Here, I believe, the poem resonates to a sense of the precise contingencies of its own late fourteenth-century provincial milieu. In his pioneering study of the regional society of Cheshire and Lancashire, Bennett shows how intimately the gentry of the West Midlands were affected by Richard's attempts to strengthen and exploit direct royal ties to their home turf. Richard himself held the earldom of Cheshire throughout his reign and actively recruited soldiers in his palatinate to secure a personal military base of support. In addition, his expansion of the royal household offered new opportunities of patronage and office to those in the provinces unable to pursue a career at home. As a result, great numbers of ambitious Cheshire and Lancashire men left their provinces to seek their fortunes at court, in the military, and elsewhere on the national scene. Bennett highlights their cultivation by the royal family:

The palatinates of Chester and Lancaster were favoured by particularly close relations with the royal house in the later middle ages, both being in the hands of the ruling monarchs for over half of the period under discussion [ca. 1350–1430], and of princes of the blood for the rest. No other region could rival the Northwest in the puissance of its connections . . . There were few local knights and squires who were not the mesne tenants of either the earl of Chester [Richard II] or the duke of Lancaster [John of Gaunt]. Through wardship, the performance of homage, and the rendering of military service, most came into regular contact with the households of princes and kings. Many county notables and men of lesser means gained further credit with their royal lords by protecting their interests and acting as their agents in the region. Through employment in local government and estate-management, it was often possible for able careerists to bring their talents to the attention of powerful patrons, and then to secure advancement in the realm at large.[31]

Such profitable ties with the royal family and greater magnates were too alluring to refuse yet the effects of this continual drainage from the provinces to the capital and to other regions must have been noticeable, especially in regions as geographically isolated and as sparsely settled as were Cheshire and south Lancashire. And any sense of local debilitation would emerge more sharply amidst the distinctive regional culture of the West Midlands. Bennett discusses the strong unities in culture, outlook, and government that made the West Midlands distinctive provincial societies in England. The region was unusual both in its geographical isolation, and its comparative lack of past cultivation, settlement and enfeoffment—characteristics to which the Gawain-poet vividly attests as he describes Gawain's lonely journey. The soil was too poor to support the wide-scale farming necessary to maintain great baronial estates; there were few wealthy magnates with extensive holdings within the provinces to offer opportunities for patronage and careerism. Government was largely and unusually in the hands of the local gentry.

These factors established the North West Midlands as a distinct geographical and political regional society and nurtured a regional class-consciousness. In the absence of any nucleation around greater noble households, the local gentry bonded with each other. They fraternized, married, and served on the same committees and councils to an incestuous degree. To take one famous example of this solidarity, in 1386–87 when Sir Robert Grosvenor was litigating for his right to retain his coat of arms before the Court of Chivalry, the majority of his 200 dispositions came from his Cheshire neighbors, who joined together to defend him.[32] This sense of regional identity transcended the boundaries of the provinces; members of the gentry who sought careers outside often retained their sense of solidarity even after they had taken up permanent office elsewhere.[33] Even outside the North West Midlands, Cheshire had acquired a regional reputation for belligerence; at the end of the century this reputation, exacerbated by the king's flagrant partisanship, sparked the fear and hatred of the rest of England.[34]

Yet as Richard's reign progressed and he pursued his policies of drawing upon the region for both courtiers and loyal militia, the independence of the North West Midlands' gentry became seriously compromised. Bennett defines the essential dilemma—a local knight's need to maintain his status by seeking patronage where it could be found and his possible reluctance to abandon his regional self-sufficiency for a position of reliance on the crown:

The operations of royal patronage and the progress of careerism inevitably wrought major changes in Cheshire and Lincolnshire life. For the first time, it brought large sections of regional society into the mainstream of national life. It allowed many local men to attain positions of wealth and power wholly unobtainable in a provincial society. At the same time it produced its own sort of dependency. Increasingly, in order to maintain their fortunes through the vicissitudes of national politics, local families had to seek the favor of courtiers and government officials.[35]

In this passage, Bennett suggests that the new opportunities which started as incentives to seek a career outside the provinces were increasingly becoming economic imperatives—the scarcity of regional resources created a localized glass ceiling. A member of the gentry might achieve a certain status within the province but could only rise above it by seeking posts elsewhere, and was then obliged to maintain what status he had gained by soliciting further patronage. Given the conservatism and the regional solidarity of the provincial gentry, such success could not come without its costs.

The provincial gentry of Cheshire and Lancashire at the time of *Sir Gawain and the Green Knight* were thus caught in a double bind, embracing two fundamentally different perspectives. They valued their traditions of self-sufficiency but were increasingly rushing to become court dependents. On the one hand, they needed the profit and prestige that royal patronage offered, and were quick to exploit any opportunities that presented themselves. On the other hand they were bent on preserving their traditions and guarding their hereditary seigneurial rights—rights upon which the king was encroaching, even as he offered them unprecedented opportunities for individual advancement. Nigel Saul's discussion of the ambivalent behavior of the provincial gentry as a class shows how these contradictions could engender a kind of opportunistic schizophrenia:

They had the ability to switch roles with apparently effortless ease. They appear first as poachers, then as gamekeepers; first as lawbreakers, then as lawmakers. In parliament they appealed for better enforcement of the law; back home they were among the first to break it. In parliament they condemned the practice of maintenance; back home they were themselves the beneficiaries of it.[36]

And *Sir Gawain and the Green Knight* allows its provincial characters to
switch their roles with a similar miraculous ease. The poet leaves the
processes of their transformations a mystery; there seems to be no middle
ground between the courteous Bertilak and the belligerent Green Knight,
the vivid beauty of the Lady and the muffled and shadowy Morgan le Fay.
As the poem unwinds the manipulations of the provincial plotters it shows
how empowering such performative flexibility can be. For much of the
poem the duplicity of the provincial characters works for them, strengthening them on two fronts and imbuing them with authority. The Green
Knight and his wife transcend Walsingham's opposition between the true
knights of Mars and shameful knights of Venus by playing with equal
aggression in both battle and bedchamber. The Green Knight/Bertilak
exemplifies extremes of endurance by taking decapitation in stride, extremes
of courtesy in his welcoming of Sir Gawain. He alters his hunting strategy
resourcefully for each of the different beasts to enhance the enjoyment of
each kill. In the bedroom, the Lady pursues Gawain with equal strategy,
goading the master of "the techeles termes of talkyng noble" to within
an inch of his life and brilliantly turning both his courtly expertise and his
literary reputation against him while publicly preserving a flawless demure-
ness. Morgan is the most successfully underhanded poseur of all.

Yet in the poem, the provincial characters are also compromised by
this opportunistic flexibility of role. Just as a provincial knight may feel
ashamed at seeking the patronage of a king who seems determined to
trespass on his class prerogatives, the figures of the Green Knight/Bertilak
and the Lady/Morgan reek intermittently of bad faith. Although the Lady
is the one scapegoated at the end, the Green Knight also becomes occa-
sionally despicable: a duplicitous gamester and a sorceress's catspaw. He
panders his own wife to Gawain's bed, a relationship that concretizes in
the most brutal and literal way the provincial need to seek the court where
the powers of "luf-talkyng" are to be learned. And these fractures in his
character receive a corporeal expression that is profoundly violent and
ugly—a dissociation that the poem lingers over:

> þe scharp of þe schalk schyndered þe bones,
> And schranke þurȝ þe schyire grece, and schade hit in twynne,
> Þat þe bit of þe broun stele bot on þe grounde.
> Þe fayre hede fro þe halce hit to þe erþe,
> Þat fele hit foyned wyth her fete, þere hit forth roled;
> Þe blod brayd fro þe body, þat blykked on þe grene;
> And nawþer faltered ne fel þe freke neuer þe helder. . .
>> He brayde his bulk aboute,
>> Þat vgly body þat bledde;

Moni on of hym had doute,
Bi þat his resounz were redde. (425–30, 440–43)

[the shock of the sharp blow shivered the bones / And cut the flesh cleanly and
clove it in twain, / That the blade of the bright steel bit into the ground. / The head
was hewn off and fell to the floor; / Many found it at their feet, as forth it rolled;
/ The blood gushed from the body, bright on the green, / Yet fell not the fellow,
nor faltered a whit / . . . His bulk about he haled, / That fearsome body that bled;
/ There were many in the court that quailed / Before all his say were said.]

And who can blame them? The emplotment of events in this beheading scene is as suggestive as the gruesome details: a provincial ruler seeks
the court to ask a game from the king that leads to his decapitation. It is
suggestive that out of all blows to choose, the Knight offers beheading
when he kneels before Gawain and bares his neck to the sword. This scene
resonates intriguingly with the self-divisions of a provincial ruling class
eagerly sacrificing their own independent governance to that of the king—
and gaining in return a royally extended, if impossibly disjunctive, lease on
life. The descriptive abhorrence of the beheading undermines the Green
Knight's chivalric authority, and his prodigious energy becomes monstrous
as the courtiers spurn the cut-off head with their feet, rolling it around
the floor. This tendency toward mortal excess—this combination of heady
opportunism and bad faith—troubles all of the Green Knight's machinations, keeping the reader on the qui vive even in the festive castle of Hautdesert with its grim barrow gaping scarce two miles away.

The Most Dangerous Game

The contradictions that construct the provincial characters animate and
render more dangerous the games these characters play. As doubles, the
Green Knight/Bertilak and the Lady/Morgan le Fay entwine Gawain in a
network of plots as elaborately interlaid as nesting dolls. To draw him in,
they tempt him into risk-free bargains, offering him the opportunity to
hedge his bets and gain a prize at little cost. Both the exchange-of-blows
game and the exchange-of-winnings game offer Gawain the initial advantage. Gawain takes the bait because these games are familiar to him from
Arthur's court, where prizes are won without risk. The provincial characters turn the court's own inconsequential ludic paradigms against it, to
lure Gawain out of this secure realm of courtly diversion and implicate him
in a world where life is lived vividly, where death lurks in haunted barrows,
game turns to earnest, and oaths breed contradictory consequences—in

other words the world of history, as it is presented at the beginning of the poem where pain and wonder, bliss and blunder, and truth and treachery join hands and riot together down the ages.

Arthur's playful court not only reminds readers of its youth but invokes the culture of courtly gamesmanship in the later part of the fourteenth century. John Stevens has argued that throughout the late Middle Ages, the society of the royal court used game scripts (such as the "Game of Love") to provide a fictional framework for the drama of courtly community formation.[37] Chess, dice, word-plays, and riddles were appropriated to the greater games of love and loyalty because they provided metaphors and figures which courtiers could deploy to enrich their courtly self-constructions. During the late fourteenth century the royal court's weakness for prescripted diversions was so well known that non-courtly subjects could take advantage of it, ingratiating themselves by offering gifts under the guise of wagers. One such event is of particular interest. In 1377 before Richard's accession to the throne, the Commons of London honored the young prince with "great sporte and solemnity."[38] They sent a large procession of mummers through London and to the palace at Kenington, where the prince, his mother, the Duke of Lancaster, and many other magnates were celebrating Candlemas. The arrangements were lavish; the mummers were sumptuously costumed and nobly mounted. Yet this was more than a civic spectacle in the young prince's honor; they offered him a game:

When they were come before þe mansion they alighted on foot and entered into þe haule and sone after þe prince and his mother and þe other lordes came out of þe chamber into þe haule, and þe said mummers saluted them, shewing a pair of dice upon a table to play with þe prince, which dice were subtilly made that when þe prince shold cast he shold winne and þe said players and mummers set before þe prince three jewels each after other: and first a balle of gould, and then a cupp of gould, and then a gould ring, þe which þe said prince wonne at three castes *as before it was appointed* . . .[39] (emphasis added)

This game gives the prince the heady illusion of risk even as it assures him of the final outcome. When he receives the gifts he has the added delight of having won them. And this dice-loading illusion was not simply aimed at the ten-year-old. After the mummers diced with the prince they went on and wagered a gold ring against the prince's mother, the Duke of Lancaster, and every earl present. As wager followed wager and loss followed loss, the mummers must have enlivened the predictability by miming increased disappointment and belligerence, no doubt staging their mock-humiliation to intensify the court's delight. The mummers' use of this game represents their successful exploitation of a familiar courtly paradigm by which smaller games can be constructively lost to larger ends.[40]

Within the poem also, games are how Arthur's courtiers dramatize their status, famed both at battle and at court for their "gryndelayk"—fierce play—and "hendelayk"—noble play.[41] As the poem opens, they mark their Christmas celebrations by playing gift-games whose outcomes do not matter:

> And syþen riche forth runnen to reche hondeselle,
> 3e3ed 3eres-3iftes on hi3, 3elde hem bi hond,
> Debated busyly aboute þo giftes;
> Ladies la3ed ful loude, þo3 þay lost haden,
> And he þat wan watz not wrothe, þat may 3e wel trawe. (66–70)

[Then gallants gather gaily, hand-gifts to make, / Called them out clearly, claimed them by hand, / Bickered long and busily about those gifts. / Ladies laughed aloud, though losers they were, / And he that won was not angered, as well you will know.]

These games transform chance into a mutually pleasurable exchange—kisses for presents—a mock forfeit that binds the knights and ladies together with delightful exclusivity and no commitment at all.[42] No real consequence is allowed to trouble the interlude. Arthur's court is emphatically not the arena of intense display and elbowing-jabbing competition that Richard's household became; if the poet imbues Arthur's court with Ricardian resonances, he also carefully idealizes it into a fantasy world of knightly fellowship full of jest without pain and contest without loss. Even the public competitions of courtly speech that construct a courtier and instantiate his status are almost absent here.[43] Whatever their feelings and anxieties, the Arthurian courtiers in the poem speak a single language—pleasantry.

The Green Knight/Bertilak therefore tempts the court into chance-free ventures and seemingly meaningless exchanges when he proposes his bizarre games to Arthur and Gawain. Each game offers the lure of a rich prize for what seems very little risk. In the exchange-of-blows game, the beautiful ax is the prize, "a giserne ryche." And the idea of violent *exchange* seems nominal as long as Gawain has the first buffet. The exchange-of-winnings game makes the winnings themselves the prize, but the difference between Bertilak's and Gawain's daily occupations ensures that the most material advantage will fall to Gawain. One of the poem's nicer ironies emerges when Gawain, trained at court kissing games, doesn't suspect that even kisses can become consequential.[44] The Green Knight even tantalizes Gawain with the possibility that he will never have to leave the court at all: "And if I spende no speche, þenne spedez þou þe better / For þou may leng in þy londe and layt no fyrre— / bot slokes!" (410–12) ["And if I spend no speech, you shall speed the better: / You can feast with your friends, nor further trace my tracks."] This possibility—that Gawain may stay celebrating in his land and seek no further—is what the Green Knight's plots are designed to play on and frustrate. The poet depicts courtly gaming with gentle indulgence but also places it in a larger context of more serious games in order to pass a value judgment on it. Arthur's courtiers need chivvying from their playful self-enclosure and into the complex maturity that characterizes life in the provinces.[45]

To do this, the provincial characters take the simple binaries with which the Arthurian court hedges its world: loyalty and betrayal, friend and foe, game and earnest, and force them into intimate proximity. The result not only frightens the court but completely bewilders it. Although Arthur determinedly dismisses the Green Knight's intrusion as a "layking of enterludes," the contrast between the Green Knight's bloody performance with the historic interlude at Kenington shows how far the Knight's game has transgressed courtly ludic expectations. The mummers at Kenington preserve courtly decorum by maintaining strategic boundaries: the dice are loaded; the gifts go one way; the game ends with a dance where real lord is carefully insulated from play lord: "þe prince and þe lordes dansed on þe one syde, and þe mummers on þe other."[46] Any possibilities for ludic parody and a mingling of rule with misrule are left cautiously unexplored in this divided dance. The *Gawain*-poet is ruder. The Green Knight's "courtly interlude" shoves opposites together: his mummer fits the golden spurs of a knight over bare feet and flourishes both a holly branch and an ax in amity and enmity.[47] More threateningly, he intrudes into their company and entices them to investigate him in their turn; they wonderingly "stalk him near." This proximity becomes grotesque when the Green Knight's head is stricken off to be kicked among the courtier's feet. By the end of the opening scene, the Knight's blood is spilling over the floor and his body and head have literally bounded all over the court, penetrated by them and penetrating their company. Such terrible familiarity threatens the boundaries by which Arthur's court constitutes its circle of idealized self-enclosure, the endless knot of its chivalry.[48]

Both Arthur and Gawain make repeated attempts to restore their boundaries by treating the Knight as unequivocally hostile. The Knight no sooner professes his peaceful intentions than Arthur expresses his readiness for single combat: "If þou craue batayl bare, / Here faylez þou not to fyзt" (277–78) ["If contest here you crave, / You shall not fail to fight"]. The courtly characters are constrained by their own rigid adherence to their games of chivalry which conditions them to formulaic responses and idealistic self-identifications. Here Arthur claims the role of hero in one of his beloved chivalric romances responding to an appellant (challenger). So defined, the Green Knight may be dealt with swiftly and simply. But the Green Knight evades him, claiming the court insider status implicit in an exchange game.

However, the terms of his "playful" challenge define a game more dangerous and more uncontrollable than combat itself, despite his emphasis on legality and formal covenant. Kathleen Ashley brilliantly shows how the poet encodes these legal structures in order to gradually unravel them, replacing a world of secure relationships and identifications with a more ambiguous world where authorities and even contracts require constant revision.[49] The Knight's game thoroughly demolishes both the inconsequentiality of court exchange and the protocols of judicial combat. First and most nastily, in contrast to a contest where "the toon [must] preve his entent upon þe toothir, and the toothir in the same maner for [must] defend him," his terms forbid any resistance to each blow. Second, by convention, the knight appellant was to give his name to the constable overseeing the combat. The Green Knight steadfastly refuses to answer Arthur's question of "what man he is?"[50] Instead, the Knight demands first Arthur's identity and then Gawain's before agreeing to his substitution. He tantalizes the court by promising future disclosures of "my hous and my home and myn owen nome" (408), revelations that are delayed until the end of the poem. Third, although the Green Knight bears a weapon, it is neither courtly nor chosen by the court. Approved weapons in the lists were long sword, short sword, and dagger, or whatever weapon the constable should decide. The Green Knight takes the choice of weapon into his own hands, just as he usurps the court's prerogative of choosing the time and the place of the encounter. Finally and most tellingly of all, he comes armed with Morgan le Fay's magic—an act explicitly illegal in armed combat. Both appellant and defender were required to take an oath "upon the masseboke" disavowing all manner of supernatural resources:

Thou swerest, that thou ne havest ne shalt have more poyntes ne poyntes on the, ne on thy body within thise listes ... ne stone of vertue, ne herbe of vertue, ne charme, ne experiment, ne carocte, ne othir inchauntment by the, ne for thee, by the which thou trusteth the þe bettir to ovircome ... thyne adversarie, that shall come ayenst the within theise listes this day in his defence; ne that thou trustith in noon othir thyng, but oonly in God and thi body, and on thy rightfull quarell, so helpe the God and these halowes.[51]

In short, the Green Knight's ax "game" lays a mask of amity over an encounter which the court has no conventions to manage. By rescripting the encounter and deferring its resolution, the Green Knight is able to bypass the chivalric reflexes of Arthur's courtiers and draw Gawain out into unknown territory.

After the opening scene, the poem abandons its testing of Arthur's idealistic self-identifications—perhaps he is too easy, dangerous, or tedious a target—in order to tease apart those of his proxy, the Pentangle Knight. By the poem's end, Gawain will be forced to experience the complex contradictions that underlie his own chivalric practice, to question the possibility of his own ideal self-identifications, and finally to rely on other proofs of nobility than strength of the body in combat. As many commentators have pointed out, the device of the pentangle knits together battle-field virtues, like boldness and strength, with religious and social ones, like devotion and courtesy. This symbol gives an illusion of stellar unity to what eventually proves to be a loose constellation of the shifting, contingent, and often contradictory mores of chivalric behavior. As an alternative and remedy, the poet offers the open-ended negotiations of the girdle; its flagrant extrusion of the intimate, its perplexing of salvation with death, honor with shame. The poem's critique becomes, finally, a recognition that such open-endedness can yield not just strength but enjoyment. Ernst Robert Curtius suggests this: "The peculiar charm of the chivalric ethos consists precisely in fluctuation between many ideals, some of them closely related, some diametrically opposed. The possibility of this free interplay, of freedom to move within a rich and manifold world of values, must have been an inner stimulus to the courtly poet."[52] It is certainly a stimulus to this courtly poet, who delights, in Fitt III, in twisting his hero between conflicting contractual, amatory, and religious loyalties. And throughout the poem, Gawain himself seems susceptible to the exhilaration of soft-shoeing along the boundary between courtesy, virtue, and delectation.

Recognizing this does not mean dismissing chivalry as a viable system. Here my reading diverges from those commentators who read the poem as a clerical critique of fourteenth-century secular chivalry. The poet does not delight in problematizing the world of his hero simply because Gawain is a secular knight and not a Percival, but rather because he is the "childgered" Arthur's proxy. The Green Knight, in fact, teaches several areas where clerical and knightly virtues converge—most notably the stern self-restraint he demonstrates when he responds to Arthur's ferocious axe brandishing by thoughtfully stroking his beard, and when he stands rooted beneath Gawain's blow. He educates Gawain in it at the Green Chapel, goading him to stand unflinchingly beneath a death stroke. Gawain passes the Knight's test partly because he proves to possess this accepting and indrawn strength, the readiness for sudden death that is the root both of Augustinian disengagement and of military aptitude.[53] This is another link to North West Midland culture where traditions of military service ran deep on the border of restless Wales, whose proximal enmity and strangeness the poem shadows in the wild enemies that beset Gawain's journey through it. Cheshire had been a recruiting ground for English kings as early as Edward I's Welsh wars, and its investment in soldiering had broadened under the earldom of the bellicose Black Prince. Richard himself drew heavily from the region toward the end of his reign. These military traditions were so central to the regional livelihood of Cheshire that in 1393 when peace with France looked likely the Cheshire gentry actually revolted "accus[ing] Lancaster, Gloucester and Derby . . . of seeking to abolish the ancient liberties of their county."[54]

Thus, whether or not "no medieval poem demonstrates the incapacities of both fourteenth-century knighthood and twentieth-century criticism as elegantly," as Gregory J. Wilkins dryly comments, the poet nurtures the heart of fourteenth-century martial chivalry even as he targets the immature presumption of chivalric authority of Arthur's royal court.[55] At the end of the poem, the Green Knight debriefs Gawain, lauds him, and addresses him by his full knightly title of Sir Gawain for the first time in the poem; Victoria L. Weiss persuasively links this scene to the medieval knighting ceremony.[56] By the poem's end, the knighthood of Sir Gawain has been validated by presiding spirit of the West Midlands, a validation that Gawain neither recognizes nor accepts.[57] And his refusal of this accolade stems equally from his chagrin at the trickery to which he has been subjected and from the bad faith of his testers who manipulated him so intimately—and who turn out to be catpaws of his own aunt. Gawain's accolade of shame thus also suggests a failure in governance, the breakdown of the conservative ideal of a monarchy accepting of the divergent counsels of its barony and provincial chivalry. Baronial consultation loses its meaning when king and barony begin living in each other's pockets, far too familiar with each other to utilize any difference in perspective. The barons and gentry that insular romance makes the true arbiters of chivalric order in the realm have become knights of the royal *familia*, knights of the chamber. But familiarity has its charms. The poem suggests the delightful and treacherous opportunities such intimacy opens not just for the provincial knight but for the royal court itself when it sends the provincial Lady to Gawain's actual bed.

The Lady Layks Me Well

The outcome of the Green Knight's challenge to Arthur's court depends upon the result of an embedded encounter between Sir Gawain and the Lady of Hautdesert. The Lady, unnamed like the Green Knight, also commands the paradigms of courtly behavior in order to overstep them without warning.[58] Where her husband tests Gawain's reputation for "trawthe," the ability to hold to the meaning of his word, the Lady tests his mastery of courtesy, the ability to manipulate, multiply, and evade the meanings of his words. Together they explore "what speed there is in speech," (918), engaging in verbal play so pleasurable and perilous that it finally becomes an end in itself. Like her husband, whose games always incorporate the tantalizing prospect of a loss—something slipping away in the process of exchange—the Lady recognizes the appeal of risk in sharpening the pleasure of the game. In their game of courtly love the conventional roles of lady/master and knight/servant are altered and renegotiated with every speech, revealing inlaid paradoxes of power and volition.[59] As each endeavors to gain mastery over the other by seeking a position of service, Gawain is brought to experience and fight for a kind of authority unknown at Arthur's court: one that is not centralized, overarching, and already in place, but multiple, dispersed, and negotiable.[60]

As an emissary from the enchanted circle of Arthur's court, Gawain enters the provinces freighted with modes of self-definition that are formulaic and unaware of internal tensions and contradictions. Throughout the poem, Arthur's court operates through a simple logic of either/or; either the Green Knight is a friend to them, a harmless Christmas interlude, or else he is an enemy to be challenged to single combat and dispatched as quickly as possible. They are incapable of interpreting the mixed signals of his tokens, the ax and the branch of holly. But as Gawain comes increasingly under provincial influence, he is gradually seduced into a logic of both/and: both joy and terror, friend and enemy, truth and treachery, a seduction in which the very paratactic structure and syntax of the poem colludes.

Like her husband, the Lady mobilizes familiar paradigms of courtly behavior in order to trap Gawain, the champion courtier. At one point, she tutors him in his chivalric obligations by appealing to the traditions of continental romance:

> "Hit is þe tytelet token and tyxt of her werkkez
> How ledes for her lele luf hor lyuez han auntered,
> Endured for her drury dulful stoundez,

And after wenged with her walour and voyded her care,
And broȝt blysse into boure with bountees hor awen." (1515–19)

["Why, 'tis the very title and text of their deeds, / How bold knights for beauty have braved many a foe, / Suffered heavy sorrows out of secret love, / And then valorously avenged them on villainous churls / And made happy ever after the hearts of their ladies."]

Whenever Gawain refuses to respond to her advances, she accuses him not only of transgressing the literary codes of knightly romance but also of violating his own literary reputation. The Gawain of the continental romances exhibits a courtesy that verges on abjection, a predilection for too facile friendships with both men and women, and an inability to resist amorous encounters.[61] When Gawain has to be energetically inveigled into giving a single kiss to the Lady, he is flouting 200 years of continental romance characterization.

The Lady mobilizes continental traditions of *fine amor* in which the seeking lover represents himself at the mercy of his supremely powerful lady. This lady anchors a matrix of social, amatory, natural, and even religious hierarchies. Like Mary she is constructed as a figure beyond earthly desire; like Eve she teasingly instigates it. She promises her suitor the pleasures of paradise and delivers him to the abjections of hell. She can imbue him with supernatural strength or fatally enervate him. Because the lady is often the wife of a social superior, a knight's service to his mistress intersects with his service to his lord in ways that interlay sexual loyalties with political ones. These traditions, articulated by the continental troubadours and poets such as Dante and Petrarch, appear to empower the lady. However, recent readers usefully critique them as courtly constructions designed not to elevate the woman to a position of power, but to constrain her will and limit her choices to particular culturally freighted alternatives.[62] Once fixed as either the "cruel fair" or the vaguely benevolent but unthinkably unattainable goddess, the woman is frozen into an object of representation and can thereby provide a pretext and site for the self-constructive and mutually reinforcing interactions between men in the court. In *Sir Gawain*, this dynamic is nicely crystallized in a line that describes Gawain's armor and bespeaks his literary reputation as a peripatetic lady's man. On his helmet are turtledoves and true love's knots as thickly stitched as if "mony burde þereaboute had ben seuen wynter / in toune" (614) [many women had worked seven winters thereon entire], an aside that makes the loving labors of women an eloquent part of Gawain's self-presentation.

In other words, in the game of courtly love the woman is elevated and centralized not because she is the natural source of all courtly virtue, essential to knightly identity, but to make her foreign to it, an alien at the heart of the male-dominated, male-oriented court, which creates for her a particularly overdetermined position in order to delimit her potentially disruptive agency. As an object of male representation, she is locked into the specular passivity that characterizes both Gwenore at the poem's beginning and Mary, the strength-inspiring token on the privy side of Gawain's shield. At Arthur's court her choices are constrained by the knights who play the gift games at the poem's beginning, offering the ladies a choice of hands and claiming the kisses they grant with such laughing chagrin.

However, the static portrayal of the courtly woman provokes its own unease. We see Gwenore, still and secret amid the genial chaos and merriment, set off from the court up on the dais in a glittering tent that completely obscures any part of her body except for her eyes: "Þer glent with yȝen gray" (82) [she glanced with eyes of grey]. Even this window-dressed Gwenore who is the "comlokest to discrye" (81) [the comeliest that man could descry] has the capacity to look back—and the poet does not tell what she sees even as he draws attention to her looking. Gwenore's image will later polarize and split to create the two ladies at Bertilak's court: Morgan, muffled with expensive clothing from top to toe, whose eyes are her most visible feature; and the beautiful Lady who recalls and outshines Gwenore in Gawain's eyes but whose gaze is even more penetrating.

The poem's perceptions of these secret errancies shows how they arise from the very mechanisms by which Arthur's knights distance themselves from and enclose the courtly woman. In order to consolidate his social, psychological, and economic sovereignty, the knight-lover repeatedly declares his lady's amatory, aesthetic, and social supremacy over him, his helplessness before her. This game underhandedly makes the servant the master—the one who can maneuver, the one with the power of language and representation. In his conversations with the Lady, Gawain constantly seeks an inferior position, eluding her attempts to hold him to his reputation as a grand-master of courtesy by declaring his inherent unworthiness.[63] This enables him to evade her manipulations. Yet even as the affirmation of female power enables the knight to maintain his independence and exercise his capacity for representation, it also involves a calculated risk. What if this figurative, strategic, and represented power should become literal? What if women suddenly slipped the leash of representation and started actually exerting their supposed power to dictate the knight's actions and "ouertake [his] wylle"—actively wielding the kind of sexualized magic which courtly poets attribute to them. Or less threateningly, what would happen if the ladies of Arthur's court began to maneuver kisses from the knights? These prospects are imbued with both danger and pleasure in approximately equal proportions by polarized but linked characters of Morgan le Fay and the Lady.

As an ancient enchantress who seduced her way into Merlin's tutelage, the blank and muffled Morgan le Fay becomes a screen for this knightly projection of predatory feminine sexuality. In the realms of romance, where the supernatural becomes a magnifying lens for the cultural desires and fears of its audience, aversion against the aging female body becomes a full blown projection of feminine magic in all its unassimilable otherness. The fear and fascination Morgan can arouse in the poem emerges most clearly in her first description. The poet sets her against the Lady, partly so that the beauty of the young Lady might shine more brightly in the shadow of the old one. However, the emphasis on Morgan's ugliness exceeds that function. The poet lingers over it, provocatively interweaving the descriptions of these old and young women:

> vnlyke on to loke þo ladyes were,
> For if þe ȝonge watz ȝep, ȝolȝe watz þe oþer;
> Riche red on þat on rayled ayquere,
> Rugh ronkled chekez þat oþer on rolled;
> Kerchofes of þat on, wyth mony cler perlez,
> Hir brest and hir bryȝt þrote bare displayed,
> Schon schyrer þen snawe þat schedes on hillez;
> Þat oþer wyth a gorger watz gered ouer þe swyre,
> Chymbled ouer hir blake chyn with chalkquyte vayles,
> Hir frount folden in sylk, enfoubled ayquere,
> Toreted and treleted with tryflez aboute,
> Þat noȝt watz bare of þat burde bot þe blake broȝes,
> Þe tweyne yȝen and þe nase, þe naked lyppez,
> And þose were soure to se and sellyly blered;
> A mensk lady on molde mon may hir calle,
> > For Gode!
> > Hir body watz schort and þik,
> > Hir buttokez balȝ and brode,
> > More lykkerwys on to lyk
> > Watz þat scho hade on lode. (950–60)

[But unlike to look upon, those ladies were, / For if the one was fresh, the other was faded: / Bedecked in bright red was the body of one; / Flesh hung in folds on the face of the other; / On one a high headdress, hung all with pearls; / Her bright throat and bosom fair to behold, / Fresh as the first snow fallen on hills; / A wimple the other one wore around her throat; / Her swart chin well swaddled, swathed all in white; / Her forehead enfolded in flounces of silk / That framed a fair fillet, of fashion ornate, / And nothing bare beneath save the black brows, / The two eyes and the nose, the naked lips, / And they unsightly to see, and sorrily bleared. / A beldame, by God, she may well be deemed, / of pride! / She was short and thick of waist, / Her buttocks round and wide; / More toothsome, to his taste, / Was the beauty by her side.]

In this mingled description, the Lady displays herself while the "auncian" muffles herself up to the chin. This concealment is necessary to the plot; otherwise, presumably, Gawain would recognize his own aunt. However, this masking of Morgan becomes even more powerful in the context of alliterative romance's centralization of spectacle. Alliterative romances both mask and communicate interior thoughts and motives through spectacular surfaces and signs—insignia, clothing, behavior, stated reputation, costuming them in order to rivet the eye and entice questions about interiors. Here a character deliberately veils herself. By using the same strategy as the poet, Morgan seizes control of her own narration, determining what is seen and what is hidden in her representation.[64]

But the poet does not take this lying down. His emphasis on the ugliness of the few exposed parts, which are "sour to se and sellyly blered," makes the lifting of the veils a dubious pleasure but one that he cannot seem to resist. His description winds aversion and desire into an inextricable knot. Backing away, he virtually jeers, "A mensk lady on molde mon may hir calle, / for Gode!," yet not even the Lady is explored so corporeally as Morgan, whose lips and buttocks get a detailed investigation. This approach-aversion effect is heightened by intermixed descriptions drawing the two ladies so closely together that the poet ends up salivating over the "lykkerwys" Lady only after exploring the intimacies of Morgan's body.[65] Thus the poet enacts with Morgan the same titillating games of command and control over representation that all the other provincial characters are playing.

This description of Morgan recalls that of the castle Hautdesert, and thus suggests her as a resident genius. She is swathed in "chalk-quyte vayles" just as the castle sports "chalkwhyte chymnees" (795, 798). During the Christmas feast, this edifice of female ugliness is placed at the head of the table in the most honorable position, a place that at the Arthurian court was reserved for the bishop. This substitution of a grotesque old woman for an ecclesiastical dignitary departs from the traditional hierarchies of Arthur's court and introduces possibilities of a more free-floating authority. At Hautdesert, the control of the situation lies not in the exercise of a focal and focused mastery from above but rather in the profession of service with its strategic and rhetorical flexibilities—and both men and women can play. And although Bertilak impresses Gawain with his leaderly comportment, gives the orders, instigates the contests, and proposes the prizes, he also repeatedly withdraws his power, absenting himself from the castle, deliberately opening authoritative vacuums into which he invites his wife, Morgan, and Gawain himself to step. This abdication of authority is dramatized in the game he proposes on the very first night, in which he doffs his hood and hangs it on a spear as a prize for all contestants, including himself. "And I schal fonde, bi my fayth, to fylter wyth þe best / Er me wont þe wede, with help of my frendez" (986–87) [And I shall try for it, trust me—contend with the best, / Ere I go without my headgear by grace of my friends]. This figurative de-cap-itation alerts us not only to his previous identity but also to the gestures of self-deauthoritization that perplex it.

As a result, we are never sure who rules in the castle at any particular moment. As Gawain enters the castle, he himself is given mastery as an emissary from the royal court; all the servants and the company wait on him, plying him with hospitality sumptuous enough for a prince. Then we meet the master of the castle, Bertilak, who seems well able "to lede a lortschyp in lee of leudez ful gode" (849) [to be a master of men in a mighty keep]. Yet, at the Christmas feast, Morgan is accorded the highest honors, with Bertilak bearing her company at the head of the table; this leaves Gawain and the Lady free to play alone together in the midst of the company. Then, when the Lady slips into Gawain's bedroom on the first day of the exchange game, she sets up a covert operation which underscores the dialectical interdependencies of mastery and service. During the afternoons the two ladies are together, playing sovereign ladies to Gawain the servant, ruling within the castle while Bertilak commands the forest outside. Indeed, even architecturally, Hautdesert denies the hegemonic focus provided by Arthur's central hall and dais, replacing it with many disparate chambers, lofts, and hearthsides.

This continual decentering of authority becomes most insistent in the portrayal of the Lady. As the loveliest lady at the provincial court, she both echoes and displaces the static Gwenore, becoming a mobile subject of desire rather than its frozen object and more beautiful, "wener þen Wenore," through that very agency. In her characterization, the poet highlights the pleasurable possibilities of less rigid and hierarchical courtly interactions than those of Arthur's court.[66] From her first entrance, the poet dissociates the Lady from the iconic representation of her queenly double. Unlike Gwenore, she does not wait to be looked at; she actively seeks out Gawain to feast her own eyes.

Þenne lyst þe lady to loke on þe kny3t,
Þenne come ho of hir closet with mony cler burdez.
Ho watz þe fayrest in felle, of flesche and of lyre,
And of compas and colour and costes, of alle oþer,
And wener þen Wenore, as þe wy3e þo3t. (941–45)

[Then the lady, that longed to look on the knight, / Came forth from her closet
with her comely maids. / The fair hues of her flesh, her face and her hair / And her
body and her bearing were beyond praise, / And excelled the queen herself, as Sir
Gawain thought.]

The "Þenne ... Þenne" structure of the first two lines emphasizes the
swiftness with which she acts upon her desires. In contrast to Gwenore's
rigidly sartorial portrayal, the poem figuratively caresses the surfaces of her
body. Skin, flesh, and complexion come first in the enumeration of her
attributes, form and coloring are a close second, followed by manners.
By focusing on her bodily loveliness, the poet differentiates her from the
courtly ladies of Gawain's experience. Revealingly, Gawain seems less susceptible to this sheerly corporeal beauty than he is to a skillful makeup
job and haute couture; the two moments when he comes the closest to
succumbing follow descriptions of her jewelry and apparel.

Despite these differences, Gawain persists in treating the Lady as he
would Gwenore, eagerly asking to be her servant with a touching faith
that she will stay safely on the pedestal he makes for her. But she takes the
offensive, challenging his chivalric identity, testing his rhetorical skill, and
pushing his bodily restraint with dextrous brinkmanship. In the delicately
nuanced and multiply-enclosed ambiances of Bertilak's court, the roles
of amatory subject and object are thus liable to change without notice.[67]
Gawain discovers that such risky and delightful negotiations sharpen the
pleasures not only of conversation and game but, in the face of his own
rapidly approaching execution, come to stand for the pleasurable uncertainties of life itself.

This focus on pleasure through danger implicates the violent bases of
aristocratic honor culture which must hazard itself for honor and renown.
But the poet's projection of battlefield tactics into the provincial bedchamber searches out the desires which drive this chivalric self-fashioning—not
for the honor and material renown won but rather the acute and fearful
pleasures of venture itself. In this skewed but revealing provincial mirror,
the chivalric assailant becomes the knight's pleasurable conspirator in a process of mutual, heady, and profoundly dangerous self-proving. As Arthur's
custom suggests, the knight cannot sit and feast, cannot be satisfied until
the stranger arrives, an enemy who must be kept closer than friends because

that stranger is already frighteningly and exhilaratingly at the center of the knight's craving. The poem associates this insight with the provinces in the very process of moving us towards them. Refusing with a figurative yawn to indulge in Malory-like chronicles of the monstrous combats and agonies that had enlivened Gawain's winter journey, the poem hastens to transform Gawain from an intimidating warrior into a more vulnerable and sympathetic figure and his enemies from the woodwos they at times resemble into more intimate provokers of knightly identity. In this provincial castle where chivalric paradigms are driven to uncomfortable and bizarre extremes, the poem thus flouts medieval romance conventions in a profoundly revealing way, at once inviting and oversetting the snap judgments that trained readers of romance are tempted to make, even as it urges us towards chivalry's strange, fearful, and wonder-hungry heart.

Thus it is significant that Gawain's first reaction upon entering the castle is a thankful relaxation. In romance traditions, moments of knightly relaxation or disarming before the climactic encounter usually signal a dangerous temptation. An audience familiar with such traditions would be further alerted by the fact that Gawain is not just unclothed but "dispoyled" (860) of his armor—an enforced change of social identity tinged with sexual violence. And yet Gawain is endearingly grateful for his despoilment. This is the first suggestion that at Hautdesert, risk and pleasure are necessarily entwined. Gawain sheds the austere persona of the questing knight to play a more comfortable role, the champion courtier, a role anticipated and prepared for him by the folk of the castle, who have his new costume ready for him. The poem centralizes this relaxation, I believe, to provoke not wariness and resistance but rather sympathy.[68] If Gawain's eager relief to get out of the cold and away from his quest is mocked, the mockery is very gentle and stems from Gawain's own rigorous self-identification as a paragon of knightly perfection. Gawain becomes a knight who needs his sleep, who enjoys the play of verbal repartee enough to return to the company of the two ladies every afternoon, and who seems unable or reluctant each morning to scrape himself out of bed, even when after the first day he knows he will be trapped naked under its sheets. Gawain's happy lassitude becomes even more surprising when contrasted to Bertilak's terrible energy as he ranges all over the countryside, transported by the joys of the chase in three of the most strenuous hunts of medieval literature.

But the poem is pushing us into chivalry's labyrinthian interiors and to this voyage in, Gawain's passivity is key. It lulls him to sleep in order to pin him down. The architectural intricacies of castle Hautdesert encourage retreat and offer the pleasures of self-enfoldment. The denizens of Bertilak's shifty and decentered estate are continually seeking the intimacy of private conversations, withdrawing "to chambre, to chemné" (978) [to chamber, to chimney], the welcoming circles of the castle's many glowing hearths, to the upstairs rooms away from the central hall where one can enjoy the prospect of morning sunlight gleaming on the quiet walls. Even in the central hall in the midst of the Christmas feast, Gawain and the lady are able to cast a circle of delightful privacy about themselves: "Vche mon tented hys, / And þay two tented þayres" (1018–19) [Each tends his affairs / And those two tend their own]. But unlike the similar circles of happy exclusivity cast at Arthur's court, these privacies are not safe havens—they are microscopic slides, isolated for scrutiny.[69]

This emerges in the bedroom scenes of Fitt III.[70] The poem deepens the sense of sanctuary implicit in Gawain's long morning sleeps, his welcome retreats into stillness, peace, and absolute privacy. Even the poet, so adept at slipping in and out of his hero's moods and thoughts, refrains from intruding at one point. "ȝif he ne slepe soundyly, say ne dar I / For he hade muche on þe morne to mynne, ȝif he wolde / In þoȝt / Let hym lyȝe þere stille" (1991–94) [I don't dare say whether he slept soundly or not, for he had much to mull over in his mind concerning the morning if he chose; let him lie there still (my translation)]. Yet this seeming privacy inevitably becomes a peep show.

> And Gawayn þe god mon in gay bed lygez,
> Lurkkez quyl þe daylyȝt lemed on þe wowes,
> Vnder couertour ful clere, cortyned aboute;
> And as in slomerynge he slode, sleȝly he herde
> A littel dyn at the door, and dernly vpon,
> And he heuez vp his hed out of þe cloþes,
> A corner of the cortyn he caȝt vp a lyttel,
> And waytez warly þiderwarde quat hit be myȝt. (1178–86)

[And Gawain the good knight in gay bed lies, / Lingered late alone, till daylight gleamed, / under coverlet costly, curtained about. / And as he slips into slumber, slyly there comes / A little din at his door, and the latch lifted, / And he holds up his heavy head out of the clothes; / A corner of the curtain he caught back a little / And waited there warily, to see what befell.]

Here the poem's general obsession with the actions of enfolding, wrapping around, encircling, and overlapping goes into overdrive, pleasurably but relentlessly insulating its hero. Within his closed door, all is still and silent in the morning light. The curtains of his bed are closed; within the bed he is entirely buried in rich covers; and within the covers he is gliding in deep slumber. The Lady's stealthy intrusion throws him into a confusion as profound as the one which stuns Arthur's court after the Green Knight's first entrance, when all are as silent as though they were "slypped vpon slepe" (244) [slipped into sleep]. But where Arthur's court resists the Green Knight's stupefying effect, Gawain courts it, lying doggo and feigning sleep once more. Gawain is in the position of Gwenore at the poem's beginning, framed off from the activity of the castle, enveloped in rich wrappings and tapestries from which he can peer out but whose encirclements he seems unable or reluctant to leave. This presentation signals the reversal of roles he is about to undergo, when the lady slips in to make him her *prisonnier d'amour*. Yet this position is not simply a trap from which he should extricate himself with the fearful alacrity of a tempted St. Anthony (as some of the more exegetically minded commentators have argued). Gawain's anxious and pleasurable withdrawal signals the enticing interior contradictions that the poem is here, with the Lady, to tease open.

Here the poet painstakingly marks the porousness of these local havens, which like the poem's games remain available to larger scrutinies and consequences. In the solitude of Gawain's bedroom, elaborately locked away from the public central hall, the knight and the lady seem also to be isolated from an organizing central authority—the formidable or reassuring influence of the lord. However, Gawain's given word to yield up whatever prize he gains imparts a public inflection to these encounters, imbuing the bedroom with the pressures of other loyalties and obligations. The privacy is an illusion. Bertilak is simultaneously not close enough and yet all too near. Whatever goes on in the hidden precincts of the bedroom must eventually be brought out to the central hall and performed again, with gusto, to an eager and curious audience under Bertilak's ironical eye.

The poem here explores the necessary interpenetration and mutual implication of chivalry's public performance and its mysterious and conflicted interiority. And this exploration also implicates the poem's more political investigation of the conflict between center and periphery, royal court and provinces. Just as the specter of Bertilak's weirdly abrogated authority inalienably haunts the peripheries of his castle, Arthur's weirdly abrogated authority haunts the remoter peripheries of his realm. The poem drives toward the recognition that the gap between central authority and peripheral isolation is not a gap at all but a mutually implicating transaction with profound stakes for all concerned. And these transactions become more delightful even as they become more dangerous.

Fitt III sharpens the horns of these dilemmas even as it urges Gawain more and more closely toward them. The Lady presses Gawain more narrowly; the lord's hunts grow more specific, personal, and vicious; the number of kisses increases; Gawain's rendezvous with death looms larger; and his awareness of danger sharpens. Several times he attempts simply to leave, only to be detained by Bertilak. However, at the same time these anxieties press closer, Gawain's delight in the interactions of provincial life increases, not despite the dangers of Castle Hautdesert, but because of them. This becomes most noticeable as New Year's Day approaches. On the third day of the test, the adumbrations of Gawain's approaching death penetrate even his sleep. Trapped "in dreȝ droupyng of dreme" (1750) [dark muttering of dreams], for the first time he is unable to wake at the Lady's entrance. Instead of casting up the curtains of the bed, she throws open the window, and Gawain startles awake. The sudden transition from his foreboding dreams to the prospect of the beautiful lady and the window she opens into an intensity of present experience nearly undoes him:

> Wiȝt wallande joye warmed his hert.
> With smoþe smylyng and smolt þe smeten into merþe,
> Þat al watz blis and bonchef þat breke hem bitwene
> and wynne. (1762–65)

[His heart swelled swiftly with surging joys. / They melt into mirth with many a fond smile, / And there was bliss beyond telling between those two, / At height.]

In the face of his approaching death, the prospect of conversing with the Lady becomes a larger pleasurable haven, the circle of life itself in the midst of the unfathomable and inexorable processes of fate and history. Like Bede's sparrow, Gawain swings out of the darkness of his dreams into the bright chamber where the lady is laughing at him beside the open window. They break into speech with an urgency that verges on violence, emerging in the verbs "smete" and "breke." Here, for the first time, Gawain joins fully in the intense and excessive joys that seem to characterize the noble life in the provinces, a kind of bliss that only arises when the boundaries between life and death are thinnest, when the competition between gamesters involves potentially violent stakes, and when momentary perceptions are as sharp and vivid as this mortally edged consciousness can make them.

Many commentators have noted this intensity of focus, the care given by the poet to the smallest details, like the birds peeping in the wilderness of Gawain's first journey whose presence echoes and drives home Gawain's unexpressed desolation and alienation. John Ganim defines this perceptual acuity as the poem's overriding feature and Marie Borroff links it to mortality when she shows the narrator's imaginative sympathy for the vulnerabilities of mortal life as it is experienced by every living thing in the poem, from Gawain to the chill-peeping birds of the forest to the stricken and desperate animals of the hunt.[71] It seems to me that this sensual consciousness of lived experience is not merely a feature of the poem but a state of mind to which it strives to bring its hero and certainly brings its readers.

It is for this reason, among others, that the poet enfolds the secret hazards and pleasures of the bedroom scenes within the vivid hunting scenes, where slaughter, dismemberment, single combat, heroic last stands, and desperate but futile stratagems spark a delight that nearly transports the lord out of his senses:

> Þe lorde for blys abloy
> Ful oft con launce and lyȝt,
> And drof þat day wyth joy
> Thus to þe derk nyȝt. (1174–77)

[The lord for bliss was completely carried away and often broke forth and alit by turns, and thus drove that day with joy clear to the dark night.][72]

Although some commentators have read Bertilak's joy in slaughter as a sinister sidelight on his character or even an indication of his satanic affiliations, the poet is actually drawing upon a tradition which maintains that hunting's sheer physical exuberance overwhelms sin in the bounding delights of a chase which concerns itself only and joyfully with its own sensations and strategies.

Now shal I preve how hunters lyven in this world most joyfully of eny other men. For whan the hunter ryseth in the mornyng, he seeth a swete and fayr morow and the clere wedir and bryght, and hereth the songe of the smale fowles the which syngne swetely with grete melodye and ful of love ... And that is grete lykeng and joye to the hunters hert ... And than whan his houndes byn passid bifore hym, than he shal ryde after hem and he shal route and blowe as lowed as he may with gret joy and gret likyng, and I assure yow that he ne thenketh to noon other synne ne to noon other evel.[73]

In these hunting scenes, as many critics have noted, the reversals, negotiations, lurkings, and evasions between hunter and prey mirror and frame the bedroom strategies of the Lady and Gawain. But more profoundly, the formulaic unity of chivalric identity is being pried apart in the process of its enactment; altering from formula to performance, realizing itself in the contingencies of historic experience. Both Gawain and the Lady exploit and intensify the linguistic and sexual ambivalences of conventional chivalry as they wrestle for amatory roles, and these ambivalences are dizzily intensified even further as Gawain kisses Bertilak with such smacking vigor to Bertilak's appreciation before the eyes of an admiring public.[74] No one in the poem expresses discomfort—everyone in the poem is wildly delighted with a headiness it transfers vividly to its readers. These pleasurable splits in chivalric identity are literalized in the actual penetrations and dismemberments of the hunting scenes, where each animal is split and apportioned with vicious nicety. In depicting the joys of struggle and slaughter, the pleasures of carefully unbinding the intricate sinews of each body, the poem crystallizes its own mischievous investment in the similar processes by which it disarranges the "endless knot" of chivalric code and social practice that Gawain professes to embody.

By the third day of the test Gawain has been induced to taste the peculiar pleasures of a provincial life where authority is multiple, consensual, contradictory, and up for grabs. In his privy conversations with the Lady, he discovers the exhilarations and inversions of amatory performativity as well as its acute discomforts. The games Gawain plays with the lady become the more precious because, unlike the games of Arthur's court, they involve real risks, real stakes, and real prizes. The castle's denizens are joyful to the point of madness because they fall within their barrow's shadow. In short, although the sexual seduction of the Lady fails, the larger cultural seduction of provincial life succeeds.

Gawain's acceptance of the girdle confirms the effectiveness of that seduction. The girdle becomes a token of his life both magically and figurally. The Lady is not lying when she promises that it will preserve him from death at the Green Chapel, and Gawain covets it because he loves his life with a passion that the provincial plotters have painstakingly fostered.[75] By the end of the third day Gawain is no longer the idealized, earnest, and stoic knight who stubbornly commits himself to a winter journey toward death. Tempted to participate in the vivid experience of the provincial gentry, Gawain has been begun to savor the sweetness of a life that is intoxicating because of its dangers and contradictions. For Gawain, this pleasure reaches its most poignant intensity as he stands under the Green Knight's third blow. He feels the ax whisper past his neck and the warm blood following, knows himself still alive, and enjoys the most thrilling moment of his life: "Neuer syn þat he watz burne borne of his moder, / Watz he neuer in þis world wyȝe half so blyþe" (2320–21) [Not since he was a babe born of his mother / Was he once in this world one-half so blithe].

It is because Gawain is successfully seduced that when all the charms are overthrown and the plot emerges in all its bizarre manipulations that he undergoes such a backlash of shame, self-loathing, and disgust. Gawain's self-castigating, woman-scapegoating, exegetical judgment effectively hurls away as sinful or evil some of the poem's most moving and hilarious moments as well as much of its astonishing beauty. And this ending has provoked similar cries of disgust and dismay from critics who feel betrayed by a hackneyed closure that seems to sacrifice the poem's responsive, mischievous, and discerning heart. However, this ending makes sense in the light of the poem's focus on the mutually implicating conflict between provincial self-determination and royal absolutism. Ultimately, in the disaffection of this ending, the poem shows at once its subtlest and its most forceful critique of a royal authority that establishes itself by sacrificing the independent, competing, inconsistent, contingent, intensely self-interested, and self-inventing counsels and perspectives of the provincial gentry.

Gawain's encounter with the paradoxical authority of the Lady entices him to experience personally the authoritative contingencies of provincial decentralization and the acute competitive pleasures that animate them. These modes of play recall the contingent and consensual grapplings by which the gentry of Cheshire and Lancashire pursued their interests in the absence of a great nucleating magnatial households. They were practiced at keeping an indefatigable eye on the main chance. Notorious for their regional bellicosity, on the home front they established, consolidated, and plotted to extend their family holdings by energetically trading in marriages, litigating, poaching on their neighbor's estates, and competing for favor at court. The "hyƷe hode" (2297) [high hood] of provincial authority was a coveted prize for which all were contending, just as Gawain and the castle-folk contend for Bertilak's hood on the first day of the festivities. Each of the provincial plotters draws Gawain into conflicting contracts and allegiances—all are designed to destabilize his own hierarchically endowed authority by making him fight them on their own shifting ground.

Yet at the end of the poem, these flexible modes of authority evaporate, to be replaced once more by the rigid hierarchies and subservient nobility of Arthur's court—with one change: this time, it is Morgan, Gawain's aunt, rather than Arthur, his uncle, in charge. She exerts a hegemony that is universally domesticating, forbidding any possibility of negotiation. "Weldez non so hyƷe hawtesse / Þat ho ne con make ful tame" (2454) [None holds so high degree / That her arts cannot subdue]. Under her magically leveling hand all of the delicately outlined local and linguistic grapplings of the poem vanish. The Green Knight, the previous master of the narrative, becomes an errand boy running about the country in fancy dress. All his own inscrutable interests, purposes, and contradictions are subsumed by Morgan's petty plot to frighten Gwenore. The Lady is transformed from an inexplicably charming and self-determined seductress to a doubly subjugated catspaw, obeying the orders of both Morgan and her husband—

a miniature of Eve's fate after the Fall that makes the Lady's opposition to Mary in the poem even more pointed. Gawain himself, with understandable chagrin, becomes the universal dupe.

The poet thus makes a crucial move by linking Morgan to Arthur and to Gawain himself:

> "Ho is euen þyn aunt, Arthurez half-suster
> Þe duches doȝter of Tyntagelle, þat dere Vter after
> Hade Arþur vpon, þat aþel is nowþe." (2464–66)

["Your own aunt is she, Arthur's half-sister, / The Duchess's daughter of Tintagel, that dear King Uther / Got Arthur on after, that honored is now."]

Morgan's affiliations with royal authority both place her in the line of and radically compromise that authority. The callow, hyperkinetic Arthur of the poem's beginning and the ancient goddess are suddenly connected, their bloodlines entwined through Uther and the duchess of Cornwall. While Gawain humbly attributes to Arthur at the poem's beginning a singular and incontrovertible authority, what will he do when Arthur's half-sister Morgan rises at the end to take advantage of his offer? The poem's journey from kingly authority to harridan's sorcery simultaneously mystifies and disenchants the idea of a singular, all-leveling, centralizing authority. Worse than the ugliness of its realization in Morgan is its horrifying blandness— this thick-browed, white-swathed, turretted old woman with the broad buttocks is Morgan the Goddess? What does it mean to be tamed by her? Morgan's apotheosis therefore both concretizes and demonizes the incantatory power of monarchical absolutism. When the province is subsumed by rather than negotiating with the monarchy the distinction between them vanishes in a way that radically compromises both. The provincial characters lose self-determination while Gawain discovers that Arthur's noble blood and therefore his own tie them to a less than illustrious, however encompassing, ancient authority. Faced with the knowledge of such a double and dubious legacy, Gawain immediately undergoes a violent and unexpected alteration, from the joyous knight free to defend his life and prove his worth against the Green Knight in battle, to a self-castigating, woman-denouncing breast-beater, as affixed to his new treason-ridden persona as he was earlier to his trawth-ful one.[76]

Yet his reaction is eminently understandable. His own self-determination has been radically compromised by Morgan le Fay and her tools; step by step, his journey has been scripted, his reactions manipulated from beginning to end. Any courtly taste for prescripted gaming here becomes abhorrence. He directs his fury against the Lady, as the one most instrumental in his seduction but it is the prospect of meeting Morgan again that sends him racing back to Arthur's court. The provincial court from which Gawain had departed that morning is not the one to which he would return in the afternoon. It has been (and always had been) infiltrated and possessed by a royal ancestor who can not only suborn an entire castle-full of particularly headstrong and individualistic provincial gentry, but can cloak that appropriation in a kind of bland patronage for which she is highly honored by those she has subjected. Gawain will have no part in it: "he nikked him naye, he nolde bi no wayes" (2471) [the knight said him nay, that he might by no means].

By wheeling in Morgan as the agent provocateur, the poem stages the preemption of diverse and competitive provincial authorities by a singularly offensive (and offensive because mystified, unnegotiable, and above all, *boring*) royal one. The poem has sacrificed its own vivid and delicate explorations of the pleasures and dangers of provincial competition but it does so in order to highlight the humiliating costs of that sacrifice. And it pushes home its point by centering upon Gawain's disillusionment. He realizes that he has been induced to abandon his naturalized ideal self-image, "my kynde to forsake" (2380), and adopt a more open-ended one which he must reconstruct constantly (trading the pentangle for the lace). But that is not the real sting which the game holds for him. He believed he was playing games between equals whereby upping the ante—treading an ever more delicate balance between courtesy and surrender with the Lady or increasing the ardor of his kisses to Bertilak with such spectacular brinkmanship—he could prove himself a worthy and delectable opponent.[77] But instead, the scheme resembles the games offered by the mummers to Richard or the games played in Arthur's court at the poem's beginning, a fated contest against an opponent who held dice that this time were weighted cunningly against him.

And in this destruction of the dangerous contingencies of provincial gamesmanship something intense and precious is also destroyed—the vivid delights of actively negotiating the ambiguous territories between chivalric truth and betrayal, pleasure and danger, identity and performance which make life in the lands of Hautdesert worth living.

Province, History, and Narrative

The elusive and competitive provincial landscape that Gawain enters when he crosses the Ribble resonates to the perplexities of British history. This history which the poem outlines in its opening stanza previews the provincial landscape as a topography of contradictions. Its genesis is the Trojan apocalypse, its founder is a figure who knits truth and treachery together, and by that synthesis generates a line of kings as unruly and opportunistic as any of the provincial characters. Both the past and the provinces are constructed in the poem as worlds which elude easy definition and altogether escape the simple categorizations of Arthur's courtly chivalry. The provincial challenge to the royal court is thus a challenge to rethink inadequate chivalric paradigms and reenter the turbulent narrative both of its own land and its own history.

Introduced as the paragon of British sovereignty, by that very definition Arthur's court stands outside of history: a self-enclosed exemplary moment. Yet, far from crowning the historic process of conquest, foundation, and destruction, it proves to be a diversion from it. As the poem progresses, we see through Gawain how Arthur's court resists both interpretive flexibility and historical change. Its circle of courtly pleasures exists within very rigid parameters; no game or conflict is allowed to extend beyond the present moment or alter the chivalric status quo. Even such a gory exhibition as the Green Knight provides is laughed into festive insignificance. The court maintains itself by simple binarisms, ideals to which knights should aspire, and faults they must shun. The paradigmatic characters of Arthur and Gawain are etched in the foreground of a generic "douth" [company] which falls silent, laughs, and laments in a collective fashion that effaces both individual agency and the possibility of different interpretations. Arthur has succeeded in creating a brotherhood of young nobles who lack interpretive paradigms sophisticated enough to deal with the multivalent and troubling world outside their circle.

As it shapes this fantasy court, the poem is careful to avert its eyes from the tragic shape of Arthurian history (the alliterative *Morte Arthure* provides a useful contrast). Rather it concerns itself with an early unchronicled moment, sequestered from the tensions of previous or subsequent developments. Even within that moment, time has stilled. The holidays that punctuate the year do not mark the passage of time as a linear process, instead they constitute the year as a reassuring festive cycle; the court pebble-skips from Christmas to Lent, to Easter, to Michaelmas, to All Hallows, in a suspension of larger historic change that keeps Arthur and his folk firmly and permanently in their "first age."

By extracting Gawain from the festive cyclical year of the court and involving him in a game whose stake is his life and whose end has been unexpectedly deferred, the Green Knight draws him to adopt a more intense consciousness of the passage of time, the inevitability of historic change, and the knowledge that a convivial game can lead to a cruel and inexplicable end.[78] This new conceptualization situates Gawain in a different narrative, not cyclical, festive, and unchanging, but linear and irrevocable.

The poem's embedded plotlines intensify the consciousness of change and consequence by juxtaposing unlike states. These juxtapositions can occur simultaneously as with the hunting/bedroom scenes and can be embedded within each other as with the two games. In either case the juxtaposition stresses their consequential connection—as when, in the middle of the genial exchange-of-winnings game, Gawain is forcibly reminded by the severed boar's head ("This game is your own" [1635]) of the more deadly exchange-of-blows game whose ending he is rapidly approaching. The strategies of the provincial games work to undermine the oblivion of time's passage, insistently folding together "forme" and "fynisment," origin and outcome. It is only by navigating such juxtapositions of beginning and end, past and present, that Gawain may overcome the festive presentism that alienates Arthur's court from both its intransigent land and its contradictory history.

Coming to grips with such a history involves recognizing and dealing with the lack of a single stable foundation, authoritative center, or immutable system of values. If the royal court can be persuaded to acknowledge the rich complexity which waits outside of its gates, it will also gain valuable insight into the basis for its own sovereignty—which historically arose through such locally contingent competitions. The Green Knight has a stake in enlightening Arthur, but perhaps the poem also has a stake in administering a caution to an audience increasingly implicated in the ideology of royal absolutism (whether promoting, accepting, or ambivalent about it) in a land with its own stubborn history of seigneurial resistance to over-arrogant monarchs. Who that precise audience was we shall probably never know—and until more evidence turns up, it seems a little tendentious to try to pin down definitively whether the poem was circulated among a coterie of provincial literati or performed before Richard II himself by one of his Cheshire retainers.[79] The poem flexes to allow for many extrapolated audiences by inviting many nicely ambiguous identifications: Arthur as a figure like Richard who is first sought and then rejected as a target of the Green Knight's testing and tutelage; Gawain dramatizing his submission to Arthur's command even as he rises to contest it, recalling both Richard's household advisors and the greater magnates who wished, at first courteously, to overcome the king's resistance to their own role in government; and the Green Knight himself, playing a potentially self-mutilating court-game like the provincial careerists who had loosened their regional affiliations by seeking patronage at court. Over and above these interests, the fact that a lesson is to be learned through a sojourn in the provinces paradoxically centralizes the provinces as the site where history and contemporaneity interpenetrate.

In this context, the mythical resonances of the provincial characters become comprehensible; they work as avatars both of historic tradition and contemporary adaptiveness—both of which acknowledge, negotiate, and even enjoy the shifting contingencies of lived experience, past and present, and, more darkly, future. It is not surprising, then, that the poem's acute consciousness of temporal disjunction finds an echo in these characters. The Green Knight shifts back and forth from an avatar of renewal to a specter of death, a ferocious ogre lurking for Gawain at the "chapel of meschaunce" and sharpening his axe, "as one vpon a gryndelstone hade grounden a syþe" (2202) [as one who upon a grindstone whets a scythe]. Together, Morgan le Fay and the Green Knight embody both the generative and destructive principles that give both history and the narrative their shapes. Morgan instigates the plot while the Green Knight waits at the Green Chapel to end it. These characters themselves fold "forme" to "fynisement" as their plots progress; it is no wonder they preside together over Hautdesert's Christmas table.

In much the same way, the beginnings and endings of history meet in the site of the Gawain's fatal New Year's tryst, the ambiguous grave-chapel of which the Green Knight is the presiding genius. The guide who leads Gawain to it describes it as a trap where Gawain will undergo what amounts to a ritual execution and Gawain imagines it a hell-church where the devil mutters his orisons.[80] However, like almost every other provincial location the Green Chapel is a site where oppositions meet. Its name and overgrowth suggest fecundity and link to its master's regenerative aspects. It also shadows Morgan with a weird topographical explicitness. The poet describes it as a "balȝ berȝ" (2172), a swelling (smoothly rounded) barrow; the word "balȝ" is used in only one other place in the poem—the description of Morgan's buttocks: "balȝ and brode" (967). Robert J. Edgeworth shows how the topography of the Green Chapel mimics the female genitalia; the rough manuscript illustration of the barrow's gash-like opening is certainly suggestive in the light of his argument.[81] These connotations of pagan female fecundity are married to the liturgical significance of Gawain's rendezvous there on the Feast of the New Man. During the scene the poet uses both confessional and chivalric scripts to lay out a regenerative process of self-discovery and renewed nobility for Gawain—but Gawain reads it as degenerative. The gash in the earth in the manuscript illustration brings womb and tomb together and signals the cut in the flesh that will kill the old Gawain and bring forth the new—whoever he is. Thus the Green Chapel as grave site and birth place, demonic and liturgical, male and female, a place of honor and shame is a crux of temporal disjunction which will usher Gawain fully into the interlocked blunder and bliss of historic experience: the fear of death's inevitability, the exhilaration of life's continuance.

The Green Knight's first words to him signal this change:

"Gawayn," quoþ þat grene gome, "God þe mot loke!
Iwysse þou art welcom, wyȝe, to my place,
And þou hatz tymed þi trauayl as truee mon schulde." (2239–41)

["Gawain," said that green man, "God watch over you! In truth you are welcome, man, to my place, and you have timed your hard travel/labor, as true men should do."][82]

Gawain has indubitably kept his appointment with aristocratic precision, but these last lines also suggest another kind of "tyming," one that has inflected his journey and his labors and gives him the keys to the Green Knight's haunting grounds. By keeping his appointment he has entered a land where, to use Faulkner's phrase, the past is not past. It joins hands with present experience and future anticipation to inform and exercise a vital influence over Gawain's consciousness of who he is and how he should behave. It arrests him in the shadow of the fatality which haunts the whole Arthurian cycle and which was so festively elided at the poem's beginning.

This experience of time not as an unchanging cycle but as a tangled simultaneity of experience, anticipation, and memory becomes a powerful instrument of change in the poem.[83] Through his involvements with the provincial characters, Gawain has been seduced into a fundamental alteration in the way he conceives of himself. At the poem's beginning he incarnates his device—a relationship of essence and sign that does not admit any separation between them and remains inalterably true to itself.[84] By the end of the narrative, however, his self-conception has evolved into a diachronic awareness that he has changed (failed) and might do so again. He accepts his new insignia of the girdle not simply to speak forth his shame but as a reminder of a past failure he wants to make inescapable: "þer hit onez is tachched twynne wil hit neuer" (2512) [For where a fault is made fast, it is fixed forever more]. This reminder will keep him from thoughtless pride in the future: "And þus, quen pryde schal make me pryk for prowes of armes, / Þe loke to þis luf-lace shal leþe my hert" (2437–38) [And so when praise and high prowess have pleased my heart, / A look at this love-lace will lower my pride]. Though he still clutches the new formulaic identity of fallen hero, he has become someone who must recreate himself as fallen hero constantly, warily, historically. Appropriately his token changes from a seamless knot to an open-ended linear one which he must fasten anew every time he assumes it.

The poem itself does not solely authorize Gawain's chosen interpretation and in sharp contrast to its didactic treatment of the pentangle, it offers at least three possibilities for multivalent interpretations and different ways of narrating the girdle.[85] The Green Knight reads it as a memento of a good adventure carried out with superlative loyalty and courage and a sign of Gawain's chivalric maturity; he doesn't blame Gawain for loving his life—that is what good knights must do. Arthur's court also adopts the girdle as a sign of fellowship but a safer one; they recuperate it into the structure and definition of their knightly brotherhood, uncomprehending of the narrative of which it is the reminder but unified in their support of Gawain. Gawain himself, however, rejects both fellowships to read it as a sign of chivalric failure which he must always bear with him to remind himself of an essential truth about himself—though the danger of forgetting it—his need for reminder—suggests the contingent and constructed nature of such essences. His interpretation cuts him off both from the indulgent laughter of the Green Knight and the equally amiable acceptance of Arthur's court. At the end of the poem, even as he is surrounded by the green-girdled company of Arthur's court, Sir Gawain is alone, a knight nicked by human failure in a fellowship of chivalric ideologues.

By refusing to validate any of these possible interpretations, the poem both adjures and challenges the explication of readers. In its open-endedness it effectively assumes the mantle of artful silence, tempting contingency, and needful negotiation formerly enjoyed (and lost) by its provincial plotters. And its very interpretive richness drives home once more the seriousness of their loss. Yet if Arthur's court needs to recognize the interpretive complexities of its provinces and history, can those complexities offer an endurable alternative to courtly either/or formulas? The vision of history which the poem insistently performs without explaining is an incomprehensible welter of opposing forces: foundation and fall, truth and treachery, delight and destruction, "blysse" and "blunder." In one way, this vision is darkly Augustinian; we see the saeculum groping through the turbulent obscurity of its final age, offering uncertain glimpses of the two immanent cities whose relations will become clear only after history ends. But just as profoundly, with every lovingly detailed alliterative line, the poem cherishes the uncertainties of lived experience always at the threshold of disjunction. The acuity of the consciousness that can sum up a year with "And þus ȝirnez þe ȝere in ȝisterdayez mony" (520) [Thus passes/yearns the year in many yesterdays] is heart-stopping. It urges the outrageous daring to accept, endure, and, yes, even delight in the adventure of history itself. And this daring at once becomes the highest form of chivalry and transcends it.[86]

As it embraces historical contingency *Sir Gawain and the Green Knight* dramatizes how the past remains powerfully alive through the sheer force of its narrative-provoking, narrative-exceeding contradictions. Mesmerically alien and formidably familiar, it can erupt into the feasting hall to challenge the naive festivities of the royal court, while outside the court it is all-encompassing, fracturing the very provincial terrain of England to produce its own disjunct and marvelous dramas of regeneration and degeneration. In the end, the Green Knight departs "withersoever he would," remaining provocatively at large. And having pursued to the breaking point the questions opened through his challenge, the poem is unable or unwilling to discard any of them. Loftily disregarding the changes wrought by its own narrative, the poem modulates its outcome back to its origin and reprises the unresolved but vivid paradoxes of its own beginning before figuratively throwing up its hands and commending itself to heaven.[87]

Like the Green Knight who draws Gawain into a drama of courage and death only to transform it into comedy at the last moment, the poem both insists upon and draws back from the ultimate consequences of its own cultural interrogations. It delineates the fractures in the chivalric self-presentations of both royal and provincial courts without either closing them or extrapolating their eventual disastrous consequences for Arthur's society. The poem merely gestures at the impending Arthurian dissolution, content to explore the implications of contemporary divisions between monarchy and province with the same delicate attentiveness to historic experience that it tries to instill in its formula-ridden hero. The poet's Ricardian England did not have the luxury of this narrative detachment. As the century drew to its end, a vicious circle of royal alienation and magnatial belligerence was winding ever tighter to divide the nobility into increasingly insecure factions, a process which would finally end with Richard's deposition and death in 1399.[88] It is in another poem, the alliterative *Morte Arthure* completed at the end of Richard II's reign, that the apocalyptic trajectory of the royal court itself comes under a deliberate and extended scrutiny.

Sir Gawain and the Green Knight is more gentle, its elegy only an adumbration. Freer to play with multiple agendas, as it gracefully eviscerates Gawain's over-simplistic chivalric paradigms, it also teases out the perplexed heart of the provinces where most of its action is set, illuminating the multiple authorities, ambivalent perspectives, and hybrid affiliations of the provincial gentry in the light of their intimate subjection to royal policies.

4

Geography and Genealogy in
The Wars of Alexander

BOTH *St. Erkenwald* AND *Sir Gawain and the Green Knight* stage confrontations with mysterious figures interpolated into insular history.[1] The poems revive them to work toward historic transitions: the conversion of Britain into a Christian polity united under the bishop's merciful order or the possible coming of age of Arthur's youthful court, its transformation from a clique of gamesters into a true fellowship of knights in the crowning era of British history. The next two chapters, on *The Wars of Alexander* and *The Siege of Jerusalem,* also describe pivotal historic transitions but on even larger scales: the construction of new empires through confrontations with their predecessors. However, the predecessors in both *The Wars of Alexander* and *The Siege of Jerusalem* are not native; they are enticingly and terrifyingly exotic. *The Wars of Alexander* presents its hero with a myriad of powerful oriental predecessors led by Alexander's secret and secretive father, Anectanabus, an Egyptian king who is also a sorcerer, astrologer, healer, midwife, prophet, god-impersonator, and trickster. The orientalized Jews in *The Siege of Jerusalem* mount battle towers on the backs of elephants, and in one source, the *Legenda Aurea,* when one character admits he lives in Jerusalem, another replies: "Thou art from the land of sorcerers ... and therefore must possess the secret of healing."[2] In the poem itself, Jerusalem yields its conquerors both miraculous healing and miraculous wealth. It becomes not simply a city but a career.

In both poems, it is not inherent cultural difference that differentiates the two worlds of east and west but rather the violent disjuncture of conquest itself.[3] In these poems, Jews, Egyptians, Saracens, and even Old Romans die not simply for their usury, past crimes, or reliance on false philosophies but because they are too closely related to the emergent Christian or chivalric world orders that their deaths will invigorate. These poems stage the destruction of these predecessors as a means of claiming rightful inheritance of their power. They are thus driven by seemingly contradictory impulses; they mingle reverence for the past with its obliteration. This obsession with oriental predecessors intimately and intractably perplexes the troubled ideologies of western, Christian, masculine, and chivalric sovereignty. It shows them to have sprung from precisely those origins they are most anxious to alienate even as they seek to appropriate, cleanse, and flex the authority of their inheritance.

Both poems begin with a world of subtly interconnected empires and work violently to efface those connections, polarizing the world into two mythological realms: the Occident and the Orient, which they seek to realize as conqueror and the conquered. They maneuver in ways that invoke much later orientalisms but also invite us to rescrutinize later orientalisms' methodological strategies because late medieval constructions of east and west before European hegemony were necessarily more multiple, complex, and flagrantly imaginary than they later became.[4] Within the poems, the "eastern" figures are generally opposed by characters who emerge through their conflict as in some way (and often ambiguously) proto-European, either through religion, ideology, or chivalric practice. To the emergent empires of each poem, the orientalized cultures are made to represent a rich history of wealth and knowledge that their western descendants and destroyers cannot by themselves generate but which the poems attempt— often problematically—to render for appropriation.

The logic of their strategies has been described by Mary Louise Pratt (in a study of imperialism) and Naomi Schor (in a discussion of feminists Beauvoir and Irigaray) as "othering."[5] This process takes a series of complicated, elusive, and flexible relationships and it coagulates them into two unequal agents facing each other across a rift. Of these agents, one is familiar and self-like and is provisionally collected and unified by the fabricated gulf of difference, through which it can further elaborate, perform, and extend itself. Its self-unifying and self-universalizing strategies are energized by a binary logic of presence and absence, agency and passivity, knowing subject and object of knowledge, that always ensures it the upper hand. Edward Said makes this radical division between self and Oriental other a precondition for the exercise of an imperialist "will to knowledge" through which the other culture's constructed distance, difference, and potential resistance can be subjected to study, elaborated only as other, and controlled in an epistemological imperialism that keeps pace with actual colonialism in a sinister *pas de deux*.[6] Schor more succinctly suggests that "othering involves attributing to the objectified other a difference that serves to legitimate her oppression."[7] The other constituted by this difference and further defined by orientalist scrutiny is a shifting projection depending on the needs or fears of the orientalist. The other can be a dark mirror or a dumping ground for the exorcism of psychosocial demons. It can also be a realm of negativity—an extension of the gulf through which it is differenced—into which the anxious structures of "presence," logic, meaning, self-knowledge, history, and progress vanish with a dull "boum" like the fatal echo from Forster's Malabar caves. *The Wars of Alexander* explores a terrestrial cornucopia of these permutating alterities.

But there is one final other that is so perfect an adversarial gesture of the self that it takes on the self's own lineaments to become at once its producer, projection, shadow, and rival. This other is a repository of the primitive in an etymological sense, the distant first one (*primus*) that bequeaths itself as the rich *prima materia* of the self and then denies its own subsumption, thereby threatening to render that self back and subsume it in turn. When these poems catch up the late medieval obsession with eastern origins, this other becomes a powerful predecessor: alive with ancient learning, miraculously regenerative, and daunting—a lost and secret progenitor who gave life and might therefore take it away. The central conflicts of both poems are driven by fears of this ancestral determinism, the powerful stranger at the roots of the family tree. *The Wars of Alexander* desperately pursues the authoritative reflections of Alexander's sorceror-father who prophetically circumscribes Alexander even as he is killed by him. *The Siege of Jerusalem* takes umbrage at the sheer effrontery of Judaism for birthing Christianity and then continuing to flourish and rival it.

The sense of east as a point of origin was widespread in late medieval culture. Iain Higgins comments on the diversity of views intersecting late medieval writings about the genealogical relationships of east and west during this period. Troy, Greece, and Rome served as appropriable eastern points of origin for reassuring narratives of inexorably westward-tending translations of knowledge and empire, the *translatio studii* and *translatio imperii*. Judea and the Holy Land represented an even more powerful draw: the navel of the world and a "virtually fetishistic object of desire, stirring the devout, diabolical, or ambitious souls not simply of popes and princes, or even of poets, lunatics, saints, mercenaries, and propagandists, but also of ordinary men and women."[8] Paradise itself nestled unreachably on some great eastern plateau. But to many writers, more conscious of the diversity, multiplicity, geographical range, and sheer number of contemporary non-Christians, such desires for the east were coming to seem more and more illusory.

The East as it was known to Latin Christendom between the twelfth and the fifteenth centuries . . . was the fertile ground of an imagined community's noblest hopes, wildest dreams, and worst fears—at once the distant source of its chivalry, learning, and historical covenant with God, the outlandish source of its most sacred, coveted and finally unattainable sites, and the slowly expanding theater of its most reverent, bewildered, disgraceful and disturbing encounters with Otherness.[9]

Higgins vividly describes the intensifying dilemma of a culture that placed its origins in the east, but whose continual efforts to return to, convert, conquer, or assimilate those origins were increasingly resisted, demolished, or simply ignored. Both *The Siege of Jerusalem* and *The Wars of Alexander* vividly bespeak both this sense of desire for control of eastern origins and its fear and frustration. Even as both poems enforce the divides between their easts and wests and fantasize western victory, they are driven by intimations of inescapable familiarity that perplex their battle lines and drive together their binaries. These genealogical connections both compel and violate the poems' geographical campaigns, illuminating not only the fears and desires energized by the construction of these othered oriental pasts but also the fragility of their late medieval construction.

East-West

In making these older cultures exotic and marvelous, the poems draw upon an enormous literary tradition. In travel narratives, crusade narratives, and hagiographies from the fifth century onward, various easts had served as epistemological borderlands for Christian writers, places where marvels could proliferate freely in the interstices of a very sketchy knowledge. By sheer distance, they invited European literary fantasy. Mary Campbell notes usefully that in many of these sources "'the East' is a concept separable from any particular geographic area. It is essentially Elsewhere."[10] Narrators could enliven their narratives with intimations of ancient and illustrious cultures that were alluring to their audiences precisely because they were unknown to them. John Mandeville's marvelous valediction from *The Travels* invites subsequent travelers into the delectations of exotic exploration and highlights the pleasures of novelty:

For many men have great delight and desire in hearing of new things; and so I shall cease telling of the different things I saw in those countries, so that those who desire to visit those countries may find enough new things to speak of for the solace and recreation of those whom it pleases to hear them.[11]

The poets of *The Siege of Jerusalem* and *The Wars of Alexander* lavish their Jews and Egyptians with this exotic glamour, particularly the poet of *The Wars of Alexander*, who revels in mysterious eastern seductions both literal and figurative. The extreme energy of the campaigns described by both poems, in fact, suggests boundless appetite for what the eastern cultures have to offer.

However, these poems are not wholly bound to such exoticizing literary traditions. They do not echo pilgrimage narratives' traditional constructions of the Holy Land as a far-flung topographical anchor for religious meditation, even in *The Siege of Jerusalem*. The various eastern cultures they portray may be products of fantasy, but they are not as historically nebulous as the flotillas of mosques and sultanates in the French crusade romances and *chansons de gestes*. Although they collate and embroider their sources, they are also alert to historical and political developments affecting the relationships of European gentry, clergy, and aristocracy with various eastern countries throughout the medieval period and in the later fourteenth century more particularly. The poems' investment in conquest is historically charged and responds to an intercultural dialectic that intensified in the later Middle Ages: that the perceived intensity of relationships between east and west, Christendom and its neighbors, drives the need to establish lines of differentiation. In the poems, the combatants fight not because of their differences but because of their tantalizing connections.

This emerges repeatedly in the medieval history of east-west relations. During the medieval period, encounters between what are now European countries and what are now Middle and Far Eastern ones were continually energized by war, complicated by occupation (from both sides), perplexed by internal dissensions and coalition-building (within and between sides), and invigorated by mutually profitable exchange of goods, technologies, and learning. It is difficult to chart an overall trajectory of change in the set of relationships between such diverse, disunified, and continually re-coalescing agents. R. W. Southern describes an initial religious disjunction (the Crusades) followed by gradually increasing recognition on the part of western writers of theological and cultural relations between Christians and their non-Christian others.[12] Dorothee Metlitzki energetically pursues the complexity of these relationships as they mark English scientific, history, romance, theology, and travel writing as early as the eleventh century and extending through the fifteenth.[13] And Thierry Hentsch argues that complex relations throughout the medieval period gave way to strategic alienations. These alienations, which became sharpest during the late fifteenth-century and sixteenth-century imperialist programs of trade, exploration, and settlement, helped prepare for later, more deeply persuasive, orientalisms.[14]

Most salient to *The Wars of Alexander* and *The Siege of Jerusalem* is a

double-edged sense both of religiocultural relatedness (threatening or
profitable) and military desperation. These poems continually mediate the
complexities of a period perplexed by three developments: (1) After two
centuries of crusading failure, the Christian conquest of the non-Christian
world finally becomes a chimera for idealists rather than a widely endorsed
military possibility; (2) at the same time dwindling access to the eastern
systems of trade at once provokes and frustrates fantasies of enrichment;
(3) ideological acknowledgments of relatedness begin to make their way
into heterodox but often popular Christian writings which compare, for
instance, the various monotheisms of Judaism, Christianity, and Islam.
Negotiating these developments, writings that remain invested in inexorable enmities between various wests and easts become even more ideologically extreme, exhortations to utopian or apocalyptic fantasy rather than
expressions of contemporary possibility.[15]

1. East-West Bifurcations and Their Discontents

Such ideologically adversarial accounts are not, of course, confined to the
fourteenth and fifteenth centuries. Ecclesiastical writings in particular fostered enmities throughout the whole period, inventing perfidious easts
(Islam, Judaism, the polymorphous and ill-defined body of non-Saracens,
Christian schismatics, and heretics), even as they attempted to confederate
the mutually back-biting and belligerent rulers of Europe into the mobile
army of "Christendom." Christendom is the period's closest suzerainty-
crossing analogue to the idea of the West or Europe (which gets organized
and institutionalized enough to do wide-ranging, long lasting social work
only during the imperialist expansions of the Renaissance), and the difficulty of defining what Christendom comprised suggests exactly how much
work had to go into its construction, even as myth. Thierry Hentsch
shows how any medieval east-west division actually had to bifurcate the
Church itself, Rome vying historically with Byzantium for the heritage
of Roman imperio-ecclesiastical unity.[16] The ecclesiastical construction of
Christendom during this period, then, depends on the determined elision
of boundary-complicating "contact zones"—Byzantium, Spain before the
reconquista, Cyprus, Sicily, the trade networks of Genoa and Venice, and
the multiply occupied Holy Land itself.[17] In the rhetoric of many militant/
ecclesiastical ideologues—from Pope Urban II whose ferocious sermons
about the Muslim occupation of the Holy Land helped instigate the first
crusade in 1095 and through the Teutonic Knights whose empire-building
expansions sparked the fourteenth-century crusades to Lithuania and
Russia—such contact zones are necessarily turned into war zones.

The twelfth-century abbot of Cluny, Peter the Venerable, influentially fostered the model of Christendom and Islam as two antagonistic worlds. Alarmed by the avidity with which well-to-do and bedazzled Christians all over Europe were embracing Islamic cultural products, philosophies, and rhetorical styles, he visited twelfth-century al-Andalus on a fact-finding mission to translate what he thought were the most crucial Islamic scriptures in order to reveal their erroneous deceptions. The works he translated as Islamic doctrine, however, included not only the Koran but four imaginative texts. Adapting his materials to a familiar medieval Christian schema, Peter offered his readers a vision of the Islamic heaven and hell. The results, as Maria Menocal understates it, were "a very imaginative vision of Islam."[18] Peter's text represents the Islamic world as both threatening and enticing, exuding an exotic materiality that persists in many subsequent representations from Odo of Deuil to *The Wars of Alexander*.[19] This carefully tended mythological boundary granted advantages to those who deployed it. Even as it fostered persistent and often exploitable anxiety about the enemy without, it justified institutional policing of possible subversion from within and pushed towards a stronger, more intimately inquiring, and judicially buttressed ecclesiastical ministry.[20] Throughout the period of greatest contact, this helped the empire-building of conservative ecclesiastical factions in Spain, southern France and Italy, cultures that had been subject to thorough permeation by such threatening Arabic imports as Averroeism or the new Aristotelianism.[21]

Yet during this period, such accounts did not have the widespread persuasiveness they later attained. David Nirenberg discusses the regional resistance they provoked in Spain; the local negotiations which sometimes circumvented their power.[22] The medieval "threats" of the Jew, Saracen, or Turk were arguably dramatized with such vivid pathos and persistence not because they were an encroaching danger but because they were at once serviceable to the foundational strategies of Christian cultural institutions and largely irrelevant to the everyday experience of their parishes. Such "threats" required constant elaboration, performance and reperformance in violent (and therefore memorable) narratives. Miri Rubin stresses the fragility of cultural memory even where (especially where) so long-abiding and embedded an institution as medieval Christianity is concerned: "Memories require spurs, advocates . . . they need to be used and loved, inserted into narratives of life, in order to earn value. They need even more attention and care if their effect is to be directed and controlled: towards piety, uniformity or violent action against enemies."[23] We can distinguish the memory-cherishing narratives of medieval east-west enmities from their later orientalist counterparts by noting their performative contingency. They have not yet amassed the bulk of institutionally supported epistemologies and military superiorities that will suffuse post-eighteenth-century orientalist mythologies with the glamour of inevitability. They are still contested and articulated, not yet doxa woven into the thoughtless fabric of everyday assumption that is ideology's most graceful and insidious cloak. And although they energized wars, pogroms, and massacres, the accumulating weight of failure behind these enterprises helped render them more spasmodic, even if more strident. Later medieval writers, faced by their dismal crusading history, are often unable to maintain a vision of a singular, unified Christendom except as a fantasy projected into the past or the apocalyptic future. These differences between medieval and modern orientalisms work against the historical determinism that makes the myth of "western ascent" so difficult to dislodge from our own self-conceptions.

Even medieval narratives that bristle with horrified cultural incomprehension often acknowledge the more complicated relations between their proponents, the multiplicity of agendas as alliances are sought, coalitions formed, and fascinations expressed—from both sides of the divide. Crusader accounts that demonize Saracens are often conflicted about Byzantium—a fellow Christian state "tainted" with easternness but dazzlingly cultured and rich. Even Joinville's *Life of St. Louis* pauses in its unrelenting hostility to non-Christians for a fascinated disquisition on the Tartars as possible (if unlikely) allies.[24] From another perspective, Usamah Ibn-Munqidh, a Syrian scholar and warrior, recounts an illuminating incident of culture shock:

When I used to enter the Aqsa Mosque, which was occupied by the Templars [*al-dawiyyah*], who were my friends, the Templars would evacuate the little adjoining mosque so that I might pray in it. One day I entered this mosque, repeated the first formula, "Allah is great," and stood up in the act of praying, upon which one of the Franks rushed on me, got hold of me and turned my face eastward saying, "This is the way thou shouldst pray!" The Templars again came in to him and expelled him. They apologized to me, saying, "This is a stranger who has only recently arrived from the land of the Franks and he has never seen anyone praying except eastward." Thereupon I said to myself, "I have had enough prayer." So I went out and have ever been surprised at the conduct of this devil of a man, at the change in the color of his face, his trembling and his sentiment at the sight of one praying towards the *qiblah*."[25]

Throughout his memoirs, Usamah remains extremely wary of any foreigner who has not been "domesticated" by at least some time in the Holy Land, but his account stresses that such domestication is possible and that the Templars' tenure in the holy land has not only honed their reputation as strong knights but also taught a certain amount of tolerance and accommodation. *The Siege of Jerusalem* itself, one of the most inventively vicious of all the alliterative poems, is perplexed by a persistent reverence for the culture it is destroying, emerging most strongly in the equivocal characterization of Josephus, who earns both gratitude and free conduct out of the doomed city from the Roman captain he cures only to refuse them and remain, even more admirably, faithful to his people.

2. Fantasies of War and Commerce

Moreover, ideologically freighted narratives of eastern conquest were often complicated by the sense that contact zones were even more profitable and challenging to penetrate than war zones. This consciousness invigorated both knightly and merchant classes (even as it provoked new self-definitions and anxieties) and accelerated the osmotic traffic between them.[26] The countries of Europe had quickly realized the rich advantages of trade with eastern states and had, in fact, come to rely heavily upon eastern luxuries from spices to dyes to silks.[27] As consciousness grew in Europe of the extent and richness of many eastern countries and as merchant entrepreneurs sought ingress into an intricate and highly profitable system of trade that extended from Egypt and the Holy Land to China, there was a dizzying reversal in perspective. Perhaps Christian Europe, rather than being the world's religious and cultural center and the heart of the mappa mundi, was to other navigators a marginal sliver on the northwest edge of a world system larger, richer, and more various than even the Roman Empire through which Christendom imagined its own imperial inheritances.

R. W. Southern describes the traumatic effect of this slow realization upon Europeans who still cherished the dream of converting to Christianity the world of Islam, assimilating its knowledge and wealth, and uniting the world under the banner of a newly invigorated Christian world system.

There were ten, or possibly a hundred, unbelievers for every Christian. Nobody knew; and the estimate grew with each access of knowledge. One consequence of this was to make the Crusades seem either quite impossible, or in need of a drastic reassessment of its aims and methods. For the rest of the Middle Ages the Western world was divided into one or the other of these two camps: either no Crusading was called for, or very much more and better Crusading.[28]

And by the late fourteenth century, the possibility of an effective crusade, though it continued to entice, was even dimmer. The 1356 raid of Peter of Cyprus on Alexandria had won no permanent foothold. Crusades to the Low Countries, Prussia, and Hungary continued throughout the century, but foundered in campaigns against "schismatic" Christians—supporters of the pope at Avignon or of the Eastern Church—before getting anywhere near the Holy Land. Aziz Suryal Atiya emphasizes the furious activity of the English knightly contingent in these late century crusades.[29] The 1396 Nicopolis crusade was a supreme effort, significantly supported not by monarchs but by magnates and gentry on the make. But these late crusades could only pillage; they could not provide ingress into the trade system.

Their ineffectiveness only whetted an already deep-seated hunger for eastern commerce. The crusades of the eleventh through the thirteenth centuries had brought Christian soldiers into the orbits of a variety of politically disarticulated but cosmopolitan Muslim cultures, igniting widespread (and avid) veneration of the accomplishments of Muslim civilization. Despite the soldiers' unflagging military fervor, many were thoroughly and irreversibly culturally converted.[30] The appreciation was neither mutual nor unambivalent: "Muslim attitudes remained condescending at best and aghast at worst, whereas their invaders were filled with a strange mixture of hatred and romantic (if reluctant) awe and admiration."[31] This ambivalence imbues many of the French *chansons de gestes* and romances in which young European knights encounter and are completely outclassed by the wealth and knowledge of the east, winning through only by courage and perseverance—and canny alliances with breathtakingly convertible Saracen heiresses.[32] Sylvia Thrupp quips that the French nobility and prosperous merchants who were these poems' most probable audience envied the Muslims "because they know better even than the French how to live."[33] In these poems, in addition to their luxuriantly cosmopolitan life-style, Muslims possess both material wealth and arcane knowledge that can be magical without being spiritually suspect. And they are wonderfully rich. With a brashness that is almost charming, the romances make no bones about their own economic desires.[34] Where knights begin as younger sons or landless knights, they usually reap a handsome profit from their sojourn, willing or unwilling, in the Muslim lands. These narratives make the east into a profitable stomping ground for Christian knights which they can never comprehend but from which they can emerge individually enriched and fortified.

Unfortunately, by the mid-fourteenth century such fantasies were becoming even more distant. European countries could no longer easily participate in the system of mercantile exchange which had formerly knit together countries from China to England, and this was becoming a focus of increasing unease. The northern land routes over Asia had deteriorated with the fragmentation of the Mongol Empire, which had briefly created what Janet Abu-Lughod terms a *pax Mongolica*.[35] The loss of the last crusader stronghold at Acre to the Mamluks in 1291 had dealt a quietus to the trade revenues that came from the control of the westernmost posts of Palestine. These trade revenues had helped finance and maintain the crusader kingdoms which thus soon crumbled, taking with them the last remnants of a two-century bid to reestablish Christendom's control of the territory it conceived as its origin and heart. This dwindling accessibility to trade routes was aggravated after the Black Death by the Mamluk ascendancy in Egypt which had consolidated its monopoly on the southern trade route through Egypt and the Red Sea. The resentment caused by their stranglehold on trade access emerges very clearly in the accounts of the traders (European and Mediterranean) forced to undergo customs control at Alexandria.[36] Venice successfully obtained from the Mamluks a strictly regulated access to trade through this route into the fifteenth century but was obliged in return to provide them with slaves, who were trained to the ranks of the Mamluk military and thus strengthened them even further.

Most pressing to the English provincial gentry to whose interests *The Wars of Alexander* most likely appealed was the emergent Ottoman empire whose armies besieged the remnants of Byzantine Christianity, harried the borders of eastern Europe, and in 1396 thoroughly trounced at Nicopolis an ill-organized but tremendous crusade of knights from all over Europe, including sizable factions from the North West Midlands reputedly led by the noblest families in England. In sum, by the late fourteenth century, in terms of trade monopolies, assets, and military power, various eastern dynasties, sultanates, and military regimes held most of the cards, and often were quite prepared to use them.

3. East-West in Dialogue

However, even as these military and mercantile frustrations intensified, fourteenth-century continental and British writers and theologians began to elaborate more intimate relationships between Judaism, Christianity, and Islam, reimagining them as producers, foundations, and mirrors of each other. The need for these links was sharpest in the contact zones. The twelfth-century *reconquista* reduced Muslim al-Andalus to the single kingdom of Granada and incited a fury of Christian missionary activity. Yet not all of this Christian apology was inflexibly polemical. At the beginning of the fourteenth century, Ramon Llull's *The Book of the Gentile* staged an extended debate between a Jew, a Christian, and a Muslim in which each builds upon the others' sapience, monotheism, and logical and affective argumentation to convince an agonized Gentile to choose the faith that would satisfy him. In the treatise, the debaters speak a common language and share a methodology, Llull's logical Art, through which they construct glittering, tottery, conceptual structures of likeness and opposition to prove their points. As the debate continues, the Art itself assumes a fervid scholarly religiosity superceding actual religious difference. While Christianity comes to exert the most affective and logical appeal, the debate itself, provocatively, subsumes any conclusion:[37]

Many were the blessings the three wise men wished on the Gentile, and the Gentile on the three wise men ... and the end of their conversation was full of embraces, kisses, tears, and sighs. But before [they] left, the Gentile asked them in astonishment why they did not wait to hear which religion he would choose ... The three wise men answered, saying that, in order for each to be free to choose his own religion, they preferred not knowing which religion he would choose. "And all the more so since this is a question we could discuss among ourselves to see, by force of reason and by means of our intellects, which religion it must be that you will choose. And if, in front of us, you state which religion it is you prefer, then we would not have such a good subject of discussion nor such satisfaction in discovering the truth."[38]

The debate continues beyond the Gentile's decision because mutual agreement is the ultimate goal, and it cannot be reached by "war, turmoil, ill will, injury, and shame" but only by the delights of reasonable debate.[39] Ramon Llull thus gentles the honorable ferocities of battle into those of scholarly argument. He intimates not only the deep structures that link the religions but the more profound commonalities of shared intellect, passion, and exemplary courtesy activating their mutual search for truth.

If the religions shared so much, could there be no grounds also for a shared salvation? As the countries of Christian Europe realized the sheer immensity and variety of the non-Christian world, that knowledge sharpened the problem of the salvation of the heathens. Would a merciful God withhold salvation not only from the illustrious pagans of the pre-Christian past but also from the bulk of the contemporary world?[40] Yet to admit the non-necessity of Christian baptism and belief was to challenge the most basic assumptions about the Christian church's role as mediator of salvation. At least one religious philosopher, the Benedictine monk Uthred of Boldon, who was at the University of Oxford in the mid-1360s teaching theology and promoting anti-fraternal reforms, proposed a unique answer to this dilemma. He argued that salvation was offered to everyone: Christian, Jew, Saracen, or pagan, baptized or not, whatever their age, in a moment of intellectual illumination just before death. This proposal gave each individual complete responsibility for her eternal welfare; even completely innocent infants were allowed to make the wrong choice. His views along with twenty-one other heretical speculations were later formally censored and forbidden defense by Simon Langham, the Archbishop of Canterbury.[41]

Anxiety about pagan salvation galvanized the popular circulation of stories like Trajan's, which is energetically refigured in Passus XI of B-text of *Piers Plowman*.[42] In Passus XV, Langland puts some startlingly even-handed sentiments into the toothless, tongueless mouth of Anima, whose whole dialogue strives to transcend the theological and social polemics that Will interrogates throughout the poem. Anima affirms the essential unity of Christianity, Judaism, and Islam as monotheistic religions rooted in the first line of the Christian *Credo*:

> "Ac pharisees and sarsens, scribes and Jewes
> Arn folk of oon feith—the fader God thei honouren.
> And sithen that the Sarsens and also the Jewes
> Konne the first clause of oure bileve, *Credo in Deum patrem omnipotentem*
> Prelates of Cristene provinces sholde preve, if thei myghte,
> Lere hem litlum and litlum *Et in Jesum Christum filium,*
> Til thei kouth speke and spelle *Et in Spiritum sanctum,*
> And rendren it and recorden it with *remissionem peccatorum,*
> *Carnis resurreccionem et vitam eternam. Amen."* (603–11)

["But Pharisees and Saracens, scribes and Jews are folk of one faith; they honor God the father. And since both Saracens and Jews know the first clause of our belief, *I believe in God the Father almighty*, prelates of Christian provinces should pray if they can, teach them little by little, *and in his son Jesus Christ*, until they can speak and say, *And in the Holy Spirit*, and render it and rehearse it until *the forgiveness of sins, the resurrection of the body and the life everlasting, Amen."*]

This passage builds upon shared monotheism to lead non-Christians "litlum and litlum" through the *Credo* just as one would teach it to a child. Anima's touching simplicity masks a surprising perception; merely by affirming the essential monotheism of Islam, Langland goes beyond many of his contemporaries' more colorful representations of it as paganism or demonolatry.[43] Like Llull, Anima imagines a Christianization that is disciplinary but not violent, transforming the conquest of an alien into the education of a child.

But this capacity for gentle teaching is cast into doubt at earlier points in Anima's discourse, where more consequential connections are drawn between Christianity and its others to provoke Christian self-examination.

Lines 92–95 show that if Christianity is the root of all good when practiced truly, it is also the root of all evil when abused, including the fragmentation of faith into warring heresies—one of which is Islam. As part of his discourse on charity, Anima startlingly traces Islam's genesis back to a trained dove and a Christian malcontent with corn in his ear (XV, 397–409).[44] This theory not only takes allegations of Saracen "enchantment" and reduces them to corn-artistry, it also attributes them to a uniquely Christian iniquity—status-seeking within the church. The very existence of Islam is a Christian sin come home to roost. Such a view both connects Christianity with Islam and reassuringly restores to Christianity its role as universal religious source and center.

Two other widely circulating fourteenth-century writers, John Mandeville and John Wyclif, link Islam to contemporary Christendom to castigate it even more fiercely. Mandeville puts calls for Christian reform into the mouth of the Sultan of Egypt who has sent knights in disguise to infiltrate Christian society. He contrasts its corruption with the inferior but well-practiced credo of his own land, admitting if Christians ever began practicing what they preached they would conquer Islam with ease. But at other points in *The Travels* the narrator teases at deeper reflexivities between Christianity and its eastern others, as when he transforms the worship of idols and simulacra into expressions of praise for a single, generous God. Throughout *The Travels* the narrator dances provocatively between daring a profitable intimacy with even the most ferocious-seeming others (as in the tale of the knight and Hippocrates' dragon-daughter) and retreating fearfully from the greed of his own desires for profitable strangeness (as in the daunting journey through the Vale Perilous).[45] Wyclif's vision of Islam, on the other hand, sharpens a similar sense of reciprocal relationship into extreme disapproval.[46] He follows Uthred in maintaining the possibility of salvation for the Muslims[47] while his views of Islam hark back to Peter the Venerable's twelfth-century descriptions of a dangerously seductive materialistic religion. However, Wyclif makes that materialism a mirror for fourteenth-century ecclesiastical abuses.[48] In his "Tractatus de Pseudo-Freris," he echoes Langland by analogizing Islam to the spiritually corrosive Christian sects of "benet or dominic or faunciss or bernard" [Benedict, Dominic, Francis, Bernard], all impure shoots from the same troubled tree.[49] In the work of these writers, Islam reflects back to Christianity its own negative image. Reform Christianity and its others dwindle; neglect it and its others grow.

The Siege of Jerusalem and *The Wars of Alexander* both acknowledge and work to efface such contemporary intimations of relationship between west and east, Christendom and its others. They spin fantasies of more "ideal" encounters, where the "western" characters emerge as indubitable conquerors. However, the two poems indulge in very different fantasies. *The Wars of Alexander* imagines multifarious, wide-flung, and diverse enemies of profound learning, rich in lands and holdings, but nonetheless conquerable by the chivalric strength of a single extraordinary king. It plays with the idea of the impossible conquest and fantasizes the chivalric solidarity and sheer transgressive energy that might bring it about. *The Siege of Jerusalem*, by contrast, imagines an enemy who possesses all the reputed wealth and wisdom of the east, but is small, isolated, and vulnerable to western assault. Thus it brings into focus the figure of crusader as profiteer who shadows late medieval crusade romances.

Both *The Wars of Alexander* and *The Siege of Jerusalem* are revealing in their frustration, their insecurity, their alertness to the ways that boundaries between east and west may be advantageously—or fatally—constructed and questioned. These poems strive to differentiate two worlds, consolidating the strengths of one from the entrapment and dissolution of the other. Yet in both poems it is the actual processes of connection, the contacts between the Romans and the Jews, Alexander and all his predecessors, that drive the poems and constitute the reasons why in *The Siege of Jerusalem* the struggle between the nations is so horrifically prolonged and why in *The Wars of Alexander* it is so compulsively repeated.

Troubled Paternities

The Wars of Alexander describes what is simultaneously a conqueror's dream and a xenophobe's nightmare.[50] While relating the exploits of Alexander the Great, a chivalric conqueror driven to separate himself from and place himself above all the kingdoms of the east, the poem incessantly disturbs his illusions of preeminence with the intimations of affinity. After describing its hero's Egyptian parentage and his effacement of this oriental origin, the poem is a mercilessly energetic description of his campaigns. Throughout the 5,800–line poem, Alexander drives onward, seeking new boundaries to obliterate, new kingdoms to encompass, in what becomes finally a need to escape the limits of history itself. As he ranges over the length and breadth of Asia, Alexander is impelled to transcend all chivalric expectations, to exceed every military precedent, and finally to set himself over every past, present, and future authority.

But Alexander's iconoclasm is painfully contained. As his campaigns

incline farther and farther to the east, he is continually halted by the
realization that his numerous adversaries are intimates—they know him,
reflect back to him his own face, and adumbrate his own future. When this
happens, he succumbs to an awful sympathy, arrested by the intensity of
his emotions—a paralysis that ends only when he effaces the significance
of the encounter and turns to meet the next enemy. Both Alexander's identity as a world conqueror and his chivalric enterprise are thus contingent
upon his willful ignorance and rejection of his subversive resemblances
to his enemies, of his oriental genealogy, and of his eventual fate—world
conquest and sudden death, two processes that the poem seals together in
inescapable consequentiality.

The Wars of Alexander stages the conquests of a chivalric hero over
the marvelous, perilous, and incomprehensible kingdoms of the east and
shows how this geographical campaign is also a war against ancestors and
predecessors. However, The Wars of Alexander mediates this opposition in
a strikingly equivocal way. Alexander not only conquers the oriental world,
he also attempts to fathom it, and the later sections of the poem underscore the knowledge that in many cases it is far too extensive, too exotic,
and too inimical even for him to encompass. Even more than The Siege of
Jerusalem, the past-present conflicts of The Wars of Alexander are pointedly
generational, struggles that pit son against both father and mother, youth
against maturity, inexperience and obscurity against fame, and finally chivalric iconoclasm against the delimiting structures of its own origins and
history. This generational conflict establishes indissoluble links between
Alexander and his various adversaries—even as they succumb to him, they
invoke his origin, reflect his face, and mirror his future. In this way, The
Wars of Alexander conflates genealogy and geography as contested territories, two linked fronts along which Alexander wages war, striving to efface
the one and dominate the other. And while the poem shows his irresistible
geographical power, it also insists on his complete genealogical helplessness: his placement within a history that not only links him to his enemies
but subjects him to the same fate he imposes upon them.

The poem thus elaborates the essential relatedness of geographically
distinct cultures, and it constructs that relatedness in a particularly threatening and intimate way—it is based on blood in both senses: violence
and generation. As the child-sized Alexander subjugates the patriarchal
tyrants of the east, his own escalating ambitions draw him closer to them.
Where he confronts powerful female conquerors such as Candace of
Prasaica, he thrills with the same shrinking enticement that his mother,
Olympados, has instilled in him. Alexander's horrified recognition of his

oriental progenitors foregrounds, drives, and is ineffectually effaced by his subsequent military conquests. The poem ingeniously propagates modes of east-west affiliation: generation, similitude, desire, projection—by its end, war and intimacy are working themselves out on the same exotic grounds. Alexander's progress thus dramatizes a late medieval chivalric consciousness that is provocatively alert both to its desire for labile, diversified, and polysemic others and to its need to ground its self-inventions upon their alienation.

The poem is fascinated by moments in which the voices of Alexander's adversaries interrupt the strategic displacements that foreground his endeavor. Such moments are the militarily indomitable Alexander's only points of vulnerability, and the poem probes at them with sardonic persistence. In one confrontation of piercing clarity, as Alexander pauses on the banks of the impassable Ganges to question the Brahmins, they transfix him with their perception of his entire military enterprise: "It is ȝourselfe and noȝt oureself þat ai þe self hantis" (4794) [It is yourself and not us that you are forever pursuing/speaking of].[51] Alexander's military victories incessantly preface such stunning epistemological counterattacks. The idea that Alexander is chasing his own carefully exoticized shadows animates the poem in a multitude of different ways, refracting Alexander's conflicts of identity into a world of battles. And the deepest conflict is Alexander's relationship with his Egyptian progenitor, Anectanabus. His patricide models and drives his subsequent conquests of his other oriental predecessors.

And these others become bewilderingly multiple. As the poem continues and Alexander runs the gamut of adversaries from militant Persians, to ingenious Jews, to saintly Brahmins, to giant scorpions, his identity as a chivalric conqueror whose endeavor depends on singularity of will and solidarity of loyalty begins to break apart. Emily Bartels discusses a similar process in the context of the Marlovian stage which also breeds spectacles of strangeness: "Because each iteration of a type stands in conflict with a field of others, it produces a figure who is ultimately unknowable."[52] Not only is Alexander not in charge of his conquests, he has no hope of knowing who he is and what drives him. Identity implodes into a frantically riven subjectivity under the inexhaustible pressure of so many others. And the poem delights in this process. Even as it depicts a hero energetically trying to reduce endless empires to a single rule, the poem is captivated by the sheer diversity of Alexander's enemies, and it expands upon its source's descriptions of them with considerable inventiveness. Alexander's adversaries range from his secret Egyptian father, to the Jews in Jerusalem, to the great emperors Darius of Persia and Porrus of India, to the Brahmins of the Ganges, to the mysterious Master of the Temple of the Sun, and to the unnervingly self-possessed queen of Prasiaca, Candace.

As the poem continues and Alexander passes into unmappable eastern desolations, gruesome monsters erupt from the very earth to harry and decimate his forces. There is a clear sense that resistance to his encroachments is worked into the very soil of the landscape which yields doubles and monsters with equal fecundity. This overriding sense of eastern multiplicity subverts the cognitive division of the world into two halves, east and west, and even the logic of conquest itself. Thus, even as the poem depicts a relentless sovereignty in the process of foundation, it worms away at the boundaries between internal and external, self and other, by intimating their essential reflectivity, their mutual dependence upon each other, their mutual generation of each other, their contingency, their insecurity. In a world so vast and strange, Alexander's power stretches more and more thinly, devolving into a fraying web of tenuous and temporary negotiations as much psychological as military.

This recognition emerges most strongly in Alexander's intractable hybridity. Traditionally, even his eyes were of different colors and the poem actually makes him "wald-eʒed," with eyes staring in different directions. He is schooled both by Anectanabus—an adept of sorcerous, eastern knowledge—and Aristotle, whose writings were preserved and elaborated at the courts of Baghdad before they were reintroduced into Europe in the twelfth century to be translated, and claimed by scholars with such avidity that they became the center of a thirteenth-century scholastic maelstrom of urgent assimilation, synthesis, and resistance. And Alexander's genealogical ambiguity would have posed very interesting and fertile problems for the poem's audience. His Egyptian ancestry, his polytheism, and the mounting scope of his ambitions make him a figure just as easily appropriable by eastern conquerors as western ones. To cite one contemporary and well-known example, Froissart's chronicle describes the defeat of the European army at Nicopolis in terms that attribute Alexandrian ambitions to the Ottoman leader, Bayezid (Lamorabaquy), as he rejoices in the captured tents of the Christian leaders:

Than Lamorabaquy . . . made as great myrthe as myght be, and sayd how he wolde shortely with great puyssaunce passe into the realme of Hungery, and conquere the countrey, and after other countreys upon the Crysten men, and to bringe them to his obeysaunce . . . he sayd he worlde reygne lyke Alysaunder of Masydone, who was twelve yere kynge of all the worlde, of whose lynage he sayde he was dyscended. (Froissart, 237)[53]

Bayezid's ambition resounds even more menacingly when Froissart attributes to him a desire to become the new Alexander and attain the "signory" over Christendom. Froissart intensifies Bayezid's threat by showing his ability to extract one of the Nine Worthies from the crown of European chivalric exemplarity and claim him for his own predecessor.

The poem elaborates Alexander's confrontation with his own oriental history and hybrid identity, therefore, in order to draw its readers into a similar confrontation with the ambiguous past of their own chivalric fantasies. And like other alliterative romances, it returns to the past only to discover that it is still alive, still connected, immanent in the foundational enterprises and insistent misgivings of its audience. In the process the poem probes one of the most insidious anxieties of a late medieval xenophobic sensibility anxious to reduce relations between itself and its eastern neighbors to the simple, unidirectional relation of conqueror and victim. It suggests the belatedness of western culture, its debt to its eastern predecessors. It insinuates that western foundational texts and tenets, science and learning, and chivalric genealogies have been obsessively desired, seized, translated, and assimilated from cultures and countries now distanced as eastern and other, from the Jews, Greeks, Indians, and Arabs. The sense of futility that plagues Alexander—the recurrent apprehension that he is shadow-boxing his own "fonned fantasies" (5639) through Asia—ultimately implicates a late fourteenth-century audience increasingly aware of the necessary connections and complex originary debts between themselves and their numerous eastern adversaries.

Furthermore, Alexander's dilemma reimagines the political and ideological conflicts of a whole late fourteenth- and early fifteenth-century generation of British aristocracy and gentry, haunted by the specter of their military ineptitude during recent crusades—and ferociously refusing that knowledge. The poem goes well beyond its sources in spectacular inventiveness;[54] it is striking that a British poet of this period should have been energized to translate and amplify a poem of such length into such luxuriant and mordantly ironic alliterative verse.[55] I will argue that Alexander is a uniquely situated figure for the gentry of the North West Midlands who were this poem's probable audience. Themselves identified with and eager to appropriate the historical and ideological appurtenances of the English nobility, they were drawn to Alexander as a chivalric model, about whom a rich legendary history had accumulated. Alexander's ongoing appeal is attested by the five-century history of the Alexander romances which were richer and more numerous even than the other British chivalric Matters of Arthur and Charlemagne.

As a chivalric exemplum, Alexander is alluring because he fantasizes the possibility of victory over the whole eastern world. In the course of *The Wars of Alexander*, despite (or because of) his Eastern and magical origins, Alexander becomes a paragon of chivalric leadership and a worthy predecessor to fourteenth-century nobility who wished to look further back than Arthur or even Rome for desirable chivalric forefathers.[56] Yet as a Greek ruler (and in the late fourteenth century the Greeks themselves were given the ambiguous status of schismatics and were subjected to orientalist rhetoric), he himself hovers on the tenuous border between what the fourteenth century defined as east and west. As this poem makes clear, if Alexander is situated as an identification for western chivalry, he is also its other—and his contradictions and perplexities mirror its own. Thus the poem's interrogation of Alexander's conquest enables a potential self-analysis and critique for a culture still desperately invested in oriental conquest but gradually forced to realize the futility of its dreams. Alexander fascinates the late fourteenth-century poet precisely because he is so driven and self-perplexed. He performs the extremities of western chivalry's admiration for and aversion to an oriental world it can never convert or conquer and from whose learning, science, and history Europeans had drawn a great part of their own.

Oriental Fathers

The Wars of Alexander relishes easternness, from Darius of Persia's jeweled staircase to Porrus of India's army of elephants and unicorns, to Candace of Preciosa's amazing, revolving closet. Wherever possible the poem capitalizes upon the marvelous knowledge and barbaric splendor of Alexander and his enemies. However, it depicts Alexander's Egyptian forebears very equivocally. Their knowledge and wealth are shadowed by an unchivalric duplicity and monstrous audacity which surface most disturbingly in Anectanabus, Alexander's powerful and ignominious father.[57] Anectanabus expresses an oriental legacy of penetrating desire, unnerving perception, self-interest, rootlessness, and disregard for feudal obligation and chivalric honor. This apparently makes him irresistible, in both senses of the word.

The poem begins in Egypt, where live the wisest men of the world. The poet vividly recounts world-encompassing potential of their learning:

> For þai þe mesure and þe mett of all þe mulde couthe,
> Þe [graynes] of all þe grete see and of þe grym wawys,
> Of þe ordere of þat odde home þat ouir þe aire hingis,
> Knew þe kynde and þe curses of þe clere sternys . . .

Þe pasage of þe planettis, þe poyntes and þe sygnes.
Þai ware þe kiddest of þat craft knawyn in þaire tyme,
And þe sotellest vndere son seges in þaire lyfe . . .
As wide as þe werd was went worde of þaire teching,
Of sorsery and slike werkis sleȝtis enogh.
And þe kyng of þat contre was a clerke noble,
Þe athelest ane of þe werd and Anectanabus was hatten.
He was wyse enoȝe wirdis to reken,
When he þe heuyn beheld, of [hathils] opon lyfe.
Þe iapis of all gemetri gentilli he couth,
And [as] wele as Aristotill, þe artis all seuyn.
Þare preued neuir nane his prik, forpassing of witt,
Plato nor Piktagaras ne Prektane himseluen. (25–28, 31–34, 37–46)

[For they knew the size and the measure of the whole world, all the valleys of the great sea and of the fierce waves. They knew the order of that illustrious region that hangs over the atmosphere, knew the nature and the courses of the clear stars . . . the passage of the planets, the degrees and the signs of the zodiac. They were the most excellent practitioners of that craft known in their time, and the most subtle men in their lives under the sun . . . As wide as the world went the word of their teaching, of their many tricks of sorcery and such like works. And the king of that country was a noble scholar, the most lordly one in the world, and he was called Anectanabus. He was so wise he could calculate the fate of every man alive when he looked at the heavens. He excellently understood the crafts of geometry and knew the seven arts as well as Aristotle himself. Neither Plato, Pythagorus, or Priscian ever proved his equal in excelling at wit.]

As it admires the magical amplitude of Egyptian perception, this passage cross-fertilizes learning and aristocratic status. Adjectives denoting nobility saturate the description of Egyptian learning—"odde," "kiddest," "noble," "athelest," "gentilli." The Egyptians are noble because they are knowledgeable; their king is a "clerke noble," ruling over a country that is less a monarchy than an epistematocracy. This redefinition of nobility shifts nobility's center of gravity from military performance to learning while retaining a sense of world conquest: its seizure through knowledge. And as the passage progresses, this expertise gathers increasingly disturbing connotations. The rarified learning that can pierce the heights of the air and the depths of the seas is transmuted by its very intensity into a kind of esoteric craft, the "sorsery and slike werkes" that are as apt to disguise as disclose the truth. This trickery becomes more conspicuous as the passage proceeds and the "subtlety" of the Egyptians is touched by the more treacherous accents of the "slights" of a king practiced in the "japes" of geometry.

The poem confirms the nonchivalric eccentricity of Egyptian aristocratic identity when he describes Anectanabus' reaction to the news that Egypt is about to suffer an invasion.

Þoȝe [the king] þa sawis herd say, ȝit samyd he na princis,
Ne ost ordand he nane of na [athill] knyȝtis,
Bot airis euen furth him ane and entirs his chambre
To knaw by his clergi þe come of his faa. (51–54)

[Though the king heard the news, yet he did not gather any princes, nor did he prepare any of his noble knights for battle. Instead, he goes forth by himself and enters his private chamber to discover by his learning the arrival of his foe.]

Here the poet shows Anectanbus's blow-by-blow rejection of the courses of action a fourteenth-century chivalric hero might be expected to take: calling a council and gathering an army. In contrast to Titus and Vespasian in *The Siege of Jerusalem* and Arthur in the alliterative *Morte Arthure*, Anectanabus refuses to operate as the head of a political network of loyalties and lieutenancies. Anectanabus is much more interested in his magical arts than his monarchical ones. He explicitly forsakes these bonds by going alone into a private chamber to confirm his news by his own peculiar means.

And peculiar they are. The poet amplifies every nuance of magical exoticism in Anectanabus's divination, from the bowl of brass, to the magic wand, to the spirits adjured to reveal his enemies' strength. Anectanabus's command of the spirits who assist his sorcery replaces his command of his own retainers, as he ascertains that the invasion is both irresistible and at his sea gates: "Slik was þe multitude of mast so mekil and so thike / Þat all him þoȝt bot he treis, a hare wod it semyd" (69–70) [The multitude of ship masts were so enormous and thick that all of them seemed to him like trees, a hoary wood it seemed]. Having confirmed the need for instant military action, he returns to the court but not to rally his men. Instead he deliberately misleads them as to the severity of the threat. When a warden who has actually counted the invading ships rushes into the court to warn Anectanabus to ready a huge defense, the king dispels his worry with a rhetorical syllogism worthy of Plato at his most coercive. He begins with the chivalric dictum that "bignes of will" (105) [ambition, ferocity] is more crucial to victory than numbers; a small number of men who are pushed to extremities will often win over a larger but lazier army. This leads to the proposal that small numbers are better than large ones in fighting, and that an "anelepy leon þat ouir þe land rynnys / Will make to fang to þe fliȝt and flay many hertis" (109–10) [A single lion that runs over the land, will terrify many harts/hearts and make them take to flight]—a foreshadowing of his son, ironic in the context of his father's incipient betrayal. Later Alexander will use a similar argument to counter Darius's threat. When presented with Darius's glove full of poppy seeds, a token of the innumerable numbers of the Persian armies, Alexander takes a handful and easily chews them up. He then returns to Darius a glove full of peppercorns, fewer in number but as Darius discovers, far less easy to swallow. The difference between Anectanabus' and Alexander's use of this argument is that Alexander leaps to back it up militarily while Anectanabus evades it magically. Anectanabus at once places himself outside the practice of chivalry and makes it a tool for betrayal.

Having silenced the warden with this argument, Anectanabus returns to his chamber for another bout of sorcery. His brave words and supernatural powers lead the reader to believe that perhaps he can defeat the invading Persians by magic, conjuring up an army of spirits or generating a storm, Prospero-like, that will founder the forest of enemy ships. But no such synthesis of magic and military power will the poem allow. Once alone, he fashions a miniature fleet of ships from wax and fans them with a palm leaf not to totemize their destruction but to rediscover that Persia will be victorious. Egyptian magic can only discover fate not change it. With an eye to the main chance, Anectanabus doffs the regalia of a king, assembles the paraphernalia of a prophet, and blows town:

> Þan wendis he wiȝtly furth and his wede changis;
> Clede him all as a clerke and his croune shauys,
> And with a bytand blade he his bered voydis.
> Þen takis to him tresour and trusses in baggis
> As many besandis on his bake as he bere miȝt
> And oþire necessari notis as nedis to his craftis,
> To sike s[ors]ry [and sleȝt] as himself vses.
> He toke traimmes him with to tute in þe sternes;
> Astrala[b]us algate as his arte wald,
> [Qu]adrentis coruen [full quaynte] all of quyte siluyre,
> Mustours and mekil-quat mare þen a littill. (119–30)

[He goes swiftly (bravely) forth and changes his clothes, clothes himself as a cleric and shaves off his hair (crown), and with a sharp (stinging) blade cuts off his own beard. Then he goes to his treasury and stuffs into bags as many gold coins as he could carry on his back. He took other necessary devices that pertain to his craft, to such sorcery and trickery as he practices. He took instruments (war engines) with him to gaze at the stars, also astrolabes as his art required, quadrants all of white silver carved very skillfully, and more than a few examples of astrological devices and many other things as well.]

The poet again dramatizes not only the steps Anectanabus is taking but also those he is not by employing words with military and chivalric echoes. "Wiȝtly" means both "swiftly" and "bravely," and shows how the bravery that might lead to quick battle preparations instead leads to a fearful flight. When Anectanabus shaves his head with the "biting" blade, he deadens the fierce edge of chivalric leadership by turning it against itself, a self-castration only confirmed by the cutting of his beard. When he equips himself, not with sword and armor but with gold and astrological instruments, the poet uses the word "traimmes" [instruments/war engines] to describe devices not about to be used on the battlefield. These astronomical instruments further link the flight from war to the artful orient: Arab navigators introduced astrolabes and quadrants to Europe in the eleventh century. Anectanabus simultaneously unfits himself for chivalry and embraces a science that can slip too easily from discovery of the truth of the future to its fraudulent manipulation.

And the poem drives home the socially destructive consequences of Anectanabus's unchivalric (literally horseless) flight by showing how Anectanabus's leaderless court topples into a chaos of stunned misery before the Persian invaders even get there:

> Slik care kindils in his curte quen þai þaire kyng myssid
> Þat it ware tere any tonge of þaire tene to reken.
> Princes of his palas preses into chambre
> To laite þaire lord þat was lost with latis vnblythe,
> Kairis into closettis kny3tis and erlis
> Sekand þaire souerayn with many salt terys.
> Barons and bachelers balefully gretis;
> Swiers wemyle, swouned[en] ladys,
> And many was þe bald berne at banned þe quile
> Þat euir he dured þat day vndede opon erthe. (149–58)

[When they missed the king, such sorrow kindles at the court that it would be difficult to tell the extent of their anguish. The princes of the palace retire into their chambers to seek their lord who was lost with unhappy cries. Knights and earls go into private rooms, seeking their sovereign with many salt tears. Barons and knights weep in torment, squires faint and ladies swoon, and many a bold warrior cursed the time that he had ever endured alive on the earth that day.]

This vision of courtly anguish heavily underscores Anectanabus's betrayal not only of political loyalties but also personal ones. The pathetic detail of the knights rifling in vain the inner chambers and private rooms shows how well these courtiers knew their secretive king. By cutting himself away from these organizing ties of love and loyalty, Anectanabus makes the prophecy of their defeat self-fulfilling. The Egyptians beseech the gods to reveal his whereabouts and receive from the high god Siraphas the news that he has fled but will return some day in the guise of a youth to destroy the Persians—a prophecy of Alexander's birth. They then erect an enormous statue of Anectanabus so that they can mourn him in perpetuity, and succumb without battle to the Persian armies. Alexander himself will later weep before the statue that commemorates his father as king and not as sorceror. The poem dwells on these consequences both to highlight the deep affectivity of chivalric bonding and to show that Anectanabus's prophetic knowledge, however empowering it may seem, ultimately circumscribes him, inciting him to cede first his kingship, then his people, and eventually even his life.

But Anectanabus does not care. As a free agent, he is loyal to no one but his own powerful will. Once slipped from its social moorings the kingly magnetism that his people mourn transmutes into a potent force for deception, manipulation, and magical prurience. His trickery grows more culpable as it increasingly disrupts more and more consequential bondings between ruler and subject, man and wife, and mortal and god. And the sense of danger to a chivalric society invigorated by reciprocal fealties sharpens as the reader realizes that Anectanabus will get away with his increasingly impertinent freelancing. Garbed as a prophet committed to reveal the truth of the future, he instead bears out the treacherous connotations of his sorcerous trade and travels to the court of Macedonia where he will seduce a queen by disguising himself as a god.

This seduction shows Anectanabus's power at its most transgressive. By cutting himself off from the body politic this king-errant has undergone a kind of reverse castration whose socially disruptive potential emerges when he becomes a kind of wandering phallus. After leaving Egypt, Anectanabus travels by secret ways into Macedonia, where he sees Queen Olympados and falls instantly in lust with her. His desire is as naked in its intentions as it is exotic in its strategies. Costumed as a court astrologer, he approaches Olympados and offers his services. Astrological and bodily penetration converge in his invitation: "þe poyntis of all þi preuates pertly can schewe" (255) [The conditions of all your secret things I can reveal openly]. His glittering eye is no less piercing:

> Quen he þire sawis had sayd, he in his sege lened
> In stody still as a stane and starid in hire face,
> Beheld haterly þat hend þat had his hert percid,
> With depe desire of delite ay on þat dere waytis.
> Sone as hireself it sawe at he hire sa behaldis
> Þen scho talkis him to and titely him fraynes,
> "Quareon muse ȝe sa mekill, maistir?" scho sayd.
> "ȝe behald me sa hogely, quareon is ȝour mynd?"
> "My frely fode," quod þe freke, "noȝt bot þe [faire]werdes
> Of my gracious goddis, þe grettest on erde." (262–71)

[When he had said these words, he leaned forward in his chair in study still as a stone and stared in her face. He beheld fiercely (violently, keenly) the noble lady who had pierced his heart, and with deep desire for delight waited continually on the dear/noble one. As soon as she saw that he looked at her in such a manner, then she speaks to him and quickly asks, "On what do you muse so mightily, master? You behold me so forcefully, what are you thinking about?" "My lovely child (food)," said the man, "nothing but on the fair words of my gracious gods, the greatest upon earth."]

As the pun on "fode" stresses, Anectanabus is entranced—and he wastes no time. The "fair words of his god" hint at the strategy he will use to seduce her, which he instigates at once by telling her that she is predestined to sleep with one. Once informed of her fate, she, like Anectanabus, submits to it at once, becoming fortune's willing servant and Anectanabus's dupe. The poem stresses her titillated interest not in the god's power or character but in what bodily shape he will take for their encounter, and also whether she will be caught and divorced by her husband. This air of half-sanctioned, half-guilty betrayal defines her character for the rest of the poem and imbues her relations with her son with the peculiar chivalric misogyny that desecrates the lady even as it hyperbolically insists on her protection. Anectanabus is swift to smooth Olympados's fears and fan her desires, painting an exotic and beguiling picture of the god, promising her diplomatic immunity from her husband, and the affair begins—as fantastic and flamboyant a seduction as can be fantasized, involving a transformation from a flying dragon to an exotic god and back again.

Anectanabus usurps divine authority with disquieting success, catching at the prurient ambitions of his victims, enlisting them as willing conspirators in a plot that at once gratifies and debases them. He carefully presages the encounter in a dream he sends to the queen. This quells Olympados's lingering doubts; a queen might distrust the words of a wandering astrologer but a dream must have an unquestionable internal authority. Anectanabus exerts this oneiric authority once more when he sends a dream to King Philip that dramatizes the entire encounter with the "god" who afterward literally places his seal on Olympados's "belechiste" (423) and informs him that the son born of it will conquer the whole world, a vision that successfully persuades him not only to retain Olympados but to bring up the son honorably as his own. The poem makes a similarly spectacular appeal to readers when Anectanabus shape-changes into a dragon and flies through the hall to kiss the queen publicly before the eyes of her husband, who is so gratified at what he takes to be the dragon's divine condescension that he makes no objection. The description of the Anectanabus-dragon dwells on its terrifying power.

> He was sa hattir and sa hoge quen he þe hall entird,
> Lete sa lathely a late and sa loude cried,
> Þat all þe fest was aferd and oþire folke bathe.
> To þe chefe chaiare of þe qwene he chese him belyue
> And laide as hendly as a hunde his hede in his arme;
> Seþin kyssis he hire clene mouthe, enclynes her lawe,
> And braydis furth with a brym bere out at þe brade ȝatis.
> Þen sayd Philip to his fere and all his fre gestis
> "ȝone selfe dragon, forsothe, I saȝe with myne eȝen
> Quen I was stad in þe stoure; he strenthid all myne oste,
> And þare þe floure in þe filde I fanged þurȝe himselfe. (490–500)

[He was so fierce and so huge when he entered the hall, let loose so horrible a sound and cried so loudly that all the people at the feast and everyone else about were terrified. He immediately headed toward the highest chair of the queen and laid his head in her arms as tamely as a hound, then kisses her on her pure mouth, bows low to her, and suddenly rushes forth with a savage noise out at the broad gates. Then Philip addressed his companions and all his noble guests, "That same dragon, in truth, I saw with my eyes when I was in the middle of battle; he strengthened all my host, and there I took the victory of the field through his power."]

This passage leads to two seemingly opposing conclusions about Anectanabus's wayward power. The first emphasizes its dangers: Anectanabus volatilizes a previously chivalric identity into pure, performative, transgressive desire. The shape he takes, a roaring, flaring dragon with the appetites of a man, perfectly expresses his threat. The second conclusion, however, effaces it. For all his roaring this monster is ultimately as "hend[e] as a hunde" [docile/handy as a dog]. The performance is so faultless, the deception so dextrous that it has no socially disruptive consequences at all. Anectanabus's impersonation of a god is so perfect that he might as well be one. His spell-fabricated vision of a dragon can imbue Philip with a dragon's actual power on the field of battle. Alexander's birth is attended by so many earthshaking portents (not attributed to Anectanabus) that he might as well be the son of a deity. Alexander is thus gifted with three fathers, one hidden, Anectanabus, and two publicly acknowledged, Philip of Macedon and Amon the sun-god.

This overdetermined ancestry is warily negotiated by Alexander throughout the course of the poem. It enables Alexander to recognize his two public fathers and displace the specter of Anectanabus. The two public (and false) fathers, Amon and Philip, tease out strands from the tightly wound skein of power and trickery that Anectanabus represents. Alexander's putative father, Amon the sun-god of the Macedonians, provides a divinely purified non-Arabic source for Alexander's excessive energy, providential invulnerability, and incredible military success. Alexander's adoptive father, Philip of Macedon, impugns Anectanabus's shifty disregard for the socially formative links of chivalric loyalty and service. Alexander internalizes the attributes of his two putative fathers as he is brought up in Philip's court He becomes so chivalrically adept, both as a superb leader who instills and nurtures deep loyalties in his followers and as a defender of noble women, that he comes to instruct Philip himself in loyalty to his queen. Even after he discovers his true father's identity, killing him in the process, Alexander declares his affiliation only to his two public fathers throughout the poem, virtually alternating them each time he announces his ancestry to every new soon-to-be-subject ruler. Alexander is nothing if not thorough so he follows his murder of Anectanabus's person with the obliteration of Anectanabus's character and name.

During his subsequent career, Alexander takes every opportunity to challenge the oriental side of his heritage. He cherishes, reinforces, and turns to effective military uses the chivalric obligations that his father abandons; his successful conquests stem from the faith and loyalty he bestows on and commands from his followers. What Anectanabus does Alexander takes care to undo—honoring his mother where Anectanabus had dishonored her, defending his land as Anectanabus abandoned his.[58] Most of all, he disdains the submission to destiny that renders Anectanabus so cynical, Philip so gullible, and Olympados so haplessly prurient. This submission threatens at its very core a chivalric identity energized by cultivating the impossible. Alexander continually fights destiny, disdains and disregards it repeatedly, although his whole campaign reverberates with the prophecy of his irresistible victory and early death. Enemy after powerful enemy, from one end of Asia to the other, threatens this youth with defeat and death. Repeatedly Alexander answers by confirming the necessity for uncertainty, the fatality of overconfident pride. He testifies again and again that against all reason and logic, he can emerge the victor.

Despite these overt rejections, however, Alexander expresses as much of Anectanabus's heritage as he erases. As the poem continues and Alexander's conquests lead him farther and farther from home, he gradually becomes as itinerant as Anectanabus, deploying the force of his military energy just as Anectanabus directed his magical energy. This pint-sized patricide claims his father's volatility and denies its sudden taming, and for the rest of this poem rages against destiny as he transgresses every boundary of the world.

Patricide and Conquest

In challenging all the rulers of the east, Alexander expresses his need not just to avoid, but to deauthorize, break away from, and obliterate the oriental enemies who shadow his predecessor and mirror his end. Where Anectanabus succumbs to the mere vision of the wilderness of ships assembled against him, Alexander impossibly will dispatch them all. But the poem also perplexes divisive ideologies of conquest. As in the other alliterative romances, the dead do not stay dead; vanquished fathers return incessantly to insist that victorious sons die too—sooner than they think and no matter what they do to escape.

This paradoxical circumscription at the moment of victory dominates the scene where Alexander kills Anectanabus and learns the truth about his parentage. After begetting Alexander, Anectanabus takes a position as court astrologer to Philip and Olympados and occasional tutor to Alexander. When Alexander reaches adulthood, Anectanabus takes him up to a cliff above Philip's castle for some stargazing. He points out the fateful influences in the heaven that decree his own death at the hands of his son. Alexander, still ignorant of their relationship and incensed at Anectanabus's resignation, strikes him on the back with such force that the astrologer "drives down to the depths of the dike bottom" (712). As he falls, Alexander adds insult to injury: "Þou has feyned þe forwyse and fals alltogedire; / Wele semys slike a sacchell to syeȝe þus of lyfe!" (715–16) [You have pretended to be very wise when you are altogether a fraud. It well beseems such an idiot to sink thus from life!]. Here Alexander is not simply punishing fraudulence with death. He is turning his Greek tutor (Aristotle) against his Egyptian one to prove by a nicely Aristotelian syllogism that Anectanabus is fraudulent. Anectanabus must be killed by his own son; Alexander is not Anectanabus's son and Alexander has killed Anectanabus; therefore Anectanabus is a fraud. Quod erat demonstrandum. His violence is an irrefutable way to break the prophecy by anticipating it.

But Anectanabus, uncharacteristically, is not willing to vanish. Even as he succumbs, the description of his death chillingly demonstrates his preemptive power:

Þan Anectanabus, as him aȝt wele, augirly granys.
Dryues vp a dede voyce and dymly he spekis,
"Wele was þis case to me knawen and kyd many wyntir
Þat I suld dee slike a dethe be dome of my werdis.
Sayd I þe noȝt so myselfe here before
I suld be slayn of my son as now sothe worthis?"

> "What? and am I," quod Alexander, "ane of þi childer?"
> "ȝha, son! Als glad I my god, I gat þe myseluen"
> Fro he had [warpyd] hym þis worde, he wakens no more,
> Bot gaue a gremly grane and þe gast ȝheldez.
> That oþer wy for hys werkez wepys eueryllyke,
> So hard and so hertly þat neȝ hys hert brestes. (717–28)

[Then Anectanabus, as it was necessary for him, groans greatly, drives up a dead
voice and speaks darkly: "That my fate has doomed me to such a death is a thing I
have known very well for many winters. Did I not say myself just now that I should
be slain by my son as has now come truly to pass?" "What?" said Alexander, "and
am I one of your children?" "Yes, son! As it please my god, I begot you myself."
When he had uttered these words, he wakes no more, but gave a mighty groan and
yields up his spirit. The other man weeps continually for his deeds so hard and so
heartily that his heart nearly bursts.]

Here Anectanabus joins the ranks of the speaking dead in alliterative
romance: a voice from the grave animated his own fatal prophecy. And just
as Alexander's blow was an attempt to enact a proof and destroy his father's
authority, Anectanabus's revelation not only implicates Alexander in his
death but finally and irresistibly reinstates Anectanabus's prophetic authority and by extension, the validity of all the prophecies which will hound
Alexander throughout the poem. By attempting to destroy Anectanabus's
influence, Alexander has actually surrendered to it. His iconoclasm, however excessive and self-assured, is contained and rendered futile by his
ignorance of his intimacy to that which he is destroying. The poet stresses
the force of Alexander's horror by compressing it into direct dialogue.
Alexander's aghast "What? Am I one of your children?" conveys the shock
of the revelation and the way it reshapes his identity: from the son of a
god and foster son of a king, to a fakir's bastard and patricide—a shock
that Anectanabus's vigorous "ȝha! son" drives home.

This disclosure cannot be absorbed by Alexander; he melts into a
flood of tears, heavily shoulders the body, and returns home to perform
the first of many attempts to escape self-knowledge. Readers of *Sir Gawain
and the Green Knight* will not be surprised to learn that he finds a welcome
scapegoat in a woman. He blames Olympados: "Dame, now is þare none
other to do bot deme it þiseluen, / For as þi foly was before, so foloweth
aftir" (735–36) [Lady, now there is nothing to do about it but judge it to
yourself, For your folly began it; here is the result]. Yet this shared secret
of sexual betrayal implicates Alexander, binding him to his mother and
eroticizing their subsequent semi-Oedipal relationship even as it establishes a pattern for Alexander's fascinated fear of women and generation.

This scene of patricide doubly determines the shape of Alexander's subsequent conquests. First, it provides a paradigm of conquest as a zero-sum game of fall and rise. Alexander will spend the rest of his career "driving into the depths of the dike bottom" all the tremendous oriental rulers and armies that oppose him, and they, like Anectanabus, will implicate him in their own fate as they fall. Second, it outlines a pattern of reaction for Alexander once he discovers how closely he resembles his victims. The young conqueror spends much of the rest of the poem running on an emotional gerbil-wheel from sudden anger, to aghast recognition and tears, to evasion and erasure, to anger again. But the poem forcefully insists that victors inevitably become victims; the high are driven down in their turn. On numerous occasions, as the victorious Alexander stands over his fallen enemy, he receives the advice to regard the fall as the mirror of his own future and look to himself. Darius of Persia elaborates this somber injunction to self-examination:

> "Þe same ensampill of myselfe [þou sees now betid].
> So gret I grew of my gods and gold in my cofirs,
> Þat kindly gods creatoure I kend noȝt myselfe,
> Bot for his feloȝe and his fere faithly me leued.
> Þus prosperite and pride so purely me blyndid,
> I couth noȝt se fra my sege to þe soile vndire;
> Þat at me failed þan to fynd fast at myn eȝen,
> Be þe myrrour now of meknes, I may a myle knawe . . .
> If all þe limp as þe list, loke to þine ende,
> For die þe bose quen all is done, and ay þi day scortis." (3408–15, 3426–27)

["The same example of myself you can see happening now before you. I grew so mighty of my gods and had so much gold in my coffers, that I did not know myself for one of god's natural creatures, but rather believed myself firmly to be his equal and companion. Thus prosperity and pride blinded me so completely, I could not see from my throne to the soil underneath. I failed to discern what was clearly before my eyes and now through the mirror of submission I can see it from a mile away . . . When everything seems to be going as you wish, I warn you, look to your end. For you must die when all is done, and your day already shortens."]

This foreboding passage transforms the dialectic of high and low from a synchronic structure which divides victor from victim to a diachronic cycle which connects them. At the moment of his transcendence the victor is conjured back into the exigencies of history. The "myrrour . . . of meknes" into which Darius now gazes also presses home the affinities between the two players. The temptation, as Darius argues, is to be blinded by the seeming invulnerability of victory, the high throne beneath which the earth secretly, patiently waits. This trope is a commonplace in non-alliterative medieval writing and an obsession in alliterative poetry; it also surfaces in the *transi* effigies upon the tombs of medieval aristocracy—the estates that would have the most temptation to let their exalted social position obscure the fact of their mortality.[59] It is often incorporated into the paradigm of the noble life cycle as a necessary recognition. In *The Parliament of Three Ages*, another North Midlands alliterative poem of the late fourteenth century, a passage echoes Darius's in both sentiment and admonition: Age addressing Maturity and Youth:

> "I sett ensample bi myselfe and sekis it no forthire . . .
> I was als euerrous in armes as ouþer of ȝoureseluen . . .
> And as myche wirchip I wane, iwis, as ȝe bothen . . .
> Than I mukkede and marlede and made vp my howses . . .
> Gatte gude and golde full gaynly to honde . . .
> Bot elde vnderȝode me are I laste wist,
> And alle disfegurede my face and fadide my hewe
> Bothe my browes and my berde blawnchede full whitte . . .
> Makes ȝoure mirrours bi me, men, bi ȝoure trouth
> This schadowe in my schewere schunte ȝe no while."
>   (269, 271, 276, 279, 281, 283–85, 290–91)

["Seek no further for an example (proof); I give you myself . . . I was as eager in arms as either of you, . . . and won as much worship as both of you. Then I manured and spread . . . fertilizer and built up my house, quickly gathered gold and goods in my hands, . . . but age crept under me before I knew it, and disfigured my face and bleached my color, blanched my brows and my beard completely white . . . Make your mirror by me, by your faith. Avoid no more this shadow (reflection) in my mirror."]

This passage accentuates the specular connection between the humbled speaker and the still proud audience. Like Darius, Age transforms himself into a mirror of the future tendering a pale reflection that needs facing. And that mirror of the future also contains the shadow of a predecessor; *The Parliament of Three Ages* insistently connects its characters not only through likeness and reflection, but also genealogy.[60] The poem ends with Age declaring, "I am thi sire and thou my sone, the sothe for to telle, / For Elde is sire of Midill Elde, and Midill Elde of ȝouthe" (646–47) [To tell the truth of it, I am your father and you are my son, for Age is father of Maturity, and Maturity of Youth].

While *The Wars of Alexander* urges its hero to remember his inevitable mortality, other alliterative poems add insult to injury by making Alexander's mortality exemplary. In *The Parliament of Three Ages*, although Age instructs his audience to look no further than his face, with characteristic prolixity he cannot resist showcasing the Nine Worthies and in particular detail the example of Alexander of Macedon himself, who "alle þe worlde wanne, / Bothe the see and the sonde and the sadde erthe, / Þe iles of the Oryent to Ercules boundes ... He conquered with conqueste kyngdomes twelue, / And dalte thaym to his dussypers when he the dethe tholede, / And thus the worthieste of this werlde went to his ende" (332–34, 402–4) [all the world won, both the sea and the land and the stable earth, the isles of the Orient to the pillars of Hercules ... He conquered with conquest twelve kingdoms, and divided them among his famous knights when he suffered death, and thus the worthiest man in the world also went to his end]. The alliterative *Morte Arthure* casts Alexander in the same role even more chillingly as from Fortune's wheel he offers Arthur a glimpse of the same fatal reflection.

But these poems also show how the emotional force of this spectacle is muted by its exemplarity. Exemplary deaths (especially in illustrious groups) can be mourned more cleanly; dead heros do not haunt as powerfully as dead victims. This is why Alexander always mourns his victims as heroes. His tears after the death of Darius—"as a barne [he] gretis" (3449) [(he) wails like a child]—like his tears before the illustrious (and incredibly euphemistic) commemorative statue of his father Anectanabus—enable him to forget them and move on to the next enemy. The accounts of Alexander's death in *Parliament* and *Morte Arthure* do not beseech pity across the gaps of time; rather they provide a contrast between an exemplary past which has needfully accepted its mortality and the still tortured present viewer who cannot be induced to acknowledge, let alone yield to, that recognition.

The Wars of Alexander, therefore, invests its conventional lesson with drama by intensifying the personal torture it causes Alexander. It cherishes descriptions of Alexander's ferocity endlessly on the boil: from his schoolboy days where he responds to any insult from his companions by knocking them "kenely on þe croune ... with his tablis / Þat al tobrest wald þe bordis and þe blode folowe" (639–40) [fiercely on the heads with his slates so that they would burst in pieces and blood ran], to his adolescent taming of the head-ripping, rib-shredding, hand-munching horse Bucephalus, which "faunys and loutez" (785) [fawns and abases itself] at Alexander's touch, suggesting they will share a rough ride between chivalry and savagery in more ways than one. Given this temperament, Alexander is fearfully debilitated when at every turn his iconoclasm becomes a further instance of submission to fate. Each time he asks for a prophecy—and he asks constantly—he seems more desperate to get a different answer. He is forced to recognize repeatedly that as he subdues each additional realm, he only inscribes himself more profoundly into that same inescapable dialectic. This in turn spurs him more violently to further conquests, as he seeks the kind of military victory that will not only be complete but also continuous, an everlasting campaign that will obliterate his bastard heritage as the son of Anectanabus and will take him to the level of his putative father, the sun-god, Amon. The poem becomes the story of Alexander's increasingly desperate attempts to break the mirror of mortality itself, as read back to him by the "schadewe in [the] schewere" of his oriental enemy. And yet, with every king he drives down to the dust, the ground beneath his own throne becomes that much nearer. As *The Wars of Alexander* repeatedly traps its hero at this peculiar intersection, genealogical conquests against tyrannical predecessors are reenacted as spatial and geographical ones, while genealogical affinities sharpen into actual reflections.

Breaking the Terrestrial Mirror

As Alexander beats his way further east, the east throws back to him with increasing force a myriad of disquieting echoes, reflections, projections, and recognitions. The poem shows how Alexander's agonistic conquests shade fatally into self-conquests and how he is continually caught up in a projected web of his own self-fashionings. This both blinds him and makes him manipulable. The Jews are particularly perceptive in playing to Alexander's more grandiose self-conceptions. Warned by one of the omnipresent prophecies that Alexander will conquer but that his reign would be very brief, the Jews adorn Jerusalem with silks and jewels to resemble a heavenly city, dress themselves in angelic white, and welcome Alexander with great ceremony—in short, like a deity (but without ever calling him one). Their dramaturgy so charms him that he refrains from battle and grants them a tribute immunity for seven years. By that time, they know, he will be dead. They stave Alexander off by staging a picture of himself not as he is but as he wishes to be.

And they do so advisedly; Alexander cannot bear harsher reflections. In an arresting set piece (and the subject of another alliterative poem, *Alexander and Dindimus*), Alexander meets the Brahmins who live a life without rank, culture, or luxury on the opposite side of the impassable Ganges. Alexander halts on the western bank and sends over letters asking to learn of their manner of living. They send him back a description that imbues the primal innocence of the Golden Age with discourses of Christian reform.[61] They literalize Christ's sermon about the lilies of the field:

no cultivation, no building, no rulers or servants, no greed, no disease, no excess, and no inequality. They believe in a single god and regard life as a brief pilgrimage to be used and not enjoyed. Conquest is unknown but not incomprehensible, as their prescience toward Alexander suggests. Alexander replies with an aristocratic sneer, condemning them for blasphemously and foolishly trying to imitate the gods. Their answer to him presents him with a picture of himself and his own society that rivals Langland in its satirical energy: prideful, idolatrous, avaricious, blasphemous, and ultimately futile. They end by throwing his accusation back in his teeth:

> "Þe same ensampill, as me semes, into ȝoureself touches.
> For so þe qwele of qwistounes ȝoure qualite encreses
> Þat noþir gesse ȝe gouernour no god bot ȝourselfe!
> ȝe brixsill our benignite, our bonerte repreues,
> And beris apon vs blasfeme þat neuire bale thoȝt . . .
> It is ȝourselfe and noȝt oureself þat ai þe self hantis." (4786–94)

["The same proof, it seems to me, touches your own case, for as long as the wheel of fortune increases your quality, you believe in no governor or god but yourself. You upbraid our goodwill and reprove our gentleness, and attribute blasphemies to us who never intended evil . . . It is yourself and not ourselves that you continually pursue [concern yourself with."]

Alexander's response to the Brahmins resists this revelation and in a lovely anticipation of colonialist rhetoric chides them for their primitive contentment with a base state of nature which he would improve if he could only cross over to them. He then puts up a plaque boasting that he had "followed his foes" as far as the Ganges. Yet the gentleness of the Brahmins' demeanor only underscores the devastation of this revelation to Alexander's endeavor. He is not merely after conquest; he is trying to be a god—the sun-god, in fact, the father/identity that Anectanabus stole from him. And, caught in his need to erase his parentage, he is projecting his own obsessions upon everyone he meets. The military rationales of self-defense and revenge with which he began his campaigns—to defend Macedon from its enemies, to preserve his father's sovereignty, to avenge the personal insults of Darius and Porrus—all evaporate as justifications for further campaigning and we are left with a blind desire for apotheosis.

The scene that crystallizes this most compellingly follows 300 lines after Alexander's conversation with the Brahmins. After attacks by several monsters—giants, basilisks, and serpents—Alexander climbs and crosses a great plateau hedged by a great adamantine cliff. Alexander and some of his men climb the cliff and reach a bejeweled land peer to nothing but

"paradyse selfe" (5032). This land and its lord have prompted compari-
sons of the poem with the work of the *Gawain*-poet.[62] There on a golden
mountain Alexander finds a house situated in "þe hiȝe est" (5029). The
house's name—"þe hous of þe son" (5030)—echoes significantly in this tale
filled with pseudo-sun-god fathers (Anectanabus), sun-god pseudo-fathers
(Amon), and restless sons (Alexander). Alexander meets with a mysterious
lord who seems to be a living embodiment of time itself, all three ages of
man joined in one:

> Ane of þe borliest bernes þat euire body hade,
> With fell face as þe fire and ferly faire schapen,
> Balgh, brade in þe brest and on þe bely sklendire.
> His cheuelere as cha[nu]ele for changing of elde,
> And as blaȝt was his berd as any briȝt snaw.
> Sone as oure prince with his peris his person avyses,
> He gesse him wele to be gode and of na gome kind. (5048–54)

[One of the burliest men that ever had a body, with a face as fierce as the fire and
marvelously well shaped, with a broad rounded breast and a slender waist. His hair
was greying with the approach of age, and as bleached was his beard as the bright-
est snow. As soon as our prince with his companions saw his aspect, he believed
him truly to be a god and of no human nature.]

This mysterious figure is referred to by the editors as the Sun-god because
he seems to be a god and lives in the house of the sun, although he is
not linked at any point to Amon. His youthful face, vigorous body, greying hair, and white beard mark him as a timeless figure above the wheel
of history in which Alexander is trapped: he knew of Alexander's identity
"Or any drope of þ[e] deluuie drechet had þe erd" (5068) [Before any drop
of the great Deluge had drenched the earth]. From his high house he offers
Alexander a glimpse into temporality itself:

> "List þe noȝt loke on þe lindis þat leuys euiremare
> Þat has þe surname of þe son and [Cynthia] alls,
> Þat is to mene bot of þe mone, and miȝt has to speke
> And tell þe trewly all þe text quat tide sall here-eftir?" (5069–72)

["Would you not like to look at the trees that live forever which have the surname
of the sun and of Cynthia also, which is to say, the moon? They have the power to
speak and tell you truly all the text of what shall happen hereafter."]

In this quasi-paradise, the trees of the garden do not promise the knowledge of good and evil but rather the knowledge of time from the perspective of eternity. These trees of the celestial objects that regulate the day
and year are as immune to time's passage as the lord who keeps them. And

their knowledge is not free to everyone: the asker must be "wemles for woman[es] touchinge" (5075) [unstained by women's touching], that is, a virgin not yet fully implicated in the processes of generation and lineage which the poem imbues with such fear. Alexander answers that not only is he qualified but that he desires such knowledge more than anything in the world. Just as throughout the poem he seeks knowledge of the alien lands which he desires to conquer, he is driven here to seek knowledge of the generational history he desires to surpass.

And yet, predictably, standing before the trees of the sun and the moon, he once again finds confirmation of his subjection to the dialectic of father and mother, generation and mortality. The sun tree, gendered male, the ultimate father, inscribes him in a tale of doomed fatherhood even as it orphans him:

> "Sire, þou ert lele of ilk lede þe lorde and þe fadire,
> But þi sire soile in na side see sall þou neuire." (5147–48)

["Lord, you are truly of your people the lord and the father, but your fatherland you will never at any time behold."]

The moon tree, gendered female, takes on an Olympados-like aura of untrustworthy love by telling him that he will die by the treachery of a dear friend within two years. Alexander actually clasps the moon tree in his arms and asks her who this friend will be, but she refuses to answer, and the lord rebukes him sternly:

> "Lefe of þi wordis
> For writhing of þire wale treeis and willne þaim na mare.
> But graythe þe, gome, on gods behalue and agayn turne,
> For ouire þe lemetis of þire lindis may no lede founde." (5161–64)

["Leave off your words and ask these proud trees no more lest you anger them. But prepare yourself, man, in gods name, and turn around, for over the limits of these trees may no man go."]

This scene puts the kibosh on Alexander's strange xenophobic, misogynist, semi-Oedipal quest for world conquest and historic transcendence. He may deplete the world of human fathers and cringe at the grasp of needful mothers up to a point but the trees incarnate both nature and history as well as generation, and Alexander remains subject to their laws, a patricide who has become a father. He must "agayne turne" into history. Alexander reacts to this news exactly as he reacts to his father's death and to the other intimations of mortality with which the poem badgers him: he bursts out weeping and hides the knowledge from his army and even from himself. However, this incident seals the change in narrative direction that the encounter with the Brahmins initiated—an ominous shortening of Alexander's leash.

Up until these encounters, Alexander is able to ignore such shadows of affinity with relative impunity. Subsequent ones, however, no longer simply adumbrate Alexander's mortality; they actually kill. Two hundred lines after the encounter with the Brahmins, Alexander and his armies are menaced in a narrow chasm by a basilisk that crouches on the brink and destroys vast companies simply by turning the glare of its eyes in their direction. Alexander climbs up to the beast and makes himself a special shield, as large as a barn door to cover his body and mirrored on its outer surface to destroy his foe:

> Þe screwe in þe schewere his schadow behaldis,
> And so þe slaȝtir of his siȝt into himselfe entris. (4981–82)

[The wretch beholds his shadow in the mirror, and so the slaughter of his gaze enters into himself.]

Alexander's turning of the basilisk's destructive power back on itself metaphorizes his strategies of resistence to his own dark reflections—the basilisk's magical invulnerability and fatal power are Alexander's own. Alexander's shield, which both hides himself and reflects his enemy, figures his most crucial strategy, the willful non-recognition upon which his conquest depends. The danger the basilisk poses is ocular, but that is not the only avenue of ominous projection the poem explores. He encounters another when he, famously, runs out of earth:

> [he] . . . cairis on forthire
> To þe Occyan at þe erthes ende, and þare in an ile he heres
> A grete glauir and a glaam of Grekin tongis.
> Þan bad he kniȝtis þaim vncleth and to þat kith swym,
> Bot all at come into þat cole, crabbis has þaim drenchid. (5628–32)

[He goes on further to the Ocean at the earth's end and there from an island he hears a great chattering and din of Greek tongues. Then he ordered knights to unclothe themselves and swim to that land, but everyone that entered into that cold sound was drowned by great crabs.]

This island at the end of the world marks the point of greatest alterity where the earth itself gives out and can grow no stranger. It is only at that farthest point that he uncannily hears a clamor of his own language. Yet he cannot reach the island where the east becomes west and other echoes into himself; to pass across that "cold sound" is to be dragged down by monsters. These passages not only mark the desperation with which Alexander pursues his others, but in teasing at the barrier between self, other, and monster, they suggest the monstrousness of Alexander's whole endeavor, the extremity of the desires that drive him.

And in the latter part of the poem as Alexander tentatively ventures into the incessantly twinned realms of generation and mortality, the poem presents him with a final dangerous reflection. On his way back to Macedon, he pauses at the nearby land of Preciosa to challenge its conqueror-queen, Candace. Alexander has dealt with female conquerors before: the Amazons who cannily negotiate tribute with him, and the terrifying mermaids who inhabit landscapes of impassible flame. However, Candace is the first who reminds Alexander of his mother: "Him þoȝt hire like at a loke his lady his modire" (5383) [It seemed to him that she looked like the lady his mother]. Here Alexander finally faces the other half of his parental legacy, the tangle of desire, fear, guilt, and betrayal represented by Olympados. Disguising himself as one of his own knights, he rescues the queen's daughter-in-law from a neighboring king. Knowing that Candace's sons would kill him on sight, he visits the queen anonymously to receive her thanks. However, Candace has secretly sent a portrait-maker into Alexander's camp to secure his likeness, judging him a highly desirable figure. On the second day of his stay at her court, she takes him by the hand without explanation and leads him into a private chamber whose gilded walls "stremed as þe son" (5412) [gleamed like the sun]. Although they are quite secluded, she takes him and leads him further into a "clochere with a kay" (5415) [enclosed place locked with a key] which is devised to whirl around rapidly by the work of twenty tamed elephants. Once they are within, the room begins to turn and as Alexander is wondering at it, the queen calls him by his name, "Alexsandire." At this he starts and turns pale, but the queen only laughs, takes his hand and leads him even further into a "preue parlour" (5430). And it is here in this invaginated sanctum that the now sinister queen takes out his portrait and shows it to him, saying, "Se þiselfe a sampill þat I þe sothe neuyn" (5432) [See for yourself a proof that I name you truly]. Alexander is terrified. By capturing his portrait and luring him from familiar ground into her own exotically revolving sphere, the queen has conquered him. Candace mocks him, not too gently:

> "Qui fadis so þi faire hew?" said the faire lady,
> "Þe werreour of all þe werd and wastour of Ynde,
> Þou þat has brettend on the bent þe barbrins fokke,
> Þe pepill out of Panty, þe Persens and þe Medis,
> Loo, now, þe here withouten hiȝt into my handis sesed,
> Bot in womans ward for all þi wale dedis!" (5435–40)

["Why does your beautiful color fade?" asked the fair lady, "The warrior of all the world and the waster of India, you who have broken on the field all the barbarian folk, the people out of Parthia, the Persians and the Medes. Lo, now you are suddenly without warning seized into my hands, in the power of a mere woman for all your proud deeds."]

Alexander nearly explodes with rage, gnashing his teeth and shaking his head violently. When the queen teases him a little more he declares:

"I swete . . . þat I na swerd haue,
For I na wapen haue, iwis my writh with to venge!"
"Now, bald baratour on bent, if þou a brand hade,
Quat prowis miȝt þi person apreue in þis stounde?"
"For I vnwarly," quod þe [wee], "am to ȝoure will taken;
I suld þe slaa þare þou sittis and þan myselfe eftir!" (5450–56)

["I sweat with rage that I have no sword, because I have no weapon to avenge my wrath." "Now, brave knight on the field! if you had a blade, what prowess would your person prove in this place?" "Because I unwarily," said the man, "am taken within your power, I should slay you where you sit, and then myself after!"]

The violence of Alexander's reaction exceeds the queen's half-mocking innuendos, responding instead to the all too intimate (not to say incestuous) threats of her recognition, desire, and control. Yet it is utterly fitting that the person who finally bags him mirrors his mother and is threatened with the fate of his father; she captures him in paint and in the flesh with an irresistible combination of Olympados's allure and Anectanabus's guile (to say nothing of the exotic secret chamber). The queen calms him only by assuring him that she does not desire dominion, a promise that enables a brief liaison between them which the poem emphatically downplays. Within one hundred lines Alexander is on the road again looking for new enemies.

This pivotal (and dizzily pivoting) scene touches the heart of Alexander's "haunting," the tantalizing fear that drives him to pursue the shadow in the mirror which betokens his enemies, his origins, and his death. In this light it is fitting that he will be killed eventually by a much loved friend; he has already become his own worst enemy. Simultaneously the greatest warrior in history and history's greatest dupe, the self-conflicts that have been driving him onward finally begin to tear him apart. The last eight hundred lines of the poem confront him with increasingly fantastic and nightmarish enemies while his ambitions grow wilder and wilder. Attrition sets in. He battles hordes of lethal beasts: giant lions and scorpions, who pick away at his army and destroy his provisions, reducing his followers by huge numbers. His ferocious man-eating horse, Bucephalus, companion and double since his boyhood, dies of a lingering disease. At the same time, he grows tired of subjugating the terrestrial sphere and attempts to attain the celestial one, rigging a flying machine by harnessing four winged griffins to a chariot and extending a great hook baited with raw flesh over their heads. This attempt at stellification looks promising at first: the griffins rise up until "midilerth bot as mylnestane na mare to him semed, / and all the water of þe werd bot as a wrethen neddire" (5651–52) [The earth seemed no more than a millstone, and all the water of the world only a coiled serpent]. But the Christian God prevents Alexander from reaching his goal and, cursing like Lucifer, he falls to the earth, frustrated but unhurt. Undeterred he then attempts to fathom the depths of the seas in a great barrel.

With these antics (which unfailingly fascinated manuscript illuminators of Alexander romances) the narrator ironically disengages from his hero's increasingly "fonned fantasy" (5639) [foolish fantasy]. He plays on the latitude allowed by his hero's hybrid identity both to validate Alexander's chivalric leadership and to alienate the more baroque excesses of his ambition from his fourteenth-century audience. He amplifies the flamboyance and ingenuity of Alexander's griffin-flown chariot to cast a humorous half-smile at Alexander's blasphemous drive for conquest. But elsewhere, he gives it a darker tinge. Alexander battens upon violence so insatiably that he starves even as he devours the next battle: "his flesche is fostard and fedd be fiȝt and sternes" (3623) [his flesh is fostered and fed by battles and hostility]. The Brahmins tell him, "ȝe with wodnes of weris all þe werd fretis / And ȝit forfeȝtils ȝoure face, all fasting it semes" (4529–30) [with the madness of wars you devour the world and yet your face grows lean; it seems to be fasting]. As Alexander aims with increasingly maniacal frustration at godhood, he fantasizes an identity as self-sufficient, volatile, and perpetual as that of the fiery phoenix which he glimpses wistfully in the sun-god's garden. Yet with provocative ambidexterity, the poem simultaneously admires Alexander's chivalric leadership. If one recalls the ambiguous ancestry and legacy which make Alexander a model and ancestor appropriable by both European and eastern conquerors, the poem's evident relish in Alexander's imminent demise becomes spiced with a kind of vengeful fantasy. Alexander's ambition driven to these extremes is blasphemous because, as the Brahmins point out, it finally refuses to acknowledge any authority but its own self-generated one. But that very extremity makes it terribly beguiling—especially in the face of impossible odds.

And these impossible odds were precisely what the English crusaders at the end of the fourteenth century were facing. They reputedly regarded

war as their livelihood, the Turks as their enemies, and the signory of
the world as their God-given right. They might well have been fired by
Alexander's pursuit of a life of war that is perpetual, profitable, and undeterred by any entrapping sense of debt, cultural affinity, or even knowledge of himself. If, as I argue, Alexander embodies the ideology of
fourteenth-century British chivalry, his hybrid genealogy and his impossible ambitions expose the conflicts within that increasingly defensive audience. Other North West Midlands alliterative romances express a similar
interest in the quandaries of their chivalric heroes: *Sir Gawain and the Green
Knight* delights in pinching its hero between the twin imperatives of courtesy and loyalty; the alliterative *Morte Arthure* describes an Arthur whose
blend of ardent chivalry and excessive ambition echoes Alexander's own.
But rather than simply interrogating monarchical, baronial, or provincial
chivalry on its native grounds *The Wars of Alexander* displaces it to show
how it produces, desires, and fears an eastern shadow that in turn begets,
besets, and mirrors its own ambitious frustration. And in this ultimately
fatal self division, the poem pursues in extremis a chivalric ambition that at
once defines and disarticulates itself by its own historical impossibility.[63]

Similar crusading aspirations—equally desperate, fantastic, and disap-
pointed—although they increasingly failed to rouse substantial monarchical support, were by no means alien to the knighthood of Christendom,
including the English provincial gentry, the probable audience of *The Wars
of Alexander*. Their livelihood depended on war and they felt threatened by
the late century impasses of the Hundred Years War and the negotiations
for peace Richard II was pursuing in the early 1390s. In fact, the gentry and
itinerant soldiery of Cheshire and the North West Midlands—the region
from which *The Wars of Alexander* is believed to originate—were so horrified by rumors of these peace negotiations that in 1393 they led an armed
rebellion. Both Charles VI of France and Richard II of England sought to
redirect the energies of veterans disaffected with the prospect of treaty by
actively promoting crusades against the Ottoman Turks encroaching upon
Prussia and Hungary. When the Cheshire soldiery revolted, no less a per-
sonage than John of Gaunt suppressed them and, significantly, enlisted the
bulk of them into his army, first to quell his Gascon subjects, but then to
accompany him on the crusade against Nicopolis. J. J. N. Palmer describes
their fate: "Although John of Gaunt himself eventually withdrew from this
venture, there is good reason to believe that most of his Cheshire troops
marched towards the Balkans under the leadership of his illegitimate son
John Beaufort, and fought and died on the banks of the Danube."[64] Aziz
Atiya emphasizes the prominence of English knights in this campaign:

"Although no accurate estimate of their contribution to the Crusade of Nicopolis can be deduced from the sources, the fact that their forces attracted the attention of many independent chronicles in various parts of Europe proves that the English must have constituted a distinctly great and noteworthy element in the foreign contingent."[65]

And this crusade enticed cascading fantasies of perpetual victory as ambitious as Alexander's. In Froissart's account, the army was confronting not only the Turks but the rallied forces of Alexandria and Damascus, the leadership of the Khalif of Baghdad, the King of Tartary, and an army of "Sarazyns and Panyms, of Perce, of Tartary, of Arabye, and Suryens."[66] To them, this was the greatest confrontation there had ever been: the combined forces of Christian Europe facing the immeasurable hordes of the East. Victory over Bayezid's army would lead not only to the salvation of Europe but final all-vindicating victories in Syria, the Holy Land, and Jerusalem itself: "This next sommer we shall wynne the realme of Armony, and passe the brase of saynt George, and so into Surrey, and wynne the portes of Japhes and Baruth, and conquere Jherusalem, and all the Holy Lande."[67] But when the Christian armies were decimated at Nicopolis, their defeat put a humiliating cap to a century of disastrous military reverses, economic dependence upon eastern luxury goods, and, most troublingly, internal dissensions within and between European and Christian countries. To such recent developments, the traditional world-bifurcating strategy of crusade had proven a wholly inadequate response.

And in *The Wars of Alexander*, Alexander's dilemma is similarly unresolvable. The poem proposes no way for him to escape it, no sense in which he can acknowledge the deadly reflections between himself and his enemies and still remain the great world conqueror he is driven to be. In that, the history of the poem's two manuscripts have done Alexander a service. They are fragments lacking endings and therefore provide no account of his death. It is useless to speculate whether the poem was deliberately left unfinished, or whether the ending has been simply lost. The poem does, however, gesture at closure before breaking off: it ends with the list of Alexander's conquests that he inscribes upon the walls of his palace. In this, the manuscripts' history or the poem itself collaborates in the desires and aversions of its hero. The poem replaces Alexander's death with Alexander's monument, a gesture at immortality that puts a final flourish to Alexander's conquests but simultaneously redirects the reader's attention to his ambiguous and continuing legacy. Alexander's monument is, fittingly, a wall, designed both to separate and commemorate, that refuses closure by redramatizing the interminable conquests of the poem itself. It is this ambivalent, open-ended, and reverberant legacy that ties the poem so closely to the late medieval audience, the gentry of the North West Midlands. It is precisely because Alexander is in such an impossible, uncomfortable, and familiar position that his character so vividly encompasses the self-contradictions, anxieties, and fatal self-evasions of late fourteenth-century provincial chivalry.

5

Profiting from Precursors in
The Siege of Jerusalem

IN THE LAST QUARTER OF THE FOURTEENTH CENTURY a poem was written in a modest monastic establishment, Bolton Priory, in a remote and infertile area of the West Riding of Yorkshire.[1] The scope of the poem, however, is neither modest nor provincial; it essays nothing less than a foundation for Christian imperialism. The alliterative *Siege of Jerusalem* tells the tale of the conquest of Jerusalem by recently converted provincial Roman leaders who decide to launch a crusade to avenge Christ's death.[2] The siege culminates in the destruction of the temple, the subjection of the Jews, and the liquidation of their assets. Subjecting Jerusalem to the fierce pressures of siege, the poem reforges the city, the Jews, and the Orient, beating them down from religious and imperial rivals of the new Christian Roman Empire into pure, moveable wealth. It thus solves the dilemma of whether to destroy the Jews or to exploit them by doing both in one protracted campaign. And it does so with an unflinching acknowledgment of Christian violence which is perplexed by an enjoyment of the supremely fitting shapes that violence takes. The poem thus enacts the ambiguities of the Augustinian doctrines of Jewish witness and tolerance which inform its probable milieu but shadows these doctrines with later-medieval anti-Judaic narratives dramatizing harsher responses to this threatening precursor.[3] By revisiting the historical origin of Jewish dispersal with such exploitative relentlessness, the poem also explores the genealogical anxieties stemming from Christianity's supersession of its Jewish predecessor and works to transform them into imperial and economic certainties. In so doing the poem fantasizes remedies for some of the driving historical and contemporary anxieties of a late medieval Augustinian clergy during a period of economic depression: concerns about the crusades, the bullion shortage, and the continuity, unity, and identity of Christendom.[4]

Even when the poem seems most to indulge in genocidal fantasies, it stresses the desirability of continued and profitable attachments between the Christians and the Jews—that is, attachments that are profitable to the Christians. In the poem, the Christians are bound to the Jews by three needs. The first is the need to immure Jews into the past that keeps them predecessors to Christianity and not rivals. The poem literally besieges the Jews within their own walls and thus destroys at one blow both Jewish control of the Holy Land and the Jews' potential power over the newly appropiated "Christian" tradition—a power which comes from the Jews' command of their own history, religious texts, and scholarship. The second need that binds the Christians to the Jews is the need for a holy war to draw together the scattered energies of the nascent Christian/Roman Empire and cure its physical and spiritual malaise. The third is the Christian/imperial need for profit. As it constructs a relationship that increasingly enriches the Christians and desolates the Jews, the poem indulges the fantasy of a revenge that for the Christian Romans is socially productive in every sense: morally justified, militarily successful, both spiritually and physically salutary, and extremely lucrative. Most significant of all, the Christians gain a communal identity. By defining, confining, and liquidating the Jewish enemy, these newly converted provincial Romans are able to heal their bodily and body-political maladies and consolidate their own disparate forces into a powerful and unified Christian empire.

Theologizing Supersession: The Augustinian Doctrines of Jewish Witness and Tolerance

As it recounts the ferocious battles between the Christians and the Jews, the poem dramatizes a confrontation with a threatening past whose ambiguous legacy required particularly attentive supervision for medieval Christian writers. The Jews are the revered first recipients of God's election; they presage Christian identity, power, and prophetic authority, but then linger to call them into question. The poem's battles, like those of other alliterative romances, become at once generational and fraternal. The poem performs a preemptive strike on Jewish sovereignty at the moment it threatens to secede from Rome and become a self-perpetuating rival empire to Christendom; it works to abort that sovereignty and place it firmly into a dead past from which it can be rendered for Christian use. The poem's Christendom needs the generational relationship to justify its own sovereignty, needs to show that the Roman Christians are the true heirs of Christ and the Judaism that he crowns. Jews give birth to Christianity even as they kill Christ; the poem imbues their continued existence with the threat of this mortal act of paternity. But the poem also expresses a kind of separation anxiety; the gradual first-century-long detachment of

Christianity from Judaism left scars and uncertainties that perplexed the most influential New Testament writers from Paul to the John of Revelations and cast a long shadow into the writings of patristic and medieval theologians. In the poem these anxieties of relationship climax in the war over the city that centers, marks, and becomes the site for cutting the ligature of Judeo-Christian religious consanguinity, Jerusalem the *umbilicus terrae*, the navel of the earth.[5]

Paul's argumentative intricacies in the letters to the Corinthians, Hebrews, and Romans show the difficulty of marking the transition from Judaism to Christianity at its inception. How can Christianity leave Judaism when it persists within the church and within himself? He grapples with the dilemma caused by the need to preserve God's faithfulness to the Jews as his chosen people and the Jewish refusal to see Christian "truth." Paul's solution is as problematic and interesting as his own inevitable self-interrogation as the most spectacular convert from Judaism in early Christian history.

There is a hidden reason for all this, brothers, of which I do not want you to be ignorant, in case you think you know more than you do. One section of Israel has become blind, but this will last only until the whole pagan world has entered, and then after that the rest of Israel will be saved as well. As scripture says: The liberator will come from Zion, he will banish godlessness from Jacob. And this is the covenant I will make with them when I take their sins away . . . Just as you changed from being disobedient to God, and now enjoy mercy because of their disobedience, so those who are disobedient now—and only because of the mercy shown to you—will also enjoy mercy eventually. God has imprisoned all men in their own disobedience only to show mercy to all mankind. (Romans 11:25–32)[6]

Paul still thinks of himself as part of an Israel of which only a section (all practicing Jewish non-Christians) has been blinded. The non-Jewish Christians are not off the hook, either—they must not persecute the Jews out of hand but see them as part of God's plan for giving mercy to all the disobedient (which only recently included the converted pagan Christians). But in the meantime, this passage makes Jewish disobedience crucial for the spread of Christian salvation—a strategy that presages Augustine's doctrine of Jewish witness (and guarded tolerance) as well as the Augustinian tradition of Jewish utility (and exploitation) that so informs *The Siege of Jerusalem*.

This troubled relationship was aggravated and institutionalized with the codification of the Christian canonical Bible, which swallowed whole the Hebrew scriptures. The relationship between Jewish and Christian truth, Old Law and New, therefore bifurcates the canonical Bible itself and

leads to a perpetual digestion process—the continual generation of interpretive hermeneutics to relate, oppose, mine, and determine the usefulness
of one to the other. Jeremy Cohen stresses how disjunct these hermeneutics could be; his discussion of one of the most influential figures,
Augustine, highlights his constant revision of his conclusions both about
Old Testament interpretation and the historic role of the Jews so inextricably associated with it. In the early *De doctrina christiana* Augustine denigrates the stifling carnality of Jewish literal understanding of their law as
opposed to the liberating figurality of Christian exegesis. However, in the
later *Contra Faustum* and *De civitate Dei*, Augustine extolls the antiquity
and continued faithfulness of Jewish belief as incarnating the historical
authority of Old Testament scripture.[7] Augustine's perplexed attitude
toward the Jews does not always logically accord with his other conclusions, gesturing both at the complexity of the problem and at the continuing centrality of the Jews and Jewish scriptures to Christian self-definition
and proselytizing. In one particularly revealing passage, Augustine makes
the contemporary dispersal, subjugation, and enslavement of the Jews an
exhibit in the case of Christian truth. This providential incursion strikingly
departs from the deep-seated doubt in *De civitate Dei* that God's will
ever manifests itself clearly in the turbulent saeculum of contemporary
history in the last age of the world. Book 18, Chapter 46, of *De civitate
Dei* shows how Jews have always been and will continue to be intimately
bound to God's will—in both their faith (or blindness) and their subjugation. The doctrine of Jewish witness makes the Jews God's uniquely
visible thumbprint on a history through which he otherwise moves in mysterious ways:

But the Jews who killed [Christ] and refused to believe in him . . . were dispersed
all over the world—for indeed there is no part of the earth where they are not to
be found—and thus by the evidence of their own Scriptures they bear witness for
us that we have not fabricated the prophecies about Christ . . . It follows that when
the Jews do not believe in our Scriptures, their own Scriptures are fulfilled in them,
while they read them with blind eyes . . . As for us, we find those prophecies sufficient which are produced from the books of our opponents; for we recognize that
it is in order to give this testimony, which, in spite of themselves, they supply for
our benefit by their possession and preservation of those books, that they themselves are dispersed among all nations, in whatever direction the Christian Church
spreads . . . *Thus it was not enough for the psalmist to say, 'Do not slay them, lest at some
time they forget your Law,' without adding, 'Scatter them.' For if they lived with that testimony of the Scriptures only in their own land, and not everywhere, the obvious result
would be that the Church, which is everywhere, would not have them available among all
nations as witnesses to the prophecies which were given beforehand concerning Christ.*
(emphasis added)[8]

This passage makes the existence of Jews (faithfully adhering to their scriptures but subjugated to and dispersed within Christian sovereignties) a kind of thoughtful bequest to Christians from a providential God, an irony that *The Siege of Jerusalem* rethinks and violently materializes. Prophetic Jewish scripture (truly legible only to Christians) is inextricably welded to the oblivious Jews who paradoxically possess, preserve, and must scatter to bear witness to these scriptures. The Jews themselves become historic/prophetic books for Christians, readable by others, reified and blind in themselves, their faith concretized into both sign and referent of their own unknowing subjection to Christian utility. Cohen shows how medieval writers elaborated Augustine's doctrine of witness to draw the Jews even closer to Christian self-definition:

The Jew testifies to the law revealed by God [in the Old Testament]; he preserves the books that contain this law; but, even more important, he lives the law in his everyday life. At first sight, this may appear astounding: Medieval Christianity related to the Jew certain that his Judaism, his Jewish life, constituted a text of the revealed word of God. Put more bluntly, the word of God was incarnate in the Jew![9]

The Jews here become antitypes but also doubles of Christ—both incarnate God's word as Old Law and New. The grounds for reverence are as irrefutable as those for rejection.[10] By making Jews "living letters" of their own/Christian scriptures (the phrase is from Bernard of Clairvaux), medieval theologians alert to Augustinian traditions create a textualized Jewish body internal to, but also subject to and separate from the body of Christian believers. It has dead-alive/ancient-contemporary status of the other alliterative temporal disjunctions we have explored in this book: dead letter and living witness, historic acuity and present blindness, ancient reverence and contemporary revulsion. In this medieval figuration, Jews become Christian ancestors usefully frozen in time and continually on parade. "Slay them not" adjures the psalm that underwrote the doctrine of tolerance. Their centrality depends upon the medieval Christian belief that they remain admirably and immutably faithful to their own religions. Forced conversions were therefore influentially legislated against by Gregory the Great throughout his reign as well as Isidore of Seville during the Fourth Council of Toledo (with certain exceptions—Jews already forcibly baptized under the edicts of Sisebut were forbidden to recant).[11]

Yet even the more "tolerant" discourses often nurtured the potential energy of violent retribution that is *The Siege of Jerusalem*'s most vital impulse. The poem repeatedly insists on the perfidy of the Jews in killing Christ, a theme in most of the theological writings about Jews (from Paul forward) but also, and much closer to this poem, in the chronicle of William of Newburgh, thirteenth-century Augustinian chronicler. His account of the massacre at York both admits Christian acquisitiveness and condemns Jewish error. Elisa Narin Van Court rightly notes the undercurrent of sympathy for the Jews that troubles the anti-Judaism of William of Newburgh's surprisingly even-handed narrative.[12] But the anti-Judaism is not just a reflex: William energizes his pious condemnation with a resentful sense of Christian social victimization that wakes nervous echoes in a reader of the *Siege*-poet:

> the Jews in England under Henry II were by an absurd arrangement happy and renowned far more than the Christians, and swelling very impudently against Christ, owing to their great good fortune did much injury to the Christians, wherefore in the days of the new King the lives which they possessed by Christ's clemency were put in danger by his just judgment, though by the beautiful arrangement of his justice those have no excuse who brought slaughter on them by a secret rising.[13]

William here follows Augustine's *De civitate Dei* by suffusing accidental with providential history. But he also adumbrates the *Siege*-poet when he turns a recognition of Jewish social and financial power into a condemnation of their arrogant rebellion against Christ, threatens the end of Christ's clemency, and, most of all, aesthetically relishes the retributive elegance of Christ in using one group of sinners to slaughter another. And, both for William and for the *Siege*-poet, vengeance corrects the "great good fortune" of the Jews as they emerge from their providentially ordained states of subjection to claim a Christian-injuring social power. This amounts to a rebellion against their role in Augustinian providential history and it strikes against the foundations of Christian identity by threatening to reverse Christian supersession.[14] Therefore it must be forcibly quelled: in William of Newburgh by the "just judgment" of the new king; in the *Siege* by their fellow rebels against Roman rule, the provincial captains.

Killing the Future: Creating the Past

In one of the poem's most revealing moments, the *Siege*-poet recounts the tale of Mary, "a myld wyf" (1077) and an obvious antitype of Christ's mother. Caught within Jerusalem as Titus is starving out the inhabitants, she is driven by hunger to eat her own child:

> Hir owen barn þat зo bar, зo brad on þe gledis,
> Rostyþ rigge and rib with rewful wordes,
> Sayþ "Sone, vpon eche side our sorow is a-lofte,

Batail a-boute þe borwe, our bodies to quelle,
Withyn hunger so hote, þat neȝ our herte brestyþ;
Þerfor ȝeld þat I þe ȝaf and aȝen tourne,
And entr' þer þou cam out!" and etyþ a schoulder. (1078–84)

[Her own child that she had borne, she cooked on the coals, roasted its back and
its ribs with lamentable words. She said, "Son, our troubles are coming from
all sides: a battle outside the city to slay our bodies, and inside the city is hunger
so fierce that it almost bursts our hearts. Therefore, give back to me the life that
I gave you! Turn about and enter the body you came out from!" And she ate a
shoulder.][15]

In this extraordinary passage, Mary the nurturer of Christ becomes Mary
the devourer, enacting a cannibalistic Eucharist of death rather than salvation. This scene substantiates incarnation into meat, Eucharist into flesh;
it reverses Christian transubstantiation into cannibalism with vicious precision; at the same time it performs a non-Christian's view of Christian
Eucharist.[16] The exactitude of this reversal at once enacts and destroys the
generational relationships between the faiths. And it is not the only place
where the poem targets Jewish mothers in bizarrely flamboyant ways; during the siege one of the catapult stones strikes a pregnant woman knocking the baby out of her womb and two miles away over the walls of the
city. In both instances the Christian siege exerts extraordinary internal and
external pressures at once on Jewish city and bodies. It targets the generative capacities of the Jews because those capacities reflect the most intimate
and intractable site of Jewish vitality: the wombs that bring them forth,
the bodies which continue to engender their faith in the present. In these
scenes the poem takes spectacular measures to force Jews to destroy their
own capacity to generate a future. It forces them to "turn again" back into
the Christian past where supersessional logic demands they should stay.

What happened to the Augustinian doctrines of witness and of tolerance? Why does this poem make Jews witnesses to Christian truth in this
new way—not because they survive within Christendom's body as living
letters of the law but because they are compressed so relentlessly that they
are shaped into negative impressions of the faith that is crushing them?
The poem here reflects the gathering darkness of specifically late medieval
anti-Judaisms and pushes to a spectacular conclusion the family drama they
play out. Historically, late medieval anti-Judaism reflects upheavals within
Christendom and the church, the crusades, and the increasing interest in
and familiarity with Arabic and Hebrew scholarship entering Christendom
through such contact zones as Norman Sicily (especially under Frederick
II) and gradually reconquered al-Andalus. Most notable of the changes

within the church was the thirteenth-century ascendency of the Dominican and Franciscan fraternal orders with active outreach programs—translations, missions, and inquisitions.[17] Cohen describes the multitude of ways in which this evangelical emphasis intensified intolerance.[18] In addition, a number of particular judicial and political legislations specifically directed against Jews had been gradually put into play all over Europe, a process that defined them as enemies, forced them into stigmatized but necessary social occupations (like the credit economy) and then more and more systematically worked to destroy their power in society. The general evolution of these mechanisms has been traced by R. I. Moore, who describes their cumulative effect as a fundamental transformation of medieval European society into a persecuting society.[19] Cohen argues also that the twelfth-century Christian "discovery" of the "Talmudic Jew" led to changes in the trajectory of anti-Judaic writing.[20] As Christian writers realized how central were ongoing rabbinical learning and debate to the religious identities and practices of Jewish communities, the "usefulness" of Jews became compromised. Jews were not fixed and living letters of the law but historically adaptive subjects.

This recognition that Judaism was not only persisting—it was growing, changing, and regenerating itself—shadows late medieval anti-Judaic mythologies of all kinds, both ecclesiastical and popular. They become less ambivalent, less recuperative, more violent. Miri Rubin traces this later medieval escalation of hostilities in didactic narratives that centralized ecclesiastical power and its regulation—in particular the spreading stories of Jewish child abuse and desecrations of the Eucharistic host.[21] Most salient to my generational argument is the family dynamic that structures many of the most violent narratives. These tales obsessively tell about the Jewish abuse and Christian recuperation of connections between fathers, mothers, and children. A case in point is the widespread and much elaborated tale of a Jewish child who is led by his Christian friends into taking communion in a church adorned by a statue of Mary. When the child's father discovers this, he thrusts the child into a blazing oven despite the desperate protests of his mother. Christian neighbors hear her screams and pleas, rush in, and open the oven to find the unharmed child marveling at the beautiful and merciful lady, Mary, who had protected him from the flames. The mother and child convert to Christianity and the father is shoved into the oven in his turn and baked. Rubin concludes, "A family romance seems to have emerged from the tale: the Jewish Boy acquires a new parentage, an engulfing mother [the oven as womb/Mary] acting as a conduit to a new father, Christ."[22]

But versions of this adoptive drama alter between earlier and later periods; its earlier dramatization of Marian mercy shifts to a late medieval Eucharistic piety delighting in tragedies of slaughtered children and Christian vengeance. As the *Siege* strikingly figures it, Mary the generatrix becomes Mary the devourer. *The Prioress's Tale* is another famous instance. Rubin shows how such narratives increasingly work up Jews as murderous patriarchs who threaten innocent Christian children (individually and in the image of the Christ-child of the host) and who come to merit slaughter in their turn. Rubin shows how these narratives intensify the ambivalences of a legacy both problematized and energized by the echoes of an originary violence Christians cannot quite escape:

The [anti-Judaic] narrative coexisted and collided with desires for the separation and excision of Jews from central European urban communities. But even when Jews were made to leave and when their quarters were burnt, their property redistributed and their streets renamed, the memory of violence in townscape, in pious offerings, in moving images, in laments heard in home and synagogue could facilitate their return and realize their presence.[23]

Rubin's description emphasizes both the danger and the intimacy of the Jewish other to the Christian body; Jews are violently excised from the body of Christendom only to return in the memory of pain. The cruel fathers who threaten the innocent children are themselves destroyed—Rubin carefully outlines the historic murders, pogroms, and seizures such narratives helped incite and justify—but not simply through the automatic reflexes of an increasingly intolerant society. Instead Rubin usefully emphasizes situated moments of choice that spark both perceptible resistance (from Christians as well as Jews) and ambiguous responses that have to be carefully and incessantly nurtured to institutional ends. The double consciousness she finds in the performance of late medieval anti-Judaism—destruction and pity, the glorified reenactment of violence and its memorial lamentation—is the knife edge on which *The Siege of Jerusalem* painfully balances in its own exploration of the intimate viciousness within its troubled genealogy.

Affective Piety to Muscular Christianity

The poem begins by redefining Christianity, appropriating it for imperial chivalry and wedding it to war. In the process, Christianity literally changes hands, from the disparate, sorrowing, devoted hands of its private practitioners, Nathan, Veronica, and the still unrecognized pope, Peter, to the

restless, resistless, relentless hands of the provincial Roman military leaders, Titus and Vespasian. The poem thus enacts the scriptural dictum that
Christ comes not to bring peace but a sword; its first passage suspends
Christ's sword, Damocles-like, over the heads of the Jews, and the rest of
the poem is measured out by its reiterated blows:

> For al þe harme þat he hadde hasted he noȝt,
> On hem þe vyleny to venge, þat his veynys brosten,
> Bot ay taried ouer þe tyme, ȝif þey tourne wolde,
> ȝaf hem space þat hym spilide, þey hit spedde lyte,
> XL wynter, as y fynde, and no fewer ȝyrys,
> Or princes presed in hem þat hym to pyne wroȝt. (19–24)

[Despite all the injury he had undergone, Christ did not hurry to avenge the vil-
lainy on those that had torn his veins, but he waited to see if they would be converted over time, gave a little time to those that had killed him, but they did not
avail themselves of it; forty winters, I find, and no fewer years passed, before
princes assailed those that tortured Christ.]

This forty-year grace period places a severely limited Christian mercy in a
context of impending vengeance. The poem's next passages pump up this
muscular Christianity even further, translating it from private to public
domains, from provincial to international fronts, and from martyred endurance to vital fury. This happens in a flurry of salutary conversions:
the miraculous cures of a pair of Roman provincial kings, Titus, king of
Bordeaux, and his father, Vespasian, king of Galatia. Titus, afflicted by
a cancerous lip, is converted by Nathan, a merchant emissary sent from
Jerusalem to bring news of the Jewish refusal to pay their tribute to Rome.
Nathan describes Christ's death and tells Titus of the Vernacle. Titus is
infuriated by the tale of Christ's death, is immediately healed—as much by
his anger, it seems, as by divine intervention—and prays to Christ to allow
him to avenge his death. He and Nathan set out for Rome to pass the news
of the Vernacle to his sick father, Vespasian, etymologically beset by wasps
in his nose. Vespasian searches out the clandestine pope, Peter, and sends
for both Veronica and her veil to come to Rome.

　　The transfer of the Vernacle unmistakably signals the poem's selection of a military trajectory for its performance of Christianity. It briefly
articulates other Christianities—notably, feminine affective piety—in order
to close them off. The veil begins as a private love token from Christ to
Veronica: "For loue he left hit hir til hir lyues ende" (164) [For love he left
it to her while her life should last]. Casting herself at the pope's feet she
commits both it and herself into his hands: "Of þis kerchef and my cors þe
kepyng y þe take" (220) [I put both this veil and my self (literally "my

body") into your keeping]. Veronica's faith and submission passively attach her to her own veil, bandied as easily about. Yet when both she and the veil are passed along into the stewardship of Peter and Titus, the veil changes from a token of private remembrance to one of publically displayed power that is simultaneously destructive and curative. When it is brought into the Roman temple,

> a ferly byfelle forþ myd hem alle:
> In her temple bytidde tenful þynges,
> Þe mahound and þe mametes, to-mortled to peces
> And al to-crased, as þe cloþe þroȝ þe kirke passed. (233–36)

[A marvel happened before all the company, and dreadful things happened in the temple. As the cloth passed through the church, all the pagan idols crumbled to pieces and were crushed.]

The veil's power here gets a vengeful public expression which soon will expand to imperial magnitudes. Immediately after wreaking havoc on the Roman gods, the veil's itinerary continues to the palace where it acquires all the trappings of beatitude; it emits a marvelous light and a sweet savor, and Vespasian is publically cured by it. He immediately begins preparations for the invasion of Judaea. The poem lingers at this point to address the doomed Jews in Jerusalem, reveling in the forecast of destruction to come:

> Suree, Cesaris londe, þou may seken euer,
> Ful mychel wo m[o]n be wroȝte in þy [w]lonk tounes,
> Cytees vnder S[yon], now is ȝour sorow uppe:
> Þe deþ of þe derewortþ Crist der schal be ȝolden.
> Now is, Bethleem, þy bost y-broȝt to an ende. (293–97)

[Syria, Caesar's province, you will sigh forever over your fate. Much woe will be wrought in your proud towns. Cities under Zion, your sorrow is just beginning. The death of the noble Christ will be very dearly bought. Now Bethlehem, your boasting is brought to an end!]

From the outset, then, Christian initiative is directed away from remembrance, affective piety, and submission, and toward military prowess. The poem weds Christian belief to Christian violence, taking it from the hands of women and obscure prelates and entrusting it to the vengeful provincial captains. This incident, in addition to the account of Titus's cure by anger, shows the poem's interest in constructing a masculinized Christianity that inspires its proponents with a purgatory anger. When Vespasian follows his cure by immediately instigating a campaign against the Jews, he has, in fact, taken on the role and power of the veil that cured him and is duplicating its iconoclastic itinerary. By destroying the provincial Jews in the east, he will gain the power to consolidate, heal, and renew the splintering Roman Empire as an energized Christian one.

To accomplish this transformation, the poem uses strategies of destructive inversion. Because the Jews threaten to withhold their tribute to Rome, their very bodies are converted into tribute; because Judas betrayed Christ for thirty pennies, the Jews are sold into slavery, thirty for a penny. As the poem progresses, the Jewish culture is isolated, encompassed, and the paradigms historically constructed for it are turned against it. The representations that signify cultural unity to Jerusalem are coopted and rewritten to signify those cultures' disintegration. By working such inversions upon its victims, the poem accomplishes its revenges in a particularly vicious and elegant manner. One instance occurs on the first day of the battle against Jerusalem when the Jewish armies meet the three Roman battalions under Titus and Vespasian in open battle before the city. Before the battle begins, Caiaphas, the Jewish high priest, inspires his troops by recounting the founding moment of Jewish independence: the parting of the Red Sea by Moses and the drowning of all Pharoah's soldiers—the moment when the enslaved Jewish kingdom finally broke with their overlords to establish a culture and freely practiced religion of their own.[24] Yet the battle's outcome wrenches this story around to signify Jewish defeat as the Jews are utterly crushed with incalculable slaughter. When the sun sets that day:

> So was þe bent ouer-brad blody by-runne,
> With ded bodies aboute, all the brode vale.
> Myȝt no stede doun stap bot on stele wede,
> Or on burne, oþer on beste, or on bryȝt scheldes. (599–603)

[The field was so overflowing with blood, and with dead bodies strewn all about the broad valley, that no horse could take a single step without tripping on steel armor, or on man or beast or on bright shields.]

Moses' victory over Pharoah has been claimed by the Christians and inverted. The next day, the Romans plunder the bodies and glean enormous riches. Then they pile the bodies into heaps and make "wide weyes" (642) through them. This parting of the piles of bodies on the land reads Jewish body into Jewish territory and resonates with the poem's larger alienating agendas—its need to bisect the Judeo-Christian body/territory with its intricate genealogies, obligations, likenesses, and anxious assimilations through a military incision that will once and for all define their relationship in a way that keeps the Christians on top and in control. And it is a typological vivisection as well. Although the poem refrains from underlining the link between Caiaphas's lesson and the battle's outcome, the message is clear. The Red Sea has been parted anew—as a sea of Jewish flesh.

The cruel irony of such inversions seems to delight the poet; he indulges in them repeatedly, and whenever there is the possibility of incorporating one from a source, he uses and expands upon it. These scenes deflect religious retribution into a destructive economy of bodies. They gruesomely concretize the traditional letter/spirit hierarchy as a description of the relationship between Jews and Christians but make it explicitly an exercise of forceful Christian agency. Christians consolidate a newly energized and invulnerable spirituality by violently reducing Jews to passive and vulnerable bodies. The text recounts tortures of the Jews that (1) take the skin from the body; (2) force the blood from inside to outside (all the Jews); (3) force the body to consume its own flesh and blood (Mary and the Jews in the city whose water is flavored by the ashes of their burnt dead and whose air is tainted by the corpses piled in their streets); and (4) spill internal organs into the light of day (the Jewish man whose brains are hurled a mile from his head, and the Jewish woman whose unborn child is knocked out of her body and over the city walls by a catapult stone). Caiaphas's death is a tour de force: he is flayed alive, drawn with horse on the field, and then hanged on a high gallows feet upmost, with honey anointed on the "hydeles" (698) [skinless] parts, or worse, as manuscript A figures it, "hiddlills" [secret parts, crevices], with four sharp-clawed dogs and cats attached to his thighs, and two apes attached to his arms "to rend the raw flesh into red pieces" (702).[25] Ralph Hanna felicitously describes the *Siege* as the "chocolate covered tarantula of the alliterative movement."[26] I tend to see more tarantula than chocolate but that doesn't impair the metaphor. In fact many of the poem's critics note with varying degrees of repulsion the inventiveness of the poem's inseparably brilliant and gruesome imaginary. Even in a genre where battle eviscerations are more or less de rigueur, *The Siege of Jerusalem* has the dubious distinction of being the most inventively vicious poem of the alliterative revival.

Why does the poem move Christianity from the self-abnegating performances of Veronica's affective piety to the agonistic and agonizing self-productions of Titus's and Vespasian's war? And why are the Jews such desirable targets when they had been expelled from England in 1291? I believe this transformation is driven by the late medieval status of the Holy Land as an origin more and more irrevocably lost to Christian sovereignty. Like the medieval theological Jew, the Holy Land had become a textual construction haunted by bodies and topographies that it must work to reform and control. The Holy Land is where Christian history can be literally traced out in a pilgrim's own body. In the narrative of pilgrims like the fourth-century Egeria's, pilgrims enter a zone of material, textual, historical, and prophetic significance, reading, treading, and being transformed by a topographical text. With the proper meditative technology pilgrims could evoke the sacred past as they retraced the footsteps of Christ and his disciples.[27] Even as late as the early fifteenth century, this literal *imitatio Christi* made sacred history immediate, so that Margery Kempe, with her unerring grasp of the most dramatic visionary gesture, approaches Jerusalem like Christ on Palm Sunday, riding an ass and praying for anagogical revelation:

And when this creature saw Jerusalem ... she thanked God with all her heart, praying him for his mercy that, just as he had brought her to see this earthly city of Jerusalem, he would grant her grace to see the blissful city of Jerusalem above, the city of heaven.[28]

And these Christian performances rely on the dispersal of the Jews from the landscape which witnesses the Christian supersession of their ancient mastery. It is crucial that pilgrims trace their affective typologies on a landscape that the Jews no longer had the power significantly to mark or historically change.

However, by the late fourteenth century, neither did the Christians. Muslim control of the Holy Land (as well as Islamic incorporation of both Hebrew and Christian scriptures in the Koran) subjected Christendom to an all too familiar supersessional dialectic. The tenacious popularity of crusading after the beginning of the twelfth century bespeaks the need to reverse this apparently perverse turn of history. How could God have providentially sealed the Christian triumph over Judaism only to subject the Christians to such dispossession in their turn? Some writers took refuge in apocalypticism, foreseeing the end of Saracen rule as included within the divine plan for the end of the world. But the Christian supersession of the Jews still haunts their strategies for containing the Muslim threat. Roger Bacon, fascinatingly, searches Islamic scientific writing for prophecies of Islamic destruction just as the Hebrew Bible had been appropriated to signify the downfall of the Jews.

For according to what Albumazer says in the eighth chapter of the second book [the *Liber conjunctionum* of Abu Mashr, ninth-century Muslim astrologer], the law of Mohammed cannot last longer than six hundred and ninety-three years ... It is now the six hundred and sixty-fifth year of the Arabs from the time of Mohammed, and therefore it will soon be destroyed by God's grace—something which ought to be a great consolation to Christians.[29]

Other Christian writers drew consoling analogies between Jew and Muslim, imaginatively associating them in order to defuse the threat of Islam by delimiting its sovereignty.[30] William of Tripoli's *Treatise on the Conditions of the Saracens* is a case in point:

> The Saracen religion arose through the sword of Mohammed and will fall through the sword which will be God's, that is to say, it began through the sword and through the sword will end . . . The Jews had their time and state and fell, and so also the state and realm of the Saracens will fall; but the belief and state of the Christians will endure until Christ again descends from heaven where he now lives, makes all things straight and level, and slays the Antichrist.[31]

William of Tripoli here imagines a world gone terribly awry, poised for an apocalyptic rectification too long in abeyance. Its consoling analogies are imbued by the desperation of its need for God's providence finally to become visible in the welter of the saeculum, and for Christ himself violently to vindicate his state. This desperation has far flung effects. *The Siege of Jerusalem* shows how the Muslim supersession of Christianity darkens medieval Christianity's views of its own Jewish forefather. The poem reflects the troubled consciousness of an Augustinian Christianity caught in its own supersessional dialectic and, unable to dislodge its successor from the Holy Land, taking "great consolation" in turning its frustration against a more vulnerable precursor.

And when the poem translates religious piety into such immediate vengeance, it imagines a consummation devoutly to be wished for its late fourteenth-century English provincial audience. If the poem dramatizes a crusading impulse, as Mary Hamel argues, it is doing so in an era when royal subsidies of crusade were dwindling.[32] This is not to say that crusading was irrelevant to fourteenth-century English society; quite the contrary. The early part of the century has been called the "real age of propaganda for the Crusade," signaling a widespread conviction that crusade was politically and ideologically necessary, despite the increasingly incontrovertible recognition that it had become economically and militarily disastrous.[33] This dilemma was intensified by three historic developments which necessitated redefinition of relations between European interests and the countries of the east: the loss of the last Crusader stronghold at Acre in 1291, the ascendancy of the Mamluk sultanate in Egypt and Syria and its throttling of access to eastern trade routes, and most threateningly of all, the late-century incursions of Ottoman armies into eastern Europe.[34] In response to these developments throughout the century, crusade propagandists such as Thaddeo of Naples, Pierre Dubois of France, Marino Sanudo, Pierre de Lusignan of Cyprus, Philippe de Mézières, and Manuel II Paleologus of

Byzantium traversed Europe, presenting treatises to kings and pontiffs, arguing for the urgency of the eastern threat and the need for military unity among European monarchs. Many attempted to negotiate peace between warring kings to that end, proposing strategic military alliances with the Tartars, with Byzantium, with the Genoese and Venetian communes, and generating a crusade literature "bewildering in its dimensions."[35]

However, throughout most of the century English monarchs were reluctant to commit themselves or their resources to crusade. They prudently displayed their general approval of it, allowed their subjects to finance it privately, and even engaged in negotiations for it where it suited their purposes—for example, when early in the century such activities gave them access to church monies dedicated to crusade.[36] Edward III was the first king since Stephen not to declare himself a *crucesignatus*, initiating instead more profitable wars against Scotland and then France.[37] Edward III's support for the crusade remained impersonal, despite the hopeful treatise offered to him by crusade propagandist Roger of Stanegrave in the first decade of his reign. He left it to his subjects' private initiative to launch their own campaigns which they did with great enthusiasm but often indifferent success.[38] Richard II also professed great interest in crusade in the 1390s but his support seems to have been motivated more by the need to exalt his image as a monarch than by the need to devote actual monies or militia to the effort.[39] Despite the lack of royal participation, the English nobility never lost interest in crusade although no ventures were launched directly against the Holy Land, and very few yielded any military, moral, or financial benefits. Atiya points out how "the fourteenth-century Crusaders appear to have pursued their quests by devious ways" (92), attacking other important targets as a prelude to seizing the Holy Land, which receded farther and farther as a possibility the longer the century progressed. [40] All of these crusades were ephemeral or calamitous, leading to no sustained followup and often crippling European military and economic interests even further.

The English clergy, also, were greatly invested in crusade; they contributed incessantly at every ecclesiastical level to papal collectors for crusade.[41] But it was very difficult to organize a united crusade that enlisted a wide base of monarchical, aristocratic, clerical, and popular political interests. Here, the late century propagandizing of Phillippe de Mézières is particularly enlightening. His massive 1389 treatise *Le Songe du Vieil Pèlerin* decries the English for continuing the Hundred Years War rather than uniting with their Christian brethren and engaging their military energies for a more worthy cause. His 1395 *Epistre* to Richard II more amiably urges the French and the English to settle their differences as a preparation for a new crusade uniting the chivalry of Christendom into a new military order which would forge the military and religious strengths of its proponents into "une nouvelle génération de combattants qui possédera ces quatre vertus morales" [a new generation of fighters who possess the four moral virtues].[42] Once this unification was achieved, the Christian sovereigns of Europe could be certain

que par la divine bonté et naturelle débonnaireté du souverain chevetaine de l'ost de la crestienté, leurs morteles plaies seront sanée; la gloire de la foy horriblement blecie, et les royalles magestés du glaive des Turs enemies de la foy férues et deshonnourées: seront relevés et en Dieu essaucies et très-honnourées: laquelle chose Dieu nous veuille ottroier![43]

[that by the divine mercy and the natural nobility of the high sovereign of the hosts of Christianity, their mortal wounds will be cured; the glory of the faith so horribly wounded and the kingly powers struck down and destroyed by the lances of the Turks, enemies of the faith, will be restored and in God exalted and honored greatly: an outcome with which God desires to bless us!]

This passage resonates with urgencies similar to those driving *The Siege of Jerusalem*, which also connects the language of righteous vengeance with that of miraculous cure. But even more similar is its almost frantically hyperbolic tone, the certainty that divine support is only waiting (impatiently) for a divided chivalry to consolidate itself in a Christian cause. Its extremism answers the felt gravity of the situation: the disorder and disease begotten among the chivalry, monarchy, and clergy of Christendom by a century of crusading failure. When *The Siege of Jerusalem* opens by instantly and effortlessly welding its imperial, chivalric, and religious interests into one militant Christan force, it responds to a widespread misgiving that the divergences between European national, chivalric, and religious interests would bring about the disintegration of Christendom beneath the all too united onslaughts of its eastern neighbors.

From Rival Heir to Precious Heritage

The poem does not only respond to the pressures of Muslim supersession; it actually briefly suffuses Jews at the start of the campaign with a chivalric and oriental vigor that recalls the representation of Saracens in the crusade romances. At its beginning, it toys with the mirage that the Jews will be worthy chivalric enemies, rivaling the strength and ambition of the Roman armies themselves. On the first day of the battle, the arrayed armies seem

well matched, two strong provincial states equally interested in divesting
themselves of the tyranny at Rome. The very battle devices of the two
armies mirror one another in their richness and ferocity. Both sides speak
a mutually comprehensible heraldic language. The Romans erect a belfry as
a battle standard, bristling with weapons. On top of the belfry, they set a
dragon:

> Wyde gapande, of gold, gomes to swelwe,
> With arwes armed in þe mouþe, and also he hadde
> A fauch[ou]n vnder his feet, with four kene bladdys,
> Þer of þe poyntes wer piȝt in partyis four
> Of þis wlonfulle wor[l]de þer þei werr fondyn. [390–94]

[With wide gaping jaws of gold, ready to gulp men down, armed with arrows in
its mouth, and it also had a sword under its feet with four keen blades, of which
the points pierced the four corners of this proud world where they were set.]

This dragon/tower/belfry is a multipurpose device, displaying the Roman
general's wealth, ambition, and ferocity, providing a landmark and rallying
point where Roman soldiers who are weaponless or confused can go to get
aid, and looming over the city so that Vespasian can spy out enemy musters
and movements. The Jewish battle towers do exactly the same thing, with
one added advantage—mobility:

> Fyf and twenti olyfauntes, defensable bestes,
> With brode castels on bak . . .
> And on eche olyfaunte armed men manye. (445–47)

[Twenty five elephants, animals able to fight, with broad castles on their backs . . .
and on each elephant many armed men.]

One elephant carries a whole castle containing a richly adorned tabernacle
within. The two armies speak the same battle language; both blend prac-
ticality with self-advertisement. There are some differences—the Roman
dragon with its world-piercing swords bespeaks the Christian Romans'
imperial ambitions, while the Jewish tabernacle stakes a more religious
claim to sovereignty. Real elephants are also more fascinating and exotic
than modeled dragons. But just as interesting is the essential reflexivity
between the two armies. Where the Romans place a fabulous "defensable
beste" (445) on top of a weapon-bristling tower, the Jews place weapon-
bristling towers on top of fabulous defensible beasts.

The exotic strength of the untried Jewish army links them not to
the stereotypical Jew of the English cycle dramas but to the stereotypical
Saracen, the invading pagan, and the marauding Turk that haunt crusade

narratives, the thirteenth-century French Jerusalem cycles, and *chansons de gestes* such as *La Chanson de Roland*.[44] While I do not wish to suggest that the Jews of the poem are not Jews at all but merely Saracens in disguise, I would like to stress that in many influential narratives of the period, the two were persistently associated—and that association does a range of social work. Jeremy Cohen describes how the crusades themselves helped to foster it:

the anti-Jewish violence of 1096, though not a part of the official mandate of the crusaders, invariably roused many churchmen to come to grips with the problematic function of the Jew in Christian society . . . Concurrently, confrontation with the Muslim world induced many to associate Jews and Muslims, projecting the characteristics of one group onto the other and incorporating both groups into a larger genus of infidels who, by their existence and in their beliefs, challenged the supremacy of Christianity.[45]

Throughout the ensuing period, any arousal of crusader sentiment against the Saracens usually spelled trouble for the Jews as well, despite efforts to differentiate their situations by such august authorities as Pope Alexander II.[46] Every large crusade from the First to the Fourth is associated with pogroms where armed pilgrims would enliven their passage to the Holy Land by pillaging and massacring Jewish communities along the way.[47] Yet by a perverse logic this expanding European persecution and expulsion of the Jews was engendering the very association between Jew and Arab that it feared. Increasingly the Jews were expelled eastward at the same time that the Muslim emirates from Turkey to Cairo were pushing westward. Jewish colonies had settled in central and eastern Europe because many of the countries of western Europe—including France and England—had already expelled them. Often throughout the period the Jews chose to live under Muslim rule rather than in Christian countries, because Muslims generally tolerated the practice of their religion.

The specter of collaboration between Muslim and Jew surfaces also in the long and well-documented history of recurrent European anxiety that the Jews of Europe were actually in league with the Muslims abroad and plotting the demise of Christendom.[48] In eleventh-century France this conviction led to the legend that Jewish traitors had fatally betrayed Toulouse to the Islamic armies a century before (a legend that involved a certain stubborn rewriting of history, because Toulouse, in fact, never fell to Islamic armies). This legend, however erroneous, persisted and led to the inauguration of a custom designed to humiliate the Jews ceremonially each year on Easter, when a representative was ritually struck in the face before the Basilica of St. Stephen.[49]

Given this association a certain aspect of *The Siege of Jerusalem*'s focus of vengeance becomes clearer—its obsession not only with Jewish bodies but also with Jewish gold. This feature strikingly tempers anti-Judaic mythology with crusader fantasy. Jews from the ninth century on had been associated with trade in small, value-intensive commodities; for centuries the Radanite corporations trafficked in gold, jewels, pearls, silks, and rugs.[50] By the late fourteenth century, Europe, including England, had come to depend upon the luxury items traded from markets of India, Persia, Ceylon—the spices, artifacts, and exotic silks and fabrics in which *The Siege of Jerusalem* so delights to bedeck its armies. At the same time, the different trade routes which had previously been accessible to European merchants had narrowed to a single practical access point, and that had come under a monopoly formed by the association of the Venetian merchant mariners and the Mamluks in Egypt. The Mamluks controlled the single most profitable trade route to the rich ports of India and China at this time: the adit to the Red Sea. The Mamluks gave access privileges to the Genoese and Venetians (and, later, only to the Venetians), because these Italian communes provided them with slaves and war materials with which to buttress their unique social/military hegemony. This trade in goods and slaves persisted despite the well-reasoned attempts of such statesmen as Marino Sanudo to show its disastrous economic and military consequences for European interests. Even after his 1309 treatise "Secreta Fidelium Crucis" had convinced Pope Clement V and King Charles IV of France to adopt a complete trade embargo and a military blockade which would starve Egypt of military power and the economic resources to maintain it, the embargo failed, partly because the pope almost immediately started issuing lucrative dispensations to Venetian ships so that they could continue trading and partly because the Genoese continued to make quite a profit smuggling slaves and weapons to the Mamluks despite the papal blockade.[51] Mamluk regulation extended not only to who was allowed to trade but even the mechanisms of trading contact, often to the fury of the merchants involved.[52]

This Muslim regulation of eastern trade routes put European traders in a subsidiary position and contributed to the pressures that, I believe, give *The Siege of Jerusalem* such an obsession with the exotic wealth of Jerusalem. European merchants were forced to compete fiercely among themselves even for what little access they were offered. Especially in the early part of the century, England found itself exporting raw materials such as unprocessed wool to Continental manufacturers in Bruges while it continually imported and paid dearly for the rich dyes, spices and silks that only the Venetian (and for some time, the Genoan) merchants could provide. Heightening anxieties about trade imbalances, the drain of gold and silver bullion southward and eastward intensified after 1350.[53] This drain led to widespread "bullionism" (the word is J. L. Bolton's), the effort to strengthen a nation's economy by amassing more gold and silver bullion.[54] In England throughout the century, both kings and commons pursued legislation to control the outflow of cash from England. There is a rich record of royal ordinance and petitions to parliament including monarchical and parliamentary attempts to control the import of labor-intensive and expensive luxuries, prohibit the collection of Peter's pence (a penny for each Christian for the pope), and require the payment of such international debts in English goods only.[55] In 1363, Edward III passed sumptuary legislation to discourage the seemingly insatiable market for expensive southern and eastern textiles, and in about 1436, the jingoistic "Libelle of Englyshe Polycye," decried the parasitical greed of Italian exporters and the gullibility of the Englishmen for shipping out their good English wool in return for such frivolities.[56] All these developments bespeak a widespread English fear that unless trade regulation could be imposed and maintained both at home and abroad, "gold and silver would be sucked from the country."[57] These concerns would have been of particular interest to members of the provincial canonry at Bolton and in Yorkshire generally, where a period of relative prosperity in the earlier part of the century seems to have led to roughly a century of slowly sinking financial stagnation.[58]

But there is an even more intimate historic association of Augustinian monasticism, Jews, and gold to which the poem arguably responds when it offsets the Jews' rich oriental splendor with their vulnerability. There is extensive evidence that Jews and Augustinian canons had been partners in capitalism during the twelfth and thirteenth centuries. When landowners could not extricate themselves from their debts to wealthy Jewish moneylenders, monasteries often paid off the debts in return for the estate. This seems to have been a mutually beneficial arrangement, liberating land for the market, enabling the expansion of monastic holdings, and serving as a kind of security for the Jewish moneylender. H. G. Richardson lists examples drawn mostly from Yorkshire: "We can find a good deal of evidence for dealings by houses of these two orders [Cistercian monks and Augustinian canons]. Walthan Abbey, for example, not only profited by the transaction between Le Brun and Henry II, but is found, not very long after, engaged in dealings on its own account. Other houses of Augustinian canons to acquire land in this fashion in the thirteenth century were Holy Trinity, Aldgate, and Healaugh Park" (98–99).[59] Many prominent

Augustinian and Cistercian foundations were able to secure their financial vitality through these indirect transactions with Jews. However, the ideological ramifications were clearly disturbing to many, especially those clerical estate owners who borrowed directly from Jewish moneylenders and incurred debts that they could not pay off. The uneasy symmetry between the Christians' scriptural and financial debts to the Jews must have engendered doubt about the strength of the Christian foundational enterprise and impelled the preemptive appropriations continually exercised in both areas. According to William of Newburgh, at least one of the most violent rioters at York in 1290 was a Premonstratensian canon whose excesses William decries (apparently he immolated a bloodied host each morning before appearing in a white robe to urge the warriors to crush the enemies of Christ).[60] It seems that many of the riot leaders most eager to erase their debts by destroying the Jews and their financial records were connected with northern abbeys. Joseph Jacobs comments, "It was possible that even the leaders of the riot were combining business and religion in their attack on the Jews. They were all connected with various abbeys, and their names occur in the Abbey Cartularies ... The Fauconbridges were the great patrons of the Abbey of Welbeck, and Malebysse himself was afterwards the founder of Newbo in county Lincoln."[61]

The Siege of Jerusalem responds to these developments when it defines its most distinctive victimizing impulse. The Jews in the poem have two very desirable characteristics: they are exotically rich, and they are extremely malleable; in fact, the more the poem mauls them, the more gold they seem to produce. Gold is magically generated by their presence, it plasters their city and apparel—they exude surplus value. This emerges most disturbingly at a point during the siege when large numbers of starving Jews are desperate to surrender. Titus grants them safe-passage from the city with disastrous consequences. It is discovered that they have eaten their gold to preserve it from pillaging, and the Roman warriors take prompt action:

> [Wiþou]ten leue of þat lord, ledes hem slowen,
> [G]oren euereche a gome, and þe gold taken,
> Ffayn[ere] of þe floreyns [þan of] þe frekes alle. (1166–68)

[Without asking leave of their lord (Titus), men slew them, goring every one of them to extract the gold, more delighted with the money than with all of the men themselves.]

While the poem literally extracts gold from Jewish bodies, it simultaneously literalizes the abusive stereotype of money-hungry Jews and reveals the desires of the besieging Christians (willing even to go against their more compassionate leaders' orders to fulfill them) that are being served by this translation of a living culture into dead flesh and gold. In fact, the scene imposes on the Jewish body the only form of generation that the poem will allow for them. It answers that previous scene of unnatural consumption, Mary's devouring of her child, an attack on Jewish generation, and points to a more appropriable fecundity. That is why the men are "Ffayn[ere] of þe floreyns [þan of] þe frekes alle." This violent extraction is depicted as illicit and against Titus's orders—and he laments when he hears of it; as a solution to the conflict between exploiting and profiting from the Jews it is so excessive that it creates a rift between the Christian leader and his men.

But less corporeal liquidations continue. The Jews at the beginning of the poem are like the Romans; they use their wealth and culture to communicate their power and status; they are a vigorous self-generating culture. By the end of the poem, they have been forced to internalize and transform themselves into the dead tokens of power and status which they formerly controlled.

When the siege has been victorious, this terrible alchemy culminates with the mass enslavement of the Jews: literally converted into money and sold as marketable goods:

[Titus] made in myddel of [þe] ost a market to crye,—
Alle þat cheffare wolde chepe chepis to haue,
Ay for a peny of pris, who-so pay wolde,
Þrytty Jewes in a þrom, þrongen in ropis.
So wer' þey bargayned and bou3t and bro3t out of londe. (1313–17)

[Titus declared a market in the middle of the army, in which anyone who wanted to have a bargain could haggle. All for the price of a penny anyone who wanted to pay could get a crowd of thirty Jews, squeezed together in ropes. Thus were they bargained for and bought and taken out of their land.]

Here the poet indulges in another of his inversions. The Christ-sellers are sold, with the additional scornful fillip of bringing only a fraction of the price of Christ. But while the living bodies of the Jews themselves are not allowed here to yield much profit, their community's civic body, Jerusalem, and its heart, the Temple, are different stories. After a qualm that sin should destroy such a precious place, the sack is an extended, gleeful rummage through a town-sized treasure chest:

Þer was plente in þe place of precious stonys,
Grete gaddes of gold, who-so grype lyste,
Platis, pecis of peys, pulsched vessel,
Bassynes of brend gold and oþer bry3t ger,
Pelours, masly made of metals fele,

In cop[r]e craftly cast and in clene seluere;
peynted [with] pur' gold, alle the place was ouer:
Þe Romayns renten hem doun and to Rome ledyn.
Whan þey þe cyte han souȝt vpon þe same wyse,
Telle couþe no tonge þe tresours þat þei þer founden,
Jewels for joly men, je[mewes] riche,
Ffloreyns of [fyne] gold, broches and rynges,
Clene cloþes of selke many carte-fulle,
Wele wanteþ no wye, but wale[þ] what hym lykeþ. (1261–76)

[In that place, there were enormous quantities of precious stones, huge bars of gold for whoever wanted to grab them, plates, pieces of great weight, polished vessels, basins of burnished gold and other bright gear, and all over the place were pillars, massively made of many different metals, cunningly cast in copper and in bright silver and painted with pure gold. The Romans tore them down and bore them off to Rome. When they had searched the city in the same manner, no tongue can tell how many treasures they found there: jewels for gay-spirited men, rich double rings; no man lacked many coins of bright gold, furs and cloth that were rich enough for princes to wear, gold coins, gold bracelets, brooches and rings, many cartfuls of bright silk cloth; no man lacked for wealth but chose what he liked.]

This sack of the Temple does double service to the poem. Literally, it is the physical center of the Jewish nation and its destruction and pillaging consummates and finalizes their own. Figuratively as the center of Jewish religiosity, it metonymizes the Hebrew Bible itself—the edifice of the Old Law which the Christians will ravage, disassemble, and typologically appropriate. In this scene the poem reaches a desired end. It has not merely retaliated against the Jews, it has liquidated them. All the gold, the silks, and the cunning artifacts of the east are free for the taking. The Temple is literally dismantled into fungible commodities for Christian transportation—and the sensory delight in the sheer luxury of it casts a glamour over possible typological significances. The crusade that began by boasting only to avenge Christ's death has along the way reaped a considerable profit. The exultant joy of the Christian armies by its very excess actualizes the enormity of the hungers that drove this army of Christendom, the fissures at the foundations that might have gaped wider had the Jews actually succeeded in escaping their role as precursors whose supersession, subjection, and exploitation enables Christian sovereignty and prosperity.

Chivalry into Extortion

What matters in this struggle is a cruel relatedness, the tugs of war. The struggle must be prolonged in every way so this profitable conflict/contact can be maintained. To do this, the poem makes both sides strategically uncooperative; when Romans offer peace, the Jews are moved to reject it; when the Jews plead for it, it is withheld. Both sides are imbued with exactly enough pride and highhandedness to keep the conflict justifiable and therefore prolong it. Whenever idiotic stubbornness is needed, it occurs, even when it flies in the face of the progressive annihilation that the poem is underscoring. However, the Jews are never allowed seriously to threaten the Roman armies. This powerlessness contrasts with the Islamic might depicted in the *Chanson de Roland*, or Darius's military splendor in *The Wars of Alexander*. The poem, unlike the other battle-oriented alliterative romances, is not interested in whether the Jews prove the Romans chivalrically admirable by putting up a good fight. It would rather that they give the Romans a cursory run for their money.

The poem thus solicits an unequal if not usurious economic transaction, replacing a trade (an eye for an eye—a death for a death) with an extortion. If Christ's death bought all of humanity away from sin, then the reckoning for that death in the poem expands to encompass an entire nation. The struggle is prolonged so that worse and crueller sufferings can be imposed and greater and better profits can be reaped. The economic metaphor here, yet again, assimilates a paradigm imposed on Jews: payment with interest, a usury of violence at which the Romans become more adept and more successful as the poem proceeds. By the poem's end, the Jews and the Romans are caught up in the cruel intimacy of extortionist and victim. All the violence of the poem comes to a head at the bargaining table, where the Jews' value is calculated by Roman standards and they are sold as slaves.

To maintain this exploitative economy and keep the Romans on top, the poem must subordinate the chivalric paradigms upon which it depends for its emotional effect. In battle epics such as the *Chanson de Roland* and the alliterative *Morte Arthure*, the extremities of battle are high points where the opponents become almost indistinguishable in their fury. Both these poems dwell on the moment when the battle suddenly transcends all earthly, bodily, and religious limits and carries all the participants off in an ecstasy of rage, sublimating body into pure action. In *The Siege of Jerusalem*, such moments are dangerous because they conflict with the need to keep the Romans invulnerable and the Jews malleable.[62] One of the few the poem allows comes fittingly with the breaching of the walls of Jerusalem. As the Romans swarm through the gap and are met with desperate resistance, the crucial separation between Jew and Roman vanishes and only the violence itself remains, feeding on itself. There was

noȝt bot dyn and dyt as alle dye scholde
So eche lyuande lyf layeþ on oþer. (1189–90)

[nothing but din and clamor as if everyone were going to die together, so fiercely did each living life beset the other].

It is at this moment that the only Roman captain to be killed, Sir Sabyn of Syria, meets his death. Such textual moments are dangerous because they level the participants to equals in struggle, body against body, each life against the other with no differentiation. The poem continually swerves from this risky chivalric sublimity, restores the boundaries and deflects the danger onto the Jews alone. As soon as the walls are breached, for instance, the poet moves abruptly out of the melee and begins retroactively recounting portents signifying Jewish defeat that had appeared *three years before* (and outside the poem's purview): visions of a great sword and a heavenly army hanging over the city.[63] These afterthoughts of portents emphatically separate the invaders from the victims by retroactively wheeling in a vulture-like sign of Jewish doom. By situating these ancient portents unsequentially at the moment the walls of the city are finally broken and Romans are pouring in, the poem resists the disintegratory culmination toward which the battle fervor tends. It extracts the Romans from the danger presented by the breach of Jewish walls—the boundary that separates them—and narratively shelters the vulnerable Roman army beneath an invulnerable heavenly one.

This process extends over the entire poem as the poem continually courts and then resists the breakdown of boundaries between the combatants. Such approach/avoidance tactics extend to the formation of sympathies and the emotional identification of the audience with both victims and victors. While appearing to indulge all the variegated genocidal fantasies of late medieval clerical culture, the poem never loses sight of the sufferings of the Jews. In the scene where the Jewish woman, Mary, eats her own child, the poet draws attention not only to the monstrousness of the act but to the pitiable circumstances that drove her to it. Time and again the poet details the sufferings of the Jews trapped within the city, making them human and sympathetic. He laments at the fact that starvation has deprived the Jewish women of all their beauty. By continually underscoring their humanity the poem threatens its initial paradigm where the Jews are perfidious Christ-killers and the Romans the sympathetic Christian heroes.[64]

But simply because this suffering is so extreme, the poet can often in a mere twist of phrase make it monstrous. This is the emotional border the poem continually smudges, modulating from sympathy to ridicule to sheer horror. The Jews in the poem are first humanized, weeping tears of pity and suffering, and then "othered"—reduced to the levels of beasts or traitors in a way that justifies the inflictors of torture and spurs them to continue their efforts. The poem runs an emotional gamut from "Look at the poor wretches,"—to (more insidiously) "How ugly they are,"—to (subtler yet) "They're monsters, they deserve it," and finally to "You thought it would stop here—no! The worst is yet to come!" However, the very artistry with which the poem dehumanizes the Jews points to the inevitable contrivance of that dehumanization, prohibits any comfortable naturalization of it, and generates the need for its continual active reinforcement. In this, I believe, the poem participates in a very widespread medieval clerical production of the idea of the Jews as perpetually necessary and reiterable anti-types and enemies to Christians, a ritual reproduction of ideological enmity clearly visible in the clerically vetted cycle dramas produced at York as well as in *The Croxton Play of the Sacrament*. [65]

Consolidating the West

The Jews are not the only threatening precursors in the poem; the poem pinions pagan Rome as well. It targets two pasts significant to Christendom as an imperio-religious mythology, dispatching the rival religiosity of the Jews simultaneously with the crumbling imperial edifice of pagan Rome. When Titus first hears of Christ's torture and death, he does not condemn the Jews; he blames Caesar, who appointed the unjust provost, Pilate, working himself into a fury as he does so. The moment Titus finishes fulminating, he is healed of his disease and regains his strength. At first glance, this immediate condemnation of Caesar is startling, given the simple anti-Judaic revenge frame with which the poem begins. However, as the poem progresses, it becomes clear that the poem is concerned with greater changes than the repayment of a violent debt. The poem's Christianity leads beyond the Jewish war to imperial revolution, a two-pronged attack that realigns the face of the Roman Empire itself on both foreign and domestic fronts.

From the beginning, the poem pursues the distinction between Old Rome and New Rome, as vigorously as it does the distinction between Christian and Jew. Titus is constructed specifically as an enlightened Christian king in opposition to Nero, the savage pagan emperor. In the poem, the Roman emperors are depicted as not only corrupt and bestial but fatally stupid, because they are not guided by the Christian faith that motivates the emerging Christian empire. They share with the Jews the blame for Christ's death because the condemnation of Christ constitutes a failure of their just administration, and, like the Jews, they fall prey to the poem's destructive inversions. Because Nero has shown ill judgment in appointing his provincial overseers, who allowed fear of a mob to dictate their injustice, he is pursued from his palace by a mob of his own citizens, and only has time to snatch a stick of wood, which he gnaws to a point with his teeth and then stabs through his own heart. Titus, by contrast, instantiates a new kind of leadership as he is baptized to gain the divinely sanctioned and unhesitating authority of the crusader: "for[th] [th]ey fetten a font ... Made hym cristen kyng [th]at for Christ werred" (189–90) [they fetched forth a font, made him a Christian king that warred for Christ].

It is no accident that the wars at home and abroad are simultaneous and mobilize the same dynamics; both the pagan Romans and the Jews are precursors upon whose destruction the cohesion of the newly defined Christian community directly depends. The poem underlines this by linking deadly enmity against both enemies to the healing of Christian imperial bodies. Vespasian is healed once and Titus twice. Titus's second illness and cure in particular illuminate the poem's recuperative dynamic—the invigoration of imperial Christendom through carefully administered hatred. When Vespasian succeeds in gaining the Roman throne only halfway through the poem and well before Jerusalem is defeated, Titus becomes so joyful that he falls ill:

> Titus for þe tydyng ha[þ] take [so] mychel joye
> Þat in his synwys soudeynly a syknesse is fallen.
> Þe freke for þe fayndom of þe fader blysse,
> With a cramp and a colde cauȝt was so hard
> Þat þe fyngres and feet, fustes and joyntes
> Was lyþy as a leke and lost han her' strengþe.
> [He] croked aȝens kynde and as a crepel woxe,
> And whan þey sey hym so, many segge wepyþ. (1023–30)

[Titus took so much joy from the tidings that a sudden sickness struck his sinews. He was so joyful at his father's happiness that he was gripped by a cramp and a chill. It took him so strongly that his fingers and his feet, his fists and his joints were as limp as leeks and lost their strength. Against nature, he grew crooked and walked like a cripple, so that when many people saw him, they wept for pity.]

Here, Vespasian's success in Rome threatens the poem's trajectory towards a new Christian empire by introducing a premature ending, a Christian/Roman empire that has not fully assimilated the profits from the destruction of both its predecessors. Titus's new illness signals the importance of the Jewish side of the equation, and underlines the continued usefulness of the Jews. Titus sends into Jerusalem, famed for its healing, for a physician. Josephus, the Jewish clerk, Roman sympathizer, historian, military strategist, and writer of one of the sources for the poem, willingly comes out to cure him:

> Tille he haue complet his cure condit he askeþ
> For what burne of þe burwe þat he brynge wolde.
> Þe kyng was glad alle to graunte þat þe gome wylned,
> And he ferkiþ hym forth, fettes ful blyue
> A man to þe mody kyng þat he moste hated,
> And yn bryngeþ þe burne to his beddes syde.
> When Tytus saw þat segge sodeynly with eyen,
> His herte in an hote yre so hetterly riseþ,
> Þat þe blode bygan to [br]ed[e] abrode in þe vaynes
> And þe synwes [to] resorte in her self kynde.
> Ffeet and alle þe fetoures as þey byfore wer'
> Comyn in her' owen kynd. (1039–50)

[(Josephus) asked for free conduct from the city for any man he might choose that would last until Titus's cure. The king was happy to grant to him all that he wished, and Josephus went forth and fetched very quickly a man that the proud king hated the most on earth. He brought that man to the king's bedside. When Titus saw that man suddenly appearing there before his eyes, his heart rose up so fiercely in a hot rage that the blood began to race in his veins and his sinews were restored to their old strength. His feet and all his features were as they had been before, renewed in their natural state.]

In recounting this extraordinary cure, the poet has altered his sources in significant details. Its main source, the *Legenda Aurea* of Jacobus de Voragine, includes this episode simply because it was there in its own source and Jacobus repeatedly qualifies it as apocryphal and denigrates its significance. The *Siege*-poet alters it from an interesting diversion of uncertain worth to an episode that crystallizes the need of the Christian Romans to preserve the Jews so that their own imperial successes do not enfeeble them. Other adjustments are also significant. First and most important, the hated man is not Titus's own slave as in Jacobus's account but a man from the city, a Jew. In addition, Titus is not constrained to acknowledge his enemy publicly as an honored guest at a banquet as Jacobus tells; he is only forced to face him within the confines of his own sick chamber, and as a result, the power of his antipathy becomes more surprising. Finally, the poet omits Jacobus's account of Josephus's rationale for the cure: that contrary should cure contrary. This change that makes the mechanics of the cure more miraculous, intense, and essential; the cure springs directly from the hatred in Titus's heart without any intervening logical framework. These changes knit the incident tightly into the poem's network of desires. The scene dramatizes the healthful consequences of balancing the furious need to destroy the Jews against the material profits of their continued existence. Hatred of them becomes not merely economically but physically salutary. The Jews are not simply an enemy that the Romans by divine sanction can love to hate, but one that it is energizing and healthy to hate, a truly desirable enemy.

In creating this economy of salutary hatred, the poet recognizes and constructs an originary mythology for the historic exploitation of the Jews from the twelfth century onward by courts, nobles, and city governments throughout Europe. The Jews in England were supremely useful to thirteenth-century monarchs for the tallages that could be levied on them, some of them amounting to one fifth of total monarchical income. P. Elman argues that the Jews were finally expelled from England in 1291 because their resources had already been effectively depleted; they were no longer a good investment.[66] In addition to direct taxation, their services as moneylenders could be exploited not only by aristocratic and clerical landowners but by the kings themselves. All over Europe, rulers repeatedly captured the services of the Jews as money-lenders, only to expel or kill them when they were unable to meet their obligations for repayment.[67]

The Siege of Jerusalem acknowledges the usefulness of the Jews when it undergirds the foundations of Christian empire with its own extortionist economies. But Josephus's knowing dramaturgy in this scene is chilling; by healing his enemy he colludes in his city's demise. And the poem strikes this home by following it with a description of the massacre of noncombatants in the trammeled starvation of the town. Historically, Josephus's ambiguous self-positioning as Jewish apologist for Roman authority has always exerted its own troubling prurience—for historians, for Biblical scholars, and for Christian writers seeking a Jewish fifth-columnist. Josephus's histories exerted an authority almost certainly familiar to the *Siege*-poet who seems to draw on them as sources; other Christian writers both bespoke and laid claim to that historic authority by interpolating accounts of Christ's incarnation into them. A leader in the Judaean rebellion against Rome, Josephus also counseled fiercely against revolt; as one of two survivors in a mass-suicide pact he bears the stigma (or rationality) of refusing religious self-sacrifice as well. In the poem, as a soldier, scholar, and strategist he stands in opposition to the bloated priest Caiaphas. Caiaphas becomes the dangerous father of the late medieval anti-Judaic family romance—the slaughterer of the innocent Christ—upon whom the poem wreaks a revenge of unprecedented ferocity. Josephus, on the other hand, is a "good" father to the Roman Christians; if a Jewish figure can be coopted to agree to his own supersession, Josephus is he. Yet his insistence on returning to the city, the lesson in forgiveness he teaches Titus by urging him to spare the man who angered/cured him, his refusal to accept Christian fees, and his faithfulness to his people haunt across the great fissures between Jew and Christian that the poem incessantly carves, faintly intimating possibilities of paternal respect, gratitude, and even love.[68]

In at least two additional ways, the poem reveals an anxiety about its own strategies. First, the boundaries it constructs have to be obsessively policed; they are always in danger of collapsing as their violence threatens to reduce the Romans to the bestial level of their Jewish victims or their Roman predecessor Nero. It is this danger, I believe, that impels the undercurrent of pity for their victims which both Titus and Vespasian at times express, differentiating them not only from their Jewish precursors but their Roman ones, and showing a Christianity capable of horror at its own appropriative strategies, although this consciousness does not change the outcome.

Second, the very extremity of the poem's obsessive need to master the denizens of the Holy Land in every possible way (torture, civic disintegration, mass slaughter, vengeful inversion, economic exploitation) seems uncalled for given the relative weakness of the Jews after their first day of battle. I would argue that this insatiability for vengeance satisfies a wider need. The poem is so eager to revisit the Christian supersession of the Jews because, at the time of the poem's composition, the Mamluks in Egypt and the Holy Land and, especially, the Ottomans in Turkey were turning the tables on the monarchs of Christian Europe and putting the kibosh on the last eager hopes of a final successful crusade. Lord Kinross underlines the sense of inversion: "Thanks initially to Murad, the West was now to fall to the East as the East had fallen to the West in the centuries of the Greeks and the Romans."[69]

The Turks were in fact in the process of founding an empire that would not only rival in extent the Christian/Roman Empire constructed in *The Siege of Jerusalem* but also last much longer.[70] And while Murad I was circumspect in his dealings with Christians, mandating religious tolerance among his new subjects and not forcing conversions, his successor was less diplomatic. Murad's son, Bayezed, renewed the Ottoman Expansion, reputedly declaring himself the sword of Islam and apparently boasting to envoys from Italy that "after conquering Hungary, he would ride to Rome and would feed his horse with oats on the altar of St. Peter's."[71] In 1391 he instigated the first Ottoman siege of Constantinople, the center of Eastern Orthodox Christianity.

These depredations did not go unnoticed in Europe. King Sigismund of Hungary began to agitate for a new crusade and was gratified by an enormous response from nobility of all ranks and countries, including a large contingent from England

For the last time in history, the finest flower of European chivalry gathered together for a crusade as much secular as religious in impulse, whose objective was to check Bayezid's lightning advance and eject the Turks, once and for all, from the Balkans. Thus an "international" army, composed with Sigismund's own force and the contingents of knights with their retinues and mercenary bands of some hundred thousand men, mustered at Buda in the early summer of 1396—the largest Christian force that had ever confronted the infidel.[72]

This European force was utterly defeated by Bayezid, largely through its own chivalric arrogance. In Froissart's account, when Sigismund of Hungary with his knowledge of their enemy advised his international allies to wait for his own reinforcements, Sir Philip of Artois was enraged and declaimed that "the kynge of Hungery wolde have the floure and chiefe honour of this journey; we have the vowarde, he hath graunted it to us, and nowe he wolde take it fro us again: beleve hym who wyll, for I do nat!"[73] Penetrating the enticingly weak Ottoman vanguard, they came face to face with the main bulk of Bayezid's army, 60,000 men, and were decimated or taken prisoner. The following day, Bayezid massacred the prisoners in a scene that grimly echoes the ending of *The Siege of Jerusalem*, as the European warriors are roped together in groups, forced to kneel, and beheaded. 10,000 people are said to have died that day.[74] Froissart laments the European idiocy: "Lo, beholde the great foly and outrage, for if they had taryed for the kynge of Hungery, who were threscore thousande men, they had been lykely to have doone a great acte: and by them and by their pride all was lost, and they receyved suche dommange, that sythe the batayle of Rounsevalx where as the xii. peres of Fraunce were slayne, Crystendome receyved nat so great a dommage." The parallel with Roland's battle is suggestive of the importance invested in this confrontation and of the narrator's need to ennoble, even narratively, this crushing defeat.[75]

I am not arguing for a direct relationship between this campaign and *The Siege of Jerusalem*, though a very late dating of the poem, just before its terminus ad quem of about 1400, would allow for it. What is more important, however, is that the motivations and anxieties that impel this last immense gathering of the knighthood of Europe are also at the heart of the poem, spiced by clerical traditions of anti-Judaism. The poem assuages these anxieties in its exuberance over the isolation, conquest, and torture of the one eastern culture that is not only rich but imaginable as vulnerable. In its stress on the need to preserve the Jews for exploitation, the poem appeals in one final way to the Augustinian interpretation of the need for Christian tolerance of the Jews. William of Newburgh again crystallizes this logic:

Indeed with the same reason of Christian utility the perfidious Jew, the crucifer of our Lord Christ, is allowed to live among Christians as the form of the Lord's cross is painted in the Church of Christ, viz., for the continual and most helpful remembrance by all of the faithful of our Lord's Passion . . . and thus the Jews ought to live among Christians for our use, but serve us for their own iniquity.[76]

In the bland word "utility," this passage illuminates the link between the nurturing of social memory, economic need, and the cultural reproduction of Christian community, and lays the groundwork for *The Siege of Jerusalem*'s spectacular dramatization of a simultaneously just, pitiable, and vicious reiterative economy of violent exploitation. In its very elegance, the poem reveals its fictionality; its active and anxious interest in carving "wide ways" through a territory of genealogical and geographical relationship, desire, and debt. The Christendom it produces, the unities between violence and religiosity it asserts, and the economic transactions in which it revels are beautifully and viciously contrived. As this Christendom seizes, disassembles, and liquidates its ancestral religious "birthright" by subjugating its Jewish rivals, it both kills and entreasures its own past, striving to ameliorate the seemingly unresolvable tensions of its own cultural provenance.

Both *The Siege of Jerusalem* and *The Wars of Alexander* in their diverse ways react to and in turn reshape the increasingly widespread consciousness that whatever the outcome, the fates and identities of Christian Europe and the lands to the east were irrevocably linked. Each poem distances this consciousness by constructing a deep history of difference. This strategy echoes the past-reviving strategies in many other alliterative romances, working not only to displace anxieties but also, more interestingly, to show that these anxieties have long histories and that the past is still alive in the present. They construct violent foundational mythologies so that more violent work may be done, but also shift uneasily beneath their weight, suggesting their guilt, futility, and sometimes their cruelty. What is striking is how different are the responses of each poem to this consciousness. *The Siege of Jerusalem* fantasizes the foundations of the opposition between Christian and Jew, west and east, forcing the two apart into a brutal but problematic relationship of torturer and victim, exploiter and source of wealth. *The Wars of Alexander* traces a more troubled genealogy, exploring the subversive contiguities between east and west, past and present, parents and children, ultimately intimating that they cannot be escaped. Taken together, the sheer diversity of responses to the Matter of Araby, its different embodiments as Jew, Saracen, Egyptian trickster, Greek schismatic, Persian and Indian tyrant, or inchoate monster drawn from the oriental soil—all demonstrate an understanding of the relations between east and west that complicates simple distinctions and oppositions between them. Each grows out of the other in ways that not only polarize but reflect. Although *The Siege of Jerusalem* describes an empire in the process of foundation and *The Wars of Alexander* perplexes the whole concept of a successful and lasting conquest, both poems reluctantly agree on one thing about the identities of east and west, Christian, Muslim, Pagan, and Jew, past and present. Their relationality is what determines them.

6

King Takes Knight: Signifying War in the Alliterative *Morte Arthure*

> "Now wakkenyse þe were, wyrchipide be Cryste!"
> [War is wakening, praise the Lord!]

WAR, SHUNTED ASIDE IN *Sir Gawain and the Green Knight* and suffused with imperial longings in both *The Wars of Alexander* and *The Siege of Jerusalem*, is pushed to further extremes in the alliterative *Morte Arthure*.[1] In the poem's battles, war becomes a chivalric sacrament where surpassing violence intersects with the structured materials of knightly display: insignia, armor, and body. Sir Cador's war prayer above makes war into knighthood's animating spirit, a hoard-bound dragon, always astir and craving for conflagration. The *Morte Arthure* describes the last great campaign of King Arthur against a range of enemies from the past, at once ancestors and rivals, doubles and others: the Giant of St. Michael's Mount, Sir Priamus, Sir Lucius, and the hordes of his Roman, Greek, Schismatic, Saracen, and giantish cohorts. The poem shows how Arthur's confrontations with Britain's imperial predecessors at once prove the strength of Arthur's kingly solidarity with his knights and impel their greatest triumphs—only to bring about their utter destruction. Like *Sir Gawain and the Green Knight* and *The Wars of Alexander*, the *Morte Arthure* focuses on a particular elite—the king and his circle of greater magnates. However, it deliberately averts its gaze from late fourteenth-century tensions between the landed nobility and the royal court when it depicts intense and naturalized solidarities between king and noble. It reaches back instead to an earlier fourteenth-century monarch who attentively nurtured those solidarities.

The parallels between the romance's Arthur and Edward III are both inescapable and, intriguingly, mutually cultivated.[2] On the one hand, scholars have long noted the resemblance of Arthur's justifications for the invasion of Rome to Edward III's for his invasion of France at the beginning of the Hundred Years War, and have read the poem as a commentary on the English reverses suffered throughout the later part of his reign.[3] Arthur's military fervor recalls the early career of Edward III, when the war in France was going well and the king along with his greater magnates and nobles were celebrating the victory of Crécy. In the *Morte Arthure* even the details of the armor and arms borne by Arthur and his knights date from the beginning of the Hundred Years War. On the other hand, Edward III, like his grandfather Edward I, found it in his political interests to promote himself as a second Arthur in the tradition of the Nine Worthies; he likely devised the Order of the Garter as a reenactment of Arthur's Round Table. His original scheme included a large hall at Windsor where a brotherhood of 300 knights could meet once yearly at Pentecost to reaffirm their fellowship and enjoy whatever staged marvels the king could produce. Its eventual expression, a band of twenty-six select aristocrats from a range of social backgrounds, probably did even better political work for him in its valuable exclusivity. Edward used the cultural currency of Arthur's legendary monarchy to help cement loyalties among the restless nobles and forestall the rivalries and differences between royal and magnatial interests that beset both the reign of his father Edward II and that of his grandson, Richard II.[4]

The *Morte Arthure* also recalls Edward's policies when it adapts the king to the military ideology of his knights, making Arthur a paragon not of royalty but of seigneurial chivalry. "Sir Arthur," as he is called during his final battles, is a far cry from the Gawain-poet's "sumquat childgered" Arthur whose prowess is condescendingly dismissed by the Green Knight. The *Morte Arthure*'s Arthur proves his nobility in combat as vigorously as any of his knights. By making Arthur at heart an ideal knight with a thin veneering of royalty, the poet constructs a fantasy of solidarity between king and noble at a time of intensifying factional division and alienation between royalty and nobility climaxing in the deposition of Richard II.[5] In the poem, these solidarities extend beyond oaths and even bloodlines and infuse their corporeal identities until king and nobility become virtually one body; the poem's Arthur both incarnates and contains the chivalric self-expressions of his knights and captains, while they in turn express his own fierce emotions and desires.

The poem thus invokes a very recent British past when it makes Arthur resemble Edward III. But the poem's Arthur also reaches back further to become a portmanteau of chivalric nostalgias. Arthur and his knights belligerently repudiate the practical economics of fourteenth-century warfare as livelihood in favor of an archaic feudal purism. Arthur gathers his knights and allies by feudal levies and sworn pledges of support which are utterly outmoded by the fourteenth century, when military service was far more likely to be a contractual rather than a feudal arrangement. Arthur refuses to indulge in the profitable exchange of prisoners for ransom, which throughout the Hundred Years War was one of the most enticing incentives for campaigning at all. Arthur and his knights construct a military solidarity that at first seems all the more illustrious for its disdain of contemporary contractual feudalisms.[6]

The poem gives its Arthur this antique finish to deepen his patina of vintage worthiness but also, more crucially, to urge its outmodedness. This poem treasures imperial ambitions recalling those of *The Siege of Jerusalem* and *The Wars of Alexander*, and the shadows of various oriental predecessors stretch over this poem as well: the Genoese Giants (Genoa and Venice were the two Italian trade cities allowed conditional and temporary access to eastern trade routes) and the Saracen, Greek, and eastern kings of Lucius's army. The *Morte Arthure* also draws its line in the sand by seeking the "pure" plunder of war against these enemies, refusing indulgence in medieval warfare's binding and familiarizing economic, political, and cultural exchanges. The poem even resonates with a familiar threat of eastern intimacy, when Mordred calls Saracens, not Saxons, into Britain to strengthen his armies against Arthur's. Yet within this orientalist frame, the poem seems more interested in the relationships within Arthur's army—the theater of give and take, command and control, explosion and escape that plays out between Arthur and his aristocratic captains. Through this more inward focus the poem is able to put pressure upon the political fantasy of a monarch and his knights bound together into powerful solidarity by war. At first, the synergies between war-leader/king and warrior knights are productive. But the poem shows how these imperial ambitions ultimately consume the chivalry they drive. It criticizes the nostalgia for such solidarities between the king and his chivalry when it stages their implosion.

This extends the poem's critique to a foundational theme in chivalric writing: the idea of chivalric decline used as a spur to present achievement. Chivalric writing from its very inception constitutes itself as belated: the present is a time of degradation and deterioration from an always truer and more illustrious chivalric past.[7] This nostalgic strain has tempted both critics and historians to conclude that during this period chivalry was actually in decline, that when the knights of England and France fought the Hundred Years War or the Wars of the Roses or engaged in incessant tournaments, they were performing ideologically overdetermined exercises in self-performance, going through the motions of what was increasingly becoming a game. But this myth of late medieval chivalric decline has been usefully countered by K. B. McFarlane who describes the necessity of such wars as both economic venture and livelihood for members of the nobility and gentry. Louise Fradenburg attacks it from another angle by arguing that gamesmanship and violence are continuous rather than oppositional terms, and their interplay animates and theatricalizes even the most brutal battlefields and tourneys—a major reflex in this poem.[8]

I will not argue, then, that the poem simply reanimates this typical nostalgic fantasy of a time before chivalric decline from the belated perspective of that decline. Chivalry is going to flourish, regenerate, change, and opportunistically recreate itself for at least the next two hundred years. Rather, I will argue that the poem looks at this nostalgia critically. It goes back to a time of past and "pure" chivalric practice and it shows its horrendous costs. Thus the poem does not scrutinize a moment of chivalric weakness and decline but, with traditional knightly bravado, takes its subject at its greatest strength. The result unflinchingly dramatizes the structural rather than the accidental weaknesses in the traditional chivalric ideal of strong warriors bound by their loyalty to an illustrious king. The poet shows how the practice of war, in particular, becomes both chivalry's "life force and death rattle" as Thomas Hahn inimitably puts it. As the poem searches the meaning and costs of war not only for its civilian victims but for its chivalric victors, it participates in an important strain in medieval chivalric narrative whose critique of war is all the more serious because it is internal, born of long experience of its exhilarations and exhaustions.[9] The poem begins by wedding (both by military oath and intimate loyalty) the knights to Arthur as they set off joyously together to a war that will make Arthur emperor; it ends with Arthur alone and "widowed" amidst the corpses of his knights, lamenting the ambitions that led to their slaughter and yet clinging to his revenge. The poem shows that to use war as a means to chivalric solidarity between king and aristocracy and to instantiate the king's honor by leading knights violently to execute it on others is to perform a nostalgic fantasy not only of a world that never was but a world that never could be, futureless, feeding on its own expenditure, and blindly fantasizing the indefinite deferral of its own mortal consequences.

Thus, although the poem aggressively denies conflict between king and noble, it strains with a sense of internal conflict, monarchical alienation, and aristocratic restlessness that existed at the end of Richard's reign. Especially during the period of Richard's tyranny, from 1377 to his deposition in 1399, the nobility and parliament were riven by different factions: royalists, supporters of the executed Lords Appellant, supporters of Henry of Lancaster, and conservatives like Northumberland who were distressed alike at the king's partisanship and at his enemies' temerity.[10]

And yet the failure of solidarity between king and noble was sometimes very enabling for careerist aristocrats and gentry. Aside from the brief monarchical consolidations of Henry IV and Henry V, the fifteenth century in particular was to become a kind of amazed golden-age for aristocratic self-fashioning, allowing the rise of fantastically powerful families like the Percys and the Stantons and culminating in the Wars of the Roses. In his political history of the north of England, Frank Musgrove shows how throughout the medieval period periods of monarchical centralization alternate with periods of dispersal of power to the provincial peripheries, and especially the border zones of the realm. Times of demographic, economic, and military expansion tended to favor the centralization of monarchical power, but times of stasis or decline encouraged entrenchment. Kings invested in fortifying the realm's border zones, enriching the outriding baronies with royal support for their militarization. Additional power shifted to the peripheries with the balance tipping from more traditional land-based feudalisms to more contractual and economic feudalisms.

Bastard feudalism was the perfect recipe for a very loose confederation of regional magnates unconstrained by a powerful centre. To a far greater degree than the far-northern regalities, bastard feudalism stood outside and endangered royal authority. It was entirely congruent with, and indeed promoted, a weak centre and powerful perimeters.[11]

And the fourteenth and fifteenth centuries were high points of such aristocratically profitable decentralization: "of a perimeter awash with power from Calais through Normandy and Gascony to the marches of Wales and the frontier province towards Scotland."[12] Written at the midpoint of this process, the *Morte Arthure* accommodates both the divisions and the ambitious energies of its provincial milieu when it directs a measured gaze backward to a monarchy which both exercises and battens upon the energies of the nobility, finally devouring them altogether and thus destroying itself.

Chivalry and War

At the beginning of the poem in the Giant's Tower council, the poet takes care to justify Arthur's campaign against Lucius. Arthur and his nobles will be fighting to gain retribution for Roman depredations in Britain, to restore justice to territory that is Arthur's by right of ancestral conquest, and most importantly to free the people of that territory from the depredations of a tyrant. At this point, all Arthur's adversaries are defined as oppressors. The bear of Arthur's dream "betakyns the tyrauntez þat tourmentez thy pople" (824) [betokens the tyrants that torment your people], the Giant is "a teraunt besyde that tourmentez thi pople" (842) [a tyrant that torments your people], and Lucius is told by his emissaries that he "dosse bot tynnez [his] tym and turmenttez [his] pople" (1954) [does but lose (his) time and torment (his) people]. However, as the poem proceeds the emphasis changes; the farther Arthur gets from the Giant's Tower where his reasons for conquest were laid out and his war justified, the more his own acts begin to seem like the arbitrary pillaging he is supposedly contesting. We remember that his initial justifications were performed in Giant's Tower when he begins to resemble a giant:

> Into Tuskane he tournez . . .
> Takes townnes full tyte with towrres full heghe;
> Walles he welte down, wondyd knyghtez,
> Towres he turnes and turmentez þe pople;
> Wroghte wedewes ful wlonke, wrotherayle syngens,
> Ofte wery and wepe and wryngen theire handis,
> And all he wastes with werre thare he awaye rydes—
> Thaire welthes and theire wonny[n]ges wandrethe he wroghte!
> Thus they spryngen and sprede and sparis bot lyttill,
> Spoylles dispetouslye and spillis theire vynes,
> Spendis vnsparely þat sparede was lange . . .
> Fro Spayne into Spruyslande, the word of hym sprynges
> and spekynngs of his spencis—disspite es full hugge!! (3150–52)

[Into Tuscany he turns . . . rapidly conquers towns with very high towers; he hurled down their walls and wounded knights, overturns towers and torments the people. He made beautiful widows to sing with misery, often to curse and weep and wring their hands. And wherever he rides he wastes with war; turned their wealth and their winnings into sorrow. Thus they drive and spread and spare but little, despoiling without pity, and killing their vines, expends without sparing that which was long saved up . . . From Spain to Prussia the word of him springs and tidings of his expenditures—at which there is much bitterness.]

Before this, the poem had celebrated Arthur's campaign as a productive activity: one that endowed its practitioners with honor, manhood, livelihood, and worship. In this passage we see that large-scale war is also produced at considerable expense. It has become a self-feeding process with its own economy of display and waste. The poet no longer rehearses the justifications for each conquest; war has become the aristocrats' industry, with its own rules and timings, accruing them profit at the people's loss. By refocusing on aristocratic economic predation, this passage's critique goes beyond the context of justification for war and strikes at the heart of monarchical authority itself. In this passage, as in the earlier alliterative poem *Winnere and Wastoure*, the land is divided up into producers and consumers with Arthur and his knights gaining an international notoriety for the dissipation of the garnered wealth of the people: "Spoiling without pity . . . and spending unsparingly that which was hoarded up for a long time." This is precisely one of the accusations leveled throughout the century at the royal courts of Richard II and at the provincial courts of the greater magnates. In *Winnere and Wastoure*, the producer or Winner voices a perennial complaint against the aristocracy when he gripes that Wastoure "destroys my goods in playing and waking on winter nights, / in excess and unthrift, and arrogant pride" (l. 266–67).[13] In the midst of a more bellicose consumption, Arthur "torments the people"—the exact accusation which, applied to his tyrannical adversaries, furnished him with a just reason for going to war in the first place.

These fairly widespread late fourteenth-century challenges to the self-involvement and conspicuous consumption of the aristocracy are sharpened even further in the poem.[14] The *Morte Arthure* takes aim at the violence by which nobility performs itself in the poem—a violence that feeds upon and is fed by monarchical ambition. John Barnie comments on how intricately honor and violence are linked: "Honour . . . is an aggressive concept. The honorable man must demonstrate his honour continually before his peers and this in turn often involves challenging the honour of others." And Pitt-Rivers observes, "The ultimate vindication of honour lies in physical violence."[15] This dependence upon physical confrontation and its largest and most profitable manifestation, war, not only gave the nobility a livelihood and social justification but enabled them, for a while, to consolidate themselves as a class against upstarts and interlopers. Other signs of noble identity—seals and heraldic coats of arms—could be and were assumed by anyone and everyone, from the prosperous guildsmen to the commons, but it was harder to make a mark on the battlefield—at least up to the mid-fourteenth century when the demographics of war began to shift downward and the yeoman archer emerged as a potent force on the battlefield in competition with the traditional mounted knight. War also provided support for the expenses of honorable display—noblemen were obligated to put on a good show at court and cultivate relations with their peers by displaying magnificence and exchanging gifts. War offered opportunities for advancement, grants of land, and continued service under richer and more influential lords.[16]

The *Morte Arthure* reflects this logic of violent vindication by making the battlefield the central domain upon which knights and kings are created and their status justified: an illustrious ruler is necessarily a conqueror.

At the poem's beginning when Arthur sets off to war, he appoints his nephew Mordred regent in charge of his queen and his holdings, and promises him a kingdom (not England) for good service. Mordred bitterly protests his exclusion from his uncle's military expedition. He fears that in later days his lack of war experience will make him less respected and his advice in council less worthy than that of war-seasoned commanders. In a power play designed to keep his nephew subservient, Arthur rebukes him, addressing him in terms that emphasize Mordred's lack of maturity as well as his ties of obligation to his uncle: "Thowe arte my neuewe full nere, my nurree of olde / That I haue chastyede and chosen, a childe of my chambyre . . . That thow ne wyrk my will, thow watte whatte it menes" (689–90, 692) [You are my close nephew, my former fosterling whom I have brought up with discipline and chosen, a knight/child of my chamber . . . If you do not work my will, you know what will happen]. The court thus becomes a playpen for "children of the chamber" like Mordred—a place where a knight is provided with nurture and education available nowhere else but that is incapable of proving him a knight among other knights. When Arthur leaves the young Mordred at court, he consigns him to a neoteny that will undermine his future authority. Later Mordred engineers his own military route to power, hiring Saracen mercenaries to defend England from Arthur and claim it as his own. So powerful is the cultural imperative that war determines true nobility that it invalidates more peaceable transfers of power and instigates an intensely competitive and increasingly fractured system of rivalries, both fraternal and generational, that undermines the very system of chivalric solidarity on which Arthur's rule depends.

As the poem focuses on war as a means by which noble rank is produced and proven, the poem repudiates another other crucial arena of chivalric practice—life at court. The *Morte Arthure*'s militarism stands in sharp contrast to the courtly preoccupations of *Sir Gawain and the Green Knight* which reduces its hero's battles with giants and ogres on the Welsh border to mere episodes in his journey to Bertilak's court. But the *Morte Arthure* leaves no engagement unmagnified. In *Sir Gawain and the Green Knight*, the two elements of seigneurial life, court and battlefield, reinforce each other, but Gawain is less famous (at least at Bertilak's court) for his military prowess than for his skill at the "techless termes of talkyng noble." In the *Morte Arthure*, by contrast, Arthur scorns the delicate sliding innuendoes and double meanings which the Gawain-poet manipulates, indulging instead a taste for grisly irony. The poem is interested in courtly articulations only if they express the violence of the battlefield. Arthur's "crewelle lates" [menacing manners] have a physical force: in the opening scene the sight of his angry face actually throws the Roman ambassadors to the floor.

And the prospect of real war introduced by the Roman ambassadors causes Cador of Cornwall to heave a great sigh of relief:

> "I thanke Gode of þat thraa þat vs þus thretys . . .
> Þe lettres of sir Lucius lyghttys myn herte:
> We hafe as losels liffyde many longe daye
> Wyth delyttes in this lande with lordchipez many,
> And forelytenede the loos þat we are layttede.
> I was abaischite, be oure Lorde, of oure beste bernes,
> For gret dule of dessuse of dedez of armes.
> Now wakkenyse þe were, wyrchipide be Cryste!" (249–57)

["I thank God for this anger that threatens us . . . The letters of Sir Lucius lighten my heart. We have lived as wastrels for many a long day, enjoying delights in this land, with many lordships, and as a result we have diminished the fame that we used to seek. I was worried, by our Lord, about our best warriors, because of the great sorrow that comes from the disuse of deeds of arms. Now war is wakening: praise the Lord!"]

The king rebukes Cador for this recklessness but agrees that his counsel is noble. This passage transforms the prospect of an extended peace into a dangerous temptation to live "with delyttes in this lande with lorchipez many," an existence that will turn the best knights into "losels." To Arthur's court, peace is emasculating; knights will grow flaccid if they are not out continually tempering their weapons in mortal combat. When Mordred is excluded from Arthur's campaign and given the regency, he is instructed to take care of Guenever and indulge her by allowing her to hunt in the royal forests, thus associating the court (humiliatingly in this poem) with the care and cosseting of women.

By repudiating a focus on the court as a place of noble discourse, couture, and display simply for their own sake, the poem reflects a strain of contemporary uneasiness about the royal court. Many fourteenth-century chroniclers believed that excessive courtliness actually weakened the ruler, diminishing his inclination and ability to wage war. Thomas Walsingham placed the two facets of the noble life in opposition when he criticized Richard II's favorites for being "knights of Venus rather than knights of Bellona, more valiant in the bedchamber than on the field, armed with words rather than weapons, prompt in speaking but slow in performing the acts of war."[17] Richard in fact was no pace-setter; he was pursuing monarchical fashions for greater display, extended hierarchies, and more

formal modes of address that at this time were growing increasingly elaborate at courts all over Europe. These included the Aquitaine court of his
father, Edward the Black Prince, and the French court of his closest rival
monarch, Charles V, as well as courts in Italy and Bohemia.[18] Ralph A.
Griffiths notes Richard had "a mind that was fascinated with heraldry and
kingly dignity, and besotted with things French."[19] He was interested in
the language and trappings of courtliness and used them to exalt the king's
status as proprietor of the signs and tokens of chivalric rank, a gesture that
the nobility resented. However, Richard received criticism for his unusually dramatic cultivation of the formal, historical, and legal prerogatives of
kingship, for his retinue building, and for his extravagant ennoblements
(which included investing his greatest friend Robert de Vere with the unprecedented rank of marquis).[20] The nobility were very sensitive to the
Richard II's seemingly absolutist tendencies. Regardless of the truth of the
famous anecdote from the *Vita Ricardi Secundi* that Richard would sit
silently amidst his nobles, forcing them to kneel at his nod, the chroniclers
who compiled such stories were manipulating an anxiety about absolutism
that was already prevalent among the nobility, emerging sharply in the
criticisms of the Lords Appellant.

With the benefit of twenty-twenty hindsight, the anonymous poet of
Richard the Redeless criticizes Richard for attempting to extend his royal
court over the entire land by recklessly multiplying his liveried retainers
until they "swarmed . . . thikke / Þoru-oute his lond in lengþe and in brede"
(Passus II, 21–22) [swarmed thick throughout the length and breadth of his
land].[21] In attempting to construct a system of his own retainers to deal
directly with the people, Richard works to replace the intricate fretwork
of seigneurial jurisdictions with a singular royal one—exerting over the
land the exclusive dominance he might exert over the circles of his household. According to the *Richard*-poet, this attempt to consolidate his own
authority ends paradoxically by dispersing it. His hart-liveried retainers
abuse their authority and break the laws both of the realm and of nature
by devouring Richard's true nobility. The punning upshot is that Richard
burdens England with the sign of the White Hart and thereby loses the
people's hearts. The *Richard*-poet applauds the martial energy of Henry IV
who sweeps away this predatory network.

The *Morte Arthure* has a more oblique and critical response to the
dangers of royal absolutism and courtly effeminacy. It interrogates the
fantasy of an ideal king at one with his nobility. Arthur is the polar opposite of the Richard II of the chronicles. Canny but forthright, he whole-
heartedly participates in the beliefs and interests of his nobles in order to

govern them sympathetically. He literally *feels with* them and they *feel for* him. He can rebuke without alienating them; he carefully rewards them for services rendered. He listens to his nobles in council rather than relying on hired advisors and household retainers. He does not indulge in favoritism although he is particularly close to those barons who are also his kinsmen. At the poem's beginning he does not revel in emotional excesses such as Richard's reputed destruction of Shene manor after the queen's death; on the contrary when he takes his leave of Guenever, her weeping and fainting contrast almost parodically to his self-possession and icy resolution.

Yet this fantasy of ideal leadership darkens as the poem progresses. The solidarity of Arthur and his knights is disrupted by the very mechanisms of martial display that at first cemented it. During Arthur's last battles, even his taciturnity fails and he falls prey to bouts of dramatic emotional display; after Gawain's death, he has to be rebuked by Ewaine for weeping like a woman over his nephew's corpse. In his last speech as he surveys the bodies of his slain knights, he compares himself to a widow stripped of all she held dear. Paradoxically the battlefield has engendered the same process of softening and feminization that Arthurian chivalry supposedly escaped by abandoning the court to go to war.[22]

Thus the poem mobilizes anxieties about maturity and masculinity to force a rift between two important aspects of noble life, the court and the battlefield. It effectively isolates the culturally privileged antique and traditional figure of the nobleman as warrior and creates a field where this figure's status, experience, and social impact can be put to the test—and found wanting at the height of its greatest triumphs. The chivalric performances by which noble masculinity can prove and reprove itself on the poem's many battlefields become subject to increasingly devastating reproofs.[23] The rest of this chapter examines the process of this slowly coalescing critique, exploring how the mechanisms which create knightly (and masculine) identity end up engendering their opposites.

Criticizing Arthur

The central tension between war as a socially productive and socially destructive practice runs beneath the rhetoric of chivalric virtue in the poem and is part of a larger web of critical instabilities. John Barnie discusses the contradictions of a chivalric code whose "noblest virtues contain *in potentia* the very vices it strove to overcome . . . prowess is often indistinguishable from foolhardiness and overweening pride."[24] And the *Morte*

Arthure teeters on the line of this uncertainty. It divides the criticism of
the poem into two camps: those who think the poem is an ironic portrayal
of the increasing corruptions of military power—an Augustinian tragedy of
sin and retribution; and those who think it is a glorification of chivalric
leadership that like all earthly endeavor meets a tragic end—a Boethian
tragedy.[25] The numbers for each side are fairly even and both arguments
find textual support.

Appeals to contemporary writing to arbitrate the problem only magnify the confusion. For those who feel that Arthur's portrayal is a critique
of imperialism, there are many contemporary condemnations of tyranny
from chroniclers such as Froissart to poets such as Gower. William
Matthews gathers the most extensive list of these sources.[26] Among many
others, he quotes Jean de Montreuil's letter of 1395, raging against the war
in France:

> who shall describe the slaughter, especially of so many nobles of the highest rank,
> and even of kings? Who shall tell the robbery and the burning of even sacred
> places? Who shall set forth the sacrilege, the raping, the violence, the oppression,
> the extortion, the plundering, the pillaging, the banditry, and the rioting. Finally,
> to embrace many crimes in a few words, who shall portray the inhuman savagery
> committed in this horrible and most cruel war?[27]

Matthews's answer is the *Morte*-poet, whose graphic descriptions of battle
atrocities undercut Arthur's victories. In Matthews's argument then, the
poem topically alludes to a growing strain of criticism of war in late
fourteenth-century England and becomes an innovative and daring tract
constituting "for the first time a critical portrait of the national hero on the
basis of deep concern with the moral problem of war [and thus] distinctly
a minority report."[28] The pro-chivalry contingent consider this the weak
point of Matthews's argument. They argue for an overwhelmingly conservative trend within the poem and within contemporary alliterative poetry
generally, due to the extent to which the poem's probable audience and
author were implicated within the chivalric ideologies of the magnates and
lesser gentry. They point to other fourteenth-century figures such as Henry
of Grosmont and the Black Prince, whose conquests and battles were no
less gory and "imperialistic" in the modern sense, but who were almost
universally glorified as military heroes and models of knightly behavior.
John Barnie underlines the great differences in cultural sensibilities that
make these figures appear at least equivocal to a post–World War II vision,
where to their biographers their lives and conduct are exemplary.[29]

Larry D. Benson finds a middle ground by saying that the poem eludes
categorization and demands of its readers an ability that we have lost: "to

maintain contradictory viewpoints, sincerely admiring and just as sincerely rejecting worldly ideals." In his view, modern criticism is an either/or proposition, subordinating one ideal to the other in a way that the poem itself resists.[30] Benson rightly insists upon the fact that the poem itself at once invites and frustrates both readings. However, the opposition between religious and worldly ideals Benson deploys is complicated by the way the poem overlays battle with sanctification. We can call Arthur's military ideals worldly, but the poem loves to show how thoroughly, powerfully, and disturbingly the intensities of chivalric bloodshed and the intensities of religious ritual can interpenetrate. Why else make Arthur's combat with the giant into a pilgrimage, recount miraculous battlefield healings like that of Priamus and Gawain, show Arthur canonizing Gawain's blood, and show Arthur himself aspiring toward a Christlike sacrifice on his last battlefield? With such play, the poem puts pressure upon late fourteenth-century paradigms of chivalric virtue: the allure and danger of their extremities.

And it maintains this pressure by manipulating its own focal range. The closer and more immediate the actual individual battlefield experience is, the more war seems to invigorate: hence the unabated relish for combat of Cador, Gawain, and the rest of Arthur's captains. In an analogous way, K. B. McFarlane argues that throughout the late fourteenth and fifteenth century, individual nobility were justified in thinking of war as a productive livelihood, even though their countries may have been bankrupted by it. Campaigns offered many opportunities for individual enrichment and for the formation of mutually advantageous relationships with other knights. He cites the example of two English esquires who swore to be brothers-in-arms "loyal one to the other without any dissimulation or fraud," a relationship that involved mutual promises to ransom the other or to stand hostage for him until enough ransom money could be raised. Their partnership was a profitable business venture; fifteen years after its beginning they were buying up manors in south London.[31]

A broader view, however, often highlights war's debilitating effects. When Arthur ravages Italy, he is doing nothing that he has not done repeatedly in his prior campaigns; the only differences between this passage and previous descriptions of Arthur are its uncharacteristic cursoriness and the inclusion of a non-noble perspective—the audience of "pople" left aghast at Arthur's extravagance. Yet this distancing of events is sufficient to turn a captain rejoicing over a hard-won victory into a wastrel tyrant. Throughout the poem, the reader is constantly reminded of how delicate a balance Arthur treads between laudable nobility and arrogance.

For instance, his self-confidence reaches the point of arrogance when he rides within arrow range of the walls of Metz boasting of his immunity, as an anointed king, from death at the hands of a mere yeoman, an incident that recalls Richard I's fatal audacity at Chalus, where he received the arrow wound that later killed him.[32] Robert Thornton, the scribe of the poem's only manuscript, evidently read Arthur's pride as both excessive and characteristic of his class; there is a drawing of a peacock with a helmed human head at the beginning of this section of the narrative.[33] Yet Arthur keeps well within the bounds of late fourteenth-century military protocol even when he ravages Italy. In the line following the passage quoted above, the poet calls Arthur valiant.

Thus, even as the poem stirringly advocates the invigorations of warfare as a way of life, it broadens its view to pursue the contradictions within the monarchical prowess that Arthur represents and that the poem continually stages. It draws into question the whole ideology that makes the pursuit of the king's wars the basis for chivalric practice. And when it does this, it grips one of the mainstays of alliterative romance as a genre: its sense of provinciality which energizes critical scrutiny of the royal court. Rosalind Field brilliantly suggests that Arthur is so closely associated with monarchical self-promotion that the aristocracy-centered writers of Anglo-Norman and early Middle English romance refuse to touch him at all. Aside from the Breton lays, fourteenth-century alliterative romances are the first insular romances to seize on the matter of Britain—and they usually regard Arthur from a skeptical distance.[34]

The alliterative *Morte Arthure*, accordingly, portrays a rather troubling ideal when it shows an aristocracy wholly bonded to the king's military ambitions. Whose ideal is it? The affective appeal of solidarity between king and barony is going to depend a great deal upon who is levying it and why. Solidarity can arise from genuinely if temporarily shared interests; but solidarity can also camouflage manipulation and coercion. Richard Kaeuper points out that for late medieval culture "we have good reasons for thinking that the union of chivalry and kingship was a marriage of convenience . . . Kingship and chivalry were moving on divergent courses which only for a time appeared to be parallel."[35] Here it is interesting to note that both Edward I and Edward III were Arthurian romance enthusiasts who sought to cultivate this apparent parallelism by performing Round Tables of their own. The *Morte Arthur*'s criticism of the nostalgia for this old comitatus-type solidarity between king and knight based on the pursuit of national wars is sharpened by an alertness to how conveniently and effectively that ideal had been manipulated by recent English kings.

Edward I, in particular, gained an international reputation for chivalric virtue that drew heavily upon Arthurian scripts. Whether or not he was an Arthurian enthusiast as Roger Loomis argues or merely a canny manipulator of the cultural power of Arthurian romance as Maurice Powicke suggests, throughout his reign Edward I claimed, played, and deployed the Matter of Britain for his own purposes. Invoking Arthur, he could broadcast his own sovereignty as a conqueror of England's border realms in Wales and Scotland and mark his suppression of baronial rebellions within his own realm.[36] In 1278 he ceremonially translated the supposed bodies of Arthur and Guenever from Glastonbury to Westminster.[37] In 1279 he attended a magnificent Round Table held by his supporter and friend Roger Mortimer and staged another himself in 1284 at Nefyn in Snowdonia to celebrate his acquisition of Wales. The following summer he brought the putative ancient crown of Arthur back to Westminster as a sign of his sovereignty over the Arthurian heartland (he made a similar trophy of the Stone of Scone in 1296 and the crown of John Balliol in 1299). And in the last year of his reign, in 1306, he staged a Feast of the Swans, evocative of romance in its dramatic interpellation of participants to pledge support to the king's military aspirations. In each case, Edward drew upon Arthurian romance dramatically to reinforce a variety of military and political consolidations. The Feast of the Swans is particularly interesting since it also marks his last-ditch attempt to draw his heir and barons away from their own disorganized fractiousness and toward a new campaign against Robert Bruce in Scotland. Powicke stresses the self-consciousness of this dramaturgy:

Edward was a political realist. He lived in an age of historical propaganda and knew the value of it. He was conscious of the danger latent in the mingling of the passion for tournaments with the disorderly impulses to self-help ... In his later years the danger was serious ... It is probable that at the feast of the Swans the king sought to divert this undisciplined energy into the channels cut by his own wrath, just as, more than forty years before, he had rallied the Marcher lords against Earl Simon.[38]

After Edward II polarized the barony even further with fatal consequences, Edward III seems to have taken a leaf from his grandfather's book. Driven by an implacable sense of his own sovereign rights, he nonetheless succeeded in reinventing the monarchy in a way that appealed to the chivalric fantasies of his barony. Juliet Vale argues that Edward III reworked to his own ends a recognizable aristocratic tradition of cultivating Arthurian cult status within chivalric performances like jousts, tournaments, and feasts. Edward III held Round Tables, staged feasts and tournaments, and carefully instituted the Order of the Garter to mark his victory at Crécy and model the possibility of monarchical support in an Arthurian vein to a deliberately wide range of chivalric contenders at different levels of experience, reputation, and status.[39] In this,

his simultaneous political achievement was two-fold: to provide a perpetual memorial to the justification of his own kingly claims [successfully defended at Crécy]; and also to create a prestigious chivalric elite comprising representatives of every section of society that could aspire to inclusion—established noble families and allies abroad, as well as members of his own household and family—who were characterised first and foremost by loyalty to the order's head.[40]

In fact Edward III founded the Order of the Garter with exquisite timing; it followed and helped ameliorate a political crisis brought on by the effort of funding and cultivating alliances for first massive campaigns of the Hundred Years War.[41] The Order and Edward's other efforts to offer his aristocracy and gentry arenas for self-promotion within "the channels cut by his own wrath"[42] succeeded resoundingly in engaging the cooperation, financial support, and campaigning skills of an aristocracy that hitherto had had to be strong-armed into the wars of their monarchs from Henry III through Edward II. This enthusiasm culminated in a level of aristocratic recruitment in 1359 and 1360 so high (over 3,000 English men of arms) that the king was able to turn away foreign mercenaries as an unnecessary expense.[43]

Yet this aristocratic enthusiasm did not quell a more widespread consciousness that this ongoing national war was unprecedented and expensive. Its economic and political repercussions went far beyond the monarchy and aristocracy, leading to debate and in some cases to criticism and resistance. Gerald L. Harriss argues that in England the responsibility of parliament to oversee taxation both toward the defense of the realm (the argument used by Edward for war financing) and for the common profit actually brought parliament into a "defensive dialogue with the Crown," which exercised and strengthened their potential for political opposition.[44] The monarchy was bolstered but at the same time forced to negotiate with an increasingly expert parliamentary body drawn from the aristocracy and gentry of the realm and at least as alert to local interests as they were to international ones.[45] And Richard Kaeuper shows that the unprecedented scope and duration of fourteenth-century war efforts exacerbated a growing economic depression and intensified problems of authority, justice, and livelihood that perplexed not only the noble classes but medieval society at large:

The kings of England and France . . . channeled vast resources in the form of money, goods, and services to the conduct of war; the campaigns which these resources sustained brought dislocations to the common economic life of northwestern Europe and serious devastation to much of France . . . If the vigour of medieval warfare expanded as the vigour of the medieval economy slumped, the role of war looms very large indeed in the constellation of late medieval problems.[46]

Kaeuper finds in the *Morte Arthure* an example of this attritional consciousness.[47] And it would not be the only alliterative poem to exhibit it. The ending of *Winnere and Wastoure* highlights the king's willingness to overturn the estates themselves if he could thereby channel civilian resources into his military endeavors. The debate which occupies the poem ends with the king separating the combatants, sending "each to a land where he is loved the most" (459). The aristocratic warriors who consume of the wealth of the realm (Waster) are to go to Cheapside in London, where they will spend their resources in setting up shelters where drunk men can be made drunker, and the already sated can be further stuffed. This parodically co-opts Waster's previous injunctions to charity and deliberately billets the military strength of the realm within a setting of urban consumption which will consume their own energies and resources. On the other hand, the mercantile, legal, and religious producers (Winner) should go to the papal court where they can display their acquisitive expertise before the real pros and then be lured (along with their wealth) to swell the ranks of the king's army before Paris by the promise of more wealth:

> "Wayte to me, þou Wynnere, if þou wilt wele chefe,
> When I wende appon werre my wyes to lede . . .
> I thynk to do it in ded and dub þe to knyghte
> And giff giftes full grete of gold and of siluer
> To ledes of my legyance þat lufen me in hert." (496–97, 499–501)

["Look to me, Winner, if you want to prosper, when I go to lead my men to war . . . I intend to put it into effect and dub you a knight, and give very great gifts of gold to men of my allegiance that love me in their hearts."][48]

Here the poem completely divorces the aristocracy from military practice, while at the same time recruiting the rich, nonaristocratic, merchants, fraternal orders, and lawyers to the king's war efforts, ironically rewarding their weirdly expanded military heraldic display at the poem's beginning with the promise of actual military indenture and knighthood. Given that *Winnere and Wastoure* was probably written between 1352 and 1370, it does not even require a late century perspective to spark an ironic commentary on how the king manipulates the realm's economic forces and not for either the maintenance of traditional modes of chivalry (as Edward's Arthurian rhetoric would suggest) or the good of the realm, but for his own military self-promotions.

If the gentry and aristocracy became disengaged from monarchical military endeavors during the late fourteenth century, that disengagement sharpened into actual resistance under Richard II. This is not because the king was less expert than his grandfather in chivalric propaganda—or less interested in traditional chivalric ideals.[49] Rather, I would argue, he relied on favorites too much, targeting too narrowly, partially, or episodically and without the consistent broadness of appeal shown in Edward III's formation of the Order of the Garter, which had included "representatives of every section of society that could aspire to inclusion."[50] There is no doubt that Richard II could manipulate the image of the king as war leader with amazing effect. During the Rising of 1381 at Smithfield, as part of an apparently well-executed plot to isolate and kill the rebel leader, Richard dramatically marshaled the insurgents almost before the body of Wat Tyler had hit the ground. He rode into the crowd shouting, "You shall have no captain but me," before directing them away from the indefensible heart of London to Clerkenwell.[51]

In 1385, he attempted an inaugural expedition to Scotland distinguished more by its glamorous appeal to chivalric tradition than by its military results. Desiring to assemble the third largest army of English fourteenth-century warfare, he enacted an old-style feudal levy, the last in English history though its anachronistic appeal belied the contractual mechanisms by which it was actually assembled. This tactical maneuver was intended both to enhance Richard's prestige by recalling his grandfather Edward III's levy of 1337, the start of a brilliant military career, and to save the government money by forcing the larger tenants to recruit men without the single or double "regard" which under ordinary circumstances they would have expected.[52] The ensuing brief campaign bespoke both martial implacability and strategic restraint. Richard chased the retreating Scottish army for a week, torching Melrose Abbey, Newbattle Abbey, and Holyrood en route. But he wisely refused to risk campaigning across the Firth of Forth, resisting the bellicose advice of John of Gaunt, whose Lancastrians made up the bulk of Richard's army. The campaign achieved its military objectives without either bringing the Scottish army to bay or exciting the admiration that a large victory could bring.

Throughout his reign, Richard waged wars that by and large achieved their military ends but failed to excite popular loyalty. In 1394, a well-executed military expedition to Ireland foundered politically, according to

James L. Gillespie, because Richard let his cultivation of the image of law-giving and beneficent king overcome political realism.[53] At home, he propagated an image of stern justice and prudence.[54] Writing after his death and from across the channel with no obvious motive to praise him and apparently little interest in his deposition, Christine de Pisan mused on the gulf between his misfortune and his reputation:

> Renowned
> Very highly for taking up arms;
> Willingly, he was praised
> For being *preux*, a true Lancelot,
> It was said of him, without fault,
> In matters of arms and battles."[55]

Gillespie attributes Richard's dismal military reputation among modern historians not to ineptness but rather to an inability to project successfully an image of himself as victorious leader, quipping that "He never fought in France; and he used a handkerchief! His critics have looked no further."[56]

But more crucially, both Richard's excluded barony and the increasingly factionalized aristocracy were becoming much less receptive to monarchical dramaturgies of national war—and not simply because they disliked the monarch. Indeed as early as the 1370s and 1380s many among the aristocracy and gentry with domestic commitments were bailing out of the king's wars. Within the armies their proportion waned from about twenty percent to less than ten percent. Instead, armies became dominated by mounted bowmen as well as nonaristocratic careerist soldiers on the make; the tactical combination of mounted knights and bowmen was very effective and strategies were altered accordingly.[57] This downward shift in the social composition of warfare is crystallized in Chaucer's *General Prologue* portrayal of the old-style (literally rusty) knight at arms, his courtly squire, followed by the trim, weapon-bristling yeoman of nebulous estate, as the shape of things to come—a potted military history. Andrew Ayton sums up the disappointing effects of this shift on the aristocratic warrior:

No sooner had the provision of pay and a major continental war provided him with an opportunity to convert the ideal of a warrior class into a functioning reality, than he found himself no longer the only really important component of the military community . . . the aristocratic fighter had become the partner of the bowman in a tactical system which depended upon them both. Moreover, he was now increasingly likely to find himself fighting shoulder to shoulder with *parvenu* men at arms, men who were certainly not of gentle blood . . . The fading of the gentry's interest in war . . . may well be connected with this change in military status, as with the heavier demands of shire administration and local justice.[58]

By the end of the century, Andrew Ayton concludes, "war was no longer an activity which set the minor aristocrat apart from his social inferiors."[59] Imbued by this late century consciousness of change, the *Morte Arthure* looks backward to propose a critique at once brutal and wistful. It highlights the way that war had been manipulated as an arena both for chivalric self-fashioning and monarchical convenience. To do so, it pushes the languages of war—as they constitute armor, body, blood, and loyalty—to theatrical extremes to show them for the wonderful, savage, and ultimately fatal beguilements that they are.

Wandering Signs

The confrontation between Arthur and Lucius in the poem shows a chivalry whose visual mechanisms of self-expression have become untrustworthy. This semiotic instability sharpens the skirmish between Sir Clegis and the King of Syria, who has a much larger army. To even the odds Clegis proposes a mini-tournament—three courses of war with champions from both sides. But the King of Syria stops the proceedings:

> Þane sais þe Kynge of Surry, "Alls saue me oure lorde,
> ȝif þow hufe all þe daye, þou bees noghte delyuerede
> Bot thow sekerly ensure with certayne knyghtez
> Þat þi cote and thi creste be knawen with lordez,
> Of armes of ancestrye entyrde with londez."   (1687–91)

[Then says the King of Syria, "God save me, but you can stand here all day and you won't get a fight unless you give some surety with trustworthy knights that your coat and crest are known among lords, and your ancestral arms entered in the registers along with your lands."]

In this passage, Clegis is asked with insulting politeness to produce his knightly credentials. The knight gives an impressive list of justifications for his right to bear arms: his arms are inherited, have been confirmed by lords, and have been observed in battle, and his ancestry dates back to Brutus and thence to Troy, the nonpareil origin for all European nobility. These credentials combine genealogical rationales with recognition by peers and thus show familiarity with such contemporary procedures for legally justifying arms as were followed during the famous Scrope/Grosvenor trial where battlefield witnesses were amassed. However, the King of Syria does not believe them. In the end Sir Clegis and his commander Sir Cador have to prove their worthiness to fight simply by fighting en masse even though they are cruelly outnumbered and end by losing fourteen knights.

This unreliability of the signs that designate nobility infects the poem as a whole but becomes even more acute when the signs not only designate family, lineage, and property but also reflect personal identity. Susan Crane argues that within chivalric signifying systems, the stable and codified heraldic signs of family status, coat of arms, crest, and seal are continually in tension with the more personal and flexible signs of personal identity such as motto, colors, and badge, which knights could abandon and invent over the course of a single career and which therefore can historicize chivalric identity as changing and performative. In addition, both the stable and the historical signs of chivalric identity are flagrantly opaque, highlighting what is withheld in order to rivet the eye and engage the imagination of the viewer.[60]

The *Morte Arthure* imbues the signs of chivalric self-performance with exactly such provocative ambiguity when it attaches multiple devices and figures to participants in the conflict, inviting interpretation of their characters but pushing semiotic flexibility to dizzying extremes. For instance, Arthur's first dream links him to the dragon, and Lucius and the Giant to the bear. The dragon is an ambiguous authority who comes over the western sea both to kill the foreign tyrant and to destroy his own people. Arthur's association with a dragon is not surprising; in the poem's sources, the dragon is Arthur's emblem in battle, a legacy from his father, Uther Pendragon. Yet Lucius, Arthur's "bearlike" enemy, claims the dragon emblem as well when he "drawes into douce Fraunce . . . dresside with his dragouns, dredfull to schewe" (1251–52). A dragon turns up on the banner of one of Lucius's allies, the Viscount of Rome, and finally appears on Lucius's own standard when he "dresses vp dredfully the dragone of golde" (2026). Mary Hamel argues that the assignment of the dragon banner to Lucius was a late addition because after describing the battle of Sessye, the poet reverts to his chronicle sources and gives Lucius only the imperial eagle in subsequent lines. This suggests that the poet began by trying to keep the sides of the conflict distinct and then deliberately began adding things to perplex them.[61] Both leaders become dragons, figures of equivocal power that end by destroying their own people.

Arthur's fight with the Giant transmits the symbols of oppressive authority even more disturbingly. The Giant rules by (literally) naked force, emblematizing his power with two symbols, his great blunt club and the cloak trimmed with the beards of subjugated and figuratively emasculated kings. Arthur slaughters him in a flurry of crusading zeal, but although he erects a shrine to commemorate the event he retains both the club and the cloak as trophies, inciting wonder about Arthur's own

hypermasculine desires. By virtue of these shared emblems the poem shat-
ters the ideological boundaries between different sides of the conflict just
as Arthur transgresses the boundaries of England, France, and Italy. As
Arthur moves into Lucius's territory across the sea in France, he acquires
symbols that recall Lucius' tyranny, while Lucius is linked to symbols originally associated with Arthur. Since each sign is a term in a binary that validates one side at the expense of the other (primal club/chivalric sword;
brutal bear/bright dragon; tyrant/just king), this tendency for symbols to
cross over and attach themselves to both sides of the equation troubles
the self-justifying work of each binary. The very terms that individuate a
knight, ennoble him, legitimize him as a warrior and not a murderer, and
designate his conquest righteous and not rapacious, gradually collapse into
their opposites.

And these signs continue to proliferate. Where *Sir Gawain and the
Green Knight* assumes the elegant sufficiency of pentangle and girdle, the
Morte Arthure pranks itself out beyond superfluity, offering multitudes
of pseudoheraldic tokens through which to read Arthur's character but
nothing definitive. We do not even know Arthur's actual battle standard
until he turns back to England to fight Mordred, and when we discover it,
it is double; the poet created it by amalgamating two traditions. The
French prose romance tradition gives Arthur three gold crowns on a red
field while the chronicles give him a white virgin with child. Arthur's banner in the *Morte Arthure* gives him both: the crowns below and the virgin
on the upper third (3646–49). How are we supposed to relate imperial
longings to merciful piety? Is this another one of the poem's many moving
and troubling conflations of the language of sanctity with the language of
battle? Or can it signify the disjunction between Arthur's masculine imperial battle-play and the femininized, courtly, and eventually generational
labors he refuses? Ideally these symbols should signify Arthur's synthesis of
these diverse virtues, but their very multiplicity is suggestive and difficult.
Even if we dwell on any single symbol (say, the dragon), we find ambiguities which the poem is at pains to foster and multiply further.

This semiotic chivalric excess resonates with late fourteenth-century
changes in chivalric self-definition and display. Although in the late fourteenth and early fifteenth century in England the protocols and regulations
of heraldry were not so rigid as they afterward became, knightly insignia
still denoted family, lineage, and property. However, by the late fourteenth
century, heraldic emblems were not exclusive to the noble classes and could
be simply adopted by anyone from prosperous urban capitalists to peasants.
Even fraternal orders had their emblems, as *Winnere and Wastoure* shows.

Fourteenth-century upward mobility accentuated this proliferation of armorial signs. Christine de Pisan approvingly discusses the "arms that everyday are assumed at pleasure, as it sometimes happens that Fortune at her pleasure raises men to higher estate."[62] A bearer-of-arms could be a knight by distraint, struggling for the income to maintain his equipment; a wealthy merchant who had left the city to purchase an estate and thus bought his way into the gentry; a provincial man-at-arms who did well enough at Poitiers or Crécy to win a post in a gentry household; a land-owner who got the means to maintain himself by venturing himself or seeding some of his family into trade; or a civil servant ennobled by the king. One could inherit gentle status, be granted it, purchase it, or simply claim it. Sylvia Thrupp holds that there were four ways for a merchant to acquire arms in medieval London: inheritance, a grant from the king, pur-chasing a patent from a herald, and simple appropriation. The first three were comparatively rare but the fourth method was rampant. Merchants and artisans chose devices that sometimes reflected their trade (two pikes for the fishmongers, for instance) but more often claimed the same fantas-tic and predatory beasts that enlivened the banners of the greater nobility. Some tradesmen chose emblems that abjured the laws of heraldry, turning shields more or less into billboards.[63] Freeborn peasants could also claim coats of arms.

Such widespread adoptions of the signs of seigneurial status fed the need for more organization of heraldry. Throughout this time, heralds were refining their discipline by writing treatises and compiling Rolls of Arms.[64] By the end of the fourteenth century, armorial trials such as Scrope versus Grosvenor and Lovel versus Moreley were being arbitrated at court, while more forceful disputes often enlivened the battlefield. Christine de Pisan, drawing from Bonet's *Tree of Battles* and other sources, argues that knights from separate countries should not dispute each other's claims to identical arms, but they often did.[65] Froissart leads up to the battle of Poitiers by describing an altercation between Sir John Chandos and the French Marshal, Lord Jean de Clermont, in which they discover that they each, like Arthur, bear an image of the Virgin:

Than the lorde Cleremont sayd, Chandos, howe long have ye taken on you to bere my devyce? Nay, ye bere myne, sayd Chandos, for it is as well myne as yours. I deny that, sayd Cleremont, but and it were nat for the truse this day bytwene us, I shulde make it good on you incontynent that ye have no right to bere my devyce. A sir, sayd Chandos, ye shall fynde me to morowe redy to defend you and to prove by feate of armes that it is as well myne as yours. Than Cleremont sayd, Chandos, these be well the wordes of you Englysshmen, for ye can devyce nothyng of newe, but all that ye se is good and fayre.[66]

Cleremont accuses Chandos of stealing an attractive personal device from the culturally superior French—a personal insult jagged with a slight about the derivative nature of English chivalry. And while this conflict is enlivened because its proponents are on opposing sides of a crucial battle in the Hundred Years War, the Scrope/Grosvenor trial demonstrates serious disputes within English chivalry as well.

These inevitable convergences between devices are further complicated by the flexibility of fourteenth-century personal badges, mottos, and signs. These insignia, like the figures associated with Arthur in the *Morte Arthure*, could be altered and multiplied. Edward III adopted a series of devices and several different personal mottos throughout his reign. Some of the higher nobility, the Black Prince among them, had two insignia, one for peace and one for war. The family heraldic device in the late fourteenth century was often altered to reflect not only its bearer's family but his personal identity and changing fortunes. For instance, the eldest son alone would inherit his father's coat of arms; other sons were obliged to difference them, making changes within the paternal design to show that they belonged to a cadet branch of the family.[67] Insignia could also be changed to reflect seigneurial acquisitions and changes of status, the most flamboyant example being Edward III's appropriation and inclusion of the arms of France in his own requartered coat of arms as he claimed the French crown at the beginning of the Hundred Years War. Such constant adjustment of sign to present identity demonstrates an increasingly inflected heraldic system of signification, necessarily accompanied by the growing professional specialization of the heralds employed to keep tabs on it.

Seals were even more personal. Predating the coat of arms as an authenticating personal mark, the seal usually depicted the seated or riding figure of its owner.[68] The seal gradually came to include the coat of arms (usually engraved on a shield carried by the figure of the proprietor or adorning his horse's trappings) and is thus one of the best surviving sources in heraldry, charting the rise, elaborations, and changes of the entire heraldic system of familial and knightly signification. But seals could also be changed according to the personal fortunes of their owner: marriage, inheritance, promotion, and acquisition of new holdings. The seal was often publicly canceled and broken into pieces at the death of its owner or buried with him or her, not simply to prevent its theft and misuse but to identify the body in case of an exhumation.[69] Another ceremony tightened the association between the seal and the body of its owner; at the end of the Middle Ages in France, it was placed alone on a horse to lead the procession of a royal entry, shadowing forth the body of its owner.[70]

Thus by the later Middle Ages, there were not only strong familial and lineal resonances linked to heraldic devices but also personal ones. They had civic and social as well as military uses. They were not static but constantly updated, not single but often multiple (one proprietor could have many seals of various kinds, scaled in importance and type of use). Furthermore, although they were originally limited to rulers, by the end of the fourteenth century, they were no longer the prerogative and identifying mark of any particular class.[71] The *Morte Arthure* offers an extreme and colorful response to the problem of signifying chivalric identity and true nobility. It tests the culturally accepted signs of nobility, from heraldic devices, to ancient lineage, to reputation in battle, and finds them ineffective. In the course of the poem, such signs of chivalry are stripped away and disregarded. Finally, true nobility becomes defined not by what it wears or by what people say about it but by what it does, the violent exercise of battle that makes noble blood truly visible—all over the field.

The Brethe of Kings

The Arthur of the poem is a crux of chivalric identity yet his fractured critical reputation shows he is a difficult character to sum up. Throughout the poem he acts like an epic hero, speaking always before an audience in order to cement the social cohesion of his knights. He does not articulate his private thoughts in a solitary setting until the poem's end, when he grieves for his dead knights in some of the most moving passages in the poem. One could dismiss this reticence as an epic convention; R. Howard Bloch argues that epic language as a public discourse abjures metaphorical language as well as the expression of individual interiority and self-construction.[72] Whether or not this is so (and Sarah Kay has persuasively challenged it), the *Morte Arthure* is at least an epic with metaphorical seizures.[73] While we cannot know Arthur's interiority and while the poem's incredibly rich examination of chivalric showmanship makes all its identities extrinsic and performative, we have a sense that some interiority is there. The poet incessantly draws attention to it by depicting the unusual force of Arthur's emotions while destabilizing our interpretation of them. The poem's narration of battles and skirmishes will suddenly give way to an episode that without advancing the action encapsulates the tensions perplexing Arthur's enterprise, presenting us with figural riddles to be read.

The prolific vividness of these figures—dragon, bear, giant, virgin, crusader—signals something unseen and under pressure, elusive to readers and absolutely terrifying to Arthur himself. His first dream of the embattled dragon and bear so affrights him that "nere he bristez for bale on bede whare he lyggez" (805) [he nearly bursts with anguish on the bed where he lies]. Unless he knows the dream's meaning immediately, he will die at once (813). Arthur's second dream also fills him with mortal fear. He encounters Fortune in a particularly seductive mood, whirling a wheel on which are caught the Nine Worthies, heroes from classical, biblical, and medieval history. In the dream Arthur ignores the warnings and laments of the Worthies to take his own delightful tour on the Wheel, with its predictable ending. "And when his dredefull drem whas drefen to þe ende, / The kynge dares fore dowte, dye as he scholde" (3224–25) [And when his fearful dream drew to its end the king shivers for fear as if he were going to die]. These are the only two moments in a poem filled with hideous confrontations where Arthur is said to feel fear, and crucially they are moments of half-obscured self-envisioning. It does not matter that the first dream signifies victory and the second signifies death. He trembles before the prospect of his own signification.

However, one aspect of Arthur's interiority does receive forceful visceral expression, the beating pulse of Arthur's chivalry and his prime mover. It is a vital anger that the poem calls "brethe." The poet locks this anger to monarchical authority; it enables Arthur both to overawe his enemies at court and to overpower his enemies on the battlefield. The word "brethe" is associated exclusively with Arthur (with one quasi-exception which I will discuss below)—only Arthur "wreaks his brethe" on the battlefield (2213) and even in peaceful situations his eyes can burn "full brymly for breth" (117) if he is provoked. His "brethe" at the Roman ambassadors, tightly restrained, instigates his conquests and it also drives their ending. After his dream of Fortune, he goes out "with brethe at his herte" to meet Cradok, who brings the news of Mordred's treachery and the beginning of his doom. The phrase "with brethe at his heart" denotes his state of mind no less than four times at crucial moments in the poem. According to Mary Hamel, "brethe" means "anger, wrath, and vengeful spirit" but also "breath," and connotes both life and anger.[74] The poet makes Arthur a creature of "brethe" to show that he is sustained by a constitutional rage. By placing this self-creating anger at the heart of Arthur's character, the poet captures the cruelty inherent in monarchical rule, its intimacy to the king's military ambition, its effectiveness as a source of energy, and also its potential for self-destruction.

"Brethe" is suitably expressed in the text by fire imagery. When Arthur is angry, his eyes actually smoulder: "full brymly for breth brynte as the gledys" (117) [very fiercely for anger burnt like coals]. This incendiary Arthur radically departs from Continental traditions of Arthurian portrayal, which make the king a stationary and rather feeble figurehead shadowed by the restless knights striving within or against his court for chivalric recognition. The *Morte Arthure* by contrast gives the king the force of a barely controlled explosion. We see the potential of that chivalric energy in Arthur's hunger for empire. Lucius falls midway through the poem, but Arthur goes on, to Metz, to Tuscany, to Rome. Yet Arthur is not simply a loose cannon; he both channels his own potential for explosion and directs the martial exhilaration of his knights. If Arthur were as headstrong as his knights, he would have incurred terrible losses throughout the campaign, as Cador does when he attacks an army of 50,000 men with a prisoner escort, or perhaps might have lost his own life in a bout of battle frenzy as Gawain does. Arthur is an effective commander because he orchestrates the ferocity that drives him.

This restraint actually intensifies his anger's effect by allowing for more elaborate theater. After the challenge of the Roman ambassadors he discharges glares of such ferocity that the ambassadors fall prostrate before his gaze. But Arthur collects himself (with visible effort), and engages in diplomatic protocols, expressing his violence in more subtle and indirect ways lest he "wilfully in þis wrethe ... wreken my seluen" (151) [willfully in this wrath destroy myself] — not an idle threat in this poem. Then Arthur plans a feast of which the lavish and cosmopolitan fare expresses his mastery of vast and diverse territories — the tarts come from Turkey; the wine from Venice. The sheer variety of exotic animals trussed up and exhibited to the ambassadors further bespeaks the wide range of Arthur's power, particularly as he accompanies the feast with mock apologies for its provincial sparsity. The feast also expresses his violence. It glitters and flames with metallic glazes and piercing lights, from the burnished boar's head to the glimmering fountains of wine served by ingenious faucets at the table. The astonished ambassadors are served a flaming bestiary including "Bareheueds þat ware bryghte, burnyste with syluer" (177) [bright boar heads, burnished with silver], "sewes ... owndé of azure all over, and ardant þem semyde / Of ilke a leche þe lowe launschide full hye" (192–94) [stews ... rippling all over with azure-blue sauces and they seemed to be blazing — the flame shot very high from each slice], and "fesauntez enflurischit in flammande siluer" (198) [pheasants embellished with flaming silver]. The feast substitutes for the king's scorching gaze and works only a slightly more circumspect dazzlement on the messengers. However,

the most striking image of the feast comes last, a figure that becomes a metaphor not only for Arthur's power but for Arthur himself and his court:

> There was a cheeffe buttlere, a cheualere noble,
> Sir Cayous þe curtaise þat of þe cowpe seruede:
> Sexty cowpes of suyte fore þe kyng seluyn,
> Crafty and curious, coruen full faire,
> In ever ilk a party pyghte with precyous stones,
> That nan enpoyson sulde goo preuely þer vndyre
> Bot þe bryght golde fore brethe sulde briste al to peces,
> Or ells þe venym sulde voyde thurghe vertue of þe stones. (208–15)

[There was a chief butler, a noble knight called Sir Kay the courteous who brought
in the wine: sixty cups in a set before the king himself, crafty and curious, carved
very beautifully, and set all over with precious stones in every part, so that no poison might slip secretly thereunder without the bright gold bursting into pieces
with anger, or else the poison vanishing through the power of the stones.]

The sixty cups correspond to the knights of Arthur's court—one
apiece—and crystallize the tensions that perplex chivalric identity in the
poem. The cups are rich and well made and, like the armor that Arthur and
his companions bear into battle, "crafty and curious." Their "bryght golde"
corresponds to Arthur's "clene gold" (217) colors and those of his knights.
They are "of suyte," a matched set, which makes them a community united
by likeness to each other, just as Arthur's court boasts of its solidarity
and the unity of interests between king and nobles. However, the description of their adorning jewels leads not to a metaphoric elaboration of
the virtues of the court but to more lapidary intimations of secret poison
within and it does so with an ease that is startling. "Venym" is another
carefully deployed word. Throughout the poem it is applied to Arthur's
enemies, to the Saracen allies of Mordred, to Sir Priamus's sword before
he joins Arthur's army, and to Sir Lucius. Yet the poet also applies it to the
dragon that is judged to symbolize Arthur in the dream of the dragon and
the bear. The dragon lets fly "syche a venymmous flayre . . . fro his lyppez /
That the flode of þe flawez all on fyre semyde"(773–4) [such a venomous
flare . . . from his lips that the water seemed all afire with its flames]. The
poison is linked here to the fire imagery that plays about Arthur.

In the description of the cups, the poison can catalyze one of two
possible reactions; either the cup will render the poison harmless through
the virtues of its adorning stones or the cup will become so furious ("fore
brethe") that it self-destructs. The first possibility is the fantasy that motivates Arthur's court, the image of an authority whose glittering representations and displays of exterior virtues can expel and nullify secret interior

poisons. The second possibility is the scenario that the poem will eventually enact.

Knightly Bodies

In one of the poem's most arresting scenes, Arthur comes across the body of his nephew, Gawain, amidst his downed banners surrounded by a wall of dead Saracens. Arthur lifts up Gawain's visor and kisses his lead-colored face, dabbling his own beard in the blood. His cousin Sir Ewaine rebukes his grief as unknightly behavior: "Blyne . . . thou blodies þi selfen . . . / Be knyghtly of contenaunce, als a kyng scholde, / And leue siche clamoure, for Cristes lufe of heuen!" (3975, 3979–80) [Cease! . . . You are bloodying yourself . . . Keep a knightly countenance as a king should and leave such clamor, for the love of Christ!]. Arthur's reply defends his grief as respect for his noble kinsman, locating kingliness and virtue specifically in Gawain's blood: "Þis ryall rede blode ryn appon erthe! / It ware worthy to be schrede and schrynede in golde, / For it es sakles of syn, sa helpe me oure Lorde" (3990–92). [This royal red blood spilled upon the earth! It were worthy to be arrayed and shrined in gold, for it is stainless of sin, so help me our Lord]. Arthur then gathers up some of Gawain's blood in a helmet and carries his body carefully back to camp. This scene shows the extent to which knightly power and authority can be located in a knight's body and blood. The fact that royal blood is shamefully spilled on the ground is a direct blow to Arthur's own power and status. Gawain's devastated body and blood incarnate a chivalric virtue that Arthur feels to have been destroyed in himself by Gawain's death. This scene makes explicit the resonances that complicate problems of chivalric identity in the poem. Throughout the *Morte Arthure*, bodies and blood, both living and dead, express knightly subjectivity in a more palpable and unmediated way than can the more social signs of chivalric status—the armor, the crest, the coat of arms, and the acknowledged reputation on the battlefield. Where Arthur expresses his ferocity in "brethe," his knights do so in blood.

This reliance on the corporeal is most explicit during the battles, where true nobility is proven. There, the knights are encased in armor which, like heraldic banners and coats of arms, expresses the wearer's social status and identity. The poem is fascinated by the individuating details of a knight's armor, returning again and again to the mechanisms of the visor piece, the particular shape of each bacinet. Each arming scene is lovingly detailed as the knight is gradually enclosed in the multilayered surface of cloth and metal that becomes his social and ancestral identity, ideally contiguous with and expressive of the individual knight's body, his might at arms, and his physical endurance. A case in point is the description of the armor Arthur dons before battling the giant which manifests his station as a preeminent commander. Arthur's exotic and unique armor reflects his double identity as sovereign and knight by sporting both crest and coronal.[75] When Arthur dons his armor he becomes an ambulatory self-advertisement. The armor further attests to Arthur's internal ferocity by recalling the appearance of the dragon in his dream. The dragon's tattered tail corresponds to Arthur's "shredded jupon," the dragon's golden claws, to Arthur's gilded gauntlets. Both wear silver scale mail, glittering with jewels and enamel, and both give a sense of airborne motion; the dragon is flying and Arthur "stridez on lofte" (916) [loftily strides]. More figuratively, both are filled with a burning force which expresses itself powerfully and venomously. One "shrympe" or armored monster is meant to recall the other, both as an entity in itself and a sign of Arthur's character, the volatile sovereign knight.

However, the poem pursues not only the individuating creation of a knight's social persona but its rupture. Once battle is joined, these signs of seigneurial authority are discarded as irrelevant to the real criteria of knighthood. The battlefield is where the anger that broods in knightly hearts is allowed to burst forth, destroying the traditional visual signs of knightly status to institute a more visceral insignia—not by victory but by wounding. Elaine Scarry argues that the shock of the opened body confers its own sense of reality upon the more ungrounded signs, ideologies, and rationales that can be associated with it. It bleeds conviction into them: "the injuring [of war] . . . provides, by its massive opening of human bodies, a way of reconnecting the derealized and disembodied beliefs with the force and power of the material world."[76]

And in the *Morte Arthure* there is a transubstantial countermovement as well. The impossibly wounded bodies of the knights gain a transcendent and supernatural energy which ultimately transforms the loss of life into a chivalric sacrament as shocking in its outrageousness as it is compelling in its appeal. The poet delights in verbs of splitting, breaking, thrust, and amputation, a taste for which his unusually inventive alliterative breadth of vocabulary well equips him. Although not quite as excruciatingly detailed in its dismemberments as *The Siege of Jerusalem*, the poem vividly depicts castrated giants, impaled kings, and wounded knights who are galloping about with their entrails entangled in their horse's hooves. When Cador makes his boast about the oncoming battle he describes it in terms of the violent transgression of both enemy lines and bodies.

"I sall, at þe reuerence of þe Rounde Table,
Ryde thrughte all þe rowtte, rerewarde and oþer,
Redy wayes to make and renkkes full rowme,
Rynnande on rede blode as my stede ruschez;
He þat folowes my fare and fyrste commes aftyre
Sall fynde in my fare-waye many fay leuyde." (389–94)

["For the honor of the Round Table, I shall ride straight through the rout, back-ward and forward, carving easy passages and jousting spaces full wide, running on red blood, as my steed rushes. He that follows my passage and comes first after me shall find many dying men in my wake."]

In the face of such penetrating energy, at times even fundamental distinc-tions between life and death break down. In the battle of Sessye, Lucius suffers not one but two mortal wounds, first impaled by Launcelot's spear so that "the hede haylede owtt behynde ane halfe-fote large" (2077) [the head stuck out behind by the length of a half foot] and finally dispatched by Arthur 200 lines later. The fey bodies of these exemplary warriors acquire the mortal temper of the other bodies that roam the landscapes of alliterative romance.

This extreme transgressive energy comes to constitute knighthood in the poem. Like his armor and sword, the knight is hammered out on the fields of the battles that occupy the main part of the narrative. The process of combat metaphorically echoes the forging of armor and weapons; it involves both fire to heat the metal and liquid to temper it. The smiting of weapon on armor ignites the air so that "flawes of fyre flawmes on theire helmes" (2556) [tongues of fire flame on their helms], while the blood flows freely over armor, and bodies fall into the many streams that inter-sect the poem's battlegrounds. The violent process of creating knighthood by battle is ratified by Arthur's battlefield ennoblements, as when he endows the messenger who tells him of the British victory in the first battle with the province of Toulouse (1566–70). As Mordred recognizes, it is only after war experience that knights become peers in council and join the circle of Arthur's trusted magnates.

Although this process of ennoblement through war underwrites almost every battle in the poem, one combat is particularly emblematic. Just after Arthur defeats Lucius at Sessye and continues into Lorraine to subdue the rebellious Duke, he sends Gawain out with a foraging party. After marching all night, the knights pause in a meadow to rest and Gawain moves apart from them to encounter a single mysterious knight at the edge of the woods, Sir Priamus. They fight in the manner of courtly romantic knights, for no reason except to see who is mightier. At one point in the combat between Priamus and Gawain, Gawain's armor is breached with a dreamlike slowness; the poet follows the weapon's passage step by step through the intervening layers of armor until it reaches a vein:

And awkewarde, egerly, sore he hym smyttes.
And alet enamelde he oches in sondire,
Bristes þe rerebrace with the bronde ryche,
Kerues of at þe coutere with þe clene egge,
Aue[n]tis the avawmbrace vyrallede with siluer;
Thorowe a dowble vesture of veluett ryche,
With þe venymous swerde a vayne has he towchede,
That voydes so violently þat all his witte changede—
The vesere, the aventaile, his vesturis ryche
With the valyant blode was verrede all ouer! (2564–73)

[And backhanded, eagerly, he smites him sorely, an enameled ailette he slashes asunder, bursts the shoulderpiece of the plate armor with the rich sword, carves it off at the elbowpiece with the pure edge, makes a vent in the forearmpiece decorated with silver; through a double vestment of rich velvet, with the venomous sword he has touched a vein, which empties so violently that he nearly lost his senses—the visor, the neck-protector, all these rich clothes were with the valiant blood spotted all over.]

In this combat the knights' armored social personae undergo the rupture that enables their flesh to speak through their armored bodies. During the fight, significantly, it is Gawain's ailette that is split first, a plate at the shoulder enameled with his coat of arms. This detail is an anachronism in Gawain's armor, a pre-1350 plate in a late fourteenth-century outfit. But its inclusion here, as well as showing the poet's armorial erudition, allows the poet to play out a dynamic that occurs elsewhere in the poem, when the first thing destroyed in the combat is the knight's insignia-bearing shield (in fact, Gawain has just split Priamus's shield). The ailette is important here precisely because it individuates Gawain as a knight of a particular family and a certain reputation, and its destruction shows a shift in the means by which his identity is expressed. During the battle of Sessye itself, this defacement of armorial bearings reaches epidemic proportions; the weapon play is so fierce that men "freten of orfrayes feste appon scheldez" (2142); they scrape off the gilded decorations fastened upon their shields in concerted iconoclasm. This obliteration of the outward signs allows the knight to demonstrate a more corporeal and convincing identity.

The battle between Gawain and Priamus makes this explicit. The rupture of Gawain's armor allows his own blood to replace his armorial insignia; "his vesturis ryche / With the valyant blood was verrede all ouer."

Interior and exterior, body and armor reverse and intermingle. At the end of this combat, Gawain is wearing his blood, while Sir Priamus's side has been split until his liver can be seen "with þe lyghte of þe sonne" (2561) [by the light of the sun]. This mutual wounding—not victory—is the object of this battle. Neither knight triumphs over the other; they simply proceed until each feels a violent change within his body: "þat all his witte changede." Only after this transformation do the knights stop fighting and speak to each other; it takes a death blow and a near loss of consciousness to convince them that their opponent must surely be of noble ancestry. Priamus promptly abandons his alliance with the Duke of Lorraine and joins Arthur's side. Their wounds are miraculously cured with water from the rivers of paradise.

This fight projects an ideal of battle as productive, a win-win contest with chivalric brotherhood as its prize. Even its wounds are erased. And crucially, it is a battle where the king is absent—a digression from the main campaign where two knights settle matters to their own satisfaction. Bodily extremity creates a chivalric recognition that transcends enemy lines. It provides an interesting counterfantasy to the poem's other digressive but emblematic single combat, Arthur's zero-sum fight with the giant of St. Michael's Mount whose apparent prize is Arthur's heroic superiority to tyrannical oppressors, a judgment which the poem later underhandedly rescinds. In Scarry's terms, these are the unreal signs that are violently materialized by combat.

But the poem also stresses the fictionality of both episodes—inviting disbelief and criticism of the violent methods by which belief is enticed. Arthur's battle with the fantastically horrible giant wears its romance affiliations on its face and Gawain's battle with Sir Priamus is almost parodically crammed with romance conventions. The geographically explicit itinerary of Arthur's campaigns melts suddenly into a *locus amoenus* so lovely that it lulls the knights to sleep, like the introduction to an alliterative dream-vision: "Lordes lenande lowe on lemande scheldes, / With lowde laghttirs on lofte for lykynge of byrdes . . . And some was sleghte one slepe with [a] slaughte . . ." (2672–73, 2675). [Lords leaned low upon their gleaming shields, raising loud laughter for delight at the sound of the birds . . . and some fell into sleep instantly]. The fight itself is a typical romance combat between unknown knights: no provocation; sparks ringing off the armor; the post-battle conversation when both knights should be gasping out their lives on the field; the one-on-one, blow-by-blow intensity of the combat itself. But the point that proclaims most clearly the battle's fantastic nature is the *deus ex machina* cure of both knights. The battle results not in mutual death but, miraculously, in chivalric solidarity.

Gawain's battle with Priamus dramatizes the positive alternative offered by the golden cups that figured Arthurian chivalry at the end of the New Year's feast. There, the jewels in the cup had the capacity to "voyde [the venom] thurghe vertue of þe stones" (215). Priamus bears a "venymous swerde" (2570) which deals wounds of supernatural fatality, but he is also provisioned with magically curative paradisial waters. The strength and honor Sir Gawain shows during the combat are enough to convert Priamus to Arthur's service, in effect turning him from venom to remedy.

This promise comprises battle's dangerous allure. Battle offers the possibility of a constructive transformation that draws the knights together as members of a warrior class. It replaces the unstable heraldic insignia of chivalric status with a more universal visceral insignia—mutual violent exchange. The social signs of a knight's identity may be ruptured or obscured as his armor is pierced, but his own body is enabled to speak through the armor in a way that joins him in class, gender, profit, and distinction to all the other knights on the battlefield—even his enemies. In the poem, battle allows the knights' inaccessible interiority a violent corporeal expression, but one that can dream of constructive rather than destructive ends. The language of bodily violence consolidates loyalties in a multitude of different ways: making knights into comrades, fellow-wounded, worthy enemies, and business partners in acquiring new lands and subjects. In the poem, the camaraderie of Arthur's court, the imperial hungers that lock king and noble together into an unstoppable band of chivalric brothers, require ongoing war.

Band of Brothers

In the poem, this knightly camaraderie replaces generation as a guarantor of social stability and continuity. The poem stresses the horizontal bonds between Arthur and his knights and downplays the vertical bonds linking generations and ensuring the transfer of authority and social stability. Among Arthur's knights even fathers and sons like Ewaine and Idris are seen as comrades-in-arms, their duties owed primarily to Arthur; their obligations to each other are strictly subsidiary, even in life and death situations. This is demonstrated forcibly in the final battle with Mordred, when Arthur sees Idris's father, Ewaine, overset by a horde of Saracens. He urges Idris to go to his father's aid but Idris refuses, saying:

"He es my fadire in faithe, forsake sall I neuer:
He has me fosteride and fedde, and my faire bretheren;
Bot I forsake this gate so me Gode helpe,
And sothely all sybredyn bot thy selfe one!" (4142–45)

["He is my father in faith, and I will never forsake him. He fostered and fed me
and all my fair brethren, but I refuse this departure, so God help me, and forsake
all kindred but you alone!"]

Idris does not betray his father here because it was his father who instructed him to put his loyalty to Arthur first. When this passage subordi-
nates the bonds of "sybredyn" [family relationships] to the bonds of fealty,
it not only revives a version of feudal loyalty that was by the late fourteenth century intensely anachronistic, but it drives even that anachronism
to an extreme.

This transference from bonds of generation to bonds of military loyalty reflects a more general distrust of generation and of the familial transmission of sovereignty throughout the poem. In the poem generational
bonds are subordinated to the system of knightly camaraderie because
generational bonds fray at the intimacy of knightly solidarity and threaten
to infect it with their inherent mutability. This is most evident in the suspicion with which the knights view women, who are associated with the
transmission of sovereignty between generations. There are only three
women in the poem: Guenever, her cousin the duchess of Brittany, and
the duchess's widowed attendant on St. Michael's Mount. These women
are represented either as having a pernicious effect on knightly solidarity
or as victims of the knightly livelihood of war. Mordred is told to stay in
England and look after Guenever, and the next time we see him, he has
betrayed the bonds of fealty to Arthur by impregnating Guenever and seizing the crown, apparently with Guenever's help—she gives him Arthur's
sword, Clarent, to which she alone has access. The other two women are
victims of the giant who at once opposes and obliquely prefigures the
darker and more suspect exercise of chivalric power. In either case the poem
constructs women/generation and the men/chivalry as mutually inimical.

Yet just as Arthur's device underwrites the sign of the virgin and child
with the three crowns of empire, the poem's martial brotherhood cannot
divest itself from the generation it attempts to exclude. Far from being
absent on the battlefield, the language of generation mingles with the language of competitive violence as combat after combat is sexualized. Gawain
threatens to bring the enemy to heel like a woman brought to bed: "We
sall blenke theire boste, for all theire bolde profire—/ Als bouxom as birde
es in bede to hir lorde" (2857–58) [We shall frustrate their boasts, for all

their bold challenges, they will be as submissive as a woman in bed is to her lord]. Military domination connotes sexual domination, the slash and thrust of battle includes the penetrations of rape. In siege warfare in particular if a town refused to surrender and fell to the besieger, rape of the inhabitants was the invader's legal prerogative. Christine de Pisan cautioned the defenders of a fallen town to sell their lives very dearly, attacking with any weapons even from the roofs of houses after an enemy has pierced the walls since they can expect no mercy at all.[77] Mary Hamel makes the point that Arthur shows unusual forbearance when he accedes to the plea of the ladies of Metz and forbids his victorious men to rape the women even while he makes them free of all property.

The figure who most clearly joins domination of the knightly enemy with the rape of women is of course the Giant of St. Michael's Mount, whose appetitive energies find three outlets: (1) the castrating enforcement of his dominion over other male rulers (when he demands their beards as homage to trim his cloak); (2) the fatal rape of women such as the duchess of Brittany, Guenever's cousin, which is indistinguishable in its begetting of death from the splittings and penetrations of the battlefield; and finally (3) the preying on children. Thus the Giant's bill of fare attacks family and generation in all its aspects. When Arthur battles the Giant, he may see himself as a knight destroying a monster; but he jokes to his men that he is a pilgrim seeking a saint. Arthur ends by adopting the Giant's strategies for enforcing his own power. His battle with the Giant is imbued with sexual overtones absent in the scene's sources. Arthur himself loses his sword early in the fight and is obliged to grapple closely with the half-naked Giant. Finally, the two roll down the entire length of St. Michael's Mount in each other's arms, before Arthur is able to dispatch the Giant with his dagger and claim the Giant's club and cloak of beards. When Arthur castrates the Giant, he is following the castrating Giant's example. But Arthur's power resembles the Giant's in an even more important regard; the way his authority is promoted destroys the possibility of its transmission. The Giant eats children, and Arthur's own "children"—his knights, younger nephews, and heirs—are ultimately devoured on his battlefields.[78] When Arthur jokes about seeking the Giant as a pilgrim would seek a saint, his irony is perplexed by a grain of truth; in a sense, the Giant will eventually become the patron saint of Arthur's own imperial enterprise.

This brutalization darkens Arthur's last battles as the costs of his war expand to encompass possessions, blood, wits, manhood, and life. The account of Gawain's death is an accelerating tour de force both of bravery and idiocy. In the notes to her edition of the poem Mary Hamel traces the degenerative stages Gawain undergoes in his final battle against Mordred: "In line 3817 Gawain is compared to a 'woodwose,' uncivilized and 'unwise' but still human, in 3831, to a lion, fierce but still noble; [finally] he is simply 'ferocious.'"[79] At the end, Gawain no longer knows even why he is fighting and has lost all strategy: "for wondsom and will all his wit failede, / that wode alls a wylde beste he wente at þe gayneste" (3836–37) [for fierceness and willfulness all his wit failed, so that he drove in by the quickest way, as mad as a wild beast]. In a move that recalls Arthur's drawing of the misericorde to dispatch the Giant, Gawain attempts to draw a "short knife" but, falling, cannot penetrate Mordred's armor. His prone position makes it easy for Mordred to deal the head wound that kills him. In this scene the carefully orchestrated rage the poem makes fundamental to knightly subjectivity receives more and more disastrously direct expression. The poem thus probes closer to a recognition of darkness at the center of the honor culture—the knightly potential for self-destruction foreshadowed at Arthur's feast by the cup that burst with rage at the poison within it.

It is precisely because the poem has just shown Gawain's devolution into a figure of pure, untrammeled, and ultimately suicidal fury that it selects him for a fantasy of chivalric canonization. The closer we get to the heart of chivalry as this poem depicts it, the more purely and preciously explosive it becomes. Arthur reenacts Gawain's death both as savagery and as sacrament when he laments over Gawain's body and dabbles in his blood. He tries to invest that elusive, volatile liquid with the material transcendence of a relic by gathering it up in his helmet, a figure that nicely crystallizes the way throughout the poem he has channeled the blood of his knights into his own military leadership with ultimately mortal consequences. Arthur's behavior is as disturbing to Arthur's watching knights as it is to modern critics. For all his chivalric aspirations and powerfully sanctifying language, we are acutely aware that he is laving his beard in his knight's blood, rather than forcefully expressing his own on the battlefield as his knights have done for him. The poem touches out this predatory undertone: "his burliche berde was blody berown, / Alls he had bestes birtenede and broghte owt of life" (3971–72) [his burly beard was covered with blood as if he had beaten down beasts and killed them].

Throughout, the poet has highlighted the death-in-life characterization of the warrior, his already doomed state even before the battle is under way. From Arthur's first answer to the Roman ambassadors where he promises that the "flour of his faire folke full fay sall be leuyde" (438) [the flower of his fair folk shall be left quite dead] to the last battle where the "feye blod rynnys / Of þe frekkeste on frounte, vnfers ere belevede" (4122–32) [fey blood runs / of the boldest in the vanguard, all are left meek], the boldest and strongest knights are overshadowed by the loss in battle of their animating anger—in this citation "vnfers" (unfierce) equals dead. Even when Arthur's war band has been decimated and Arthur stands alone, lamenting amidst a great heap of the corpses of his former companions, the poem does not let go of the ideology of knightly conquest—rather it is at the moment of its self-destruction that it speaks most eloquently and memorably. "Qwy then [ne] hade Dryghttyn destaynd at His dere will / Þat He hade demyd me to-daye to dy for ʒow all? / That had I leuer than be lorde all my lyfe tym / Off all þat Alexandere aughte qwhills he in erthe lengede" (4157–60) [Why has not God ordained at his own will that he had judged for me today to die for you all? I would rather have that fate then be lord for my entire life of all that Alexander owned while he was on earth]. Arthur's words are edged with a messianic glamour as he longs to die for his men rather than watch them die for him. In this the *Morte Arthure* takes a perverse step beyond *The Wars of Alexander*, which never sees death as anything but a betrayal of conquest and a final reluctant defeat. Arthur's last speeches imagine death in battle unalterably sealing a knightly concord finally more precious than the peacetime jurisdiction of lands, more valuable even than the vigorous exercise of arms. It disregards generation, rejects the possibility of merely continuing the lineage, passing its authority duly to heirs and vanishing away into history. It immortalizes its own suicidal ferocity.

Nobility, Generation, and History

The *Morte Arthure* aims, ultimately, at apocalypse. In the course of the poem, Arthur not only faces and attacks the threatening predecessors of British sovereignty as his present challengers, but he also targets the whole process of generation itself, with its possibilities of future continuity. And where other alliterative romances tend to content themselves with one or two threatening predecessors, the *Morte Arthure,* like *The Wars of Alexander,* carves its way through a horde of them: primitive, oriental, and classical, in order to show how Arthur breaks with and exceeds them. As Arthur battles toward Italy, he actually backtracks along the trail of the *translatio imperii* by which British sovereignty was justified, a geographical foray back into imperial history which offers him, fascinatingly, enemies that become more and more up-to-date. Of all the romances considered in this book, the *Morte Arthure* is the most schematic in the way it weaves the intimacy of the past with the present.[80] Although the kings in the poem predicate their status on the paradigms of genealogy and venerable origin, they finally seek a self-sufficiency from lineage and precedent, to excel all their ancestors and obliterate the divisions and doubtful antecedents of a troubled history. The poem shows the unraveling of all social bonds which knit together the chivalric body, when the next generation uses the same parricidal logic to establish itself. The poem ends with Arthur's orders that all of Mordred's descendants should be hunted down and killed. After expending his aristocracy in the fight and thus destroying the natural-ized relationship between king and knight which exemplifies his chivalric strength, Arthur targets this "child of his chamber" who has stolen a leaf from his uncle's book and thus cuts off that chivalry's transmission into the future, a last echo of the Giant's castration.

From the beginning of the poem, this multi-episodic colonization of the past is framed as the conquest of a rival line of descent in an either-or conquest over legitimate sovereignty. Arthur decides to conquer Rome for the same reason Lucius demands Britain's subjugation—that it was actually Britain's (or Rome's) by right of ancient conquests of Belinus and Brennius (or Julius Caesar). In reconquering Rome, Arthur aims to remedy the injus-tices of history and remove from the imperial throne his illegitimate brother, presumably a descendant of Brennius. The poem thus conflates two family conflicts: (1) a generational battle between two countries which are ancestor and descendant according to the historiographic tracings of the *translatio imperii*; and (2) a sibling rivalry between two brothers, both descendants of their ancient fathers, both endowed with ancestral claims to the empire.

These two conflicts decenter each other throughout the poem. The clean lines of the generational conflict are smudged by the conflict between siblings who come strongly to resemble each other. If Lucius's Roman hegemony is characterized as a decrepit but devouring Cronus figure eager to swallow his own children (like the Giant of St. Michael's Mount or the brutish bear of Arthur's dream), Arthur is legitimated as the Jovian con-queror, renovater and legitimate heir to the empire by the naturalized transfer of its center westward. He becomes the ideal of modern lawful rule and chivalric practice. Yet this perspective is problematized when the generational distinctions break down to reveal telling similarities between Lucius at his most bloodthirstily atavistic and Arthur at his most illustri-ously modern. The two become alternates, their self-representations in heraldry and visionary insignia indistinguishable from each other, in a way that undercuts distinctions between England and other, the present and the past, to show an ideology of self-definition by chivalric conquest ultimately at odds with itself.

This internal conflict is dramatized in the chiasmus between the geographical mapping of Arthur's itinerary and the temporal characterization of his antagonists. Since the overall structure of the poem delineates England's conquest of its Roman origins, the shape of Arthur's campaign might be expected to retrace Brutus's journey backward into Britain's past, each conflict dealing with a more ancient enemy until it climaxed with the conquest of Rome as its oldest living ancestor. Yet rather than casting backward along the trail of the *translatio imperii*, the narrative reverses the temporal order and traces a journey into the present and the future. We start with the Giant and end with Mordred, Arthur's own nephew.

The Giant works as an atavistic reminder of Britain's original inhabitants. The poet accentuates this native primitivism through significant departures from his sources. First, the Giant is utterly brutish; incapable of human speech, he attacks Arthur without challenge while in Geoffrey of Monmouth and Laȝamon's *Brut*, he addresses the old woman or Arthur himself. Second, the poet transposes the battle of St. Michael's Mount with a more foundational battle against the last remaining Giant of pre-settlement Britain. Laȝamon's account of Arthur's fight against the Giant of St. Michael's Mount bears no resemblance to *Morte Arthure*'s. Arthur wards off the Giant's first blow with his shield and wounds him in the chin. He then jumps behind a tree, which blocks the next blow, runs quickly around the tree three times, and knocks the Giant to the ground with a blow to the thigh. Finally, he instructs his knight Bedwyr to strike off the Giant's head. Geoffrey of Monmouth's account of the same battle is somewhat closer to the *Morte Arthure* in that the battle is not conducted wholly at sword's length; the Giant manages to grab Arthur around his middle at one point—but Arthur quickly escapes and dispatches him with a sword blow to the brain pan. Both versions differ significantly from *Morte Arthure*'s clutching and grappling brawl.

In fact, Arthur's battle with the Giant most resembles the accounts of a wrestling match staged by the Duke Corineus just after arriving on the island of Britain. Corineus—a giantish fellow himself—enjoys wrestling with the island's aboriginal Giants and after capturing the largest specimen, Gogmagog, dramatizes the match before numerous spectators. In Laȝamon this combat parallels the *Morte Arthure*'s in length, difficulty, the presence of witnesses, technique, and the final fall from a great height. Even more interestingly, Laȝamon also stresses the similarity between the combatants:

Often the two crashed down as if they would lie there; often they jumped up as if they would flee. Each man's eyes looked hatefully upon the others; each man's teeth gnashed together as the raging boar's do. Sometimes the men were pale, hatefully enraged; sometimes they were red as they struggled mightily. Each desired to dominate the other by tricks, guile and great strength.[81]

The Giant grabs Corineus, breaking four of his ribs, and nearly kills him. At the last moment Corineus reaches out, grips the Giant so violently that he breaks the Giant's back and flings him over a cliff into the sea. The episode ends: "so the Giants were destroyed, and all the land came into Brutus's hand." Geoffrey's account is similar but less elaborate. The *Morte Arthure* speaks closely to these foundational combats:

> Wrothely þai wrythyn and wrystill togederz,
> Welters and walowes ouer within þase buskez,
> Tumbellez and turnes faste and terez þaire wedez;
> Vntenderly fro þe toppe þai tiltin togederz;
> Whilom Arthure ouer and oþer-while vndyre,
> Fro þe heghe of þe hyll vnto þe harde roche;
> They feyne neuer are they fall at þe flode merkes. (1141–47)

[Fiercely they writhe and wrestle together, weltering and wallowing within the bushes, tumbling and turning fast and tearing their clothing. Violently from the summit they tumbled together; sometimes Arthur was over and sometimes under. From the height of the hill onto the hard rocks they do not hold back until they reach the water line.]

Both battles occur by the sea cliffs and end with a fall; both feature wounds to the ribs; both involve wrestling as much as swordplay; both are staged for an audience (in the *Brut* the companions of Corineus and in the *Morte Arthure* the Giant's captives). In both, the Giant is compared to a wild boar; the *Morte Arthure*, ever expansive, compares him additionally to a bestiary-length catalogue of savage animals. By echoing the combat of Corineus and Gogmagog, the poet insularizes the Giant, allowing Arthur to redramatize the original conquest of Britain, the ferocious and enjoyable expulsion of its original inhabitants by a captain at least as outsized and appallingly vigorous as they.

The ensuing conflict between Arthur's and Lucius's army echoes the battle of St. Michael's Mount when the Giant's elemental chaos resurfaces in the characterization of Lucius's armies as a motley of heathens, witches, and giants. Arthur similarly uses a combination of strategy and ruthlessness, utterly eradicating Lucius's army. Even Lucius's fleeing knights are hunted down, until the rivers are choked with bodies and literally run with blood.

The second combat with Priamus, on the other hand, engages more chivalric if orientalized classical origins for British sovereignty.[82] Priamus's name associates him with Troy; he comes from the east, and he claims to be the heir of a great eastern empire in the line of the classical and biblical Worthies from whom the British kings trace their lineage and to whom they look as chivalric models:

"My name es sir Priamus, a prynce es my fadyre . . .
He es of Alexandire blode, ouerlynge of kynges,
The vncle of his ayele sir Ector of Troye,
And here es the kynreden that I of come—
And Judas and Josue, þise gentill knyghtes." (2595, 2602–6)

["My name is Sir Priamus, a prince is my father . . . he is of Alexander's blood, the overlord of kings, the uncle of his heir Sir Ector of Troy, and here is the kindred of which I come: and from Judas and Joshua, these noble knights."]

As a figure from a less primitive past than the Giant, and one who incorporates many of the Nine Worthies in his ancestry, Priamus is more recuperable; it is not necessary for Gawain to kill him. However, his loyalty must be secured, since as an alternate descendant of Britain's lineage, and (like Lamorabaquy in Froissart) a descendant of Alexander, he is a threat to Arthur's sovereignty. The ensuing account of Arthur's conquest of Lorraine (with its army of schismatics) allows the poet carefully to establish Arthur's adherence to and even generosity within the late medieval laws of war.[83] The Duke of Lorraine and his subjects in Metz are treated not as atavistic eruptions from a primal past but as late fourteenth-century schismatics, whose cities can be pillaged but who are not wholly alien.

Arthur's Italian adversaries reveal an even more contemporary familiarity with the practices of fourteenth-century warfare. The survival-minded Count of Milan, a cosmopolitan adept at military diplomacy, surrenders unconditionally to Arthur. Arthur accepts his surrender and extremely lucrative homage without any hint of the avenging crusade or salutary extermination that characterized his combat with the Giant. This restraint is especially noteworthy, given the late fourteenth-century reputation of the "tyraunts of Lumbardye, / That usen wilfulhed and tyrannye" and their troops of professional soldiers.[84] Instead Italy allows Arthur to take his own turn toward tyranny. More and more clearly, he begins to take on the lineaments of his opponents.

The last confrontation of the narrative moves from the present to the future and extrapolates the logical outcome of the genealogical iconoclasm characterizing Arthur's colonization of the past. Given the poem's pursuit of cross-generational violence, it comes as no surprise that the "child of Arthur's chamber," Mordred, turns against his foster-father to establish his own authority. Mordred steals Arthur's own regalia, his wife, and England itself, deploying the same infectious strategies against Arthur that Arthur had directed against his own former enemies. The ancient alternate lines of descent that end in Lucius, and less dangerously in Priamus, divide again in the present generation as Arthur's possible heirs, his knightly nephews, polarize into competitive versions of each other.

Here, once again the doubling of characters fractures the generational conflict into a fraternal one. Just as Arthur positioned himself as a true emperor to Lucius as upstart (both descendants of Belinus and Brennius), and Gawain modeled as a feudal warrior to Priamus as a mercenary captain (both heirs of a Trojan past), Gawain and Mordred are good and bad nephews to Arthur. Gawain is the knight who most closely embodies Arthur's restless pride and anger.[85] Thus when Mordred kills Gawain, he strikes a direct blow at Arthur's heart. Arthur laments his loss as a loss of all that makes him king and warrior:

> "For nowe my wirchipe es wente and my were endide.
> Here es þe hope of my hele, my happynge of armes;
> My herte and my hardyness hale one hym lengede—
> My concell, my comforthe þat kepide my herte!
> Of all knyghtes þe kynge þat vndir Criste lifede,
> Þou was worthy to be kynge, þofe I þe corown bare . . .
> I am vttirly vndon in myn awen landes." (3957–63, 3966)

["For my worship now is departed and my war ended; here is the hope of my prosperity, the good fortune of my arms. My heart and my hardiness relied wholly upon him, my council, my comfort that preserved my heart. Of all knights that lived under Christ you were the king; you were worthy to be king itself, though I bore the crown . . . I am utterly undone, here in my own land."]

It is only here that Arthur realizes the extent to which his own kingly power is bound up with that of his knights. He stands aside from his own sovereign rights for the first time in the poem and recognizes the implicit sovereignty of his knights as crucial to his own authority, identity, and even body. The loss of Gawain leaves Arthur not simply weakened but "unfers," emasculated, and, ultimately, dead. In a reversal of fealty, Arthur swears to devote the rest of his life to avenging Gawain.

Yet even as Arthur is granting Gawain sovereignty, Mordred the Malebranche (wicked child, ill-begotten), Arthur's other nephew, is seizing it. And if Gawain incarnated the fey and ungraspable virtue that drives chivalry, Mordred claims its outer show. He alters his saltire insignia to three silver lions on a purple field, which nicely mixes the cowardice of disguise with the proud claim of a new, fierce, imperial heraldic identity. The outrage of Mordred's easy appropriation of the signs of chivalry deepens when Arthur recognizes the sword Mordred is carrying against him as one only Guenever could have given him: his ritual sword Clarent, kept from battle and used only for the anointing of kings and the dubbing of knights. Thus the final battle poises Arthur at the moment he is bereft of both ways chivalry can express itself: internal ferocity (Gawain died and took Arthur's heart with him) and chivalric insignia (stolen by Mordred). His nephews have taken from Arthur everything that made him a king as they become kings themselves.

At the moment when knight bleeds most completely into king and king into knight, the moment when breath, heart, and chivalric insignia pass from a king to his successors, Arthur's apparatus of war-created sovereignty self-destructs. Only on the last battlefield does Arthur recognize, with horror, that his knights have been too close to him, loved him too much, followed him too far, that their own triumphant loyalty has devoured his men to leave him "a wafull wedowe þat wanttes hir beryn" (4285) [a woeful widow longing for her child]. The last battle thus revisits the scene of the first combat on St. Michael's Mount, with Arthur shadowing forth simultaneously both the beard-collecting Giant and the weeping widow, the child-killing victor and bereft victim. In coming full circle, he cannot detach himself either from his fosterlings' graves or from the imperial ambitions that killed them. The mourning procession of barons and clerics who mark his end do not even give tribute to the glories that he won. This ideal king who drove together with his knights to conquer his rivalrous predecessors has ended by reenacting the piteous hungers of the first and worst of them. Where Alexander beat incessantly against the contours of his past, Arthur's past swallows him.

Coda: *Gologras and Gawain*

Could a better end have been achieved had Arthur and his knights not been so intimately bound together? If this poem criticizes a fantasy of chivalric solidarity between a knightly king and the kingly knights who reach the apogee of chivalry only by dying in his service, does it suggest any better relation between king and barony? I would answer these questions with a wary yes. This poem thrives on war. It loves the excesses that energize its battle scenes; it drives them to extremes because it is as enamored of the performance of chivalric honor through blood as any of Arthur's knights. But it suspects national war on a large scale. Even in its narration the poem filigrees its large-scale battles with an absorbing fretwork of smaller combats, jousts, scouting forays, prisoner escorts, and flank engagements that cast into sharp relief the deeds of Arthur's captains. Knights are freer to pursue such volatile but self-limiting performances; they gamble for honor with their own lives. But when kings go to such extremes they take whole realms down with them. Valiant or not, in this poem leaders who hunger perpetually for greater empires become tyrants, whether they be Lucius, the Giant, or Arthur himself, and the massive ongoing wars they incite are shown to be both self-feeding and ravening. If Arthur's knights had not been so intimately bound to their king's ambition, the very ferocity by which they sought to demonstrate their honor, share its recognition, and bind themselves honorably to their fellow combatants (even across enemy lines—like Gawain and Priamus) might have counteracted the zero-sum appropriations of their leader.

Another late alliterative romance, *Golagras and Gawain*, searches out the terrain of this unexplored possibility. Where the *Morte Arthure* weds king to barony, *Golagras and Gawain* negotiates with extraordinary delicacy the imperatives that divide them. While maintaining the honor of the king, it exalts the strength, honor, and self-determination of provincial lords more than any other alliterative romance: it is a crown jewel for J. R. Hulbert's argument about the alliterative revival as an expression of baronial resistence.[86] In its late date (a little before 1507) and Scottish provenance it has both thoroughly digested and provocatively reimagined the defining features of its selected genre. It shares its intricately rhymed alliterative thirteen-line stanza with *The Awntyrs off Arthure* and *De Tribus Regibus Mortuis*; it thrusts together chivalric spectacle and explosive violence with the vigor of the *Morte Arthure* itself; while to an unprecedented degree it asserts a worthy provincialism that demands and is granted respect.[87] Its two parts dramatize the relationships between Arthur and two baronial lords, one his feudal subject and the other unbound to any lord. As it brings both king and powerful barons to a recognition of each other's sovereign rights, it replaces war between king and nobility with an economy of salutary generosity like that which binds together knight, squire, and clerk at the end of the *Franklin's Tale*.

While as enamored of the theater of knightly violence as the alliterative *Morte Arthure*, *Golagras and Gawain* replaces a king's harsh siege with more personal combats between knights. Although technically Arthur wins, the poem ends by underscoring the limits of what a king can lawfully demand of his chivalric subjects and what a baron is obliged to yield up, as it dramatizes what happens when either side goes too far in its own sovereign claims. The poem tells two parables of royal courtly arrogance toward baronial sovereignty in order to urge gestures of mutual respect from king and barony. Reversing Marx's quip on historical repetition, the first episode of *Gologras and Gawain* plays as a farce what the second and longer episode will draw out as near tragedy. The problem of monarchical avidity is nuanced accordingly. In the first episode while searching for provisions for Arthur's army, Kay pilfers a swan drumstick from a lord's great hall. In the second, Arthur himself craves first a supremely well-defended castle, and then the virgin fealty of the lord who controls it. The parallelism between the first and second episode subtly but unmistakably deflates Arthur's ambitious hunger for Sir Gologras's fealty to Sir Kay's rude grabbing of the swan drumstick.[88] In both episodes Gawain's extraordinary "gentrice" [worthiness], an idiosyncratic combination of daring generosity and surpassing ferocity, induces the desired grant. Each lord tests Gawain, tempting him to arrogant appropriation, and to each Gawain carefully tenders a self-sacrificing acknowledgment of the lord's honor and sovereignty. Gawain's knightly courtesy thus offsets and educates Arthur's kingly appetites.

It all comes down to a single combat between Sir Gologras and Sir Gawain. This fight, like the combat between Gawain and Priamus in the alliterative *Morte Arthure*, forges bonds of mutual trust between Gologras and Gawain, but significantly excludes the king from their chivalric economy. The knights isolate themselves from the other contestants and begin a ferocious battle which continues until both rage-blinded, wounded, shield-scraped, shoulder-hewn warriors can barely walk and Gologras misses his footing. In a line that tersely plays on the transformation of pride to a fall: Gologras (analogue to "orgulous," prideful) is brought to "Grulingis" (groveling): "Schir Gologras graithly can ga / Grulingis to erd" (1023–24) [Sir Gologras immediately goes groveling to the earth]. Before he can rise again, Gawain, anxious to end the fight, presses a dagger to his throat, and orders him to accompany him to Arthur's camp. Gologras refuses to yield. He swears he would sooner die than betray his free ancestors (a pointed comment on the origins of Scottish resistance to English imperialism) and dares Gawain to kill him. Gawain asks him if there is a way he can leave the field with both life and honor intact and Gologras makes a startling request. If Gawain will appear to yield and return to Gologras's castle with him, Gologras promises to repay that trust in the sight of his court and all his knights. Gawain muses to Gologras that if he puts himself needlessly in an enemy's hands and is betrayed, he will be betraying his own tenants and captains (he does not mention Arthur). However, he concludes, Gologras's chivalric ferocity shows him to be trustworthy:

> "Bot I knaw thou art kene, and alse cruell;
> Or thow be fulyeit fey, freke, in the fight,
> I do me in thi gentrice, be Drightin sa deir!" (1109–1111)

["But I know that you are eager and also fierce before you are done to death, man, in the fight. I put myself into the power of your worthiness (gentrice), by the Lord so dear."]

Gologras leads Gawain to his stronghold like a captive. Arthur is left alone, confused and weeping, wracked by the same crippling sorrow he displays at Gawain's death in the *Morte Arthure*. Back in his stronghold, Gologras asks his own assembled lords a crucial question. Would they rather have him alive but Arthur's liege, or would they rather have him honorably dead and another free lord in his place. Unanimously they profess their personal devotion to him, preferring him alive on almost any terms. He tells them of Gawain's spectacular trust and, with great consciousness of show, declares his willingness to concede to Arthur—his court concurs. Arthur is overjoyed to receive his concession; both armies celebrate together, and, just before packing up camp and returning home, Arthur makes the final gesture in this economy of mutual chivalric respect and frees Gologras from his grant of fealty.

The poem makes it clear that Arthur has learned to respect baronial self-determination, just as Gologras has been taught that fortune can destroy even such a perfect and self-sufficient sovereignty as his. The poem also shows that Gawain chose rightly to relinquish the chivalric spectacle of victory and instead trust in the more essential knowledge of a knight's "gentrice," which is only experienced through the intimate ferocity of combat with him. *Gologras and Gawain* flirts with the tragedy of attrition through war, but, unlike the *Morte Arthure*, successfully evades it by diverting a war of monarchical appropriation permanently into a series of well-fought chivalric single combats. This effectively displaces the real power from the king's hands into that of his knights, and then replaces the zero-sum predation of massive warfare and siege with an individuating and contagious economy of knightly generosities. The poem's two episodes underline the same lesson. Sovereignty inheres not in the power to take from one's enemies—which becomes both boorish and tyrannical—but in the power to give to them. And that power of concession and mutual respect is generated through the surpassing violence that grounds chivalric identity and belongs most intimately to knights. Finally, by dramatizing the social value of baronial sovereignty, *Gologras and Gawain* works to preserve the distance between king and knight, the space for negotiation, mutual deference, and mutual instruction between them. In so doing, it evades the beguiling synergies that send the king and knights of the *Morte Arthure* plunging together gorily and gloriously toward the end of history.

Grave Misgivings in *De Tribus Regibus Mortuis, The Awntyrs off Arthure*, and *Somer Sunday*

WHILE ALL OF THE ALLITERATIVE ROMANCES treated in this book explore and exploit the disjunctions between past and present, few alliterative poems face the dark backward and abysm of time with the directness of *De Tribus Regibus Mortuis* and *The Awntyrs off Arthure*. These didactic alliterative poems isolate, crystallize, and drive to extremes defining features of the other alliterative romances in this study in order to pronounce judgment upon them. The past distills itself into the shape of the dead, as monarchs are brought face to face with their dead fathers and mothers. The disruptions of death and temporality which trouble the chivalric performances of Gawain, Alexander, and Arthur here loom like leviathans and take on a wider social urgency. In the long-ago epigraph to this book, the dead are invested with the task of forcing the living to confront their most cherished evasions and that is precisely what happens in these poems: the past becomes intimate enough to the present to take on the roles of social reminder and self-interrogator. Both of these poems highlight the continuing role of the dead in society not just in the form of the legacies they leave, or the prayers they solicit, but also in the kinds of social/self-examinations they adjure.[1] In this they refuse the conventions of penitential social disengagement—the Augustinian wariness toward too much investment in the earthly city as one peregrinates toward the heavenly one or the almshouse austerities promoted by fifteenth-century *Learn to Die* treatises. In these poems, the welfare of the dead is entrusted less to the judgments of God than to the practices of their living descendants, and the poems call the living to account in two ways. First, they present the living with the horrific consequences of forgetting the dead: death at large, rotting and burning as it roams the landscape, refusing to stay decently underground. Second, and even more interestingly, they put reformatory pressure upon the rituals and formal practices by which the late medieval society domesticated the disruptions of death.

Two such practices are elucidated with particular intensity: (1) the way the living resocialize the dead *as* the dead by drawing them into mutually

beneficial gift economies through ritual exchanges of recognition, commemoration, capital, and prayer; (2) the way the living take on the social
responsibilities of the dead in the inexact and anxious performances that
Joseph Roach calls surrogation.[2] These poems dramatize death to enforce
recognition of the active role in late medieval society played by the dead
and to interrogate the obligations of the living, not only to their dead but
to their neighbors and fellow members in the social body. In these poems,
to forget the dead is to corrode both self and society. This is an abiding
preoccupation throughout the medieval period. Patrick Geary shows that
the dead—saintly and secular, collective and individual—laid so many social
and religious obligations upon earlier medieval societies that they actually
functioned as an age group.[3] He explores the range of pressures the dead
exerted and the exchanges though with they are bound back into social
life both to honor their heritages and delimit their social force. Throughout the period, the living traffic with the dead in seemingly incommensurate goods: prayer, property, relics, tombs, institutions, commemorations,
and the construction of patronage. This devotion to the dead not only
supports religious faith and its institutions but also becomes an engine
for social work.

Yet institutionalized means of remembrance and redress (proper funerary rites, trentals, commemorations) are not always adequate to assuage
the guilt over the profit derived from the dead: their names, goods, and
seigneurial power which the kings, queens, and courtiers of these poems
have inherited and wield with such joy. Therefore, the experience of the
past as death translates into an urgent concern with past, present, and
future social life—the ways the noble characters have been living, the social
hierarchies and institutions through which they enact their authority and
enjoy their luxuries, and the eventual outcomes, not simply of the individual survivors but of their social ethos. The poems turn fear of individual
death into an audit of the costs of an aristocratic status quo which is linch-
pinned by a monarchy indulging in paradigms of social redress that have
become cosmetic, opportunities for self-display rather than genuine justice. These poems disinter the dead to bare the inequities upon which
courtly society depends for its continuance and to point out the inadequa-
cies of existing systems of social expiation. In so doing they dramatize
intensifying anxieties about the ritual superintendence of death within
the late medieval society—how effective such rituals were, who benefitted
from them, and at what cost.

Focusing on the sociality of death in late medieval culture yields a
picture of energetic representational and interpretive innovation. This is a

far cry from the over ritualized, baroque, and luxuriant decline so vividly depicted by Huizinga in *The Autumn of the Middle Ages* where the weighty consciousness of death's inevitability drags at a late medieval society whose lassitudes effloresce in the *ars moriendi* literature and the *transi* figures mordantly disintegrating beneath serene effigies. Compelling as Huizinga's vision is, it does not account for the sheer inventiveness surrounding late medieval discourses of death. Rituals for processing death—the writing of wills, the drama of the deathbed, funerals and commemorations to ensure remembrance, trentals and masses to curtail time in purgatory—are constantly changing throughout this period to accommodate a much wider variety of individual and social needs. Clergy and laity are negotiating for agency in the late medieval industry of death, proliferating religious confraternities, and changing the shape of churches. Death becomes an engine harnessed for a myriad of cultural functions. Such rituals go beyond institutionalizing the recognition of the inevitability of loss and the universality of decay; they also script social reintegrations which extend in at least two directions. The first incorporates the dead as social donors and recipients whose power lingers in their legacies and whose pathos speaks in their hunger for prayers, masses, and commemorations. The second and even more crucial extends to the social body of the living and in particular the gulfs between its richer and poorer members.

Both of these dramaturgies are illuminated by Marcel Mauss's classic essay *The Gift.* Mauss's description of gift economies extends to encompass relationships between living and dead. It underwrites the power of gifts to enforce circulation between clans with more profound obligations between the gods who endow, the dead ancestors who receive and endow in their turn, and the living who must receive and give back to both. In each case gift economies ritualize and diffuse the potential threats of both extreme enmity and extreme dependence.

Gift economies shape the competitive amities linking clans and generations but they are just as crucial within a particular society where they help redress the obligations the rich owe to the poor. These interclass exchanges are sparked by the sense that extreme social inequities exert a socially corrosive potential energy which tends to violent release if it is not mediated. In other words, the extraction of surplus value from the worker creates an obligation in those who benefit. Some modern societies redress this obligation at least nominally by social security; medieval society generally exhorted aristocratic charity. In fourteenth- and fifteenth-century English society, where aristocratic charity was ritualized (though the extent of its actual impact is dubious), it is significant that such socially regenerative "repayments" became associated with funerals. Philippe Ariès, Eamon Duffy, and Robert Dinn describe how the poor come to be included in funeral processions and given food, drink, and alms at funerals in order to bind the well-off dead to the needy living, who in turn were expected to apply their unusually potent prayers to the state of their benefactors' souls in purgatory.[4] More forebodingly, John Mirk's *Festial*'s homily for Advent Sunday stresses the eschatological exchanges that funerary redress to the poor anticipate:

Thys, good men, ȝe schull know well þat yn þe day of dome pore men schull be domes-men wyth Cryst, and dome þe ryche. For all þe woo þat pore men hauen, hit ys by þe ryche men; and þogh þay haue moche wrong, þay may not gete amendes, tyll þay come to þat dome; and þer þay schall haue all hor one lust of hom. For when þay haue wrong, and mow gete non amendys, þen þay pray ful hertely to God forto qwyt hom yn þe day of dome; and woll he truly . . . Wherefor, syrs, for Goddys loue, whyll ȝe byn here, makyth amendes for your mys-dedys, and makyþ hom your frendes þat schall be our domes-men, and tryst ȝe not to hom þat schall come aftyr you, lest ȝe ben deseyuet.[5]

[This, good men, you should know well, that on judgment day poor men shall be judges with Christ and judge the rich. For all the woe that poor men have is through rich men, and though they endure much wrong, they may not get redress until they come to that judgment and there they shall have whatever they please from them. For when they endure wrong and may get no redress, then they pray very heartily to God to pay them back on the day of doom, and he will truly do so . . . Therefore, sirs, for the love of God, while you are here, make amends for your misdeeds, and make friends of those who will be our judges, and trust not to those who come after you, lest you be deceived.]

Mirk's description not only highlights the social injustices suffered by the poor at the hands of the rich and the need to redress that balance, but maintains that the poor will be in a unique position to render back an even more profound service (or revenge) to the rich by virtue of the reversals in status of poor and rich on Judgment Day. As judges beside Christ, they are more reliable even than potentially untrustworthy descendants. Yet even the poor were not felt to be entirely trustworthy; Duffy points out that when alms distribution became pro forma in the sixteenth century, several wills stipulated that alms be given only to poor who knew the deceased, were from his town, or were in unusually dire straits—in other words, poor whose personal gratitude for largesse could be relied upon more securely.[6] This aura of creeping suspicion—that the investment of alms would not be reciprocated and the circulation of prayers and payments, intercession and commemoration would halt and fester—recalls the uneasy potential for imbalance implicit even in successful gift exchanges.[7]

In late medieval society, therefore, three sets of gift exchanges coincide in the rituals surrounding death, burial, and commemoration: (1) between different and possibly hostile social groups (i.e., clergy and laity, different civic factions, etc.), (2) between the dead and the living, and (3) between the well-off and the poor—and they all provoke anxiety. The uneasy delicacy of these exchanges is attested to by their constant fostering and renegotiation. There is a suspicious sense of the lurking potential of a ritual exchange to fail. Late medieval strategies for ameliorating the impact of death and resocializing the dead arbitrate the anxieties of both individuals and institutions: their fears of change or loss, their pursuit of advantageous innovations. As the two poems *De Tribus Regibus Mortuis* and *The Awntyrs off Arthure* make plain, these strategies are often not sufficient either to redress the dead or genuinely to heal the trauma of their loss. However, as they stage the shortcomings and failures of these exchanges and their uneasily commercial underpinnings, these poems envision opportunities for more profound repayments, more widely ranging social critiques, challenges to political hegemonies, redistributions of social, religious, and economic power. At their most trenchant, they intimate the inadequacy of the institutional processes by which the dead are redressed; they sabotage the funerary and commemorative liturgies that harnessed commemorative performance to institutional profit or individual status-display. These poems dramatize the utter helplessness of the abandoned dead in order to investigate the deeper, socially structuring abandonments and inequities perpetuated by their powerful descendants and by the religious and social institutions through which they exercise power.

De Tribus Regibus Mortuis, or The Head Bone Connects to the Neck Bone

The *De Tribus Regibus Mortuis (The Three Dead Kings)* is the only extant English poem devoted to a didactic encounter between the three Living and three Dead which was popular in continental writing and art. It was also often painted onto the walls of late medieval English churches—in fact, the poem ends with the painting of its dramatic encounter within just such a newly built church. The poem has been surprisingly little treated, nor has its relationship to these haunting images been explored except to note their similarities.[8] I would like to begin by discussing two of these images in manuscript depictions, the *De Lisle Psalter* BL Arundel 83 and the *Psalter of Bonne of Luxembourg* (fols. 321v-322), because they present a paradigm that the poem both draws upon and alters.[9] Where the images stress the shock of the encounter between the living and the dead and rely upon the viewer to connect the frames and read the mortal lesson, the poem guides readers through the moment of disjunction by an inventive variety of routes, putting living and dead, present and past into a number of different relationships to provoke reform. *De Tribus Regibus Mortuis* thus softens the nightmare of its initial representation of death by worrying away at the barriers between living and dead. The dead reveal themselves to be the generous and still-watchful fathers of the living and enter into a conversation with them. They appear to the three Kings not simply to confront them with the unwelcome (but surely unsurprising) revelation that they are going to die, but also to urge them to forsake their tyrannical exclusivity and acknowledge necessary obligations both to their predecessors and to their inferiors.

Both poem and images dramatize a conflict central to alliterative romance: the need to forget the past versus the need to remember it. They stage this conflict as a battle of competing interests: the piteous dead adjure remembrance and the horrified living cling to their forgetfulness. In a useful study of the differences between premodern and modern social attitudes toward death, Robert Blauner powerfully counterposes these impulses:

Modern studies of death in society emphasize the importance of the paradoxical need both to push the dead away, so the living can reestablish their normal activity, and to "keep them alive," to maintain social bonds in spite of death. This paradox is at the core of the system of exchanges informing the relationship of mutual dependence between the living and the dead in the early Middle Ages. The gifts the living had received from the dead were so great as to threaten the receivers unless balanced by equally worthy countergifts. The gifts of the dead included nothing less than life itself, property, and personal identity. Without suitable countergifts, the imbalance would become intolerable; for as the anthropologists observed, a donor keeps eternal rights in the gift and hence in the recipient. Only by finding a suitable countergift could a recipient "revenge himself or herself" on the giver (the Latin term talio can mean both countergift and vengeance). Hostile or dominating intrusions by the dead in the society of the living could only be prevented by restoring balance between the parties to gift transactions. But because social bonds were based largely on these same gifts from the dead, the dead could not be banished entirely from the society of the living; a benevolent relationship had to be established and continued.[10]

Blauner focuses usefully on the sense of indebtedness, the uneasiness and guilt it produced, the range of responses it could instigate—from devotional repayment to a violent retaliation. The past is not dead in this passage because the living feel themselves to be informed, animated, enabled, indebted by their dead and invest them in turn with the guilty power of their own necessary and renormalizing neglect.

This conflict of needs between dead and living are precisely what pictorial representations of the three Living and the three Dead dramatize. They show the impossibility of suturing over the ruptures that death inflicts, as they magnify the gaping bellies, the excoriated flesh, the wintry grins. The effect is analogous to alliterative romances' habitual thrusting together of disjunct temporal states (old and new, past and present, death and life) to compel a sense of urgent mutability. These pictures fold time, arrest succession, refuse the replacement and forgetting of the dead. And they defy outright the process of social reconstitution that Joseph Roach describes in *Cities of the Dead* as surrogation. Surrogation enables survivors to step into the shoes and don the costumes of their predecessors in constantly improvised performances that strive to construct and re-create a dead original they enflesh with inevitable imprecision. Surrogates for the dead fill, define, rework, and elide their predecessors' functions, transmit and improvise their legacies, mend (or sometimes inadvertently intensify) the trauma of their disappearance, and urge (successfully or not) a necessary forgetting. Surrogation as social performance transmits historic authority and appropriates the past, but only uneasily and with perceptible deficiency. Such performances are inevitably uncanny, inexact, haunted by the persistence and diversity of memories they are trying to encapsulate or alter in a troubled anamnesis.[11] The medieval pictorial tradition of the three Living and the three Dead brings surrogates face to face with their predecessors but also reinterprets them. Here, the past does not take the shape of an approximated original, "forgotten but not gone," as Roach quips (2), or, more poignantly, a phantasm of authentic presence, precious, inimitable, putting the lie to subsequent performances. Rather, we are presented with the worst-case scenario of ineffectual forgetting: a corporeal haunt, rotten and gaping, creaking for attention from its would-be surrogates, refusing to leave.

The early fourteenth-century *De Lisle Psalter* shows a pair of framed panels which share a border. Unusually, it makes the Living into three kings. To the left they stand, gracefully clothed and crowned to stress their effortless exercise of power: the first carries a hunting hawk, the third a scepter. Hawk in hand, as the first King gazes soberly across the frame to where the Dead are standing, he strains backward and reaches behind him for the hand of the second King, who takes it, clutching his own chest in a gesture of horror. The third King stands apart from the first two, facing out of the page but looking askance at the Dead. He leans his scepter against his shoulder and communicates vividly a wish to be anywhere else. In the second frame are the Dead, their bony angularities offsetting the graceful folds of the robes of the Living. The first is turned slightly toward the Living, arms crossed on his breast and worms enlivening the shroud above his belly. The second nods his head toward the Living and points at them with his right hand while his left touches his own chest, a gesture that communicates clearly "You are next," countering the second Living's chest-clutching gesture of "What, me?" The third figure implicates the viewer in this dialogue; he stares directly out of the picture with a wide toothy grin on his skull. The only corpse unshrouded and ungesturing, he displays the gaping cavity of his belly with grisly composure.

The *Psalter of Bonne of Luxembourg* gives a diptych presentation where the three dead confront the living across facing pages. It is even more effective than the *De Lisle Psalter* at conveying the trauma of the confrontation. On the verso three beautifully appointed noblemen are caught in mid-hunt and careen backward on horses whose contorted necks and averted eyes communicate their riders' horror as well as their own. The foremost and crowned rider wries completely around with his back to the vision while his horse bows its head to the ground and looks away. The second rider, in a handsome hat, points across the page with his left hand and with his right holds a cloth to his face to escape the stench of corruption; his horse has turned entirely and is ready to gallop off. The last, bareheaded rider holds a hawk on his left wrist which gazes over its shoulder at the corpses; with his right hand he also points across the page, mouth open in shock. If their headgear is any indication, the riders are arranged in descending order of rank, and it is the noblest figure, the rider with the crown, who finds the specter of death the most unbearable as well as the most proximal.

On the recto, in austere contrast to the flurry they have caused, stand the dead in accelerating order of decomposition. The first and nearest still bears the impression of his interrer's care—hands still crossed on his breast and shroud mostly undamaged, a greying but intact body nods down with closed eyes and open mouth to an open coffin beneath him. The second figure is the most animated. He raises a bony hand in salutation while his shroud hangs in shreds and his flesh falls away from his legs. He vividly bespeaks the shame implicit in mortification as he clutches his ragged shroud across his chest while below it falls away to bare his genitals. The third is the starkest. Almost completely skeletonized, he makes no gesture, his arms hang from their sockets, his intestinal organs are bared, and he faces the Living across the page with gaping jaw, a horror of silent eloquence.

Both the psalters press their points home with an inscription; the De Lisle's inscription virtually paraphrases lines from De Tribus as Turville-Petre points out: "Ich am afert. Lo whet ich se. Me þinkeþ hit beþ deueles þre." "Ich wes wel fair. Such scheltou be. For godes loue be wer by me" ["I am terrified at what I see. It seems to be three devils." "I used to be very fair. This is what you will come to. For God's love, take heed of me"].[12] Here the verbal exchange, like the visual presentation, is reduced to conflicting urgencies: the living distancing themselves from the demonized apparitions of the dead and the dead reaching out to claim affinities that are both pathetic and chilling. This sense of unresolved conflict is heightened by the visible divisions which both psalters place between the two parties. The Psalter of Bonne of Luxembourg sets them on different pages, so that dead and living touch only—and invisibly—when the book is closed. The De Lisle Psalter frames them separately; the shared margin is a double line which the hawk held by the first king actually crosses, but the backgrounds behind the two parties indicate separate realms—a light, unadorned vacancy for the living, and a dark field patterned by torchlike flowers for the dead. The two backgrounds are as different as air and grave, and walking from one to the other seems at once as effortless and as preposterous as Hamlet will later suggest.

Both psalter images capitalize upon a paradox: the viewer must not trust the image which so graphically stresses the contrast between states. In fact the grislier and more shocking the differences between the living and the dead, the more it is crucial to recognize the connections between them, the echoing of gestures which makes a mirror of the margin or frame: "Ich wes wel fair. Such scheltou be." This was, in fact, a common epitaph in the fourteenth century, directed not to friends or family but to the passing stranger. An admonition, it also tendered an invitation to further exchange between living and dead by adjuring a mutual recognition across time and the barrier of the grave. In this it echoes fourteenth-century tomb inscriptions that for the first time begin to exhort the passer's prayer for the deceased soul.[13] It is this recognition that the alliterative poem fosters when it translates the initial horrific encounter first into an exchange of words and prayers and then into a wider circulation of socially regenerative exchanges.

De Tribus Regibus Mortuis knows the pictorial tradition of the three

Living and the three Dead. It incorporates it when the three kings return from their gruesome meeting to build a church on whose walls their encounter is commemorated. The poem also depicts a conflict between the needs of the Dead and the desires of the Living, but it is careful to move its characters through a series of interventions that will render reconciliation more possible. Thus, the poem's kingly hunters are not halted mid-step in their full-blown puissance with a sudden mirror of their ends—they approach the confrontation through a series of chastening reminders of the limits of their power.

But first that power is displayed. The poem begins with the vividness and freedom expressed in the hunt where the kings

> With tonyng and tryffylyng and talis . . . telde;
> Vche a wy þat þer was wroȝt as þai wold,
> Þese wodis and þese wastis þai waltyn al to welde . . .
> Ham lakyd no lorchip in lare" (19–21, 25)

[with blowing horns and frivolity and tales/tallies . . . told/figured. Every man there did what they wished. Those woods and wastes they wished to control entirely . . . They lacked no lordship in earth].

Here the hunting kings exercise a dominion that, unsatisfied by the obedience of their followers, fantasizes about control even of the woods and the wastes outside society. However, their energetic delight in dominance lasts exactly one stanza. They are not aware that they are about to encounter the real experts in the art of preternatural indomitability, the dead who have eluded social control, spurning their funerary rituals to roam at large in a wasteland of wild air and entangling thickets. This association of the dead with a bewildering trackless wildness signifies their exclusion from society; it will emerge again in *The Awntyrs off Arthure* and even more incongruously in *Awntyr*'s more cheery twin, *The Trentals of Pope Gregory*, where mist and black fog incongruously accompany the ghost of the Pope's mother into the church itself. All three works barricade the dead with natural forces that also exceed, resist, and threaten human/social jurisdiction.

It is unsurprising, therefore, that a thick mist presages the dead kings' arrival, separating the living kings from their followers—an isolation which forcefully reminds them how much their power derives from their own sociality. Servantless and alone, they contemplate the notion that their pride may have precipitated this accident and they acknowledge that they can do nothing but trust in God and hope that the mist will lift by morning. As they are seeking cover, the three Dead come forth from a thicket:

> Schadows vnschene were chapid to chow,
> With lymes long and lene and leggys ful lew,
> Hadyn lost þe lyp and þe lyuer seþyn þai were layd loue. (43–45)

[Horribly shaped shadows to see, with long, lean limbs and fragile legs—they had lost lips and livers since they were laid low.]

The description of the dead from their first emergence mingles horror with a sense of pitiable loss. The revulsion of the kings and the horses recalls the contorted aversion found in the *Psalter of Bonne of Luxembourg* and is the scene that will be depicted in the church murals at the poem's end. Yet dramatic as this moment is, the poem does not linger with it. By the beginning of the next stanza a qualm of recognition complicates the alien monstrosity of the dead.

> The furst kyng he had care, his hert ourcast,
> Fore he knew þe cros of the cloþ þat couerd þe cyst. (53–54)

[The first king was distressed - care shadowed his heart, for he recognized the cross on the cloth that had covered the coffin.]

This recognition transforms the narrative in two ways. First it takes it out of the realm of the conventional chivalric encounters with monstrous enemies. The estrangements of the sword are ineffective against the familiar dead; they are already alarmingly within one's guard. And the dead are sources of the kings' power: they have given blood, name, strength, and authority even as they have lost lips and livers.

Second, this recognition flouts the masking rituals by which medieval society had progressively averted its face from the dead. Ariès describes the gradual evolution of a euphemistic funerary architecture designed to hide the face of the dead. Between antiquity and the late medieval period, bodies are gradually covered over, first by shrouds, then coffins to hide the shape of the shroud, then palls to muffle the shape of the coffin, and finally catafalques to hide all under an ornate structure which transforms the shame and vulnerability of the naked corpse into an apparatus for display. The fourteenth-century word for catafalque was "representation"—and the distancing of representation from its referent was precisely the point.[14] But in the poem, the bodies demand recognition, in all its senses. The pall cloth which the first king recognizes is the one he himself had draped over the coffin to hide both "cyst" and occupant—now it has come loose and the all-too-apparent apparition is sporting it about with posthumous heraldry.

The poem follows this recognition by spotlighting each king's reactions, which vary considerably. The first king responds with a terrified fatalism:

"Now al my gladchip is gone, I grue and am agast
Of þre gostis ful grym þat gare me be gryst,
Fore oft haue I walkon be wodys and be wast,
Bot was me neuer so wo in þis word þat Y wyst." (57–60)

["Now all my happiness is gone; I shudder and am aghast at three very grim ghosts
that terrify me, for as often as I've walked in wood and wilderness, I've never
known so much woe in this world until now."]

The second king has more fortitude; he reiterates the terror of the meeting but adds a trace of pity at the "þre ledys ful layþ þat lorne haþ þe ly3t"
[three very horrible men that have lost the light], and suggests that the
meeting might be salutary—if they had gotten back to town as they had
intended, they might be even more unfortunate. He advises them to face
the procession of the dead or they will immediately rue their frivolity.

The third king is having none of this. He hides his eyes with his hands
and urges retreat—at any cost:

"Hit bene warlaws þre þat walkyn on þis woldis.
Oure Lord wyss vs þe redé way þat al þe word weldus!
My hert fars fore fre3t as flagge when hit foldus
Vche fyngyr of my hond fore ferdchip hit feldus.
          Fers am I ferd of oure fare.
          Fle we ful fast þerfore.
          Can Y no cownsel bot care,
          Þese dewyls wil do vs to dare
          Fore drede lest þai duttyn vche a dore." (83–91)

["These are three demons that walk these hills! May our Lord who rules the world
show us a quick way out. Fear bends my heart like a reed. Each finger of my hand
weakens with terror. I'm violently afraid of our situation. Let us therefore quickly
flee. I know no council but distress. These devils will make us cower for dread that
they will shut off every means of escape."]

The poem takes care to show these different reactions even before the
corpses begin speaking, individuating the kings and alerting the reader
to a multitude of possible reactions to death ranging from petrification, to
courage, to horrified evasion. These variations among the living introduce
a more complicated texture to the encounter by replacing the single great
boundary between living and dead with a range of possible barriers, some
permeable, some resistant.

And the first corpse presses against such resistance, denying the demo-
nization of the third king and proposing an alternative that puts the living in the debt of the dead who were their fathers and benefactors. By so
doing he implicates the living in their inevitable fate.

"Nay, are we no fyndus," quod furst, "þat ȝe before ȝou fynden.
We wer ȝour faders of fold þat fayre ȝou haue fondon." (92–93)

["No, we are not fiends," said the first, "who are here before you. We were your fathers on earth that have well provided for you."]

This sense of spatial and temporal connection ("before" can indicate both) intensifies as the corpse demonstrates that just as the corpse's decomposition, worms and all, is played out on a body only recently "ful cumlé to kysse" (103) [very pleasant to kiss], the kings' own sovereignty is subject to change without notice. Even more seriously, the kings have neglected their fathers by letting their memories die and not interceding for the state of their souls—and the ghosts are more than a little surly about this ingratitude:

"Bot we haue made ȝoue mastyrs amys
Þat now nyl not mynn vs with a mas." (103–4)

["But we have mistakenly made you masters who will now not even commemorate us with a mass."]

But the corpses are not there just to solicit masses; they have a lesson to endow as well. The second corpse gives it: to distrust the pleasurable security of the flesh. His reason? "Hit lyus" (113). This conventional dictum from the *ars moriendi* comes as no shock but it puts another dent in the barrier between life and death—the living should live as if they were already dead. The visual pun on "Lyus" ("lies") and "Lyues" ("lives") suggests that life itself begets delusion. The living are eaten by their wicked deeds just as the dead are eaten by worms; if the living are unconscious of their state of decay, then the truth of their deaths can be a salutary admonition. In the words of the last corpse, relationship sharpens into performed identity: "Makis ȝour merour be me!" (120) a phrase familiar from *The Wars of Alexander* and *The Parliament of Three Ages*; the living have a duty to see themselves in the dead.

Moreover, the living must recognize not only their individual misdemeanors but their culpability as members of a dominant social class who owe their present mastery to those decrepit fathers. As "masters," the living are insidiously liable to let their power blind them both to the source of their mastery and to their inevitable fate. The corpse's final words drive that home: once a king arrogant and overbearing to the point of tyranny, now no one who will pay him service "Bot ȝif he be cappid or kyme" (127) [Unless he is mad or an idiot]. With that the ghosts glide off, day dawns, and the three kings cheer up considerably. However, even as they ride quickly away from the encounter, the poem stresses that they take the lessons with them. They stop oppressing the people, become kinder of heart, and help the afflicted. They also build a church:

A mynster þai made with masse
Fore metyng þe men on þe mosse (139–40)

[A church they made with masses for/because of meeting the men on the moor].

This stanza culminates the poem's dramaturgy of inclusion as the dead are figuratively returned from the moor into the church on whose walls the encounter is depicted. Through the two meanings of "fore," the anachronistic reference to the meeting that incited the church's construction becomes an invitation to further meetings within its walls, in the commemorative masses. And the rhyming of "masse" and "mosse" overlays the untrammeled asociality of the dead's previous domain—in wood and in waste—by the powerful ritual socializations of the celebration of the mass—that drama of religious and social incorporation. However, the poem is clear that this ecclesiastical restoration would be ineffective without the change of heart that precedes it. The kings have renounced oppression and embraced charitable works and are now more socially beneficial governors. Their transformation from domineering hunters to civic-minded monarchs parallels the dead's transformation from ghastly gliding apparitions on the borders of society to participants with the living in mutually profitable social and religious exchanges.

This idea that the nobility in particular need to remember that they can die is widespread in medieval poetry generally and emerges powerfully in both *The Wars of Alexander* and the alliterative *Morte Arthure*. In the fourteenth and fifteenth centuries it extended beyond the aristocracy to the moneyed population in general, generating hundreds of *ars moriendi* tracts which were widely circulated. In the *Series* Thomas Hoccleve makes such a *Learn to Die* treatise part of the dramatization of his continually frustrated progress from social ostracism and psychic/bodily disintegration to resocialization and psychic/bodily healing. (One of the frustrations, in fact, is his failure to finish reading the treatise). What distinguishes *De Tribus Regibus Mortuis* from many of these treatises and brings it closer to Hoccleve's *Series* itself is the figural fluency with which it elaborates metaphors of corporeality and disintegration. The poem teems with the dissociative bodily sensations of fear. Hearts are chilled like a knife or a key at the knuckles (82) or bend like a reed (85), fingers grow weak (86), and wits fade or fly away altogether (62). The kings are instantly infected with the graphic disintegrations of the dead, a transference that alludes not only to their incipient putrefaction but to their present corrupt arrogance which has estranged them from any social body.

More metaphorically, when the poem gentrifies the three Living into three monarchs, it intriguingly suggests that the encounter between Living and Dead is simultaneously an encounter between head (of state) and body (of the corpses). As heads of the body politic whose heads are more than a little overblown with fantasies of dominance or transcendence, the three kings are forced to acknowledge their own corporeal nature and their vulnerability to corruption both in life and after. Simultaneously, they begin to admit their connections to the social body they are obligated by birth not just to dominate but to govern. Their own resocialization and the renewal of society itself is signaled when they tender their social obligations to the poor and the oppressed as well as to the dead. Their transformation—from tyrants into good governors—parallels and completes the resocialization of the dead. The poem ends with a plea to the reader to continue the process.

In coming to this conclusion, *De Tribus Regibus Mortuis* suggests the inadequacy of late medieval institutional modes of redress between the living and the dead. Many responses are called for; it is not enough just to build a church, or arrange for commemorative masses, or give to the poor; one must do all three. Moreover, one must further disseminate this somber recognition of mortality and the need for reintegration. The poem's final exhortation to its readers verbally replicates the impact of the painted church image; it also reflects the emergent fourteenth-century tombstone practice of inscribing tombstones with addresses to passing strangers to remember and pray for the dead. This proliferation of responses signals an anxiety about systems of redress between dead and living, rich and poor, king and subject, the need to draw as many people as possible into its economy, to elaborate and multiply means of expiation, and to keep the prayers and remembrances coming. *The Awntyrs off Arthure* pushes even further to suggest that even such rituals of redress can become a means of resisting the self-incriminating alterations required for real social justice.

The Awntyrs off Arthure: Things Fall Apart

If *De Tribus Regibus Mortuis* shows how the living can lay their dead fathers to rest by performing their encounter, *The Awntyrs off Arthure* suggests a grimmer conclusion—that the living will ignore the lessons of the dead. In this poem, Gaynour's (Guenever's) dead mother appears to her daughter to convey a warning similar to that in *De Tribus Regibus Mortuis* but she provokes only a perfunctory expiation and no self-examination at all on the part of Gaynour. This may be because the ghost is so bitter and implacable in her criticism of Arthur's court: real reform would require all of the members of Arthur's court retiring immediately to monasteries to sweat out their sins in prayer and good works for the rest of their lives.[15] But the poem as a whole suggests smaller concrete steps that would provoke reforms similar to those enacted at the end of *De Tribus*: real charity to the poor, real redress to Galeron, a cessation of land acquisition for Arthur. The failure of Arthur's court to learn from its dead darkens the poem's picture of a doomed aristocracy more invested in their possessions and self-inflating performances than in the justice they are entrusted to serve.

The poem falls into two distinct episodes, a ghost sighting and a trial of arms, and scholars are divided as to whether the two should be related or not. Ralph Hanna, the poem's most recent editor, supports and elaborates the 1883 theory of Hermann Lübke that the first episode was a complete romance which a second and inferior poet seized and amalgamated with his less skillful continuation; he treats them as essentially separate.[16] A. C. Spearing and Thorlac Turville-Petre argue for its cumulative unity by pointing out shared chivalric concerns that link the two episodes. Helen Phillips makes a similar argument through textual analysis of the manuscript, specifically countering Hanna's characterization and suggesting a three-part structure for the poem (on the basis of its Irish manuscript) unified by a central concern with territorial sovereignty and its reluctance to see its own mutability.[17] Spearing gives it a diptych structure, a narrative analogue to the pictorial diptych of the three Living and the three Dead. The disconnection between the episodes thus becomes part of the overall message: a failure of communication between the living and the dead rather than the construction of a successful series of exchanges.[18] A diptych suggests a cumulative unity but its structural separations visually dissociate the two parts unless the viewer is provoked into interpreting across the divide—which becomes the whole point.[19]

The poem's first episode replays *De Tribus Regibus Mortuis* with tremulo and gothic effects. It opens with an Arthurian hunting party to Tarn Wadling which expresses the surpassing dominance of the court even more vividly than the initial hunt in *De Tribus Regibus Mortuis*. Gaynour and Gawain, the superlatives of courtly performance, fall behind to dally suggestively beside the lake. A sudden storm whips up, blackening the sky, an ominous sign that Gawain shrugs off by pedantically reassuring Gaynour

that according to a clerk it is only an eclipse of the sun. This is the first inti-
mation (of many) that the complacency of Arthur's courtiers will be difficult to penetrate, and the poem harrows itself up for the task accordingly:
a blazing ghost appears in the darkness across the lake. The ghost declares
itself Gaynour's mother, condemned to the torments of hell for her sins of
pride and illicit love. Unlike the succinct and mannerly dead in *De Tribus
Regibus Mortuis,* Gaynour's ghostly mother is a prima donna; death has
not simply shut her out of chivalric society into the wilds of the lake, it
has landed her at least temporarily in the hinterlands of hell whence she
appears in the operatic costume of Lucifer himself. Not content with the
separate anguishes of bodily decomposition and the flames of hell, her self-
display layers them together. However, she also shadows her daughter
across the mirror of death. Where Gaynour wears a gown "with saffres
and saladynes sercled on þe sides" (22) [with sapphires and celadonies circling the sides], her mother glides about in "a cloude of cleþyng vnclere; /
Serkeled with serpentes þat sat to þe sides" (119–20) [a cloud of dark
clothing circled with serpents that clung to the sides]. After exhorting her
daughter at length to repent of her sinful indulgence and engage in charity
to the poor, the ghost widens her critique to the entire Arthurian imperial
enterprise which she condemns as socially authorized covetousness. She
predicts the destruction of Arthur's court, the deaths of Gawain and
Arthur himself and ends with a chilling little picture of Mordred, currently
a child at the court. After instructing Gaynour once more to feed the poor
and commemorate her with masses, the ghost vanishes, the clouds lift,
and all of Arthur's hunters return to the hall. The first episode thus sweep-
ingly indicts the courtly life from its pleasures to its predations and fore-
tells its downfall.

The second episode depicts a conventional but lively challenge by the
strange knight, Galeron, asserting his right to Scottish land in Galloway
that Arthur has seized and given to Gawain. The choice of the contested
border-zone of Galloway is politically interesting, implicating Arthur in
the imperial ambitions of later medieval kings; Edward I pillaged in
Galloway after his victory against Wallace at Falkirk in 1298, but had been
unable to complete his campaign.[20] Galeron's challenge is met by Gawain,
who battles Galeron the following day, giving and receiving near mortal wounds. Finally Galeron surrenders through sheer exhaustion and
concedes his rights to the land. Gaynour, appalled by the carnage, mediates a settlement with Arthur in which Galeron receives Galloway back
and Gawain is recompensed for the loss with extensive other lands in
also southwest Scotland. The episode ends without any graver long-term

consequences to the court than the death of Gawain's horse. In the last stanza, Gaynour returns belatedly to her mother's business, instructing clergy all over the realm to commemorate her mother with "a mylion of masses" (706). The poem then reprises its beginning, a circular ending like that of *Sir Gawain and the Green Knight*.

Whether or not the poem is by one or two poets, there are enough thematic and structural resonances between the two halves to make consideration of their cumulative effect profitable. If there were two poets and the poem is an amalgamation, the second poet may not have been as metrically skillful as the first, but he succeeds in conveying an interesting judgment. Contrast with the profitable exchanges set up in *De Tribus Regibus Mortuis* sheds additional light on the significance of what fails to happen in both halves of the poem. The poem begins by isolating Gaynour and Gawain from the rest of the court, and each dominates one episode. Both episodes centralize the courtly greed for land acquisition, suggestive in the light of the probable late fourteenth- or early fifteenth-century dating of the poem and the recent dismal history of the two great failed late medieval English land grabs, the Scottish Wars and the Hundred Years War.[21]

More tellingly, both halves of the poem feature attempts at negotiation that achieve nominal resolutions but fail to address the fundamental problems. The ghost pleads three times for Gaynour to do what the three kings in *De Tribus Regibus Mortuis* do without such exhortation: to rejoin the larger body of society by works of "Mekeness and mercy . . . and [to] haue pité on þe poer . . . Siþen charité is chef, and þew of þe chaste, / And þen almessedede ouer al oþer þing" (250–53) [Meekness and mercy . . . and to have pity on the poor . . . and since charity is the chief of all the virtues for the pure, and then alms-deeds over all other activities]. Gaynour is deaf to this charitable emphasis, asking repeatedly if her mother could be helped by prayers and masses, which the ghost concedes (219–21, 230). At the poem's end, Gaynour limits herself to this institutional solution but takes it to flamboyant extremes. She impresses an army of priests and bishops into commemorative service by organizing a million-mass-march into the west, dramatizing her daughterly piety with a desperation that only underscores her neglect of the ghost's repeated call for charity (173, 230–34, 251). Thus Gaynour remains isolated and high-handed, peremptory even in penance. This ending has disturbing implications for the relationship between a court in need of expiation and resocialization and a church which serves as its eager procurer. The court is too easily solaced by ecclesiastical rituals, which, while honorable and effective as the poem agrees, are triage more than cure.[22]

The second part of the poem extends the inadequacy of institutional ritual to the court itself which brokers futile exchanges first in the battle between Gawain and Galeron and then in the land settlement Gaynour negotiates. The battle is notable for the delirious intensity of the slow-motion blows exchanged by the two knights. Unlike many romance descriptions of single combat, these achieve their impact by their scarcity and the relentless reciprocity of their exchange. After the battle, the tally gives a severed collarbone, two impalements, a debilitating blow from above, and a decapitated horse whom Gawain pauses to commemorate with a heart-felt but florid epitaph and flood of tears. Yet these murderous blows do not check the dogged battle as both knights continue scraping the decorations from each other's armor in an echo of the alliterative *Morte Arthure* and *Gologras and Gawain*. Gawain gives a last thump which leaves Galeron groveling on the ground. Gawain grabs him by the collar. At this point Galeron's lover, who has been enlivening the intervals between blows by shrieking, prays Gaynour to stop the battle, which she does, asking Arthur to settle the battle peaceably. Galeron promptly surrenders to Gawain, walking over to Arthur, who receives his "bright burnished" sword and commands peace, almost too tardily given the lamentable state of both combatants.

And although Gawain is the victor and "Gode [stood] with þe riȝt" (469) [God (stood) with the right] to the extent that Arthur's side won, the fundamental question of who justly owns the lands in dispute remains unresolved. What Arthur won by conquest is rewon by Gawain's combat—if one covetous war is questionable, than so is the other. The poem acknowledges this when Arthur restores Galeron's lands anyway. Yet the recompensing of Gawain with "al þe londes and þe lithes fro Lauer to Ayre, / Connok and Carrak, Conyngham and Kile" (677–78) [all the lands and the vassels from Lauer to Ayre, Cumnock and Carrak, Conyngham and Kile] does not solve the problem either; if Arthur has been acquiring Scottish land through conquests, Gawain's acceptance of these new Scottish lands may involve him in future challenges which will also not settle the fundamental question of the justice of Arthur's conquests.

In highlighting the number of ways such exchanges can go wrong, these alliterative poems pose crucial questions about the late medieval social performance of death. Were the goods given in these gift exchanges—alms for prayers—really commensurate? Did the poor really stand for the dead as they were invited to funeral and commemoration feasts, fed on bread and cheese, given a few pence in the funeral dole—or is their token presence an easy gesture to reinforce the hierarchies of largesse, surrogate the dead in a more subjugable form, or alleviate guilt? What are the costs of such resocializations to the living and who pays most, the donor or his heirs? Liabilities to heirs both in money and in spiritual capital could be considerable. The deceased withheld from their heirs when they bought masses, willed trentals, anniversaries, and other commemorations, and endowed temporary or, at tremendous expense, perpetual chantries. And the deceased threatened his heirs with God's judgment or sometimes his own curse if they did not persist generation after generation in upholding their commemorative obligations—even when those obligations required costly reinvestment to refund impoverished perpetual chantries, keep them staffed, or guard against their imperceptible dilapidation.

Most pressing of all was the question of whether the class inequities that persist on earth should be allowed to persist into the afterlife. Death, as Virginia R. Bainbridge and others point out, was a mirror of society in late medieval ritual practice; the dead were resocialized according to their social resources—luxuriously if they were of a high social class, meagerly if not.[23] How does this connect with Mirk's sermon on the poor as watchful judges beside Christ, or the revolutionary gospel parables where the last are first, first are last, and Dives ends up craving the services of Lazarus—in vain? These doubts, though they do not trouble the documentary surface of wills, chantry foundation deeds, or the 1389 returns in which Richard II called upon confraternities to declare themselves, surface in questions raised by heterodox or institutionally interrogatory medieval writers whose influence persisted despite official sanctions against them—Langland and Wyclif—and also in some equally influential orthodox ones, like John Mirk with his stress on real charity. Wyclif waxed particularly bitter about the damage done both to living and dead by the conspicuous consumption of the industry of death:

Many men ben disseyved in founding of chauntries, in coostli sepulcris, and in solempne sepulturis; and all these feden the world, and done no profit to the soule; but as thei harmen men lyviynge, so thei done harm to the soul.[24]

[Many men are deceived in founding chantries, in costly tombs, and solemn burials; and all these feed the world and do no profit to the soul but as they harm living men so they do harm to the soul].

And feeding the world with a spectacular and expensive display was at least partly the point. Wood-Legh notes trenchantly how the "blend of pride and humility from which would spring the decision to found a chantry was paralleled by the mixture of selfishness and altruism in the object of the prescribed prayers."[25] These rituals flourished because they simultaneously profited religious institutions and allowed individuals to dramatize a social presence after death. By the late fourteenth century, death and the rituals communicating its significance to society were providing ever richer opportunities for institutional profit and the display of social rank. Robert Dinn describes burial and commemorative rituals in Bury St. Edmunds where "the social position of the deceased was explicitly and constantly affirmed during the funeral ritual."[26] Churches charged for burials and thus privileged the rich in the placement of their tombs—optimally in ecclesiastical atria, within churches, and if possible close to the altar. Such placement promised a greater certainty of durability—particularly in urban settings where space was dear and graves were periodically excavated and emptied into charnels and ossuaries to make room for more burials.[27] The poor could not afford tombs; charity burials often landed them in mass graves, which were also subject to subsequent excavation. Funeral processions, trentals, and commemorations also had to be financed privately and could be lavish enough to draw in a town or the gathered clergy from an entire area.[28]

These developments opened the way to more active lay participation on a number of different fronts as individuals increasingly superintended not only their passage into eternity but also their enduring legacies at home. Wills became more dictatorial, commemorative rituals more elaborate, and religious fraternities more common. Ariès's description of the will as a kind of insurance policy brokering earthly and religious interests is particularly suggestive—wills allow mutually advantageous transactions between the living and the dead to intersect with negotiations between individuals and institutions: "The will was the religious and quasi-sacramental means of obtaining the *aeterna* without altogether losing the *temporalia*, a way of combining wealth with the work of salvation."[29] Because they transact such culturally freighted and crucial exchanges, late medieval wills offer glimpses into the lives, possessions, desires, and emotions of their writers that are unparalleled in their detail and explicitness. In addition to disposing of property (charitably, as a donation to a church, and to families and friends), fourteenth century wills began to express an intensifying concern for the provisioning and performance of burial and commemorative ritual. Some wills exhibit a micro-managerial anxiety that reveals the stakes not only in terms of property but also of identity. In the will an individual can stake a claim (however tenuous) in what kind of social role he will play after death. This attention to funerary and commemorative detail thus reveals a concern at least as great for that lingering social apparition as for the eternity-embarked soul.[30]

And individuals could also bond together to increase each others' powers of post-mortem social capital. Horizontally binding organizations like the religious fraternities provided a measure of posthumous insurance for those within their brother/sisterhoods since they traditionally accepted members of widely differing social classes and were formed on just about every social level. Surviving gild documents give a rich and probably deliberately understated account of the extent of gild activities. They showcase not only the fading merchant gilds, and the craft gilds that gradually gained in power and influence, but also the late medieval proliferation of religious gilds. Religious fraternities encompassed a huge range of activities, from the maintenance of lights and statues, and solemn processions, feast day masses, feasts, and plays (Gild of the Lord's Prayer in York), to the funerals, burials, and commemorative masses of their members. Their social heterogeneity made them profitable (if sometimes edgy and disruptive) sites for negotiation between classes.[31] However, they also served solidarities within a range of estates, incorporating not only wealthy burgesses (like the expensive gilds of Corpus Christi at York, of the Resurrection at Lincoln, and of St. Thomas of Canterbury at Lynn) but also Young Scholars "to mayntene and kepen an ymage of seynt Wylyam, standyng in a tabernakle, in þe chirche of seynt Margarete of Lenne (Lynn),"[32] and Poor Men devoted to St. Austyn at Norwich whose activities stressed monetary relief to needy members equally with their religious obligations.

This proliferation of religious gilds profited both laity and clergy, even as it tightened, sometimes uncomfortably, the extent of interrelationship between them. It generated the friction of not-quite-intersecting interests even as it facilitated mutually beneficial alliances. These coinciding but sometimes competing interests were often worked out on the grounds of the churches themselves. Rood screens were rebuilt or moved to wall off the nave (associated with the laity) from the choir. In order to accommodate the masses said continuously during the week for the dead and prevent the disruption of regular masses and ceremonies, some churches were forced to construct supplementary altars and chapels along the nave.[33] These grew so popular during the fourteenth century that churches had to alter their physical shape to accommodate them, often with a certain amount of white-knuckled renegotiation between clergy and laity concerning their respective rights and duties in physical maintenance for the church, and the scheduling and staffing of ritual services.[34] Yet this lay interest benefited the secular clergy as well, multiplying jobs for chantry priests since each could celebrate only one mass per day and therefore could not take on more than one daily chantry Service. Many priests had no other means of income than commemorative and trental masses. However the gradual impoverishment of many chantries depreciated such minimally paying appointments. Chopchurches, semi-illicit ecclesiastical job-brokers, proliferated to help ambitious minor clergy find better appointments.[35]

Confraternities often ordained charitable work in their foundation deeds, thus providing another late medieval site where service to the poor and service to the dead coincided. However, charity to the living seems to have been strictly subordinated. Confraternities scrupulously assured their members of post-mortem benefits they would not have been able to afford on their own, including burial in the confraternity's chapel, funeral processions of members, and commemorative prayers and services.[36] But they were often much more finicky about financial relief to members, stipulating that their need could not stem from their own neglect or excessiveness. And members always took precedence over outsiders although confraternities did bury and service the poor, especially in towns where anonymous death was a fast ticket to a mass grave. So much of their work was associated with the death industry that in local parishes they virtually became institutions of death, overwhelmingly associated with grave and burial processions. They provided instant labor pools which the urban elite or the aristocracy could draw on to amplify funeral attendance or fill out a procession. However, their traditional emphasis on charities to the living and to non-members seems to have been cosmetic at best.[37]

In fact, the very popularity of confraternities—with the ceaseless regulation that inevitably accompanied it—raised doubts about where the profits of post-mortem exchange were accruing, misgivings about the effects of death, and a persistent suspicion that existing ecclesiastical and social institutions were not able effectively to cope with them. K. Wood-Legh draws attention to the disquieting emphasis on numerical quantity and unrelenting ritual repetition with which the material economies of investment invade the spiritual economies of charity, the way that the vision of God brokered through such economizing of salvation yields a rather grim picture of God as a unrelentingly legalistic banker:

a being of infinite severity in whose dealings with men there are few signs of love, who prefers the endless repetition of the sacrifice of the altar to any manifestation of Christian character, and who, for all his majesty, has so little magnanimity that he will allow the souls in Purgatory to suffer, if, despite all the precautions a pious founder could devise, the services of his chantry, long after he and all his friends were dead, should be discontinued.[38]

In a less theological direction, the regulated exchanges that drew living and dead together are spurred, troubled, and enlivened by hints that their interests, like those of individuals and institutions, like those between the rich and the poor, like the relationship between material and spiritual value, did not always perfectly coincide. Servicing one could sometimes be stealing from, or invading, or presuming upon the other. It is this consciousness of troubled incommensurability that these alliterative poems tease out, as much in the multi-tasked redemption of the Three Dead Kings as in the disquieting miscommunications of *The Awntyrs off Arthure* where elaborate formal settlements like a million masses and a shuffle of royal endowments ineffectively surrogate fundamental reform.

Uncanny Forms

The poems themselves declare the strains between formal management and dramatized disruption in the stanzaic forms they choose, arguably the most intricate in English poetry. The thirteen-line stanza adds a rigid rhyme scheme to its alliterative exigencies which themselves go into overdrive, often enriched with alliteration on every stress, and internal patterns of concatenation. The rhyme scheme plays variations on *ababababab-c-ddd-c*, where *c* is a bob and *d* lines form a short wheel. Thorlac Turville-Petre reviews its features and gives a bibliography of its uses which proves it the most popular alliterative stanza.[39] Like the complaint stanza, it allows poets to spectacularize their skills at prosodic management while dramatizing coloratura extremes of emotion, from the elation of the hunt to the horror of the returned dead. The poets of *De Tribus* and *Awntyrs* seek dramatic variation within a frame of rigid repetition, animating their narratives within extraordinary forms in a way that echoes the repetition, excess, formality, and search for new strategies characterizing late medieval practices for the management of death.

But if *De Tribus* and *Awntyrs* metrically and thematically put such managerial practices on the line, *Somer Sunday*, another poem in the same stanza on the same mortal theme, blows them clean away. Where *De Tribus* and *Awntyrs* mobilize a drama of mortal disruption to urge redress, renewed continuity, and resocialization, *Somer Sunday* reverses the process. It leads its narrator from the usual delights of hunting into the wilderness to encounter not the dead but the time-at-a-glance spectacle of Fortune and her wheel, dead-ending in the vision of a corpse. Conventional as this sounds, the poet's treatment gives it extraordinary animation: the first-person narrative of the vision combines with an unusually compressed alliterative line to generate an almost jangling narrative immediacy; the vision teems with motto-like first-person declarations that draw the reader in.

This sense of sociality and movement is accentuated both by the picture of Fortune, vivid and beguiling, and by the men who refuse passive specularity and declare themselves from her wheel in short *versus,* compressed and repetitive to the point of singsong. Fortune's gorgeous fickleness forms an enticing contrast to the dark certainty of the lesson she shadows forth; she embodies the attractive uncertainty of historical mutability as well as its cruelty. And the men on the wheel—grasping, gleeful, and glum—form a transient chivalric company in her honor, the Order of the Wheel rather than the Round Table. The brevity of their speeches heightens their frenetic courtliness; the first two call out to the narrator in intimate terms: "Seestow, swetyng?" (76, 97) [Do you see, my sweet?]. Their "Look at me!" delight in their rising or triumphant sovereignty gives their regnal boasts a chiming pleasure. The first is due for a kingship: "Be kynde it me come / To cleyme kyngene kyngdom, / Kyngdom by kinde;" (79–81) [By birthright it comes to me, / to claim of kings a kingdom / a kingdom by birthright]. The second is charmed by his own power: "Lordlich lif led I / No lord lyuynde me iliche" (104–5) [I live a lordly life / no living lord is like to me]. But in the speech of the third, the chime turns plaintive, expressing the frictionless rapidity of attrition with startling compression: "Lond, luþe, litel, lo! last!" (124) [Land, property, little, lo!, last]. To the narrator, this is bad enough, but he immediately sees a sorrier sight: the voiceless figure beneath the wheel.

> A bare body in a bed, a bere ibrouth him by,
> A duk drawe to þe deþ wiþ drouping and dare. (132–133)

[A naked body in a bed, a bier brought near to him, a duke drawn to death with mourning and grief.]

At this vision grief steals the voice of the poem itself and it abruptly ends. The poem's breaking off at this point dramatically enacts the lesson of mortality. All the chiming, elaborate, winding, circling forms cease, leaving the reader at the brink, with no processing, no resocialization, only the prospect of the corpse—naked, uneuphemized, and about to be discarded.[40]

When *Somer Sunday* plays alliterative form against such piteous "fynisment," it does so to underline the inevitable tragedy of earthly sovereignty and to give it a startling personal immediacy. The narrator is affectively implicated at every stage in this vision, made responsive, and hence, responsible. In this, the poem fully participates in what Ralph Hanna describes as alliterative poetry's "overt consciousness of blameworthiness," a reminder of the tyranny inherent in rule which is displaced into historic mutability itself: "history itself produces guilt, a determinism which in some measure exculpates the well-intentioned alliterative subject."[41]

But offsetting this exculpation is the continued need for alertness, remembrance, and, I believe, ongoing critique: a call to reexamination and reinvention. In *The Awntyrs* the shortcomings and blindnessess of Arthur's court emerge not as inevitable but as chosen, cherished, and ritually culti-vated. Even more interestingly, the poem tinges its contemplation of their tragic fall with a tantalizing glimmer of renovation. We glimpse this when the ghost is in full cry, prophesying the end of Arthur's court at Mordred's hands. She gives a frightening vision of Arthur's last battlefield, with knights falling, Gawain slain in a muddy embankment, and Arthur perilously wounded: "All the rial rowte of þe Round Table / Þei shullen dye on a day ... Suppriset with a subjet" (304–5) [all the royal company of the Round Table, they shall die in a single day ... overpowered by a vassal/ subject/inferior]. This subject, Mordred, strides terrifyingly across the bat-tlefield bearing a silver saltire cross, formed by crossing a bend with a bend sinister—a tiny figure of his canceling effect on the power of Arthur's court. And yet this vision of the apocalyptic shadow of destiny who will make all of Arthur's court "dye on a day" (305) cuts back suddenly into the present:

"In riche Arthures halle,
The barne playes at þe balle
Þat outray shall you alle,
Derfely þat day." (309–12)

["In rich Arthur's hall, the child plays at ball who shall overcome you all, fero-ciously that day."]

This sudden intimate vision of the child-Mordred playing with a ball inter-sects the previous figure of cancellation and opens a glimpse of playful if spooky regeneration. The contrast between innocent present and dark future induces a kind of interpretive indeterminacy. Since the poem depicts Arthur's court as acquisitive, sinful, and formula-blinded, are we to shud-der away from Mordred's ferocity or see him as a breath of the new? Fate or freedom: there is nothing to be done about Mordred, yet at the same time there is a strangely comforting assurance that whether Mordred is tossing a ball or flattening Arthur's world (seigneury is often also sym-bolized by an orb) he will retain the inventive absorption of a child at play. If this image makes Mordred the fatal force of history for Arthur, then it broadens that force's energy from tragic fall to game, from blunder to bliss. It hints at the playful, innocent, devastating regenerations that will eventually altogether blow away illustrious past forms despite their most devout strategies of self-maintenance. It foreshadows their replacement by the unguessable sovereignties of their already present but unregarded "subjets," and thus renders imaginable the end of aristocracy. And here the poem joins hands with other late fourteenth-century texts—alliterative or not—making trouble at the border zones of English aristocratic culture.

When all three of these poems simultaneously spectacularize the disjunctions of death and perplex the rituals for its management, they invite readers to question the surrogations and exchanges by which the shape of the present is normalized, nurtured, and preserved—a questioning that leads to the conception of new forms, new rituals, new social bodies. Anthropologists Maurice Bloch and Jonathan Parry see an overwhelmingly conservative function for the cultural shaping of death. Intimations of regeneration and temporal continuity not only console us for the disruptions of death but also are deployed to privilege particular social structures and reinforce dominant ideologies of gender and class:[42]

At several points we have stressed the relationship between mortuary beliefs and practices and the legitimation of the social order and its authority structure. This relationship is perhaps clearest in those instances where that order is built up by transforming the dead into a transcendent and eternal force . . . In these instances the social group is anchored, not just by political power, but by some of the deepest emotions, beliefs and fears of people everywhere. Society is made both emotionally and intellectually unassailable by means of that alchemy which transforms death into fertility. This fertility is represented as a gift made by those in authority which they bestow by their blessings.[43]

This emphasis on the reinforcement of authoritarian structures is undoubtedly an ideal or a cultural imperative, particularly for the rituals and practices that are more or less controlled by socially empowered classes. What makes Bloch and Parry's description most interesting to me, however, is the extent to which it does *not* fit the constant reshaping of death in late medieval culture and in these alliterative poems, where the dead are brought back not as eternal but as devastatingly mortal and where their social role is not immutable and secure but endlessly reinvented and performed. Moreover, late medieval mortuary rituals and beliefs were in constant contest and many different social interests were negotiated through them, especially as they fell into the hands of the lay population, serving urban merchant, artisans, and rural gildsmen and -women as well as the aristocracy and clergy. Fertility and regeneration may be represented as a gift from the authorities but these poems conspicuously target those in authority as needing to reexamine their own representations of death: to see themselves not merely as donors but, more humblingly, as recipients of the benefits of the dead. *De Tribus Regibus Mortuis*, *The Awntyrs off Arthure,* and *Somer Sunday* strip away the euphemistic and spectacular edifice of aristocratic self-representations to bare the donor corpse beneath, and thus model more equitable social reconsolidations where the authorities will acknowledge their debts to the people. In this, these poems mark their distance from the aristocratic ideologies they impeach, not by rejecting the gifts of the authorities but rather by reminding them of their own social embeddedness within a system of exchange where they are recipients as well as donors of gifts that must be returned.

8

Conclusion:
The Body in Question—Again

IT SEEMED APT TO CLOSE THIS BOOK, which began with a medieval exhumation, by describing a very different Renaissance one:

On the third day of which Month [September] it was, that the great and dreadful Fire of London began in a narrow Lane amongst old rotten Buildings, near to the lower end of Gracechurch Street, which in a short time, notwithstanding all the Help that could be, consumed the greatest Part of the City; in which not only the Parochial Churches were destroyed, but also this ancient Cathedral: The Roof whereof falling down with a mighty Force, broke through those Vaults, called the Undercroft so that under the Floor of our Lady Chapel . . . over the Roof of St. Faith's Church, a Coffin of Lead, lying there, was broke open, and in it found the Body of Robert Braybroke, sometime Bishop of London . . . having been there laid two hundred and sixty Years before; whose Corpse was so dried up, the Flesh, Sinews, and Skin cleaving fast to the Bones, that being set upon the Feet, it stood stiff as a Plank, the Skin being taut like Leather, and not at all inclined to Putrefaction, which some attributed to the sanctity of the Person, offering much money for it . . . But herein was nothing supernatural; for that which caused the Flesh, Skin, and Sinews to become thus hard and tough, was the Driness and Heat of the Dust wherein those Bodies lay, which was for the most part of Rubbish Lime, mix'd with a Sandy Earth.[1]

Robert Braybroke was the bishop of St. Paul's Cathedral at the time of *St. Erkenwald*'s probable composition; he legislated and politicked for the respect due the London saint, promoted the commemoration of St. Erkenwald's feast day along with that of St. Paul himself, and refurbished St. Erkenwald's shrine so that the holy relics would once again be a nexus of spiritual transformation and an asset to the cathedral. By an irony of history, this account in Dugdale's history of the cathedral shows Braybroke himself in circumstances similar both to those of the saint he promoted and the pagan in *St. Erkenwald*. His grave is broken by cataclysm, his tomb bared to the eyes of the curious, his body is uncorrupted. In Dugdale's history, the body even surfaces between the destruction of the Old Cathedral and Christopher Wren's energetic rebuilding of the New One.

What makes this body at first seem the most pathetic and most powerless of all the bodies considered in this book is its isolation from the institutions under whose aegis it was buried and in which its authority was rooted. And this lack of institution and social continuity is not just a matter of time but of doctrinal change—the Reformation, its denial of purgatory and its construction of new and (often tragically felt) absolute boundaries between the living and the dead. Michael Neill quotes Natalie Zemon Davis to describe the impact of this new consciousness of death's irrevocability:

> In Protestant churches [the] liturgy of remembrance fell abruptly silent; and when it was no longer possible for the living to assist the dead by such pious interventions, then death became a more absolute annihilation than ever . . . In the process, as Natalie Zemon Davis puts it, "All the forms of exchange and communication between souls in the other world and the living were to be swept away. God had not assigned to the saints the care of our salvation, Calvin said, but only to Christ. As for the dead, they were beyond our help, on their own: 'There is nothing more that we can add or take away' . . . Thus the dead were to be done away with as an 'age group' in Protestant society."[2]

This description casts a shadow of cataclysm between medieval and renaissance periods, defining them as it forces them apart. In a similar way, Dugdale himself carefully averts his eyes from the medieval trope of pious foundational *inventio*; he demystifies the body's preservation, casting a cool eye at the belief that sanctity could express itself through bodies in a socially valuable way.[3] Yet that belief is still attractive to the onlookers who offer money for the body with the opportunistic alacrity of any medieval trafficker in relics. Here the change between pre-reformation and post-reformation attitudes toward the dead is at least somewhat more complicated than the sudden silencing Neill describes.

And Dugdale's description of the cathedral's destruction itself modulates from describing a cataclysm—a disruption that constitutes past and future by separating them, gelling history into epoch and rendering it graspable—to describing a quandary, a resistance at the foundations of the break between old and new. We follow the fall of the cathedral's great roof through the floor, into the vault, and finally into the very coffins to discover a bizarre persistence where we least expect it, in the body beneath the collapsing institution: "the Flesh, Sinews, and Skin cleaving fast to the Bones, that being set upon the Feet, it stood stiff as a Plank, the Skin being taut like Leather, and not at all inclined to Putrefaction." Braybroke's weird medieval body has acquired a curious toughness. Its sojourn in the earth has imbued it with earth's stubborn materiality. Even orphaned from the religious institution to which Braybroke devoted his professional career and in which he had become a fixture, his body clings fast to its shape with every hardened sinew, stiff as a plank and determined to endure.

Within Dugdale's foundational history of St. Paul's, Braybroke's body complicates the strategic division between old work and new work, medieval past and renaissance present, just as the emergence of the pagan judge's preserved body complicates and comes to mediate the transition from Old Work to New Work which does so much social work in *St. Erkenwald*. The stubborn, epoch-complicating, persistence of this material body makes it powerful. Like the bodies in the alliterative romances treated in this book it survives to become a source of speculation to onlookers and, to Dugdale, a testament to the capacities of the mortal earth itself—without any supernatural prompting at all—to preserve the past and suddenly bring forth the resistant dead. This body yields neither to religious nor to foundational explanation but persists as an intractable remnant whose strength comes from the dry dust and detritus that mummified it, "rubbish Lime, mix'd with a Sandy Earth," a figure for the tangible ungraspability of history itself.

It is this same irreducible mortality that gives the other animated bodies of these alliterative romances their interrogatory power. These bodies perform the palpable resistance of broken flesh across time, daring and eluding symbolic recontainment, or, in yielding, forcing into visibility the complex urgencies that drive their conquerors, narrators, and successors to found themselves in the spaces preoccupied by those ancient bones. These alliterative romances relish the mortality of the past in the weird walking bodies of the three dead kings, and Gaynour's mother, the riven, green elvish body of the Green Knight and his bloated goddess Morgan le Fay, the primitive appetitive grossly corporeal giant of St. Michael's Mount, the Jewish mothers tortured within Jerusalem, the dying Anectanabus, the *Morte Arthure*'s battlefield symphonies of mutilation, the pagan in *St. Erkenwald* turning suddenly and dizzyingly into rotting powder. These bodies dramatize the dead, absent, powerful past as both adversary and producer of the present, interrupting surrogation, challenging ritual expiation; questioning supersessional narratives by spurring them to revealing extremes.

In performing history as conflict, these alliterative romances unmask the present's foundational exigencies, limelighting ideologies that are not hegemonic, authorities that are in contention, identities that are riven by internal contradictions. The very titles given to them by scribes or editors describe their polarizing and contentious logic: *Winner and Wastour, The*

Parliament of Three Ages, *Sir Gawain and the Green Knight*, *The Siege of Jerusalem*, *The Wars of Alexander*, the *Morte Arthure*, *Gologrus and Gawain*. In a late medieval heterogeneous society that was clutching at the mantle of tradition while questing after innovations—commercial, political, monarchical, and religious—these alliterative poems make the dry bones of history dance, reviving the past to disturb its divisions, confound its epochs, and challenge, complicate, and persuade performances of the new.

Notes

Introduction

1. Scholars interested in exploring the wider breadth of alliterative writing have recently decried the undue scholarly privileging of this formal strain as ignoring the diversity of alliterative poetic traditions: Salter, *English and International*, 170–79; McIntosh, "Early Middle English Alliterative Verse"; Hanna, "Defining." I do not wish to further this privilege by selecting only these poems out for treatment, but it does seem to me that the shared themes that mark them as noteworthy within (rather than exemplary of) alliterative writing have been underexplored. To see what makes these alliterative romances unusual within alliterative poetry arguably will cast light on the breadth of the tradition itself. For a study which admirably explores the breadth and variety of alliterative poetry, see Scattergood, *Lost Tradition*.

2. Lawton, *Middle English Alliterative Poetry*, 1–19.

3. A historical interest has been consistently noted in descriptions of late medieval alliterative romance and the most recent assessments make it a major theme. To my knowledge, however, this book is the first to pursue it within and between separate poems and to discuss it in terms of the performance of past/present confrontations. In his 1970 Israel Gollancz Memorial Lecture ("Nature of Alliterative Poetry") Geoffrey Shepherd compellingly generalized about "these backward gazing poets" (68) who play in genre-transcending ways along the continuum between "moral insight and historical truth" (72). Ralph Hanna argues that alliterative poetry in general pursues its historic investigations in order to provoke suspicion about the violent foundations of lordship. "Alliterative Poetry." Within Lawton's collection, both Derek Pearsall and Rosalind Field treat historicity as a distinguishing mark. *Middle English Alliterative Poetry*, 45–47, 57.

4. Rosalind Field discusses the correspondences between Anglo-Norman and alliterative romance and the ways their concern with historical specificity sets them apart from continental romance: "Anglo-Norman Background." Susan Crane explores how Anglo-Norman romance and its Middle English descendants construct specifically insular romance traditions that are very useful in foregrounding alliterative romance. *Insular Romance.* My study does not centralize alliterative dream-visions, allegories, and satires, such as *Winner and Wastoure, Piers Plowman* and its followers, the didactic *Cleanness* and *Patience*, and the otherworldly *Pearl*— even though *Pearl* spectacularly stages the incommensurabilities between historical and eschatological ways of knowing through a difficult conversation with a dead

girl. For a detailed study which historicizes *Pearl* within the milieu of the court of Richard II, see Bowers, "*Pearl* in its Royal Setting," and *The Politics of* Pearl. I omitted other alliterative romances, such as *William of Palerne* and the indefatigable *Destruction of Troy*, for reasons of space.

5. Lawton, "Unity"; Hanna, "Defining," 55.

6. Stephen H. A. Shepherd interestingly suggests that the romance theme of the value of others and outsiders (virtuous pagans, chivalric sultans, admirable enemies, etc.) links Langland's *Piers Plowman* to many of the romances which accompany it in manuscripts. "Langland's Romances."

7. The poems I have chosen experiment along each of these three generic axes; the third in particular is one of the most profitable tensions in the whole genre and is a particular crux in *St. Erkenwald,* which uses the soteriological framework of the *inventio* genre to probe at the foundational strategies of civic institutions. Monika Otter shows how historically self-conscious and institutionally strategic the *inventio* genre (and its textual/historical extensions) can be; her *Inventiones* ends by showing how *St. Erkenwald* transforms the conventions of the hagiographical *inventio* genre by metaphorically expanding the range of past-present interactions and thus fostering a historical self-consciousness that can acknowledge historical difference. *Inventiones*, 157–58.

8. Patterson, *Negotiating the Past;* Patterson, *Chaucer*; Knapp, *Social Contest*; Strohm, *Social Chaucer*; Strohm, *Hochon's Arrow*; Strohm *England's Empty Throne;* Fradenburg, "'Voice Memorial'"; Carolyn Dinshaw discusses the late twentieth-century use of the medieval as a space for the abjection of the primitive and the perverse. *Getting Medieval,* 183–206.

9. See Chapter 1.

10. Lawton, *Middle English Alliterative Poetry,* 2

11. Hanna, "Defining," 55.

12. Paul Strohm approaches this incident psychoanalytically as a Lancastrian resignification of Richard II's deposition in "Trouble with Richard" and it becomes a centerpiece in his book, *England's Empty Throne,* 101–27.

13. *The Brut,* 2: 373.

14. *Versus Rhythmici*, in *Memorials of Henry V,* 63–75.

15. Froissart, *Chronicle*, 398.

16. Ibid., 399.

17. *Elmhami Liber Metricus de Henrico Quinto*, in *Memorials of Henry V,* 158; Walsingham, *St. Albans Chronicle*, 117.

18. Strohm mobilizes Kantorowicz's description of the king's two bodies to argue that the haste and comparative scantiness of this first burial puts paid to the king's earthly body only to leave at large his eternal and symbolic body, inciting the deposed king's subsequent and astonishingly persistent apparitional career. "Trouble with Richard," 96–105.

19. "Hoc anno levatum fuit corpus quondam regis Anglie domini Ricardi de Burdegalia . . . et deportatum Londonias ac apud Wesmonasterium regaliter tumulatum, non sine maximis expensis regiis, qui fatebatur se tantum sibi venerationis debere quantum patri suo carnali." [In this year was raised the body of Lord Richard of Bordeaux, formerly the King of England . . . and carried to London and at the house of Westminster magnificently buried, not without great expense for

the king, who exhibited thus as great a veneration as toward his own father in the flesh.] Walsingham, *St. Albans Chronicle,* 77.

20. Labarge, *Henry V,* 43.

21. Strohm usefully stresses that this symbolic re-encompassment may be only as effective as a particular cultural moment permits—that when the political situation changed and the Yorkists came to power later in the century, Richard could be resymbolized yet again as a Lancastrian victim rather than its progenitor. "Trouble with Richard," 110–11.

22. Ibid., 19; Saul, *Richard II,* 237, 323.

23. In fact, Thomas of Lancaster (Edward II's near nemesis) had his own developing cult at the Pontefract, the scene of his execution by Edward II. Bennett, *Richard II,* 27, 41.

24. My thanks to the anonymous reader for the University of Pennsylvania Press who suggested this parallel.

25. Bennett, *Richard II,* 103, 112.

26. Ann Astell discusses this exhumation and reburial at greater length, positing that *Sir Gawain* persistently alludes to and allegorizes it. *Political Allegory,* 122.

27. Otter discusses the dialectical relations between "distancing the past and appropriating it . . . a sense of continuity and a sense of discontinuity" (389) in medieval writing. She usefully questions scholarly generalizations about the ahistoricism of the medieval sense of the past and urges a more nuanced study of particular textual traditions. "'New Werke."

28. *Confessions,* 269.

29. Fradenburg, "'Voice Memorial'"; Stewart, *On Longing*; Bloom, *Anxieties*; Roach, *Cities.*

30. This view of the past surfaces powerfully in medieval historiography. Spiegel, *Past as Text.*

31. The idea of a medieval past of genuine difference has been productive in Chaucer studies. Lee Patterson has analyzed the recursions of a threatening sense of historic alterity in his discussions of Theban poetics. *Chaucer and the Subject of History,* 47–230. Louise Fradenburg assigns a more melancholic alterity to Chaucer's poetic struggles with a sense of a past which is irretrievably lost, mourned incessantly, used to construct socially functional nostalgias, or plastered over by tropes of reparation. "'Voice Memorial.'"

32. Freud, "The Uncanny," 368–407.

33. "Alliterative Poetry," 511–12.

34. *Living with the Dead,* 5–8.

35. Patterson, *Negotiating the Past.*

36. Anne Middleton explores the historical precision with which this claim both invokes and frustrates powerful fourteenth-century statutory and ideological categorizations. "Acts of Vagrancy." See also Pearsall, ed., *Piers Plowman.*

37. Such monarchical concerns speak powerfully to individual poems, as is evidenced by John M. Bower's acute imbrication of *Pearl* with Ricardian court culture, and political debate, and Frank Grady's reading of *St. Erkenwald* in the light of the empire-building of the Westminster government. Bowers, "*Pearl* in its Royal Setting"; Grady, "*St. Erkenwald* and the Merciless Parliament."

38. J. R. Hulbert's much-questioned theory proposed that alliterative poetry expressed baronial tension against the monarchy: "Hypothesis," 405–22.

39. Hanna, "Alliterative Poetry," 488–512.

40. Chapter 1 treats the formal, generic, and thematic coherences these alliterative romances do exhibit.

41. Salter, "Alliterative Modes," 170.

42. In fact, these poems' obsessive self-situating sets them apart from continental romances employing what Eric Auerbach in *Mimesis* calls "ethical" topographies, externalizing the processual vicissitudes of chivalric introspection. The alliterative romances, by contrast, reflect the insular romances' concern for historical specificity, venturing only briefly into this socio-subjective *terra incognita* for particular ends.

Chapter 1

1. All quotes from *St. Erkenwald* are from Turville-Petre's edition in *Alliterative Poetry*, while translations are mine. "Roynyshe" arguably connotes not only *mysterious* but mysterious *inscription*—harking back to its dual derivation from Anglo-Saxon "ryne" [mystery] and "rune" [private counsel, secret, magical writing, a letter] according to the *Middle English Dictionary* (*MED*) and Toller's *Anglo-Saxon Dictionary*. It appears in two other poems, *Cleanness* and *Sir Gawain and the Green Knight*. In *Cleanness* it is used three times, once [in the sense of outlandish or foreign] to refer to the strangers invited to the feast in the parable (*Cleanness*, 95) but twice to refer to the mysterious writing on the wall at Belshazar's feast. In *Sir Gawain* its Middle English confusion with "renishe" [rough, fierce—from ON "hrjonn"] emerges.

2. Or even a minor baron's to read Anglo-Norman, so predominant had the English mother-tongue become at the expense of the French dialect. This had been artificially nurtured as a status language among the nobility and gentry from as early as the mid twelfth century and by the late fourteenth-century was likely spoken with proficiency only by the exclusive greater nobility: Crane, *Insular Romance*, 4–7.

3. I am grateful to D. Vance Smith for his powerful reading of this lost and mourned inscription at the plenary panel "The Medieval Renaissance Divide," at the "Wrinkles in Time" conference, University of Pennsylvania, October 7, 2000.

4. Both Hoyt Duggan and Thomas Cable, in fact, recently decentralize alliteration, concentrating instead on discerning patterns of strong dips (consecutive unstressed syllables) and stresses. If alliteration is working more as a visible ornament than an essential metrical signal, arguably, in addition to the work it does to bridge the caesura of the half-line, it also functions as a way to perform visible continuities with past traditions even amidst the innovative metre.

5. Thomas Cable finds that both *Joseph* and *Destruction* depart from the structure of alliterative meter that he discovers, and work out their own metrical rules. *English Alliterative Tradition*, 86, 89, 111.

6. Cable, *English Alliterative Tradition*, 86–113; Duggan, "Shape of the B-Verse"; "Alliterative Patterning"; "Final -*e*."

7. Field argues that both formal alliteration and *laisse* share a concern with historical material (often with deliberate archaism) and religious seriousness, exhibit the stances of court-outsiders, and are treated as equivalents by contemporary writers. "Anglo-Norman Background," 60–63.

8. Chambers, "Continuity."

9. Pearsall, "Origins."

10. Hanna, "Contextualizing."

11. Hanna, "Alliterative Poetry."

12. For a supporting example, Turville-Petre traces the development of the characteristically fourteenth-century unalliterated final stress and persuasively shows it to be a logical development rather than adherence to historical tradition. He concludes that "the fourteenth-century poets did not inherit a tradition of 'correct verse' miraculously preserved, but instead they consciously—and by gradual stages—remodelled a written tradition of alliterative composition that led back only by rather tortuous routes to Old English verse." *Alliterative Revival*, 17.

13. Turville-Petre, *Alliterative Revival*, 1–25.

14. Pearsall, "Origins," 35.

15. The essay, originally published in *Neuphilologische Mitteilungen* 79 (1978): 25–35, was reprinted in her posthumous essay collection, *English and International*, 170–79.

16. See also "Defining."

17. Translation is Marie Borroff's. *Sir Gawain*.

18. For useful recent work that explores the body as a site for medieval conflicts of gender, estate, and occupation, see Bynum, *Fragmentation*; Beckwith, *Christ's Body*; Lomperis and Stanbury, eds., *Feminist Approaches*; Kay and Rubin, *Framing Medieval Bodies*; and Sponsler, *Drama and Resistance*.

19. Strohm, *Social Chaucer*, especially the first and the last chapters; and Wallace, *Chaucerian Polity*.

20. White, "Historical Text"; Ricoeur, *Time and Narrative*, 1: 161–69.

21. Translation is Marie Borroff's.

22. In the introduction to his edition of *Golagros and Gawain*, Thomas Hahn brilliantly notes the complementarity between the poem's lexical richness and "the lavish ornamentation and conspicuous consumption that mark the chivalry it describes." Many of the formally styled alliterative romances play upon this correspondence when they elaborate with such lexical exuberance the details of armor, heraldic display, and the thrust and slash of battle. *Sir Gawain: Eleven Romances*.

23. Barney thoroughly reviews recent scholarship on this subject; for reasons of space and currency my analysis will focus primarily upon Duggan and Cable.

24. I am oversimplifying this history; for notable interventions in alliterative metrical theory since Oakden, see Borroff, *Stylistic and Metrical Study*; Sapora, *Theory*; Matonis, "Reexamination"; Schmidt, *Clerkly Maker*.

25. Oakden, *Alliterative Poetry*, 1: 243.

26. Angus McIntosh also notes a return to earlier forms, a purging of elements he assigns to the thirteenth century (link rhyme, etc.) to conclude that "even if the verse of the revival is—as was suggested earlier—a new creation, whatever in it stems from the past comes from elsewhere than the kind of alliterative verse

which the thirteenth century has bequeathed to us" (26). "Middle English Alliterative Verse."

27. For instance, Cable's hypothesis requires a voiced final *-e* in particular categories of words even when received linguistic histories show it to be disappearing from late fourteenth-century usage. He treats this retentiveness as a metrical choice rather than a linguistic symptom. *English Alliterative Tradition*, 67–85; Duggan disagrees. "Final *-e*," 135–43.

28. Barney, "Langland's Prosody," 70–72.

29. "Evidential Basis," 152.

30. "Evidential Basis," 152–53; "Alliterative Patterning," 77–78; "Final *-e*," 144.

31. "Shape of the B-Verse," 569–70; "Alliterative Patterning," 77–79; "Stress Assignment."

32. "Alliterative Patterning."

33. Cable, *English Alliterative Tradition*, 92–93. Barney tests and tentatively corroborates this last rule as a promising line of future statistical research. "Langland's Prosody," 82–85.

34. Duggan's theory does not meet Cable's criteria either.

35. Cable argues in fact that strong-stress meter relies on strong dips—the "gabble" of unstressed syllables against which metrical stresses can rise to a more contrastive prominence. *English Alliterative Meter*, 9–10.

36. Ibid., 64–65.

37. E. G. Stanley argues for precisely this kind of self-consciously reinventive archaism in Laȝamon's *Brut*. "Laȝamon's Antiquarian Sentiments," 33.

38. "Langland certainly and perhaps also the *Gawain*-poet appear to be closer to Eliot than to the *Beowulf*-poet in their freedom to diverge from the norm. Although Borroff and I do not always agree on the specifics of the basic pattern, we agree that there *is* a basic pattern and that it is not always adhered to." Cable, *English Alliterative Tradition*, 101.

39. Ibid., 201–16. For Rolle and for Latin antecedents in the *ars rhythmica*, see Lawton, *Middle English Alliterative Poetry*, 15–19.

40. I am not trying to construct prescriptive generic boundaries in this section but rather constellating narrative questions which these alliterative romances pose with particular intensity. Other poems, alliterative or not, romance and otherwise, may express similar concerns and thus speak to these poems in interesting ways; other critics may regard, for instance, *St. Erkenwald*, as predominantly concerned with soteriology rather than history and thus would not include it in this group. I myself have been having second thoughts about *Pearl* ever since completing the project. This continual open-endedness between genres is what makes keeps them evolving, inflectional and thus useful for recreating themselves and their audiences.

41. Fichte gives a useful outline of general relations between alliterative romances and continental romances. "Middle English Verse Romance."

42. Field, "Anglo-Norman Background," 59; Shepherd, "Nature of Alliterative Poetry."

43. David Aers usefully questions the rift between religious and secular values in *Sir Gawain* in *Community, Gender, and Individual Experience*, 153–78.

44. "Langland's Romances."

45. Pierre Macherey, *Theory of Literary Production*.

46. Certeau, *Practice of Everyday Life*, xvii.

47. Turville-Petre, *Alliterative Revival*, 27.

48. Bourdieu, *Language*, 106.

49. Loomis, "Auchinleck Manuscript."

50. Oakden, *Alliterative Poetry*, 174.

51. Hanna, "Alliterative Poetry," 501–2.

52. Richard Firth Green similarly discusses the difference in flexibility between oral and written legal practices. When he describes the transition from an oral folklaw to a law based on a set of written documents, he quotes Fritz Kern that "a law which 'itself remains young, always in the belief that is old' was ousted by a law in which 'the dead text retains power over life'" (179). *Crisis of Truth*, 127.

53. Derek Pearsall summarizes the wide range of sources used by various alliterative poems in order to argue that only monastic libraries could supply the needs of the poets." Origins."

54. Richard Firth Green gives a thorough account of the difficulties of establishing non-aristocratic professional literary practice in England in the comparative absence of systems of courtly patronage and after the decline of the minstrel as a professional poet. *Poets and Prince-Pleasers*, 103–8. Derek Pearsall argues vigorously for a monastic origin of alliterative poetry, stressing the semi-aristocratic urbanity and secularism common in even strict monastic establishments at this time. "Origins."

55. This conclusion is based partly on the evidence of the manuscripts. The actual surviving manuscripts that include these poems bear no resemblance to the beautiful and lavishly produced French works that were the pride of aristocratic libraries at this time. They are small and businesslike, featuring few or primitive illustrations and rubrications, many of them evidently home-produced. The Thornton manuscript offers a particularly striking combination of editorial energy with paleographic pallor. Thompson, *Robert Thornton*, 56–63.

56. *Alliterative Revival*, 47. Turville-Petre also points out the gap between actual and imagined audience: "The 'audience' is created to match the poem, and this audience may be as fictional as the action of the poem itself." Turville-Petre, *Alliterative Revival*, 38. Michael J. Bennett takes umbrage at the idea of a backwoods "gouty bailiff" as primary audience, proposing instead the lesser knights with recent battle experience in the Hundred Years War and knowledge of the capital and greater courts to draw on. "Historical Background," 78.

57. Saul, "Conflict and Consensus," 40.

58. This is only one half of Crane's argument, which centralizes Dorigen's gendered exclusion as well: *Gender and Romance*, 93–131.

59. Salter, *English and International*, 109.

Chapter 2

1. I have consulted four editions: those of Savage, Morse, Peterson, and Turville-Petre. Quotations are from Turville-Petre's edition.

2. Whatley, "Middle English *St. Erkenwald*," and "Heathens and Saints."

3. Otter, "'New Werke,'" 404.

4. Nissé, "'Coroun Ful Riche.'"

5. John Scattergood usefully politicizes this sense of willful mystery by showing how the poem systematically erodes any access to the past—memorial, documentary, or symbolic—but that of the miraculous conversation given only to the bishop by God in order to reinstate a providential view of history and give back "to ecclesiastics sole custody of the past in a London that never was." *Lost Tradition*, 199.

6. This focus on divine mercy dominated earlier scholarship. Critics generally adopted one of two routes to it: soteriological and literary. Some place it in a context of intellectual or theological history, considering its stance on the theological issue of the salvation of the virtuous pagan, its use and redefinition of hagiography, or its efficacy as a devotional piece. Faigley, "Typology and Justice"; Frantzen, "*St. Erkenwald*"; Vitto, *Virtuous Pagan*; Clark and Wasserman, "*St. Erkenwald's*"; Wenzel, "*St. Erkenwald*"; and Stouck, "'Mourning and Myrthe.'" Others consider the poem's literary unity, the way its structure fits its substance, how various sources are woven into a tightly focused and richly poignant narration about a saint's salvific piety. Peck, "Number Structure"; Davidson, "Mystery, Miracle"; McAlindon, "Hagiography"; and Petronella, "St. Erkenwald."

7. This dating depends on its connection with the establishment of two feast days honoring St. Erkenwald in a 1386 pastoral letter from the Bishop of London, Robert de Braybroke: Savage, ed., *St. Erkenwald*, 75–79. Gollanz came to the same conclusion earlier, but tied it to his theory that the author was Ralph Strode, a man caught up in London city politics who backed Nicholas Brembre, the accused "Duke of New Troy," executed by the Merciless Parliament. These connections have been plausibly challenged by Clifford Peterson, who puts the poem between 1380 and 1420 with a bias toward the latter on the basis of a dozen neologisms. I am not convinced by the dating from lexicon: alliterative verse, early and late (as far as we can tell), abounds with hapax legomena, archaisms, and innovative kennings. The references to "New Troy" alone evoke the rumors and accusations of the 1380s even aside from its Braybroke-like promotion of the saint. I argue that the poem responds to the culture of London after the 1381 rising and also to larger movements of late medieval lay piety, religious dissent, and civic reorganization extending into the fifteenth century.

8. Rodney Hilton discusses the concordance between the interests of the London commons and the rural rebels. *Bond Men Made Free*, 186–213.

9. Bird, *Turbulent London*, 61–63; Thrupp, *Merchant Class*, 77–81.

10. Thrupp shows the extent and tenacity of relationships between urban and rural areas and the constant migration between them. *Merchant Class*, 222–33.

11. Anne Middleton discusses the identity-fixing impulse in such legislation. "Acts of Vagrancy."

12. On the increasing identification of Lollardy with religious heresy, see Aston, *Lollards and Reformers*. Rodney Hilton tentatively connects the subsequent outbreak of Lollardry with the revolt to suggest that such institutional suspicion might not have been entirely paranoid. *Bond Men Made Free*, 213.

13. Leeson, *Travelling Brothers*, 44.

14. Butcher, "English Urban Society," 97; Hilton and Aston, eds., *English Rising*, 333–43.

15. Steven Justice argues that this characterization arises because chroniclers are unable to read the insurgents' revolutionary idiom. *Writing and Rebellion*. Andrew Galloway counters this by discerning in Walsingham's chronicle a parodic, acute, but also knowing and sensitive dismissal of the way the rebels were claiming legal authority by citation (or invention) of ancient traditional rights and charters—like much of the rest of fourteenth-century legal establishment, "Making History Legal," 7–39. See also Green, *Crisis of Truth*, 248-92.

16. Barron, "Parish Fraternities," 33.

17. Ibid., 33–34.

18. Ibid., 35.

19. All citations from the *Vita* are from Whatley's excellent edition, *The Saint of London*, and translations are also his.

20. Whatley, ed., *Saint of London*, 91.

21. Ibid.

22. Ibid., 93.

23. Ibid.

24. Ibid.

25. Ibid.

26. Savage shows how Braybroke's letter commands that St. Erkenwald is to be accorded as much respect as St. Paul himself. *St. Erkenwald*, 75–76.

27. C. N. L. Brooke describes the gradual dispersion and redistribution of authority from the bishop and his *familia* to a wider circle of parochial clergy with a much smaller nucleus of central control. By the fourteenth century, the bishop was often forced to negotiate with the cathedral chapter, adopting conciliatory measures especially if, like Robert Braybroke at St. Paul's, the bishop was an outside appointee and had not been a canon at his cathedral: "Earliest Times," 6–7.

28. Nissé, "'Coroun Ful Riche,'" 277–95.

29. Nissé's argument illuminates many of the poem's deliberate occlusions. The pagan is a judge with kingly authority, rather than an actual king, because judges have a position outside the traditional feudal order, and thus are more a part of a living community than the class-isolated monarchs and nobles that dominate much medieval historiography. He is nameless because medieval historiographies like Geoffrey of Monmouth's regnal genealogy contain no extra-regnal center of communal authority. The pagan becomes the natural head of a body politic in John of Salisbury's model, rather than simply a war leader. Thus the poem interrogates the disjunction between regal government and authentic civil custom, ecclesiastically purifying the violent pollutions of regal history. Ibid.

30. Longo, "Vision of History."

31. Clark and Wasserman, "St. Erkenwald's," 382; Petronella, "St. Erkenwald"; McAlindon, "Hagiography"; Stouck, "'Mourning and Myrthe.'"

32. Although in the twelfth-century *Vita* he is depicted as the founder of two monasteries, he is portrayed merely as the bishop of London, not as the builder of its cathedral. Whatley, ed., *Saint of London*, 91.

33. Dugdale, *History of St. Paul's*, 24.

34. Stouck, "'Mourning and Myrthe,'" 253.

35. Morse, ed., *St. Erkenwald*, 66.

36. Benham, *Old St. Paul's*, 15.

37. Hudson, ed., *English Wycliffite Writings*, 84.

38. Ibid., 101.

39. During the fifteenth and sixteenth centuries, ugly stories were associated with this tower. Bishop Bonner, bishop of London from 1539 to 1550, confined a man named Hunne in the tower for owning Lollard tracts. When Hunne was found hanged, the official verdict was suicide, but the citizens of London blamed Bonner and hated him bitterly after that. There was also the sixteenth-century imprisonment and "persuasion" of Peter Burcher. Longman, *History*, 34; Benham, *Old St. Paul's*, 12.

40. In 1378 Archbishop Sudbury excommunicated two of the king's agents who violated sanctuary by recapturing at the altar of Westminster Abbey two refugees from the Tower of London. When the royal council retaliated by confiscating the abbot's temporalities, he extended the excommunication to the entire province, and eventually, after a parliamentary session in which he countered the crown's proposal to deny sanctuary to felons, he obtained the humiliations of the two agents. Warren, "Reappraisal," 139–52.

41. Dugdale, *History of St. Paul's*, 24.

42. Ibid., 24.

43. Ibid., 57.

44. Bird, *Turbulent London*, 82–83.

45. City of London *Memorials*, ed. Riley, 415–16, quoted in Bird, *Turbulent London*, 68.

46. Bird, *Turbulent London*, 82.

47. Ibid., 82–83.

48. Dugdale, *History of St. Paul's*, 129

49. "Crux alta ... ubi verbum Dei consuevit populo praedicari." Dugdale, *History of St. Paul's*, 130.

50. Brooke, "Earliest Times," 69.

51. Ibid., 69.

52. Cited in Longman, *History*, 45.

53. The sexton is the church official responsible for the integrity and maintenance of both cathedral building and grounds; he also oversees the business of the graveyard, arranging burials and digging graves, so his presence here as church authority is peculiarly appropriate. Peterson, ed., *St. Erkenwald*, 92 n. 66.

54. Dimock, *Cathedral Church*, 10.

55. Leeson, *Travelling Brothers*, 44.

56. Ibid., 33.

57. Hudson, *English Wycliffite Writings*, 86–87.

58. Clark and Wasserman, "*St. Erkenwald*'s," 257–69.

59. Brooke, "Earliest Times," 77.

60. Dugdale, *History of St. Paul's*, 130.

61. Gordon Whatley and Cindy L. Vitto give particularly cogent discussions. Whatley, "Heathens and Saints"; Vitto, *Virtuous Pagan*, 51–59.

62. Grady argues propitiously for an analogy operating between the bishop's saving of the pagan and the poem's tribute to an illustrious past—a kind of secular, poetic, and historical baptism of the forgotten into the culturally cherished. My reading is a little less redemptive, charting persistent anxieties about the

pagan's virtue and the transfer of its power to the bishop. Grady, *"Piers Plowman, St. Erkenwald,"* 61–86.

63. Beckwith discusses control of the host as one of the most dramatically effective and fiercely contested church monopolies. *Christ's Body.*

64. Whatley, ed., *Saint of London,* 91. Like the pagan, St. Erkenwald's true virtue emerges predominantly after his death. He dies on the second page of his *Vita;* the rest of the narrative and the whole of the twelfth-century *Miracula* concern themselves with his far-reaching posthumous miracles.

65. "'New Werke,'" 404.

Chapter 3

1. The edition of *Sir Gawain and the Green Knight* cited throughout is that of Tolkien and Gordon.

2. Unless otherwise noted, translations are Marie Borroff's.

3. Ann Astell interestingly reads the poem as a political allegory referencing specific events of the Appellants' challenge to Richard II, his execution of Arundel, and exhumation of his body: *Political Allegory,* 117–37; my own address is wary of specific allegory and pursues a broader range of historical engagements and interpellations, though Astell's centralization of an exhumation speaks wonderfully to my focus.

4. The poem has been generally dated to the latter part of the fourteenth century, although most commentators venture a more limited span depending upon their arguments about the identity of the poet and whether he wrote any or all of the other three poems in the manuscript. When Gollancz reedited *Pearl* in 1921, he placed *Sir Gawain and the Green Knight* after 1373, possibly because he wanted to attribute it to Ralph Strode. *Pearl,* xxxvi. In his 1925 edition, J. R. R. Tolkien cautiously assigns it to the latter half of the fourteenth century, venturing a *terminus ad quem* date of 1400 for the manuscript itself. In his 1974 edition, Theodore Silverstein stretches this manuscript *terminus ad quem* to the early part of the fifteenth century but sees the poem as late fourteenth-century. *Sir Gawain,* 14–16. Michael J. Bennett agrees, but wishes to argue for several reworkings of the composition, one as late as 1399, after Richard's fall and the retreat of his Cheshire archers along the route of Gawain's journey to the province. "Courtly Literature." Latest of all is J. Eadie who places the poem as late as 1415, arguing an influence from Christine de Pisan's *Livre de la Mutacion de Fortune.* "New Source." More recently still, however, W. G. Cooke argues for a much earlier date, between 1330 and 1360, well within the reign of Edward III, basing his theory on descriptions of armor and dress. *"Sir Gawain and the Green Knight."* I would question Cooke's premise that the poet would incorporate only contemporary fashions in dress and armor; alliterative romance obsessively functionalizes nostalgia. The poet of the alliterative *Morte Arthure* incorporated anachronisms in both dress and armor, perhaps to give Arthur's court a patina of historic distance and to create a nostalgic parallel between the heyday of Arthurian chivalry and the successes of Edward III's early reign. My argument presupposes a dating after 1377, as late as 1399. Certainly if it is indirectly alluding to Richard's court at all, it is the court of the young king,

before the tensions between king and the Lords Appellant, Arundel and Gloucester, had sharpened to the bitter divisions of the Merciless Parliament in 1388 and its
vengeful aftermaths. The situation in the poem seems still negotiable; there is a
possibility that the recognition it is trying to instill in Gawain can take hold. But
the fact that the gap between royal court and provinces is never quite bridged could
argue the hindsight of a later date.

5. John Bowers usefully contrasts the more provincial and earlier-seeming
preoccupations of *Gawain* with the more court-centered and later-seeming preoccupations of *Pearl* to place *Gawain* in the mid-1380s "when northern interests were
braced against a royal court mostly concentrated in the southeast during Richard's
minority." *Politics of* Pearl, 23.

6. Bishop, "Time and Temporality," 611.

7. Spearing, "Central and Displaced Sovereignty."

8. Field, "Anglo-Norman Background," 63–65. Arlyn Diamond sees in the
poem an ongoing tension between "heroic" and "courtly" codes of behavior that
disarms recourse to either the continental romance tradition or the British alliterative one to explain and judge the behavior and motivations of the poem's characters. *Sir Gawain.* David Aers shows how incommensurable are the poem's reliance
on public chivalric codes and its use of individual moral codes of behavior. *Community, Gender,* 153–78.

9. The link between Arthur and Richard is a critical commonplace. Ian Bishop
assigns this description to "the period when the king was not only 'sumquat
childgered' but actually little more than a child in years." "Time and Tempo," 612.
H. Bergner speculates about the influence of contemporary alliances between the
royal court of Richard II and his Cheshire and Lancashire protégés. Bergner proposes more continuity between the courts than I have noted. "Two Courts."

10. Spearing, *Gawain-Poet,* 1–18. The poet's knowledge of the nobility is indi-
cated by his extensive use of French loan words (750 out of 2,650), and his familiarity with specialized vocabularies that describe seigneurial areas of expertise (i.e.,
the technologies of armor and architecture, and the protocols of venery). Clough,
"French Element." My argument does not assume a particular audience or a single
performance either at the royal court or in the provinces, since the poem seems
more interested exploring the complexity of their relations than in making a particular appeal. Jill Mann proposes a London audience because of the poem's over-
lay of mercantile language. "Price and Value." However, both Michael J. Bennett
and Sylvia Thrupp rightly emphasize how very porous was the division between
urban merchant and provincial gentry. Bennett, *Community, Class and Careerism*;
Thrupp, *Merchant Class,* 234–79.

11. John Bowers interestingly discusses the way these connections between
royal court and province become more fraught in the aftermath of the Merciless
Parliament. *Politics of* Pearl, 69–76.

12. Tuck, *Richard II,* 1–87.

13. Tuck makes the point that this campaign was extremely deliberate;
Richard consciously modeled his own household upon the royal household in the
later years of the reign of his great-grandfather, Edward II. Ibid., 71.

14. Walsingham, *Historia Anglicana,* 2: 156.

15. *Westminster Chronicle,* 116–17; Stowe, "Chronicles Versus Records," 157–58.

16. Stowe, "Chronicles Versus Records."

17. The Court of Chivalry, along with the Court of Admiralty, were originally adjuncts to the common law courts, dealing with cases beyond their jurisdiction. In the 1370s and '80s, however, the Court of Chivalry began to trespass on common law territory. Since its jurisdictions were uncertain, both nobility and king tried to exploit it as a political tribunal. During the Merciless Parliament, it was under Gloucester's constableship and the Lords Appellant probably intended to have the king's protégés tried before it, until the king suggested parliamentary hearings. By 1398, the king was attempting to use it to suppress those who had criticized his regime. Tuck, *Richard II*, 146–47, 197–98.

18. *"Ordenaunce and Fourme of Fightyng within Listes,"* 303.

19. Ibid.

20. Tuck, *Richard II*, 71–72.

21. *Reports from the Lords Commitees touching the dignity of a peer of the realm*, v. 5 (London, 1834), 64–65, cited in Tuck, *Richard II*, 84.

22. Tuck, *Richard II*, 84.

23. Griffiths, "Crown and the Royal Family."

24. I am indebted for this section of my argument to unpublished work by Rob Talbot, who helpfully suggested the relevance of Michael J. Bennett to the dynamics of the poem. For a good encapsulation of Bennett's views of the poem's North West Midlands milieu, see "Historical Background." For useful discussions of the provincialism of the poem, see Field, "Anglo-Norman Background"; Kamps, "Magic, Women, and Incest," 314.

25. Bennett notes that Gawain's journey traces the path of Richard II's retreat in July of 1399. He envisions a very late reworking of the poem that stressed this itinerary and made Gawain's journey even more poignant. "Courtly Literature." See also Eadie, "Sir Gawain"; Elliot, *Gawain Country*.

26. M. W. Thompson, "Green Knight's Castle."

27. Hanneke Wirtjes convincingly links the lord of Hautdesert with the romance character of the provincial vavasour. "Bertilak de Hautdesert."

28. Burrow, "Reading"; Benson, *Art and Tradition*, 58–95; Besserman, "Idea"; Walker, "Green Knight's Challenge."

29. Bennett, *Community, Class, and Careerism*. This is true not only for these provinces but for late fourteenth-century England as a whole. Residual feudal structures and conventions (such as the ancient levy) were often carefully preserved at least in name, even when in actual practice they were often being deployed to completely strategic and commercial ends. For one late fourteenth-century example of how traditional feudal structures were adapted to contemporary economic exigencies, see Lewis, "Last Medieval Summoning."

30. Ashley, "'Trawthe.'"

31. Bennett, *Community, Class, and Careerism*, 204.

32. Ibid., 16.

33. Ibid., 15.

34. *Richard the Redeless*, passus 3–4.

35. Bennett, *Community, Class, and Careerism*, 223–24.

36. Saul, "Conflict and Consensus," 40.

37. Stevens, *Music and Poetry*, 154–202.

38. This episode appears in a fragment of an English chronicle, in a sixteenth-century hand in Harley MS 247, f. 172v. E. K. Chambers cites the entire episode in *Medieval Stage*, 1: 394–95, n.4.

39. Chambers, *Medieval Stage*, 1: 394–95, n.4.

40. John Stevens cites Froissart's tale of a chess game which King James deliberately loses in order to force a lady to receive his token. *Music and Poetry*, 154–202.

41. Lauren M. Goodlad explores the multiple valences of the word "gomen" and its analogues throughout the poem. "Games of *Sir Gawain*," 49.

42. Andrew, ed., *Poems of the Pearl Manuscript*, 210, nn. 66f.

43. Green, *Poets and Prince-Pleasers*, 118.

44. At Arthur's court, the ladies' kisses are laughingly yielded prizes. On Bertilak's provincial estate, their playful commodification becomes complete alienation as they are set loose between men, a process that raises interesting questions (not answered or acknowledged) about the homoerotic consequences of the chivalrically homosocial traffic in women. Dinshaw, "Kiss."

45. Clark and Wasserman argue that the idea that even limited actions have greater consequences is an ongoing preoccupation of the *Gawain*-poet. "Passing,"15. Elizabeth Kirk, on the contrary, finds a resolution of tensions between the festive and the didactic in the poem's use of the liturgical structures of the medieval celebration of Christmas. "'Wel Bycommes Such Craft.'"

46. Ibid.

47. Clark and Wasserman read these two conflicting signs exegetically as betokening a choice of salvation or damnation, which it is up to Arthur's court to select. For other critics who blame Arthur's court for choosing such a lethal game, see Shoaf, "'Syngne of Surfet'"; Weiss, "Gawain's First Failure," 361.

48. In an analogous reading Jill Mann shows how mercantile language takes Gawain from Arthur's court into the open market. "Price and Value."

49. "'Trawthe'"; also Blanch and Wasserman, "Medieval Contracts"; "'To Ouertake your wylle'"; Blanch, "Legal Framework." Richard Firth Green also alludes to the judicial function of the exchange-of-blows game in "Gawain's Five Fingers," 16–17.

50. "*Ordenaunce and Fourme of Fightyng within Listes*," 309.

51. Ibid., 317.

52. Curtius, *European Literature*, 535.

53. Twentieth-century military training also builds a readiness to kill with one's companions upon the intense mutual bonds that make one willing to die with them: Grossman, *On Killing*, 149–55.

54. Saul, *Richard II*, 218–20.

55. Wilkins, "Dissolution," 109.

56. Weiss, "Gawain's First Failure," 183.

57. Marie Borroff notes that this judgment is justified by an appeal not to the poem's romance sources but to the audience's familiarity with contemporary systems of rank. "Passing of Judgment," 122.

58. Freeman and Thormann, "Anatomy of Chastity," 400.

59. John Stevens discusses the extent to which the game of courtly love provided a whole framework, epistemological, psychological, and social, for aristocratic self-fashioning. *Music and Poetry*, 167.

60. Lindley shows how the dynamics of power and identity at Hautdesert operate according to the carnivalesque illogic of boundary transgression and hierarchy inversion. "'Ther he watz."

61. This scene in particular offers a clue to the way the poet reworks his continental romance sources, assuming familiarity with them even as he critiques them. For instance, the characters of Morgan and of Bertilak, Helmut Nickel convincingly argues, reference the *Merlin*-Continuation, where Bertilak le Rous along with his wife, an illegitimate Guinevere, stepsister and namesake to the real Guinevere, attempt to oust the queen by trickery and end up exiled—but the poet transforms this bizarre plot into a much larger examination. "Why Was the Green Knight Green?" 58–64. Finlayson shows how the poet mobilizes his profound knowledge of continental romances both to use and comment critically upon them. "Expectations of Romance," and "Sir Gawain, Knight of the Queen." See also Larry D. Benson's thorough discussion in *Art and Tradition*; Joerg O. Fichte, "Middle English Verse Romance."

62. Fisher and Halley, "The Lady Vanishes"; Sheila Fisher, "Taken Men and Token Women"; also Burns and Krueger, "Introduction."

63. Campbell, "Lesson in Polite Non-Compliance."

64. Crane, "Knights in Disguise."

65. Maureen Duffy considers the Lady and Morgan as essentially identical, arguing from the poem's supposed mythical sources that the Lady is a fairy woman as well. *Erotic World of Faery*, 54–63.

66. Geraldine Heng brilliantly explores this fluidity as opening up the realm of sexuality itself—extending it from physical interaction to speech, gender-construction, and subjectivity and rendering possible a less determined articulation of female desire. "A Woman Wants."

67. Astell, "Rhetoric of Romance."

68. See the interesting counterargument of John Scattergood, who reads Gawain's lassitude as a critique of the idle ways of late fourteenth-century aristocracy. *Lost Tradition*, 100–124.

69. Edmund Wilson reads the architectural intricacies of Castle Hautdesert as indicative of an innate tendency to intrigue and deceit that draws the ethics of Bertilak's test into question. *Gawain Poet*, 113–31.

70. Karma Lochrie fascinatingly reads this same dialectic in the context of late medieval and Foucauldian theories of confession as a crux of pleasure and control. *Covert Operations*, 42–55.

71. Ganim, "Disorientation"; Borroff, "Passing of Judgement." See also *Seeing the Gawain-Poet*, Sarah Stanbury's extended treatment of the philosophical dimensions of the poem's inventive use of the visual and the perceptual.

72. Translation is mine.

73. Edward Duke of York's translation of Gaston "Phoebus's" *Livre de Chasse*, in *Oxford Book of Late Medieval Verse and Prose*, 145.

74. Carolyn Dinshaw argues that this analogy and its ramifications disrupt heteronormative relations and male/female gender hierarchies only in order eventually to reaffirm them, and thus makes visible the processes by which they are constructed. "Kiss." But Karma Lochrie places more stress on how the poem's pursuit of its inquisitional and confessional pleasures actually "veers on the dislocations in

masculine and heterosexual identity that are crucial to the Christian chivalric ethos of the poem." It doesn't simply show how that ethos is constructed, it unlooses a subversive pleasure in the process of urging it to disjunctive extremes. *Covert Operations*, 51.

75. My argument diverges here from those of critics who believe the poem wants us to blame Gawain for a spiritual failure to use the world and not love it. Donald Howard's observations are worth considering: "However richly the work suggests fundamental Christian doctrine, the poet betrays at the center of everything a concern rather for the World itself, as he betrays a delight in his story per se." *Three Temptations*, 252.

76. Virginia Carmichael analyzes Gawain's tendency to identify himself rigidly with extremes of virtue and vice. "Green is for Growth," 25–38. Harvey De Roo reads Gawain's denunciation as symptomatic of his habit of psychological denial and the evasion of commitment. "Undressing Lady Bertilak."

77. Lochrie, *Covert Operations*, 51.

78. Shichtman, "Terror of History"; Bishop, "Time and Tempo."

79. Both Michael J. Bennett and John M. Bowers argue strongly for the appropriateness of a royal court audience respectively for *Sir Gawain* and *Pearl*. Bennett, "Court of Richard II," 13–14; Bowers, *"Pearl* in Its Royal Setting."

80. Carson, "Green Chapel"; Andrews, "Diabolical Chapel."

81. Edgeworth outlines the topographical similarities feature by feature: "The features of the chapel and its setting are readily identifiable with the features of the feminine genitalia. The poet mentions a ravine (the vulva) with steep banks on either side (the labia) and a stream in it (the vulva is associated with moisture for many reasons: menstruation, urination, mucous secretion and natural lubrication), and the mound above (the mons Veneris) overgrown with grass (pubic hair). The mysterious three openings correspond to the meatus, the vagina, and the anus." "Anatomical Geography," 318–19.

82. Translation is mine.

83. Ashley, "'Trawthe'"; Johnson, "Four Levels of Time." See also Juliet Dor's sensitive discussion of the way the poet repeated layers, experiments and perplexes competing temporalities: internal, external, and experiential and liturgical. "Time and Times."

84. Ashley, "'Trawthe.'"

85. Since Donald R. Howard argued that pentangle and lace should be considered as opposing but symmetrical symbols, their comparison has been an ongoing topic: "Structure and Symmetry"; Hieatt, *"Sir Gawain*: Pentangle"; Green, "Sir Gawain and the *Sacra Cinctola.*" John Ganim describes the wider emphasis on multivalency in the poem. "Disorientation." See also Braggs, "Elusion of Charity."

86. The poem's fascination with Morgan's body resonates here. Is this trope of learning to love history identifiable enough with the figure of Gawain that another romance strain exemplified by *The Wife of Bath's Tale* and *The Marriage of Sir Gawain and Dame Ragnell* can take it up and embody it as a lesson in kissing the harridan?

87. Bishop shows that the Gawain-poet does not just elude the dilemmas

he has constructed; he eludes them with consummate artistry. "Time and Tempo," 619.

88. These divisions became particularly acute in Cheshire at the end of the century. When the Cheshire militia marched to the defense of Richard, they only confirmed their regional reputation for unusual belligerence and alienated both their less royalist compeers and the rest of the realm.

Chapter 4

1. All citations are taken from Hoyt N. Duggan and Thorlac Turville-Petre's edition of *The Wars of Alexander*. Translations are my own.

2. Jacobus de Voragine, *The Golden Legend*, 263.

3. I am using the lowercased terms "east" and "west" advisedly: they do not connote actual directions but rather symbolic realms which correspond to Saidian gestures of othering and self-instantiation. They are not necessarily the way that medieval writers thought about these relationships, which were much more varied and inchoate. However, they are critically familiar and a useful way of describing the constructed separations which are so much at issue in these texts.

4. Abu-Lughod, *Before European Hegemony*; Akbari, "From Due East."

5. Schor, *Bad Objects*, 51; Pratt, *Imperial Eyes*, 139.

6. Said's description of orientalism is itself historically situated and cannot be imported wholesale to fit a medieval situation which predates the cultural/epistemological formations he describes. This does not mean that the logic he outlines can not be mobilized on a smaller scale and for situational and often fascinatingly reversible ends. Thierry Hentsch usefully reevaluates Said's relevance to pre-eighteenth-century societies. *Imagining*, ix-20; Said, *Orientalism*.

7. Schor, *Bad Objects*, 51.

8. Higgins, *Writing East*, 1.

9. Ibid., 5.

10. Campbell, *Witness*, 48.

11. *Travels*, 188.

12. Southern, *Western Views*.

13. Metlitzki, *Matter of Araby*.

14. Hentsch, *Imagining*. I am also indebted to Emily Bartels's discussions of the alienating, self-producing, self-disintegrating strategies of the Marlovian stage and its relation to sixteenth-century imperialisms. *Spectacles of Strangeness*.

15. McGinn illustrates the tendency after the twelfth century to take refuge in apocalyptic fantasies; at least the end of the world spelt the end of Saracen rule as well. *Visions of the End*, 145–57.

16. Hentsch demonstrates how mythical any stable east-west divide is throughout this period, gleefully eviscerating historians who anachronistically import it backwards. *Imagining*, ix-48.

17. The term "contact zone" is Mary Louise Pratt's, apt for particularizing and highlighting the relationality of cultural encounters: "A 'contact' perspective emphasizes how subjects are constituted in and by their relations to each other. It

treats the relations among colonizers and colonized, or travelers and 'travelees,' not in terms of separateness or apartheid, but in terms of copresence, interaction, inter-locking understandings and practices, often within radically asymmetrical relations of power." *Imperial Eyes*, 7.

18. Menocal, *Arabic Role*, 42, 43.

19. Odo of Deuil, for instance, works to associate the Greek Byzantine Christians with the Islamic Turks, as cultures alike "arrogant in wealth, treacherous in customs, corrupt in faith" ("superba divitiis, moribus subdola, fide corrupta") who are nonetheless cultured, sophisticated, and above all, rich. *De profectione*, 86–87.

20. Moore, *Formation*.

21. Menocal, *Arabic Role*, 27–70.

22. Nirenberg, *Communities of Violence*.

23. Rubin, *Gentile Tales*, 188.

24. Joinville and Villehardouin, *Chronicles*.

25. *Arab Syrian Gentleman and Warrior*, 163–64. Amin Maalouf gives an impassioned comprehensive description of Arab attitudes to European incursions during the crusade. See also Gabrieli, *Arab Historians*; Hillenbrand, *Crusades: Islamic Perspectives*.

26. Thrupp, "Comparison of Cultures."

27. This mercantile traffic was responsible for the devastating rapidity with which the bubonic plague spread from China to England. In fact, by far the greatest time lag between first documented cases occurred in the interval when it traveled from inland China (1320) to the Chinese port of Zaytun (1345). After that interval, it swiftly struck Caffa on the Black Sea in 1346, Cairo and Damascus in 1347, Italy, France, and Britain in 1348, Germany and Scandanavia in 1349, and Moscow in 1351. Abu-Lughod, *Before European Hegemony*, 172–73.

28. Southern, *Western Views*, 43.

29. *Crusade of Nicopolis*, 44–45.

30. The phrase is Maria Menocal's who illuminates how the enormous cultural transference between western and eastern cultures during this period depends both upon their intermittent military conflicts and their unflagging religious ones. *Arabic Role*, 47.

31. Abu-Lughod, *Before European Hegemony*, 106.

32. Dorothee Metlitzki discusses the marriage theme as a model for Christian-Muslim relations in romance. *Matter of Araby*, 136–60.

33. Thrupp, "Comparison," 82.

34. Kathleen Ann Kelly showed how Middle English as well as French romances imbue marriage with trade in a paper given at the 27th National Congress on Medieval Studies at Kalamazoo on May 7, 1992. "The Bartering of Blanchfleur in the Middle English *Floris and Blanchfleur*."

35. Abu-Lughod, *Before European Hegemony*, 141

36. Ibid., 236–41.

37. Though it is safe to say from the Gentile's responses to the scholars' argumentation that it will be Christianity. Llull himself invests the Artful exposition of Christianity with more persuasive power than the other two, a cogency left available to the reader's own discernment, not pounded home.

38. Llull, "Book of the Gentile," 167.

39. Ibid., 169–70.

40. M. D. Knowles links the widespread contemporary concern for these questions to mid-century affective transformations of religious experience and its social expression. "Censured Opinions."

41. Despite this swift response against his theological speculations, Uthred himself was not personally named in the condemnatory article, and although he resigned from Oxford in 1367 and became Prior of Finchale, his subsequent career was not ruined; he went on to become sub-prior of Durham, a very illustrious position. Knowles, "Censured Opinions."

42. Grady, *"Piers Plowman, St. Erkenwald."*

43. The civic cycle pageants of the late fourteenth and fifteenth centuries, for instance, make Mahound into an infernal deity.

44. Langland, *Vision of Piers Plowman.*

45. Mandeville, *Travels.*

46. Southern, *Western Views,* 79–80.

47. Ibid., 82.

48. Menocal, *Arabic Role,* 43–44.

49. Wyclif, *English Works,* 301.

50. *The Wars of Alexander* survives in two fragmentary manuscript copies, Ashmole 44, in a mid-fifteenth-century hand, and Dublin MS 213, in a late fifteenth-century hand. As with most of the late fourteenth-century alliterative poems, the author is unknown, though the poem's most recent editors speculate on the grounds of an unusual number of shared phrases and some intriguing descriptive echoes that the author may have originated in the North West Midlands and have influenced or been influenced by the Gawain-poet. The poem's dating is extremely tenuous—suggestions have ranged from 1361 to just before 1450. My argument does not presuppose a particular date but I treat the poem mainly as dating from the late fourteenth century or early fifteenth century. Duggan and Turville-Petre, eds., *Wars of Alexander,* ix-li.

51. All citations are from Hoyt N. Duggan and Thorlac Turville-Petre's edition.

52. Bartels, *Spectacles of Strangeness,* 7.

53. Froissart, *Chronicle,* 6: 237.

54. Dronke, "Poetic Originality."

55. The poem's main source is the I3 version of the immensely popular late twelfth-century Historia de preliis Alexandri Magni, of which forty-five manuscript copies survive. *The Wars of Alexander* is a faithful translation, though the poet freely expands upon his source, introducing new episodes at several points, many of which are notable for their biting irony. The fact that it is a translation does not detract from its fantastic originality or from the significance attributable to the choice to translate it in the late fourteenth century. Duggan and Turville-Petre, *Wars of Alexander,* xiii-xvii.

56. Thrupp, "Comparison of Cultures," 73.

57. Donna Crawford perceptively discusses the intersection of fatherhood with destiny, the way "Anectanabus has the power to inspire prophecy, while Alexander is only able to perform the actions that fulfill it" (414). Crawford's argument about fatherhood parallels the one I will make about parentage but puts more

interpretive pressure on the role of prophecy in the poem and the historiographically sophisticated interaction of the poem with its Latin sources. "Prophecy and Paternity."

58. At one point he turns back to Macedon on the brink of a decisive victory over a cornered Darius because he hears his mother is sick.

59. Though the socially equalizing universality of death (the indistinguishable mingling of bones in the charnels and ossuaries) could also be exploited to critique lordly authority, as in the cycle dramas' performance of the grisly death of Herod—eaten alive by worms—and in the three poems treated in the last chapter, *De Tribus Regibus Mortuis*, *The Awntyrs off Arthure*, and *Somer Sunday*.

60. David Lawton observes a stylistic difference between Age and Youth that may reflect historical self-consciousness about changes in alliterative style: Age speaks in the "stern style of Langlandian homily" (10) and Youth in the formal alliterative style of alliterative romance. *Middle English Alliterative Poetry*, 10–11.

61. There is no time here to explore how this exchange between Alexander and the Brahmins focuses fourteenth-century ecclesiastical and seigneurial anxieties about the social effects of a literal imitatio Christi, but such concerns clearly animate the episode.

62. Duggan and Turville-Petre, *Wars of Alexander*, xlii-xliii.

63. This does not mean that I think chivalry itself is in decline at this time; I am simply claiming that its hopes of recovering the Holy Land were becoming more and more illusory.

64. Palmer, *England, France, and Christendom*, 184–85.

65. Atiya, *Crusade of Nicopolis*, 44–45. Thierry Hentsch downplays the significance of this crusade, describing instead a state of overall European indifference to the Ottoman incursions, but this is possibly a result of his much longer and less precisely English focus. *Imagining*, 51–56.

66. Froissart, *Chronicle*, 6: 238.

67. Ibid., 231.

Chapter 5

1. To be able to pinpoint an origin for any alliterative poem is an astonishing feat of scholarship and persistence. Ralph Hanna and David Lawton have persuasively traced the poem to Bolton. They are editing a forthcoming edition of the poem, but for a foretaste, see Hanna, "Contextualizing." I thank both of them for generously sharing their expertise; any mistakes or infelicities that remain are despite their help. Bonnie Millar performs a beautiful deep contextualization of this poem in the only book-length study so far, pursuing the way it expands the boundaries of romance by intelligently and obliquely reworking an enormous variety of romance, historiographical, and devotional sources. Comparing *The Siege* to other nonalliterative romances such as *The Sowdone of Babylone* and *Richard Coeur de Lion*, she discerns much less influence from popular anti-Judaism and crusading romance than do I, arguing for a doctrinal anti-Judaism turned to powerful literary and romance ends. *Siege*.

2. Hamel, "*Siege* as Crusading Poem."

3. For useful overviews of medieval Judeo-Christian relations, see Moore, *Formation*; Nirenberg, *Communities of Violence*; Langmuir, *History,* and *Toward a Definition*. Jeremy Cohen carefully traces influential medieval patristic and ecclesiastical theories about Judaism and its relation to Christianity in *Living Letters*, which follows his earlier study on later medieval anti-Judaism, *Friars and the Jews*. Miri Rubin shifts the focus from theology to ritual, symbol, and social practice in her study of late medieval host-desecration accusations, *Gentile Tales*.

4. Narin Van Court effectively links the poem's descriptive dynamic to the thirteenth-century Augustinian chronicle tradition exemplified by William of Newburgh. "Augustinian Historians."

5. For Jerusalem (and Calvary) as earthly center and sacred *omphalos*, see Higgins, "Defining," and also Dorothea French, "Journeys to the Center."

6. Jerusalem Bible.

7. Cohen, *Living Letters*, 23–65.

8. Augustine, *City of God,* 827–28.

9. Cohen, *Living Letters*, 397.

10. Narin Van Court shows persuasively how the Jews are both revered and reviled within medieval Christian rhetoric. "Augustinian Historians."

11. Cohen, *Living Letters*, 67–122.

12. Narin Van Court, "Augustinian Historians," 239–41.

13. Jacobs, *Jews*, 122–23.

14. This threat emerges in ongoing legislation by popes such as Gregory the Great against any Christian being enslaved or enfeoffed by Jewish masters. Gregory's firm stand on Christian slavery by Jews is a sticking point in an otherwise relatively tolerant (but not approving) official policy. Cohen, *Living Letters*, 74–79.

15. All citations are taken from E. Kölbing and Mabel Day's edition; translations are mine unless otherwise noted.

16. Bonnie Millar gives this scene an anthropological interpretation: "Mary is a kind of priest figure at the sacrifice of her son" (91) who dies "to elucidae the horrors of war" (87) not just to the Jews but also to the Romans and the poem's readers. "Siege," 76–104.

17. Cannon, "Monastic Productions."

18. Cohen also interestingly suggests that the merchant class origins and mercantile interests of many friars may have intensified competitive hostilities, since Jews had been forced overwhelmingly into commercial occupations. *Friars and the Jews*, 43–44. For the deep links between the fraternal orders and commercial activities, see Little, *Religious Poverty*.

19. Moore, *Formation*. Nirenberg takes exception to such master narratives of generally accumulating intolerance and persecution in *Communities of Violence*. Nirenburg focuses upon Aragon, France, and Catalonia to point out that such persecutory discourse was directed by specific groups for local purposes and was often countered by other groups within the same society; in other words, persecution was always at issue during the period, tended by some groups, resisted by others, passively absorbed only after a lot of cultural nurturing. See also Rubin, *Gentile Tales*.

20. Cohen explores the emergence of rationalist arguments in Petrus Alfonsi,

Peter the Venerable, and Alanus ab Insulis. *Living Letters*, 395–96; *Friars and the Jews*, 19–32.

21. Rubin, *Gentile Tales*.

22. Ibid., 26.

23. Ibid.,131.

24. Elisa Narin Van Court shows beautifully how the subsequent description of Vespasian's inspirational speech to his own troops on Christ's passion crystallizes the differences between Jewish and Christian foundational mythologies, and re-enacts the Christian seizure and supersession of the Hebrew scriptures as the Old Testament. "Augustinian Historians," 230–31.

25. Turville-Petre, ed., *Alliterative Poetry*, 168 n. 698.

26. "Contextualizing," 109. See also Pearsall, *Old and Middle English Poetry*, 169; Spearing, *Readings*, 165–72.

27. Campbell, *Witness and the Other World*.

28. *Book of Margery Kempe*, 103.

29. Roger Bacon, *Opus Maior*, 1: 266, translated and cited in McGinn, *Visions of the End*, 155.

30. Or they anticipated another conqueror coming from the east to subjugate the Saracens in their turn—sometimes an unknown Christian leader (i.e., Prester John), sometimes the Tartars (worthy of a book in themselves: ambiguously situ-ated, potential allies against the Saracens, but pagan—though often imagined as convertible, as the thirteenth-century fraternal envoys, John of Plano Carpini and William of Rubrick, attest), sometimes the Antichrist and his army, ushering in the last things and the inevitable triumph of Christ. See McGinn, *Visions of the End*, 149–57.

31. William of Tripoli, *Treatise on the Condition of the Saracens*, from H. Prutz, *Kulturgeschichte der Kreuzzüge*, 589–90, excerpted and translated in McGinn, *Visions of the End*, 154.

32. Hamel, "Crusading Poem."

33. Atiya, *Crusade*, 94.

34. Delany, *Naked Text*, 165–73; Tyerman, *England and the Crusades*, 259–301; Palmer, *England, France, and Christendom*, 180–210.

35. Atiya, *Crusade*, 95.

36. Christopher Tyerman shows how in 1283, 1294, 1314, and 1336 secular monarchs (and even the papacy itself) tended to divert these funds to their own nationalistic ends while remaining fully invested in the ideological imperatives of crusading, *England and the Crusades*, 252–58.

37. Ibid., 293.

38. Ibid., 259–66.

39. Palmer, *England France, and Christendom*, 242–44.

40. Attiya discusses Pierre de Lusignan's 1365 sack of Alexandria, Amedeo VI's 1366 seizure of Gallipoli, the 1390 crusade alliance of the Bourbon duke Louis II and the Genoese commune against Tunis (which Sir John Clanvowe, Lollard knight and acquaintance of Chaucer, joined and died in), and the disastrous 1396 siege of Nicopolis, endorsed by both the Avignonese and Roman pontiffs, and including a thousand English knights under the leadership of John Beaufort, son of

John of Gaunt, Duke of Lancaster, as well as John Holland Earl of Huntingdon. Atiya, *Crusade*, 99–111.

41. Tyerman, *England and the Crusades*, 260.

42. Phillippe de Mézières, "L'Epistre," 467.

43. Ibid.

44. The most famous literary linkage of Jew and Saracen, in fact, comes in the *Chanson de Roland*, when Charles caps his victory by destroying not only the mosques of Sargossa but also its synagogues. In Charles's eyes, all are pagans together.

45. Cohen, *Living Letters*, 219.

46. Little, *Religious Poverty*, 447.

47. Moore, *Formation*, 31.

48. Both R. I. Moore and Lester K. Little attribute this fear partly to guilty projection. *Formation*, 30–31; *Religious Poverty*, 54–57.

49. One year the blow was fierce enough to knock a victim's eye out and kill him. Lester K. Little discusses this custom, and shows how it was not uncommon throughout the eleventh century in France. Ibid., 46–48.

50. Atiya, *Crusade*, 195–97.

51. Ibid., 98–99.

52. For the plea of a group of frustrated traders with perishable goods, see document # 168 in Lopez and Raymond, *Medieval Trade*, 335–36; Abu-Lughod, *Before European Hegemony*, 240.

53. Harry A. Miskimin outlines three principle causes for southern flow of bullion: the trade imbalances discussed above, papal taxation, and the ongoing, expensive fourteenth-century war and diplomacy costs. *Economy*, 136–50.

54. Bolton, *Medieval English Economy*, 297.

55. Miskimin, *Economy*, 141–47.

56. Holmes, "'Libel of English Policy,'"193–216.

57. Bolton, *Medieval English Economy*, 330.

58. Kershaw, *Bolton Priory*, 171–83.

59. *English Jewry*, 91–99; Dyer, *Standards of Living*, 38.

60. Jacobs, *Jews*, 123–24.

61. Ibid., 390.

62. Ralph Hanna describes another of the poem's powerful metaphorizations of this separation between conqueror and victim, that of the huntsman who calmly holds the feet of the deer and directs its flaying. "Contextualizing," 109–10.

63. Bonnie Millar thoroughly discusses the way the poem alters its sources in placing and selecting prophecies and investigates the range of uses of prophecy in both poem and sources. "Role of Prophecy," 153–78.

64. Narin Van Court, "Augustinian Historians," 233–39.

65. Glassman, *Anti-Semitic Stereotypes*.

66. Elman, "Economic Causes," 145–54.

67. Moore discusses the economic motivations behind the long exploitation and final expulsion of the Jews from Europe. *Formation*.

68. Narin Van Court convincingly argues this point. "Augustinian Historians."

69. Kinross, *Ottoman Centuries*, 43.

70. Ibid., 45.
71. Ibid., 66.
72. Ibid., 66.
73. Froissart, *Chronicle*, 6: 233.
74. Kinross, *Ottoman Centuries*, 69.
75. Froissart, *Chronicles*, 6: 234.
76. Quoted in Jacobs, *Jews*, 122.

Chapter 6

1. Citations are from Mary Hamel's critical edition, with reference to the recent TEAMS edition by Larry D. Benson. *King Arthur's Death*. Translations are my own unless otherwise noted.

2. Harder compares Arthur's feast to courtly displays by Edward III and Richard II. "Feasting," 49–62.

3. Matthews, *Tragedy of Arthur*. See also the dissenting views of Keiser, "Edward III."

4. Matthews, *Tragedy of Arthur*; Barnie, *War*, 66–7.

5. The poem's recent editors, Larry D. Benson, Mary Hamel, and Valerie Krishna, believe that the poem was completed from 1396 to1403, basing their arguments on the poem's sources and topical allusions (especially to the state of affairs in Italy, and the inclusion of the Montague family in Mordred's train). Benson, *King Arthur's Death*; Hamel, *Morte Arthure*; Krishna, *Alliterative Morte Arthure*. Larry D. Benson earlier suggested that the poem was worked and reworked throughout the last quarter of the century but definitely completed by 1403. "Date." Earlier criticism (i.e., Matthews, *Tragedy of Arthur*) tends to put the poem earlier, attempting to tie it to events and armorial fashions during the reign of Edward III.

6. The complex shifts in the late medieval balance between mutually supplementary systems of long-term feudal and short-term contractual indenture are carefully described by J. M. W. Bean, *From Lord to Patron*.

7. Maurice Keen shows how even early chivalric writings make the need to look back to a more illustrious past continually instrumental to chivalry's regeneration. *Chivalry*, 160.

8. McFarlane, *Nobility*, 19–40; Fradenburg, "Soft and Silken War."

9. Bennett, "Historical Background."

10. Tuck, *Richard II*; Saul, *Richard II*; Bennett, *Court of Richard II*.

11. Musgrove, *North of England*,158.

12. Ibid., 170.

13. Turville-Petre, *Alliterative Poetry*, 54.

14. Kaeuper, *War, Justice and Public Order*, 340.

15. Barnie, *War*, 75. See also James, *English Politics*.

16. McFarlane, *Nobility*, 19–40.

17. *Historia Anglicana*, ii, 156, cited in Stowe, *Chronicles Versus Records*, 160.

18. Saul, *Richard II*, 327–65; Bennett, *Court of Richard II*, 40–42.

19. Griffiths, "Crown and the Royal Family,"19.

20. Bennett, *Court of Richard II*, 14–55; Saul, *Richard II*, 333–55.

21. *Richard the Redeless*, 109.

22. Westover, "Arthur's End."

23. Anne Clark Bartlett discusses the complex sexual logic of the poem's construction and subversion of masculinity. "Cracking the Penile Code."

24. Barnie, *War*, 95.

25. These readings usually hinge upon the character of Arthur. For those who see Arthur as falling from ideals of good, Christian leadership toward sin and tyranny, see Matthews, *Tragedy of Arthur*; Hamel, *Morte Arthure*; Hamel, "Dream"; Boren, "Narrative Design"; Obst, "Gawain-Priamus Episode"; Pearcy, "Alliterative *Morte Arthure*"; Shoaf, "Alliterative *Morte Arthure*"; Ziolkowski, "Narrative Structure." For those who read Arthur positively as a heroic leader who pursues glory but is only human and thus victim to Fortune, see Finlayson, "Arthur and the Giant"; Finlayson, "Concept of the Hero"; Lumiansky, "Alliterative *Morte Arthure*"; Keiser, "Theme of Justice"; Keiser, "Edward III"; Vale, "Law and Diplomacy"; Eadie, "Structure and Meaning"; Porter, "Chaucer's Knight"; and Dean, "Sir Gawain."

26. Matthews, *Tragedy of Arthur*.

27. Ibid., 86.

28. Ibid., 179.

29. Barnie, *War*, 75.

30. Benson, "*Alliterative Morte Arthure* and Medieval Tragedy."

31. McFarlane, *Nobility*, 20–21.

32. Pearcy, "Alliterative *Morte Arthure*."

33. *The Thornton Manuscript*, f. 78v.

34. Field, "Anglo-Norman Background."

35. Kaeuper, *War, Justice and Public Order*, 194.

36. Roger Loomis, "Edward I," 114–27; Powicke, *Thirteenth Century*, 515–16.

37. Roger Loomis, "Edward I," 115–17; Vale, *Edward III and Chivalry*, 17.

38. Powicke, *Thirteenth Century*, 516.

39. Vale, *Edward III and Chivalry*, 93–94.

40. Ibid., 91.

41. Ibid., 87.

42. Powicke, *Thirteenth Century*, 516

43. Ayton, "English Armies," 310–11.

44. Harriss, "War and the Emergence of the English Parliament," 321.

45. Ibid., 322.

46. Kaeuper, *War, Justice and Public Order*, 114, 117.

47. Ibid., 336–38.

48. Turville-Petre, *Alliterative Poetry*, 65–66.

49. Gillespie, *Age of Richard II*, 115–38.

50. Vale, *Edward III and Chivalry*, 91.

51. Saul, *Richard II*, 72.

52. Gillespie, *Age of Richard II*, 142; Lewis, "Last Medieval Summons."

53. Ibid., 154.

54. Bennett, *Richard II*, 41–55; Saul, *Richard II*, 355–60.

55. Quoted in Gillespie, *Age of Richard II*, 118.

56. Ibid., 160.

57. Ayton, "English Armies," 312. Edge and Paddock also discuss the developments in weaponry that rendered the traditional knightly equipment outmoded, and inflicted stunning and humiliating defeats on knights, from the battle of Bannockburn in 1314, where 23,000 hand-picked knights fell to 10,000 Scottish spearsmen, to the 1386 defeat at Sempach of the Austrian army not by knights but by Swiss Confederation peasants with pikes and halberds. *Arms and Armor*, 68.

58. Ayton, "English Armies," 318.

59. Ibid.

60. Susan Crane, "Chaucer's Material Culture," presented at the New Chaucer Society Conference, London, July 2000.

61. Hamel, *Morte Arthure*, 46–52.

62. Christine de Pisan, *Book of Deeds*, 216.

63. Thrupp, *Merchant Class*, 234–87.

64. Wagner, *Heralds and Heraldry*, 12–40.

65. Christine de Pisan, *Book of Deeds*, 219.

66. Froissart, *Chronicle*, 1: 368.

67. Wagner, *Heraldry in England*, 13.

68. Pastoureau, *Les Sceaux*, 22.

69. Ibid., 40.

70. Ibid., 39.

71. Ibid., 29.

72. Bloch, *Etymologies and Genealogies*, 101, 106.

73. Ibid., chapters 3, 4, and 5. For an effective dissenting argument, see Kay, *Chanson de Geste*.

74. Hamel, *Morte Arthur*, 423.

75. Hamel, *Morte Arthure*, 288 nn.906–11.

76. Scarry, 128.

77. *Book of Deeds*, 136.

78. Lee Patterson brilliantly discusses the implications of the deaths of Chastelaine and Mordred's children in *Negotiating the Past*, 222–24.

79. *Morte Arthure*, 380 n. 3837.

80. And the present to the future: Ziolkowski shows how the two dreams, the vision of the dragon and the bear, and the vision of Fortune and the Nine Worthies, divide the poem into a dream/fulfillment, dream/fulfillment pattern. "Narrative Structure." The two single combats—with the Giant and with Priamus— similarly frame the battles that follow them.

81. *Laȝamon's Brut*, 49.

82. Patterson, *Negotiating the Past*, 217–22.

83. Porter, "Chaucer's Knight"; also Vale, "Law and Diplomacy."

84. Chaucer, *The Legend of Good Women*, ll. 354–55.

85. Dean, "Sir Gawain," 115, 119; see also Shichtman, "Gawain in Wace and Layamon," 111.

86. Hulbert, "Hypothesis," 405–422.

87. I am indebted to Thomas Hahn's excellent introduction, notes, and edition.

88. Intriguing here, given the poem's Scottish provenance, is Edward I's oath at the Feast of the Swans in 1306. He grasped the swan and swore to avenge the death of John Comyn, murdered at Dumfries, by launching a new campaign against the Scots and the newly crowned Robert Bruce—that done, he would spend his life fighting in the Holy Land. He died before he could complete the expedition. His son, Edward of Caernarvon, who in 1314 would disastrously lose the battle of Bannockburn, grasped the swan and swore not to sleep two nights in the same bed until he had reached Scotland—a vow he did not keep. Powicke, *Thirteenth Century*, 514–15. By making swan grabbing into a figure for the rude greed of English territorial acquisitiveness the fifteenth-century poem mobilizes a very retentive historical memory and trenchantly comments from an outsider's perspective on Edward's exploitation of chivalric spectacle in the service of English imperialism.

Chapter 7

1. Schmitt, *Ghosts*. I am indebted to Thorlac Turville-Petre's description of the themes shared by these poems. "Three Poems," 1–14.

2. Roach, *Cities*, 1–17.

3. Geary, *Living with the Dead*, 77.

4. Ariès, *Hour of Our Death*, 165–68; Duffy, *Stripping*, 357–66; Dinn, "Death and Rebirth,"151–69.

5. *Mirk's Festial*, 4–5.

6. Duffy, *Stripping*, 362–66.

7. Mauss, *The Gift*, 62–63.

8. Thorlac Turville-Petre gives the most complete list of English analogues and comments on the closeness of the relationship between the art and the literature. "Three Poems."

9. For a reproduction of the *De Lisle Psalter* illustration, see figure 6 in Turville-Petre, *Alliterative Poetry*. I have used this edition for all citations from the poem as well (148–57). For a color plate of the *Psalter of Bonne de Luxembourg* illustration, see plate 18B in Avril, *Manuscript Painting*.

10. Blauner, "Death and Social Structure," 378.

11. Roach, *Cities*, 1–7.

12. Turville-Petre, *Alliterative Poetry*, 149.

13. Ariès, *Hour of Our Death*, 218–21.

14. Ariès attributes this escalating camouflage to an intensifying sense of the shame of death. *Hour of Our Death*, 168–73; also Neill, *Issues of Death*, 1–15.

15. Hanna, ed., *Awntyrs off Arthure*, 27.

16. Hanna, "*Awntyrs off Arthure*: An Interpretation."

17. Phillips, "Structure and Meaning."

18. Turville-Petre, *Alliterative Revival*, 65.

19. Spearing, "*Awntyrs off Arthure*" and "Central and Displaced Sovereignty."

20. Powicke, *Thirteenth Century*, 687–700.

21. Maldwyn Mills, one of the poem's more recent editors, notes the shared problem of the "wrongful acquisition of territory" (xxix) which he stresses remains unsolved by the end of each episode. *Ywain and Gawain,* xxv-xxxiii.

22. Contrasting the *Awntyrs* to the *Trentals* of St. Gregory accentuates this sense of lingering inadequacy. The *Trentals* also features the flaming ghost of a demonic mother whom the devil had "truyled . . . with his tricherye, / And ladde . . . in to lecherye." Gregory's mother is even more culpable than Gaynour's, wringing her illegitimate child's neck, hiding her deed for fear of disgracing her station and her son, and capping the debacle by dying unshriven. When asked what can best be done, she suggests a trental, thirty masses performed three at a time on the ten great feasts of the year, which she carefully enumerates for the benefit of readers. Gregory obeys and in a year's time she appears at mass again, this time so angelically attended that Gregory mistakes her for the Blessed Virgin. The poem ends with an unabashed advertisement for the effectiveness of trental masses for saving the souls both of the dead in purgatory and of the living who offer for them. A Middle English version is included in *Minor Poems of the Vernon Ms.,* 260–68; for other sources and analogues (including the alliterative *Morte Arthure* and *Sir Gawain and the Green Knight*), see Hanna, ed., *Awntyrs off Arthure,* 24–48.

23. Bainbridge, *Gilds,* 79–98; Wood-Legh, *Perpetual Chantries*; Dinn, "Death and Rebirth,151–69.

24. Wyclif, *Select English Works,* v. 2, 213, cited in Wood-Legh, *Perpetual Chantries,* 305, n.2.

25. Wood-Legh, *Perpetual Chantries,* 307.

26. Dinn, "Death and Rebirth," 159.

27. Harding, "Burial Choice."

28. Ariès, *Hour of Our Death,*140–293.

29. Ibid., 191.

30. Dinn marks how lay fluency and inventiveness in the ritual vocabulary of death increases from the late fourteenth through the sixteenth centuries. "Death and Rebirth," 165.

31. For the profits of interclass negotiation within religious gild festivities, see Rosser, "Going to the Fraternity Feast"; for an emphasis on gilds as internally fractious, sometimes socially disordering, and therefore anxiously regulated sites of civic influence, see Ben R. McRee, "Unity or Division" and "Religious Gilds."

32. Smith, *English Gilds,* 51 (Scholars), 40 (Poor Men).

33. Ariès, *Hour of Our Death,* 188.

34. Katherine French, "Competing."

35. Wood-Legh, *Perpetual Chantries,* 75.

36. Ibid., 185.

37. Bainbridge, *Gilds,* 105.

38. Wood-Legh, *Perpetual Chantries,* 313.

39. Turville-Petre, "Three Poems."

40. Turville-Petre usefully compares the three in "Three Poems."

41. Hanna, "Alliterative Poetry," 511–12.

42. Bloch and Parry, *Death and Regeneration,* 1–44.

43. Ibid., 41.

Conclusion

1. Dugdale, *History of St. Paul's*, 124–25.

2. Neill, *Issues of Death*, 38. Neill's fascinating study of Renaissance tragedy explores how Renaissance culture invents new ways of serving the dead across this gulf—in elaborate tombs and literature, "the most enduring memorial of all" (42).

3. Otter, *Inventiones*.

Bibliography

PRIMARY SOURCES

Alliterative Morte Arthure: A Critical Edition. Ed. Valerie Krishna. New York: Burt Franklin, 1976.

Alliterative Poetry of the Later Middle Ages. Ed. Thorlac Turville-Petre. London: Routledge, 1989.

An Arab Syrian Gentleman and Warrior in the Period of the Crusades: Memoirs of Usamah Ibn-Muqidh. Trans. Philip K. Hitti. Princeton, N.J.: Princeton University Press, 1987.

Augustine of Hippo. *Concerning the City of God against the Pagans*. Trans. Henry Bettenson. Harmondsworth: Penguin, 1972.

The Awntyrs off Arthure at the Terne Wathelyn: An Edition Based on Bodleian Library Ms. Douce 324. Ed. Ralph Hanna. Manchester: Manchester University Press; New York: Barnes and Noble Books, 1974.

The Brut, or Chronicles of England. Ed. Friedrich W. B. Brie. Vol. 2. London: Kegan Paul, Trench, Trbner, and Co., 1908.

Chaucer, Geoffrey. *The Riverside Chaucer*. Ed. Larry D. Benson. Boston: Houghton Mifflin, 1987.

Christine de Pisan. *The Book of Deeds of Arms and of Chivalry*. Trans. Sumner Willard. Ed. Charity Cannon Willard. University Park: Pennsylvania State University Press, 1999.

De profectione Ludovici VII in orientem. Ed. and trans. Virginia Gingerick Berry. New York: W. W. Norton, 1948.

English Gilds. Ed. Joshua Toulmin Smith. EETS, o.s., 40. London: N. Trübner and Co., 1870.

English Wycliffite Writings. Ed. Anne Hudson. Cambridge: Cambridge University Press, 1978.

Froissart, John. *Chronicle*. Trans. John Bouchier. London: David Nutt, 1903.

Jacobus de Voragine. *The Golden Legend*. Trans. Granger Ryan and Helmut Ripperger. New York: Longmans Green, 1941.

The Jerusalem Bible. Ed. Alexander Jones. Garden City, N.Y.: Doubleday, 1966.

Joinville and Villehardouin. *Chronicles of the Crusades*. Trans. M. R. B. Shaw. Harmondsworth: Penguin, 1963.

Kempe, Margery. *The Book of Margery Kempe*. Trans. B. A. Windeatt. Harmondsworth: Penguin Books, 1985.

King Arthur's Death: The Middle English Stanzaic Morte Arthure *and* Alliterative

Morte Arthure. Ed. Larry D. Benson. Rev. Edward E. Foster. Kalamazoo,
    Mich.: Medieval Institute Publications, 1994.

Laȝamon's Brut: A History of the Britons. Trans. Donald G. Bzdyl. Binghamton,
    N.Y.: Center for Medieval and Early Renaissance Studies, 1989.

Langland, William. Piers Plowman by William Langland, an edition of the C-text. Ed.
    Derek Pearsall. York Medieval Texts, 2d ser. Berkeley: University of California
    Press, 1978.

———. The Vision of Piers Plowman. Ed. A. V. C. Schmidt. London: J. M. Dent and
    Sons Ltd., 1987.

Llull, Ramon. "Book of the Gentile." In Doctor Illuminatus: A Ramon Llull Reader,
    ed. and trans. Anthony Bonner. Princeton, N.J.: Princeton University Press,
    1985.

Mandeville, John. The Travels of Sir John Mandeville. Trans. C. W. R. D. Moseley.
    Harmondsworth: Penguin Books, 1983.

Memorials of Henry V, King of England. Ed. Charles Augustus Cole. London:
    Longman, Brown, Green, Longmans, and Roberts, 1858.

The Minor Poems of the Vernon Ms. EETS. 98. Ed. Carl Horstmann. London: Kegan
    Paul, Trench, Trübner, and Co., 1892, 260–68.

Mirk's Festial: A Collection of Homilies by Johannes Mirkus. EETS, e.s., 96. Ed.
    Theodor Erbe. London: Early English Text Society, 1905.

Morte Arthure: A Critical Edition. Ed. Mary Hamel. New York: Garland, 1984.

Mum and the Sothsegger. Ed. Mabel Day and Robert Steele. London: Oxford Uni-
    versity Press, 1936.

Mum and the Sothsegger. In The Piers Plowman Tradition, ed. Helen Barr. London:
    J. M. Dent, 1993, 135–202.

The Ordenaunce and Fourme of Fightyng within Listes. In The Black Book of the Admi-
    ralty, ed. Sir Travers Twiss. Chronicles and Memorials of Great Britain and
    Ireland During the Middle Ages, no. 55, Vol. 1, 301–29. London: Longman
    and Co., 1871.

The Oxford Book of Late Medieval Verse and Prose. Ed. Douglas Gray. Oxford: Oxford
    University Press, 1985.

Pearl. Ed. and trans. Sir Israel Gollancz. London: Chatto and Windus, 1921.

Phillippe de Mézires. "L'Epistre Lamentable et Consolatoire." Reprinted in Oeuvres
    de Froissart, ed. Kervyn de Lettenhove. Brussels: Victor Devaux, 1872.

Poems of the Pearl Manuscript. Ed. Malcolm Andrews. Berkeley: University of Cali-
    fornia Press, 1982.

Richard the Redeless. In The Piers Plowman Tradition, ed. Helen Barr. London: J. M.
    Dent, 1993, 101–33.

The Saint of London: The Life and Miracles of St. Erkenwald. Ed. and trans. Gordon
    Whatley. Binghamton, N.Y.: Medieval and Renaissance Texts and Studies,
    1989.

The Siege of Jerusalem. Ed. E. Klbing and Mabel Day. London: Humphrey Milford,
    1932.

Sir Gawain: Eleven Romances and Tales. Ed. Thomas Hahn. Kalamazoo, Mich.:
    Medieval Institute Publications, 1995.

Sir Gawain and the Green Knight. Trans. Marie Borroff. New York: W. W. Norton,
    1967.

Sir Gawain and the Green Knight. Ed. J. R. R. Tolkien and E. V. Gordon. 2d ed., rev., ed. Norman Davis. Oxford: Clarendon Press, 1967.

Sir Gawain and the Green Knight: A Critical Edition. Ed. Theodore Silverstein. Chicago: University of Chicago Press, 1974, 1984.

The Song of Roland: An Analytical Edition. Trans. Gerard J. Brault. University Park: Pennsylvania State University Press, 1978.

St. Erkenwald. Ed. Ruth Morse. Cambridge: D. S. Brewer; Totowa, N.J.: Rowman and Littlefield, 1975.

St. Erkenwald. Ed. Clifford Peterson. Philadelphia: University of Pennsylvania Press, 1977.

St. Erkenwald. Ed. Henry L. Savage. Hamden, Conn.: Archon, 1972.

St. Erkenwald. In *Alliterative Poetry of the Later Middle Ages,* ed. Thorlac Turville-Petre. London: Routledge, 1989, 101–19.

The Thornton Manuscript. London: The Scholar Press, 1975.

Walsingham, Thomas. *Historia Anglicana.* Ed. H. T. Riley. Rolls Series. London: Longman and Co., 1863–64.

——. *The St. Albans Chronicle, 1406–1420.* Ed. V. H. Galbraith. Oxford: Clarendon Press, 1937.

The Wars of Alexander. Ed. Hoyt N. Duggan and Thorlac Turville-Petre. Oxford: Oxford University Press, 1989.

The Westminster Chronicle, 1381–94. Ed. and trans. L. C. Hector and Barbara F. Harvey. Oxford: Clarendon Press; New York: Oxford University Press, 1982.

Wyclif, John. *The English Works of Wyclif.* Ed. F. D. Matthew. 1880. Rev. ed. London: Kegan Paule, Trench, and Trbner, 1902.

——. *Select English Works of John Wyclif.* Ed. Thomas Arnold. Oxford: Clarendon Press, 1869–71.

Ywain and Gawain, Sir Percyvell of Gales, The Anturs of Arther. Ed. Maldwin Mills. London: J. M. Dent Ltd.; Rutland, Vt: Charles E. Tuttle Co., Inc., 1992.

SECONDARY SOURCES

Abu-Lughod, Janet. *Before European Hegemony: The World System A.D. 1250–1350.* New York: Oxford University Press, 1989.

Aers, David, "In Arthures Day." In *Community, Gender, and Individual Experience.* London: Routledge, 1988, 153–78.

Akbari, Suzanne Conklin. "From Due East to True North: Orientalism and Orientation." In *The Postcolonial Middle Ages,* ed. Jeffrey Jerome Cohen. New York: St. Martin's Press, 2000, 19–34.

Andrews, Malcolm. "The Diabolical Chapel: A Motif in *Patience* and *Sir Gawain and the Green Knight." Neophilologus* 66 (1982): 313–19.

Ariès, Philippe. *The Hour of Our Death.* Trans. Helen Weaver. New York: Vintage Books, 1981.

Ashley, Kathleen. "'Trawthe' and Temporality: The Violation of Contracts and Conventions in *Sir Gawain and the Green Knight." Assays* 4 (1987): 3–24.

Astell, Ann. *Political Allegory in Late Medieval England.* Ithaca, N.Y.: Cornell University Press, 1999.

———. "*Sir Gawain and the Green Knight*: A Study in the Rhetoric of Romance." *Journal of English and German Philology* 84 (1985): 188–202.

Aston, Margaret. *Lollards and Reformers: Images and Literacy in Late Medieval Religion*. London: Hambledon Press, 1984.

Atiya, Aziz Suryal. *Crusade, Commerce and Culture*. Bloomington: Indiana University Press, 1962.

———. *The Crusade of Nicopolis*. London: Methuen, 1934.

Auerbach, Erich. *Mimesis: The Representation of Reality in Western Literature*. Trans. William R. Trask. Princeton, N.J.: Princeton University Press, 1974.

Avril, François. *Manuscript Painting at the Court of France: The Fourteenth Century (1310–1380)*. New York: George Braziller, 1978.

Ayton, Andrew. "English Armies in the Fourteenth Century." In *The Wars of Edward III: Sources and Interpretations*, ed. Clifford J. Rogers. Woodbridge, England: Boydell Press, 1999, 303–19.

Bainbridge, Virginia R. *Gilds in the Medieval Countryside: Social and Religious Change in Cambridgeshire c. 1350–1558*. Woodbridge, England: Boydell Press, 1996.

Barney, Stephen A. "Langland's Prosody: The State of Study." In *The Endless Knot: Essays on Old and Middle English in Honor of Marie Borroff*, ed. M. Teresa Tavormina and R. F. Yeager. Cambridge: D. S. Brewer, 1995, 65–85.

Barnie, John. *War in Medieval English Society: Social Values in the Hundred Years War 1337–99*. Ithaca, N.Y.: Cornell University Press, 1974.

Barron, Caroline. "The Parish Fraternities of Medieval London." In *The Church in Pre-Reformation Society: Essays in Honour of F.R.H. Du Boulay*, ed. Caroline M. Barron and Christopher Harper-Bill. Woodbridge, England: Boydell Press, 1985, 13–37.

Bartels, Emily. *Spectacles of Strangeness: Imperialism, Alienation, and Marlowe*. Philadelphia: University of Pennsylvania Press, 1993.

Bartlett, Anne Clark. "Cracking the Penile Code: Reading Gender and Conquest in the Alliterative *Morte Arthure*." Arthuriana 8, 2 (1998): 57–77.

Bassett, Steven, ed. *Death in Towns: Urban Responses to the Dying and the Dead, 100–1600*. London and New York: Leicester University Press, 1992.

Bean, J. M. W. *From Lord to Patron: Lordship in Late Medieval England*. Manchester: Manchester University Press, 1989.

Beckwith, Sarah. *Christ's Body: Identity, Culture, and Society in Late Medieval Writings*. London and New York: Routledge, 1993.

Benham, William. *Old St. Paul's Cathedral*. London: Seeley, 1902.

Bennett, Michael J. *Community, Class and Careerism: Cheshire and Lancashire Society in the Age of Sir Gawain and the Green Knight*. Cambridge: Cambridge University Press, 1983.

———. "Courtly Literature and Northwest England in the Later Middle Ages." In *Court and Poet*, ed. Glyn S. Burgess. Liverpool: Francis Cairns, 1981, 69–78.

———. "The Court of Richard II and the Promotion of Literature." In *Chaucer's England*, ed. Barbara Hanawalt. Minneapolis: University of Minnesota Press, 1992, 3–20.

———. "The Historical Background." In *A Companion to the Gawain-Poet*, ed. Derek Brewer and Jonathan Gibson. Cambridge: D. S. Brewer, 1997.

————. *Richard II and the Revolution of 1399*. Stroud: Sutton Publishing Ltd., 1999.

Benson, Larry D. "The Alliterative *Morte Arthure* and Medieval Tragedy." *Tennessee Studies in Literature* 11 (1966): 75–89.

————. *Art and Tradition in Sir Gawain and the Green Knight*. New Brunswick, N.J.: Rutgers University Press, 1965.

————. "The Date of the Alliterative *Morte Arthure*." In *Medieval Studies in Honor of Lillian Herlands Hornstein*, ed. Jess B. Bessinger, Jr. and Robert R. Raymo. New York: New York University Press, 1976, 19–40.

Benson, Larry D., ed. *King Arthur's Death: The Middle English* Stanzaic Morte Arthure *and* Alliterative Morte Arthure. Rev. Edward E. Foster. Kalamazoo, Mich.: Medieval Institute Publications, 1994.

Bergner, H. "The Two Courts: Two Modes of Existence in *Sir Gawain and the Green Knight*." *English Studies* 67 (1986): 401–16.

Besserman, Lawrence. "The Idea of the Green Knight." *English Literary History* 53 (1986): 219–39.

Bird, Ruth. *The Turbulent London of Richard II*. London: Longmans, Green, and Co., 1949.

Bishop, Ian. "Time and Tempo in *Sir Gawain and the Green Knight*." *Neophilologus* 69 (1985): 611–19.

Blanch, Robert J. "Imagery of Binding in Fitts One and Two of *Sir Gawain and the Green Knight*." *Studia Neophilogica* 54 (1982): 53–60.

————. "The Legal Framework of 'A Twelmonyth and a Day,' in *Sir Gawain and the Green Knight*." *Neuphilologische Mitteilungen* 84 (1983): 347–52.

Blanch, Robert J. and Julian N. Wasserman. "Medieval Contracts and Covenants: The Legal Coloring of *Sir Gawain and the Green Knight*." *Neophilologus* 68 (1984): 598–610.

————. "'To Ouertake your wylle': Volition and Obligation in *Sir Gawain and the Green Knight*." *Neophilologus* 70 (1986): 119–29.

Blauner, Robert. "Death and Social Structure." *Psychiatry* 29: 4 (1966): 378–94.

Bloch, Maurice and Jonathan Parry, eds. *Death and the Regeneration of Life*. Cambridge: Cambridge University Press, 1982.

Bloch, R. Howard. *Etymologies and Genealogies*. Chicago: University of Chicago Press, 1983.

Bloom, Harold. *Anxieties of Influence: A Theory of Poetry*. New York: Oxford University Press, 1973.

Bolton, J. L. *The Medieval English Economy, 1150–1500*. London: Dent, 1980.

Boren, James L. "Narrative Design in the Alliterative *Morte Arthure*." *Philological Quarterly* 56 (1977): 310–19.

Borroff, Marie. *Sir Gawain and the Green Knight: A Stylistic and Metrical Study*. New Haven, Conn.: Yale University Press, 1962.

————. "*Sir Gawain and the Green Knight*: The Passing of Judgement." In *The Passing of Arthur: New Essays in Arthurian Tradition*, ed. Christopher Baswell and William Sharpe. New York: Garland, 1988, 105–28.

Bourdieu, Pierre. *Language and Symbolic Power*. Trans. Gino Raymond and Matthew Adamson. Cambridge, Mass.: Harvard University Press, 1991.

Bowers, John M. "*Pearl* in Its Royal Setting." *Studies in the Age of Chaucer* 17 (1995): 111–55.

———. *The Politics of* Pearl: *Court Poetry in the Age of Richard II*. Cambridge: D. S. Brewer, 2001.

Braggs, Lois. "*Sir Gawain and the Green Knight* and the Elusion of Clarity." *Neuphilologische Mitteilungen* 86 (1985): 482–88.

Brooke, C. N. L. "The Earliest Times to 1485." In *A History of St Paul's Cathedral and the Men Associated with It,* ed. W. R. Matthews and W. M. Atkins. New York: Pitmann, 1957, 1–99.

Burns, E. Jane and Roberta L. Krueger. "Introduction." *Romance Notes* 15 (1985): 205–19.

Burrow, J. A. *A Reading of Sir Gawain and the Green Knight*. London: Routledge, 1965.

Butcher, A. F. "English Urban Society and the Revolt of 1381." In *The English Rising of 1381,* ed. Rodney H. Hilton and T. H. Aston. Cambridge: Cambridge University Press, 1984, 84–111.

Bynum, Carolyn Walker. *Fragmentation and Redemption: Essays on Gender and the Human Body in Medieval Religion*. New York: Zone Books, 1991.

Cable, Thomas. *The English Alliterative Tradition*. Philadelphia: University of Pennsylvania Press, 1991.

Campbell, Kim Sydow. "A Lesson in Polite Non-Compliance: Gawain's Conversational Strategies in Fitt 3 of *Sir Gawain and the Green Knight*." *Language Quarterly* 28 (1990): 53–62.

Campbell, Mary B. *The Witness and the Other World: Exotic European Travel Writing, 400–1600*. Ithaca, N.Y.: Cornell University Press, 1988.

Cannon, Christopher. "Monastic Productions." In *The Cambridge History of Medieval English Literature*, ed. David Wallace. Cambridge: Cambridge University Press, 1999, 316–48.

Carmichael, Virginia. "Green Is for Growth: Sir Gawain's Disjunctive Neurosis." *Assays* 4 (1987): 25–38.

Carson, Mother Angela. "The Green Chapel: Its Meaning and Function." In *Critical Studies of Sir Gawain and the Green Knight,* ed. Donald Howard and Christian Zacher. Notre Dame, Ind.: University of Notre Dame Press, 1968, 245–54.

Certeau, Michel de. *The Practice of Everyday Life*. Trans. Stephen F. Rendall. Berkeley: University of California Press, 1984.

Chambers, E. K. *The Medieval Stage*. Vol. 1. Oxford: Clarendon Press, 1903.

Chambers, R. W. "On the Continuity of English Prose from Alfred to More and His School," In *Nicholas Harpsfield's Life of Sir Thomas More*, ed. E. V. Hitchcock and R. W. Chambers. EETS 186. Oxford: Oxford University Press, 1932, xi, xiv–clxxiv.

Clark, S. L. and Julian Wasserman. "The Passing of the Seasons and the Apocalyptic in *Sir Gawain and the Green Knight*." *South Central Review* 2 (1986): 5–22.

———. "*St. Erkenwald* 's Spiritual Itinerary." *American Benedictine Review* 33 (1982): 257–69.

Clough, Andrea. "The French Element in *Sir Gawain and the Green Knight*." *Neuphilologische Mitteilungen* 86 (1985): 187–96.

Cohen, Jeremy. *The Friars and the Jews: The Evolution of Medieval Anti-Judaism*. Ithaca, N.Y.: Cornell University Press, 1982.

———. *Living Letters of the Law: Ideas of the Jew in Medieval Christianity*. Berkeley: University of California Press, 1999.

Cooke, W. G. "*Sir Gawain and the Green Knight*: A Restored Dating." *Medium Aevum* 58(1989): 34–48.

Crane, Susan. *Gender and Romance in Chaucer's Canterbury Tales*. Princeton, N.J.: Princeton University Press, 1994.

———. *Insular Romance: Politics, Faith, and Culture in Anglo-Norman and Middle English Literature*. Berkeley: University of California Press, 1986.

———. "Knights in Disguise: Identity and Incognito in Fourteenth-Century Chivalry." In *The Stranger in Medieval Society*, ed. F. R. P. Akehurst and Stephanie Cain Van D'Elden. Minneapolis: University of Minnesota Press, 1997, 63–79.

Crawford, Donna. "Prophecy and Paternity in *The Wars of Alexander*." *English Studies* 73, 5 (1992): 406–16.

Curtius, Ernst Robert. *European Literature and the Latin Middle Ages*. Trans. Willard R. Trask. Princeton, N.J.: Princeton University Press, 1983.

Davidson, Arnold E. "Mystery, Miracle, and Meaning in *St. Erkenwald*." *Papers on Language and Literature* 16 (1980): 33–44.

Dean, Christopher. "Sir Gawain in the Alliterative *Morte Arthure*." *Papers on Language and Literature* 22 (1986): 115–25.

Delany, Sheila. *The Naked Text, Chaucer's Legend of Good Women*. Berkeley: University of California Press, 1994.

De Roo, Harvey. "Undressing Lady Bertilak: Guilt and Denial in *Sir Gawain and the Green Knight*." *Chaucer Review* 27 (1993): 305–24.

Diamond, Arlyn. "*Sir Gawain and the Green Knight*: An Alliterative Romance." *Philological Quarterly* 55 (1976): 10–29.

Dimock, Arthur. *The Cathedral Church of St. Paul's*. London: George Bell, 1900.

Dinn, Robert. "Death and Rebirth in Late Medieval Bury St Edmunds." In *Death in Towns: Urban Responses to the Dying and the Dead, 1000–1600*, ed. Steven Bassett. London: Leicester University Press, 1992, 151–69.

Dinshaw, Carolyn. "Getting Medieval: *Pulp* Fiction, Foucault, and the Use of the Past." In *Getting Medieval: Sexualities and Communities, Pre- and Postmodern*. Durham, N.C.: Duke University Press, 1999, 183–206.

———. "A Kiss Is Just a Kiss: Heterosexuality and Its Consolations in *Sir Gawain and the Green Knight*." *Diacritics* 24, 2–3 (1994): 205–26.

Dobson, R. B. *The Peasants' Revolt of 1381*. 2d ed. London: Macmillan, 1970, 1983.

Dor, Juliette. "*Sir Gawain and the Green Knight*: Time and Times." In *Loyal Letters: Studies on Mediaeval Alliterative Poetry and Prose*, ed. L. A. J. R. Houwen and A. A. MacDonald, Groningen: Egbert Forsten, 1994, 207–21.

Dronke, Peter. "Poetic Originality in *The Wars of Alexander*." In *The Long Fifteenth Century: Essays for Douglas Gray*, ed. Helen Cooper and Sally Mapstone. Oxford: Clarendon Press, 1997, 123–39.

Duffy, Eamon, *The Stripping of the Altars: Traditional Religion in England c. 1400–c. 1580*. New Haven, Conn.: Yale University Press, 1992.

Duffy, Maureen. *The Erotic World of Faery*. New York: Avon, 1972.

Dugdale, Sir William. *A History of St. Paul's Cathedral*. London: George James, 1716.

Duggan, Hoyt. "Alliterative Patterning as a Basis for Emendation in Middle English Alliterative Poetry." *Studies in the Age of Chaucer* 8 (1986): 73–106.

——. "Evidential Basis for Old English Metrics." *Studies in Philology* 85 (1988): 145–63.

——. "Final -*e* and the Rhythmic Structure of the B-Verse in Middle English Alliterative Poetry." *Modern Philology* 86 (1988–89): 119–45.

——. "The Shape of the B-Verse in Middle English Alliterative Poetry." *Speculum* 61 (1986): 564–92.

——. "Stress Assignment in Middle English Alliterative Poetry." *Journal of English and Germanic Philology* 89 (1990): 309–29.

Dyer, Christopher. *Standards of Living in the Later Middle Ages.* Cambridge: Cambridge University Press, 1989.

Eadie, J. "The Alliterative *Morte Arthure*: Structure and Meaning." *English Studies* 63 (1982): 1–12.

——"A New Source for *Sir Gawain and the Green Knight.*" *Neuphilologische Mitteilungen* 87 (1986): 569–77.

—— "Sir Gawain's Travels in North Wales." *Review of English Studies*, n.s., 34 (1983): 191–95.

Edge, David and John Miles Paddock. *Arms and Armor of the Medieval Knight.* New York: Brompton Books, 1988.

Edgeworth, Robert J. "Anatomical Geography in *Sir Gawain and the Green Knight.*" *Neophilologus* 69 (1985): 318–19.

Elliot, Ralph W. V. *The Gawain Country: Essays on the Topography of Middle English Alliterative Poetry.* Leeds: University of Leeds School of English, 1984.

Elman, P. "The Economic Causes of the Expulsion of the Jews in 1290." *Economic History Review*, 1st ser., 7 (1936–37): 145–54.

Faigley, Lester L. "Typology and Justice in *St. Erkenwald.*" *American Benedictine Review* 29 (1978): 381–90.

Fichte, Joerg O. "The Middle English Verse Romance: Suggestions for the Development of a Literary Typology." *Deutsche Vierteljahrsschrift für Literaturwissenschaft und Geistesgeschicte* 55 (1981): 567–90.

Field, Rosalind. "The Anglo-Norman Background to Alliterative Romance." In *Middle English Alliterative Poetry, Seven Essays*, ed. David Lawton. Cambridge: D. S. Brewer, 1982, 56–69.

Finlayson, John. "Arthur and the Giant of St. Michael's Mount." *Medium Aevum* 32 (1964): 112–20.

——. "The Concept of the Hero in 'Morte Arthure.'" In *Chaucer und seine zeit: Symposion für Walter F. Schirmer*, ed. Arno Esch. Tübingen: Max Niemeyer, 1967, 249–74.

——. "The Expectations of Romance in *Sir Gawain and the Green Knight.*" *Genre* 12 (1979): 1–24.

——. "Sir Gawain, Knight of the Queen in *Sir Gawain and the Green Knight.*" *Modern Language Notes* 27 (1989): 7–13.

Fisher, Sheila. "Taken Men and Token Women in *Sir Gawain and the Green Knight.*" In *Seeking the Woman in Late Medieval and Renaissance Writings*, ed. Sheila Fisher and Janet E. Halley. Knoxville: University of Tennessee Press, 1989, 71–105.

Fisher, Sheila and Janet E. Halley. "The Lady Vanishes." In *Seeking the Woman in Late Medieval and Renaissance Writings*, ed. Sheila Fisher and Janet E. Halley. Knoxville: University of Tennessee Press, 1989, 1–17.

——, eds. *Seeking the Woman in Late Medieval and Renaissance Writings*. Knoxville: University of Tennessee Press, 1989.

Fradenburg, Louise Olga. *City, Marriage, Tournament: Arts of Rule in Late Medieval Scotland*. Madison: University of Wisconsin Press, 1991.

——. "Needful Things." In *Medieval Crime and Social Control*, ed. Barbara Hanawalt and David Wallace. Minneapolis: University of Minnesota Press, 1999, 49–67.

——. "Soft and Silken War." In *City, Marriage, Tournament: Arts of Rule in Late Medieval Scotland*. Madison: University of Wisconsin Press, 1991, 192–224.

——. "'Voice Memorial': Loss and Reparation in Chaucer's Poetry." *Exemplaria* 2 (1990): 169–202.

Frantzen, Allen J. "*St. Erkenwald* and the Raising of Lazarus." *Mediaevalia* 7 (1981): 157–71.

Freeman, Adam and Janet Thormann. "*Sir Gawain and the Green Knight*: An Anatomy of Chastity." *American Imago* 45 (1989): 389–400.

French, Dorothea R. "Journeys to the Center of the Earth: Medieval and Renaissance Pilgrimages to Mount Calvary." In *Journeys Toward God: Pilgrimage and Crusade*, ed. Barbara N. Sargent-Baur. Kalamazoo, Mich.: Medieval Institute Publications, 1992, 45–81.

French, Katherine L. "Competing for Space: Medieval Religious Conflict in the Monastic-Parochial Church at Dunster." *Journal of Medieval and Early Modern Studies* 27, 2 (1997): 215–44.

Freud, Sigmund. "The Uncanny" (1919). In *Collected Papers*, vol. 4, 368–407. London: Hogarth Press, 1950.

Gabrieli, Franceso. *Arab Historians of the Crusades*. Trans. E. J. Costello. New York: Dorset Press, 1989.

Galloway, Andrew. "Making History Legal: *Piers Plowman* and the Rebels of Fourteenth-Century England." In *William Langland's* Piers Plowman: *A Book of Essays*, ed. Kathleen M. Hewett-Smith. New York: Routledge, 2001, 7–39.

Ganim, John. "Disorientation, Style, and Consciousness in *Sir Gawain and the Green Knight*." *Publications of the Modern Language Association* 91 (1976): 376–84.

Geary, Patrick J. *Living with the Dead in the Middle Ages*. Ithaca, N.Y.: Cornell University Press, 1994.

Gillespie, James L., ed. *The Age of Richard II*. New York: St. Martin's Press, 1997.

Glassman, Bernard. *Anti-Semitic Stereotypes Without Jews: Images of the Jews in England: 1290–1700*. Detroit, Mich.: Wayne State University Press, 1975.

Goodlad, Lauren M. "The Games of *Sir Gawain and the Green Knight*." *Comitatus* 18 (1987): 45–58.

Grady, Frank. "*Piers Plowman*, *St. Erkenwald*, and the Rule of Exceptional Salvations." *The Yearbook of Langland Studies* 6 (1992): 61–86.

——. "*St. Erkenwald* and the Merciless Parliament." *Studies in the Age of Chaucer* 22 (2000): 179–212.

Green, Richard Firth. *The Crisis of Truth: Literature and Law in Ricardian England*. Philadelphia: University of Pennsylvania Press, 1999.

———. "Gawain's Five Fingers." *Modern Language Notes* 27 (1989): 16–17.

———. *Poets and Prince-Pleasers*. Toronto: University of Toronto Press, 1980.

———. "Sir Gawain and the *Sacra Cinctola*." *English Studies in Canada* 11 (1985): 1–11.

Greene, Thomas M. *The Light in Troy: Imitation and Recovery in Renaissance Poetry*. New Haven, Conn.: Yale University Press, 1982.

Griffiths, Ralph A. "The Crown and the Royal Family in Later Medieval England." In *Kings and Nobles in the Later Middle Ages: A Tribute to Charles Ross*, ed. Ralph A. Griffiths and James Sherborne. New York: St. Martin's Press, 1986, 17–26.

Grossman, Dave. *On Killing*. Boston: Little, Brown, 1995, 1996.

Hamel, Mary. "The Dream of a King: The Alliterative *Morte Arthure* and Dante." *Chaucer Review* 14 (1980): 298–312.

———. "*The Siege of Jerusalem* as a Crusading Poem." In *Journeys Toward God: Pilgrimage and Crusade*, ed. Barbara N. Sargent-Baur. Kalamazoo, Mich.: Medieval Institute Publications, 1992, 177–94.

Hanna, Ralph. "Alliterative Poetry." In *The Cambridge History of Medieval English Literature*, ed. David Wallace. Cambridge: Cambridge University Press, 1999, 488–512.

———. "*The Awntyrs off Arthure*: An Interpretation." *Modern Language Quarterly* 31 (1970): 275–97.

———. "Contextualizing *The Siege of Jerusalem*." *The Yearbook of Langland Studies* 6 (1992): 109–21.

———. "Defining Middle English Alliterative Poetry." In *The Endless Knot: Essays on Old and Middle English in Honor of Marie Borroff*, ed. M. Teresa Tavormina and R. F. Yeager. Cambridge: D. S. Brewer, 1995, 43–64.

Harder, Henry L. "Feasting in the Alliterative *Morte Arthure*." In *Chivalric Literature: Essays on Relations Between Literature and Life in the Later Middle Ages*, ed. Larry D. Benson and John Leyerle. Kalamazoo, Mich.: Board of the Medieval Institute, 1980, 49–62.

Harding, Vanessa. "Burial Choice and Burial Location in Later Medieval London." In *Death in Towns: Urban Responses to the Dying and the Dead, 100–1600*, ed. Steven Bassett. London: Leicester University Press, 119–35.

Harrelson, Walter and Randall M. Falk. *Jews and Christians: A Troubled Family*. Nashville, Tenn.: Abingdon Press, 1990.

Harriss, Gerald L. "War and the Emergence of the English Parliament, 1297–1360." In *The Wars of Edward III: Sources and Interpretations*, ed. Clifford Rogers. Woodbridge, England: Boydell Press, 1999, 321–41.

Heng, Geraldine. "A Woman Wants: The Lady, *Gawain*, and the Forms of Seduction." *Yale Journal of Criticism* 5, 3 (1992): 101–34

Hentsch, Thierry. *Imagining the Middle East*. Trans. Fred A. Reed. Montreal: Black Rose Books, 1992.

Hewett-Smith, Kathleen M., ed. *William Langland's* Piers Plowman: *A Book of Essays*. New York: Routledge, 2001.

Hieatt, A. Kent. "*Sir Gawain*: Pentangle, *Luf-lace*, Numerical Structure." In *Silent Poetry: Essays in Numerical Analysis*, ed. Alistair Fowler. London: Routledge and Kegan Paul, 1970, 116–40.

Higgins, Iain MacLeod. "Defining the Earth's Center in a Medieval 'Multi-Text': Jerusalem in *The Book of John Mandeville*." In *Text and Territory: Geographical Imagination in the European Middle Ages*, ed. Sylvia Tomasch and Sealy Gilles. Philadelphia: University of Pennsylvania Press, 1998, 29–53.

——. *Writing East: The "Travels" of Sir John Mandeville*. Philadelphia: University of Pennsylvania Press, 1997.

Hillenbrand, Carole. *The Crusades: Islamic Perspectives*. New York: Routledge, 2000.

Hilton, Rodney. *Bond Men Made Free: Medieval Peasant Movements and the English Rising of 1381*. London: Methuen, 1973.

——. *Class Conflict and the Crisis of Feudalism*. London: Hambledon Press, 1985.

Hilton, Rodney H. and T. H. Aston, eds. *The English Rising of 1381*. Cambridge: Cambridge University Press, 1984.

Holmes, G. A. "The 'Libel of English Policy.'" *English Historical Review* 76 (1961): 193–216.

Howard, Donald. "Structure and Symmetry in *Sir Gawain and the Green Knight*." *Speculum* 39 (1964): 425–33.

——. *The Three Temptations: Medieval Man in Search of the World*. Princeton, N.J.: Princeton University Press, 1966.

Howard, Donald and Christian Zacher, eds. *Critical Studies of Sir Gawain and the Green Knight*. Notre Dame, Ind.: University of Notre Dame Press, 1968.

Huizinga, Johan. *The Autumn of the Middle Ages*. Trans. Rodney J. Payton and Ulrich Mammitzsch. Chicago: University of Chicago Press, 1996.

Hulbert, J. R. "An Hypothesis Concerning the Alliterative Revival." *Modern Philology* 28 (1931): 405–22.

Jacobs, Joseph. *The Jews of Angevin England, Documents and Records*. London: David Nutt, 1893.

James, Mervyn. *English Politics and the Concept of Honour 1485–1642*. Oxford: Past and Present Society, 1978.

Johnson, Lynn Staley. "The Four Levels of Time in *Sir Gawain and the Green Knight*." *Annuale Medievale* 10 (1969): 65–80.

Justice, Steven. *Writing and Rebellion*. Berkeley: University of California Press, 1994.

Kaeuper, Richard. *War, Justice, and Public Order*. Oxford: Oxford University Press, 1988.

Kamps, Ivo. "Magic, Women, and Incest: The Real Challenges in *Sir Gawain and the Green Knight*." *Exemplaria* 1 (1989): 313–36.

Kay, Sarah. *The Chanson de Geste in the Age of Romance: Political Fictions*. Oxford: Clarendon Press; New York: Oxford University Press, 1995.

Kay, Sarah and Miri Rubin. *Framing Medieval Bodies*. Manchester: Manchester University Press, 1996.

Keen, Maurice. *Chivalry*. New Haven, Conn.: Yale University Press, 1984.

Keiser, George R. "Edward III and the Alliterative *Morte Arthure*." *Speculum* 48 (1973): 37–51.

——. "Narrative Structure in the Alliterative *Morte Arthure*, 26–720." *Chaucer Review* 9 (1974): 130–44.

——. "The Theme of Justice in the Alliterative *Morte Arthure*." *Annuale Medieval* 16 (1975): 94–109.

Kershaw, Ian. *Bolton Priory: The Economy of a Northern Monastery, 1286–1325*. Oxford: Oxford University Press, 1973.

Kinross, Lord. *The Ottoman Centuries: The Rise and Fall of the Turkish Empire*. New York: Morrow Quill Paperbacks, 1977.

Kirk, Elizabeth D. "'Wel Bycommes Such Craft Upon Cristmasse': The Festive and the Hermeneutic in *Sir Gawain and the Green Knight*. *Arthuriana* 4, 2 (1994): 93–137.

Knapp, Peggy. *Chaucer and the Social Contest*. New York: Routledge, 1990.

Knowles, M. D. "The Censured Opinions of Uthred of Boldon." *Proceedings of the British Academy* 37 (1951): 305–42.

Krishna, Valerie, ed. *Alliterative Morte Arthure*: A Critical Edition. New York: Burt Franklin, 1976.

Labarge, Margaret Wade. *Henry V, the Cautious Conqueror*. New York: Stein and Day, 1975.

Langmuir, Gavin. *History, Religion, and Antisemitism*. Berkeley: University of California Press, 1990.

——. *Toward a Definition of Antisemitism*. Berkeley: University of California Press, 1990.

Lawton, David, ed. *Middle English Alliterative Poetry and Its Literary Background, Seven Essays*. Cambridge: D. S. Brewer, 1982.

——."The Unity of Middle English Alliterative Poetry." *Speculum* 58(1983): 72–94.

Leeson, R. A. *Travelling Brothers: The Six Centuries' Road from Craft Fellowship to Trade Unionism*. London: George Allen and Unwin, 1979.

Levy, Bernard S. and Paul E. Szarmach, eds. *The Alliterative Tradition in the Fourteenth Century*. Kent, Ohio: Kent State University Press, 1981.

Lewis, N. B. "The Last Medieval Summons of the English Feudal Levy, 13 June 1385." *English Historical Review* 73 (1958): 1–26.

Lindley, Arthur. "'Ther he watz dispyled, with speches of myerthe': Carnival and the Undoing of Sir Gawain." *Exemplaria* 6, 1 (1994): 67–86.

Little, Lester K. *Religious Poverty and the Profit Economy in Medieval Europe*. Ithaca, N.Y.: Cornell University Press, 1978.

Lochrie, Karma. *Covert Operations: The Medieval Uses of Secrecy*. Philadelphia: University of Pennsylvania Press, 1999.

Lomperis, Linda and Sarah Stanbury, eds. *Feminist Approaches to the Body in Medieval Literature*. Philadelphia: University of Pennsylvania Press, 1993.

Longman, William. *A History of the Three Cathedrals Dedicated to St. Paul in London*. London: Longmans, Green, and Co., 1873.

Longo, John. "The Vision of History in *St. Erkenwald*." *Geardagum* 8 (1987): 35–51.

Loomis, Laura Hibbard. "The Auchinleck Manuscript and a Possible London Bookshop of 1330–40." *Publications of the Modern Language Association* 57, 3 (1942): 595–627.

Loomis, Roger Sherman. "Edward I, Arthurian Enthusiast." *Speculum* 28 (1953): 114–27.

Lopez, Robert S. and Irving W. Raymond, eds. *Medieval Trade in the Mediterranean World*. New York: Columbia University, 1955.

Lumiansky, Robert M. "The Alliterative *Morte Arthure*, the Concept of Medieval

Tragedy, and the Cardinal Virtue Fortitude." *Medieval and Renaissance Studies* 3 (1967): 95–118.

Maalouf, Amin. *The Crusades Through Arab Eyes*. New York: Schocken Books, 1985.

Macherey, Pierre. *A Theory of Literary Production*. Trans. Geoffrey Wall. Boston: Routledge and Kegan Paul, 1978.

Mann, Jill. "Price and Value in *Sir Gawain and the Green Knight*." *Essays in Criticism* 36 (1986): 294–318.

Matonis, A. T. E. "A Reexamination of the Middle English Alliterative Long Line." *Modern Philology* 81 (1984): 339–60.

Matthews, W. *The Tragedy of Arthur: A Study of the Alliterative "Morte Arthure."* Berkeley: University of California Press, 1960.

Mauss, Marcel. *The Gift: The Form and Reason for Exchange in Archaic Societies*. Trans. W. D. Halls. New York: W. W. Norton, 1990.

McAlindon, T. "Hagiography into Art: A Study of *St. Erkenwald*." *Studies in Philology* 67 (1970): 472–94.

McFarlane, K. B. *The Nobility of Later Medieval England*. Oxford: Clarendon Press, 1973.

McGinn, Bernard. *Visions of the End: Apocalyptic Traditions in the Middle Ages*. New York: Columbia University Press, 1979, 1998.

McIntosh, Angus. "Early Middle English Alliterative Verse." In *Middle English Alliterative Poetry and Its Literary Background, Seven Essays*, ed. David Lawton. Cambridge: D. S. Brewer, 1982, 30–33.

McRee, Ben R. "Religious Gilds and Civic Order: The Case of Norwich in the Late Middle Ages." *Speculum* 67 (1992): 69–97.

———. "Unity or Division: The Social Meaning of Guild Ceremony in Urban Communities." In *City and Spectacle in Medieval Europe*, ed. Barbara A. Hanawalt and Kathryn L. Reyerson. Minneapolis: University of Minnesota Press, 1994, 189–207.

Menocal, Maria Rosa. *The Arabic Role in Medieval Literary History*. Philadelphia: University of Pennsylvania Press, 1987.

Metlitzki, Dorothee. *The Matter of Araby in Medieval England*. New Haven, Conn.: Yale University Press, 1977.

Middleton, Anne. "Acts of Vagrancy." In *Written Work: Langland, Labor, and Authorship*, ed. Steven Justice and Kathryn Kerby-Fulton. Philadelphia: University of Pennsylvania Press, 1997, 208–317.

Millar, Bonnie. "The Role of Prophecy in the *Siege of Jerusalem* and Its Analogues." *The Yearbook of Langland Studies* 13 (1999): 153–78.

———. The Siege of Jerusalem *in Its Physical, Literary and Historical Contexts*. Dublin: Four Courts Press, 2000.

Miskimin, Harry A. *The Economy of Early Renaissance Europe, 1300–1460*. Cambridge: Cambridge University Press, 1975.

Moore, R. I. *The Formation of a Persecuting Society*. Oxford: Basil Blackwell, 1987.

Musgrove, Frank. *The North of England: A History from Roman Times to the Present*. Oxford: Basil Blackwell, 1990.

Narin Van Court, Elisa. "*The Siege of Jerusalem* and Augustinian Historians: Writing About Jews in Fourteenth-Century England." *The Chaucer Review* 29 (1995): 227–48.

Neaman, Judith S. "Sir Gawain's Covenant: Troth and Timor Mortis." *Philological Quarterly* 55 (1976): 30–42.

Neill, Michael. *Issues of Death: Mortality and Identity in English Renaissance Tragedy*. Oxford: Clarendon Press, 1997.

Nickel, Helmut. "Why Was the Green Knight Green?" *Arthurian Interpretations* 3 (1988): 58–64.

Nirenberg, David. *Communities of Violence: Persecution of Minorities in the Middle Ages*. Princeton, N.J.: Princeton University Press, 1998.

Nissé, Ruth. "'A Coroun Ful Riche': The Rule of History in *St. Erkenwald*." *English Literary History* 65 (1998): 277–95.

Oakden, J. P. *Alliterative Poetry in Middle English: A Survey of the Traditions*. Vols. 1–2. Manchester: Manchester University Press, 1935.

Obst, Wolfgang. "The Gawain-Priamus Episode in the Alliterative *Morte Arthure*." *Studia Neophilologica* 57 (1985): 9–18.

Otter, Monika. *Inventiones: Fiction and Referentiality in Twelfth-Century English Historical Writing*. Chapel Hill: University of North Carolina Press, 1996.

———. "'New Werke': *St. Erkenwald*, St. Albans and the Medieval Sense of the Past." *Journal of Medieval and Renaissance Studies* 24 (1994): 387–414.

Palmer, J. J. N. *England, France, and Christendom*. Chapel Hill: University of North Carolina Press, 1972.

Pastoureau, Michel. *Les Sceaux*. Tunhout-Belgium: Brepols, 1981.

Patterson, Lee. *Chaucer and the Subject of History*. Madison: University of Wisconsin Press, 1991.

———. *Negotiating the Past*. Madison: University of Wisconsin Press, 1987.

Pearcy, Roy J. "The Alliterative *Morte Arthure* vv. 2420–2447 and the Death of Richard I." *English Language Notes* 22 (1985): 16–27.

Pearsall, Derek. *Old and Middle English Poetry*. London: Routledge and Kegan Paul, 1977.

———. "The Origins of the Alliterative Revival." In *The Alliterative Tradition in the Fourteenth Century*, ed. Bernard S. Levy and Paul E. Szarmach. Kent, Ohio: Kent State University Press, 1981, 1–24.

Peck, Russell A. "Number Structure in *St. Erkenwald*." *Annuale Medieavale* 14 (1973): 9–21.

Peterson, Clifford, ed. *St. Erkenwald*. Philadelphia: University of Pennsylvania Press, 1977.

Petronella, Vincent F. "St. Erkenwald: Style as the Vehicle for Meaning." *Journal of English and Germanic Philology* 66 (1967): 532–40.

Phillips, Helen. "*The Awntyrs off Arthure*: Structure and Meaning. A Reassessment." *Arthurian Literature* 12 (1993): 63–89.

Porter, Elizabeth. "Chaucer's Knight, the Alliterative *Morte Arthure*, and Medieval Laws of War: A Reconsideration." *Nottingham Medieval Studies* 27 (1983): 56–78.

Powicke, Maurice. *The Thirteenth Century, 1216–1307*. Oxford: Clarendon Press, 1953.

Pratt, Mary Louise. *Imperial Eyes: Travel Writing and Transculturation*. London: Routledge, 1992.

———. "Scratches on the Face of the Country: Or, What Mr. Barrow Saw in the Land of the Bushmen." *Critical Inquiry* 12 (1985): 119–43.

Richardson, H. G. *The English Jewry Under Angevin Kings*. London: Methuen, 1960.

Ricoeur, Paul. *Time and Narrative*. Vol. 1. Trans. Kathleen McLaughlin and David Pellauer. Chicago: University of Chicago Press, 1984.

Roach, Joseph. *Cities of the Dead: Circum-Atlantic Performance*. New York: Columbia University Press, 1996.

Rogers, Clifford J., ed. *The Wars of Edward III: Sources and Interpretations*. Woodbridge, England: Boydell Press, 1999.

Rosser, Gervase. "Going to the Fraternity Feast: Commensality and Social Relations in Late Medieval England." *Journal of British Studies* 33 (1994): 430–46.

Rubin, Miri. *Gentile Tales: The Narrative Assault on Late Medieval Jews*. New Haven, Conn.: Yale University Press, 1999.

Rudnytsky, Peter. "*Sir Gawain and the Green Knight*: Oedipal Temptation." *American Imago* 40 (1983): 371–83.

Said, Edward. *Orientalism*. New York: Random House, 1978.

Salter, Elizabeth. *English and International: Studies in the Literature, Art and Patronage of Medieval England*. Cambridge: Cambridge University Press, 1988.

Sapora, Robert William. *A Theory of Middle English Alliterative Meter with Critical Application*. Cambridge, Mass.: Harvard University Press, 1977.

Saul, Nigel. "Conflict and Consensus in English Local Society." In *Politics and Crisis in Fourteenth-Century England*, ed. John Taylor and Wendy Childs. Wolfeboro, N.H.: Alan Sutton, 1990, 38–58.

——. *Richard II*. New Haven, Conn.: Yale University Press, 1997.

Scarry, Elaine. *The Body in Pain: The Making and Unmaking of the World*. New York: Oxford University Press, 1985.

Scattergood, John. *The Lost Tradition: Essays on Middle English Alliterative Poetry*. Dublin: Four Courts Press, 2000.

Schmidt, A. V. C. *The Clerkly Maker: Langland's Poetic Art*. Cambridge: D. S. Brewer, 1987.

Schmitt, Jean-Claude. *Ghosts in the Middle Ages: The Living and the Dead in Medieval Society*. Trans. Teresa Lavender Fagan. Chicago: University of Chicago Press, 1998.

Schor, Naomi. *Bad Objects*. Durham, N.C.: Duke University Press, 1995.

Shepherd, Geoffrey. "The Nature of Alliterative Poetry in Late Medieval England." *Proceedings of the British Academy* 56 (1970): 57–76.

Shepherd, Stephen H. A., "Langland's Romances." In *William Langland's Piers Plowman: A Book of Essays*, ed. Kathleen M. Hewitt-Smith. New York: Routledge, 2001, 69–81.

Shichtman, Martin B. "Gawain in Wace and Layamon: A Case of Metahistorical Evolution." In *Medieval Texts and Contemporary Readers*, ed. Laurie A. Finke and Martin Shichtman. Ithaca, N.Y.: Cornell University Press, 1987, 103–19.

——. "*Sir Gawain and the Green Knight*: A Lesson in the Terror of History." *Papers on Language and Literature* 22 (1986): 3–15.

Shoaf, R. A. "The Alliterative *Morte Arthure*: The Story of Britain's David." *Journal of English and German Philology* 81 (1982): 204–26.

——. "The 'Syngne of Surfet' and the Surfeit of Signs in *Sir Gawain and the Green Knight*." In *The Passing of Arthur*, ed. Christopher Baswell and William Sharpe. New York: Garland, 1988, 152–69.

Smith, Joshua Toulmin. *English Gilds*. EETS, o.s., 40. London: N. Trübner and Co., 1870.

Southern, R. W. *Western Views of Islam in the Middle Ages*. Cambridge, Mass.: Harvard University Press, 1962, 1980.

Spearing, A. C. "*Awntyrs off Arthure*." In *The Alliterative Tradition in the Fourteenth Century*, ed. Bernard S. Levy and Paul E. Szarmach. Kent, Ohio: Kent State University Press, 1981, 182–202.

———. "Central and Displaced Sovereignty in Three Medieval Poems." *Review of English Studies*, n.s., 33 (1982): 247–61.

———. *The Gawain-Poet: A Critical Study*. Cambridge: Cambridge University Press, 1970.

———. *Readings in Medieval Poetry*. Cambridge: Cambridge University Press, 1987.

Spiegel, Gabrielle. *The Past as Text: The Theory and Practice of Medieval Historiography*. Baltimore, Md.: Johns Hopkins University Press, 1997.

Sponsler, Claire. *Drama and Resistance: Bodies, Goods, and Theatricality in Late Medieval England*. Minneapolis: University of Minnesota Press, 1997.

Stanbury, Sarah. *Seeing the Gawain-Poet: Description and the Art of Perception*. Philadelphia: University of Pennsylvania Press, 1991.

Stanley, E. G. "Laȝamon's Antiquarian Sentiments." *Medium Aevum* 38 (1969): 23–37.

Stevens, John. *Music and Poetry in the Early Tudor Court*. London: Methuen, 1961.

Stewart, Susan. *On Longing: Narratives of the Miniature, the Gigantic, the Souvenir, the Collection*. Baltimore, Md.: Johns Hopkins University Press, 1984.

Stokes, Myra and John Scattergood. "Travelling in November: Sir Gawain, Thomas Usk, Charles of Orleans and the *De Re Militari*." *Medium Aevum* 53 (1984): 78–83.

Stouck, Mary-Ann. "'Mourning and Myrthe' in the Alliterative *St. Erkenwald*." *Chaucer Review* 10 (1976): 243–54.

Stowe, George B. "Chronicles Versus Records: The Character of Richard II." In *Documenting the Past: Essays in Medieval History Presented to George Peddy Cuttino*, ed. J. S. Hamilton and Patricia J. Bradley. Woodbridge, England: Boydell Press, 1989, 155–76.

Strohm, Paul. *England's Empty Throne: Usurpation and the Language of Legitimation, 1399–1422*. New Haven, Conn.: Yale University Press, 1998.

———. *Hochon's Arrow: The Social Imagination of Fourteenth-Century Texts*. Princeton: Princeton University Press, 1992.

———. *Social Chaucer*. Cambridge, Mass.: Harvard University Press, 1989.

———. "The Trouble with Richard: The Reburial of Richard II and Lancastrian Political Strategy." *Speculum* 71 (1996): 87–111.

Tavormina, M. Teresa and R. F. Yeager, eds. *The Endless Knot: Essays on Old and Middle English in Honor of Marie Borroff*. Cambridge: D. S. Brewer, 1995.

Thompson, John J. *Robert Thornton and the London Thornton Manuscript*. Cambridge: D. S. Brewer, 1987.

Thompson, M. W. "The Green Knight's Castle." In *Studies in Medieval History Presented to R. Allen Brown*, ed. Christopher Harper-Bill, Christopher J. Holdsworth, and Janet L Nelson. Woodbridge, England: Boydell Press, 1989, 317–25.

Thrupp, Sylvia. "Comparison of Cultures in the Middle Ages: Western Standards as Applied to Muslim Civilization in the 12th and 13th Centuries." In *Society and History: Essays by Sylvia L. Thrupp*, ed. Raymond Grew and Nicholas H. Steneck. Ann Arbor: University of Michigan Press, 1977, 67–88.

——. *The Merchant Class of Medieval London, 1350–1500*. Ann Arbor: University of Michigan Press, 1968.

Tuck, Anthony. *Richard II and the English Nobility*. New York: St. Martin's Press, 1974.

Turville-Petre, Thorlac. *The Alliterative Revival*. Cambridge: D. S. Brewer; Totowa N.J.: Rowman and Littlefield, 1977.

——. "'Summer Sunday,' 'De Tribus Regibus Mortuis,' and 'The Awntyrs off Arthure': Three Poems in the Thirteen-Line Stanza." *Review of English Studies*, n.s., 25 (1974): 1–14.

——, ed. *Alliterative Poetry of the Later Middle Ages*. London: Routledge, 1989.

Tyerman, Christopher. *England and the Crusades, 1095–1588*. Chicago: University of Chicago Press, 1988.

Vale, Juliet. *Edward III and Chivalry: Chivalric Society and Its Context, 1270–1350*. Woodbridge, England: Boydell Press, 1982.

——. "Law and Diplomacy in the Alliterative *Morte Arthure*." *Nottingham Medieval Studies* 23 (1979): 31–46.

Vitto, Cindy L. *The Virtuous Pagan in Middle English Literature*. Philadelphia: American Philosophical Society, 1989.

Wagner, Anthony Richard. *Heraldry in England*. London: Penguin, 1946.

——. *Heralds and Heraldry*. London: Oxford University Press, 1956.

Walker, Greg. "The Green Knight's Challenge: Heroism and Courtliness in Fitt I of *Sir Gawain and the Green Knight*." *Chaucer Review* 32, 2 (1997): 111–28.

Wallace, David. *Chaucerian Polity: Absolutist Lineages and Associational Forms in England and Italy*. Stanford: Stanford University Press, 1997.

——, ed. *The New Cambridge History of Medieval English Literature*. Cambridge: Cambridge University Press, 1999.

Warren, W. L. "A Reappraisal of Simon Sudbury, Bishop of London (1361–75) and Archbishop of Canterbury (1375–81)." *Journal of Ecclesiastical History* 10 (1950): 139–52.

Weiss, Virginia L. "Gawain's First Failure: The Beheading Scene in *Sir Gawain and the Green Knight*." *Chaucer Review* 10 (1976): 361–66.

Wenzel, Siegfried. "*St. Erkenwald* and the Uncorrupted Body." *Notes and Queries* 226 (n.s. 28) (1981): 13–14.

Westover, Jeff. "Arthur's End: The King's Emasculation in the Alliterative *Morte Arthure*." *Chaucer Review* 32, 3 (1998): 310–24.

Whatley, Gordon. "Heathens and Saints: *St. Erkenwald* in Its Legendary Context." *Speculum* 61 (1986): 330–63.

——. "The Middle English *St. Erkenwald* and Its Liturgical Context." *Medaevalia* 8 (1982): 277–306.

Whatley, Gordon., ed. and trans. *The Saint of London: The Life and Miracles of St. Erkenwald*. Binghamton, N.Y.: Medieval and Renaissance Texts and Studies, 1989.

White, Hayden. "The Historical Text as Literary Artifact." In *Tropics of Discourse:*

Essays in Cultural Criticism. Baltimore, Md.: Johns Hopkins University Press, 1978, 81–100.

Wilkins, Gregory J. "The Dissolution of the Templar Ideal in *Sir Gawain and the Green Knight*." *English Studies* 63 (1982): 109–21.

Wilson, Edmund. *The Gawain Poet*. Leiden: E. J. Brill, 1976.

Wirtjes, Hanneke. "Bertilak de Hautdesert and the Literary Vavasour." *English Studies* 65 (1984): 291–301.

Wood-Legh, K. L. *Perpetual Chantries in Britain*. Cambridge: Cambridge University Press, 1965.

Ziolkowski, Jan. "A Narrative Structure in the Alliterative *Morte Arthure*, 1–1221 and 3150–4346." *Chaucer Review* 22 (1988): 234–45.

Index

Acknowledgments

It is a pleasure to thank my teachers, colleagues, and friends for their stringent criticisms and enormous generosities during the bliss and blunder of this book. Lee Patterson has broadened the terrains of medieval literature and culture more ways than I can tell; with care, kindness, and staunch criticism he helped immeasurably in giving the argument whatever coherence it possesses. Sarah Beckwith was unfailing in her precise comments and abundant support, modeling a rare and contagious delight in scholarship. Special thanks and possibly a medal are due Larry Scanlon, who heroically read the seventh version of the introduction while also juggling four job searches, an MLA paper, and a change of residence. Affection and thanks are given to Emily Bartels, for criticism, support, and inimitable schmoozing; Susan Crane for sharing her expertise in romance, heraldry, and aristocratic display; Elin Diamond and the Rutgers Drama group for arguing wonderfully about modern performance theory and medieval drama; and Tom Hahn, Ralph Hanna, Sylvia Tomasch, Sealy Gilles, Michael Cornett, Stacy Klein, Daphne Lamothe, Peter Travis, Regina Schwartz, Scott McEathron, Anne Chandler, and Mark Amos for comments and feedback at crucial stages along the way. I thank all the friends and colleagues who gave advice and support but especially Kathryn West, Carroll Hilles, Ethan Knapp, Patricia DeMarco, Wesley Brown, and the New York Meds and I am grateful to the Rutgers University English Department for a sabbatical crucial to the revision of the manuscript. I thank Jerome Singerman at the University of Pennsylvania Press for his kind support, and the two anonymous readers for their sagacity as they played good cop and bad cop to the manuscript, pressed it to confess itself more clearly, and then generously let it go. Lastly but most profoundly, I thank my parents, whose bemused support of a daughter who decided to pursue a career not only in English but in medieval literature is itself a testament to generosity and love.